LF

D0850825

Hudson Institute
620 Union Drive
P.O. Box 648
Indianapolis, Indiana 46206

THE COMPETITION

Dealing with Japan

by
Thomas Pepper,
Merit E. Janow,
and Jimmy W. Wheeler

Foreword by Henry Rosovsky

PRAEGER SPECIAL STUDIES • PRAEGER SCIENTIFIC

New York • Philadelphia • Eastbourne, UK
Toronto • Hong Kong • Tokyo • Sydney

ALBRIGHT COLLEGE LIBRARY

Library of Congress Cataloging in Publication Data

Pepper, Thomas.
    The competition: dealing with Japan.

    Includes index.
    1. Japan--Economic conditions--1945-   .
2. Japan--Economic policy--1945-   . 3. Japan--
Foreign economic relations--United States.
4. United States--Foreign economic relations--Japan.
I. Janow, Merit E.   II. Wheeler, Jimmy W.   III. Title.
HC462.9.P42   1985   330.952'04   85-6304
ISBN 0-03-071049-9

Published in 1985 by Praeger Publishers
CBS Educational and Professional Publishing, a Division of CBS Inc.
521 Fifth Avenue, New York, NY 10175 USA

© 1985 by Hudson Institute

All rights reserved

56789 052 9876543

Printed in the United States of America on acid-free paper

INTERNATIONAL OFFICES

Orders from outside the United States should be sent to the appropriate address listed below. Orders from areas not listed below should be placed through CBS International Publishing, 383 Madison Ave., New York, NY 10175 USA

Australia, New Zealand
Holt Saunders, Pty. Ltd., 9 Waltham St., Artarmon, N.S.W. 2064, Sydney, Australia

Canada
Holt, Rinehart & Winston of Canada, 55 Horner Ave., Toronto, Ontario, Canada M8Z 4X6

Europe, the Middle East, & Africa
Holt Saunders, Ltd., 1 St. Anne's Road, Eastbourne, East Sussex, England BN21 3UN

Japan
Holt Saunders, Ltd., Ichibancho Central Building, 22-1 Ichibancho, 3rd Floor, Chiyodaku, Tokyo, Japan

Hong Kong, Southeast Asia
Holt Saunders Asia, Ltd., 10 Fl. Intercontinental Plaza, 94 Granville Road, Tsim Sha Tsui East, Kowloon, Hong Kong

Manuscript submissions should be sent to the Editorial Director, Praeger Publishers, 521 Fifth Avenue, New York, NY 10175 USA

330.952
P424c

199702

To
the memory of
Herman Kahn

FOREWORD

Henry Rosovsky

When I embarked on the first of several specialized studies of Japanese economic history in the mid-1950s, I felt a sense of awe at the task ahead—and a corresponding sense of gratitude to Professor Kazushi Ohkawa of Hitotsubashi University, who helped me gain experience in the use of Japanese-language source material and in seeing whether such data were comparable to seemingly similar data in Western countries. As a student of the traditions of quantitative and qualitative methodologies pioneered by Professors Simon Kuznets and Alexander Gerschenkron and as a novice in Japan, I considered myself extremely fortunate to have benefited from Ohkawa's willingness to examine Japanese data in a way that might make them usable in the kinds of intercountry comparisons over time that Kuznets argued were vital to an accurate understanding of economic development worldwide. Happily, for those of us who continue to believe that this approach is the best starting point for the study of economic development in any country, Japan's economic history did seem on further inquiry to follow patterns of population growth, capital formation, income distribution, industrial structure shifts, and the like that had previously been observed in other, predominantly Western developed countries. To be sure, there were significant differences, but the broad process of modern economic growth was quite similar.

Western research on Japanese economic development was still in its infancy—compared with the material available on economic development in the United States and Europe—when a group of U.S. and Japanese scholars, working with Professor Hugh Patrick and myself, embarked in the early 1970s on a study of the postwar Japanese economy under the sponsorship of the Brookings Institution. We attempted to produce a reference work that would describe the postwar Japanese economy in terms that were roughly comparable to those also used to describe other economies but at the same time flexible enough to take account of phenomena specifically characteristic of Japan.[1] Findings from this study are cited many times in the accompanying work, although, as befits a later inquiry, Thomas Pepper, Merit E. Janow, and Jimmy W. Wheeler also question some aspects of the methodology and some of the conclusions of the Brookings study. In this sense, their new study is a useful and well-timed successor to an earlier analysis of the Japanese economy that is now over a decade old.

The accompanying study is a comprehensive description of recent and likely future changes in the Japanese economy. The authors show how domestic and international factors are making the U.S. and Japanese economies increasingly similar. In line with the traditions of Hudson Institute, the authors use an interdisciplinary approach to describe certain relationships between macroeconomic and microeconomic phenomena, between the U.S. and Jap-

---

1. Hugh Patrick and Henry Rosovsky, eds., *Asia's New Giant* (Washington, D.C.: Brookings Institution, 1976).

anese economies, and between economic and political issues. For example, the authors discuss in considerable detail the unraveling of Japan's previously highly segmented financial system. They attribute this unraveling to a number of factors, among them a precipitous increase in Japanese government budget deficits beginning in the late 1970s and, in an example of an international linkage, high U.S. interest rates, which coincided with a previously scheduled deregulation of Japanese foreign exchange procedures. Similarly, the authors note that under the adverse macroeconomic conditions of the 1973–82 decade it is hardly surprising that U.S. business executives failed to show much interest in the large front-end investment costs required to break into the Japanese market. In hindsight, the interactions here between macroeconomic and microeconomic forces—and between the U.S. and Japanese economies—are clear enough.

Yet such an improved explanation of recent events may only increase the frustrations of those Americans who see U.S.-Japan trade deficits as almost entirely an issue of unfair trade practices on the part of the Japanese. As the authors go on to suggest, no purely economic interpretation of a trade deficit is likely to be as important as the political interpretations that typically dominate policy debates. In the current situation, even as a high U.S. dollar inevitably cuts into U.S. export prospects, the authors boldly but plausibly argue that specific trade disputes between the U.S. and Japanese governments are likely to be ameliorated during the second half of the 1980s by the relatively buoyant economic environment they also believe is likely to prevail in both economies.

Whether this particular judgment on their part proves correct or not, the authors have made a notable contribution to an understanding of how advanced industrial countries continue to develop and of the major policy issues between developed and developing countries. The book should naturally also be useful to four separate audiences that have recently shown an interest in trying to learn more about Japan: policy makers, scholars and students, business executives, and the general public.

I especially welcome the authors' discussion of many specific issues—trade patterns and policy, industrial policy, regulatory policy, government support for R & D, and adjustments required by declining industries—in light of a longer-term framework of economic development. By taking this appraoch, the authors have reminded specialists and laymen alike of a major challenge facing the economics profession: to deal with the increasingly recognized limitations of economics by incorporating into economic analysis lessons learned from other social sciences, the humanities, and the physical sciences.

Pepper, Janow, and Wheeler have written a book that is fundamentally optimistic about the future of Japanese-U.S. economic relations. This feeling is based neither on wishful thinking nor on sentimentality. Instead, it stems from close analysis of the past and present. Their view of the future would have a better chance of being realized if Japanese and U.S. government and business leaders studied the conclusions of this volume with care.

Henry Rosovsky
Lewis P. and Linda L. Geyser University Professor
Harvard University

ACKNOWLEDGMENTS

Preparation of this book was made possible by a grant from the United States–Japan Foundation and a commitment to the project on the part of the President and Board of Trustees of Hudson Institute.

We are extremely grateful to the Honorable Richard W. Petree, President of the United States–Japan Foundation, and to Ronald Aqua, Program Director, for their support of the basic concept of the book and their understanding of the difficulties and delays we encountered in attempting to implement the concept. We also wish to express appreciation for efforts made by the late Robert Boettcher, formerly a consultant to the United States–Japan Foundation, who helped us design the project in its initial stages.

The book is an outgrowth of research originally undertaken for a study of Japanese industrial policies for the U.S. Departments of State and Commerce and the Office of the U.S. Trade Representative, entitled *Japanese Industrial Development Policies in the 1980s: Implications for U.S. Trade and Investment*, HI-3470-RR (Croton-on-Hudson, N.Y.: Hudson Institute, October 1982). We wish to thank members of the interagency working group for that project, particularly Warren H. Reynolds of the Office of Long-Range Assessments and Research, Bureau of Intelligence and Research, in the State Department, who served as chairman of the working group, and Lester A. Davis of the Office of Trade and Investment Analysis, International Trade Administration, in the Commerce Department, for their wholehearted support of this research, even when—and in some cases particularly when—they disagreed with our conclusions. Throughout the project, members of the working group criticized draft material in ways that led to its being considerably improved and supported the idea of the final report's being revised and made available to a wider audience.

We also wish to thank Thomas D. Bell, Jr., President of Hudson Institute, for his generous support of the work needed to convert the earlier report into this book. He and other members of the Board of Trustees showed exemplary patience with the time we took to broaden and update the original research, and we shall always be grateful to them for their support.

Many other people contributed their time and ideas, both during the earlier phase of research and in the extensive revisions made for the book. In this regard, we are particularly grateful to Joseph A. DeRose of International Business Machines Corporation, Norman Achilles of the U.S. Department of State, S. J. Janow, and Peter Young of J. H. Whitney & Co. for discussing certain points at great length and commenting on portions of the manuscript. Naohiro Amaya, Special Adviser to the Japanese Ministry of International Trade and Industry (MITI), and Masahisa Naitoh, Director of the General Coordination Division, Machinery and Information Industries Bureau of MITI, provided much useful background, particularly on the evolution of Japanese industrial policy. We received extensive help from numerous participants in various Hudson seminars, especially from U.S. and Japanese members of Hudson's Corporate Environment Program. We are also grateful to the Japanese Ministry of Foreign Affairs, which invited one of the authors to Japan to talk with government, business, and academic figures on the effects of Japanese industrial policy.

Many colleagues at Hudson generously shared their time and ideas with us as portions of the manuscript were completed. In particular, Herbert I. London, a Senior Research Fellow at Hudson, read the entire manuscript and provided many useful suggestions. We are also grateful to Marianne D. Bell, William M. Brown, Owen R. Cote, Jr., Philip Deluty, Kurt Guthe, Irving Leveson, Neil Pickett, and John B. Trammell for their comments and suggestions. Midori Yamamoto, formerly a research associate in Hudson's Asia-Pacific Office, contributed much to the research for the earlier study on Japanese industrial policies.

As always, members of the Hudson support staff worked above and beyond any normal concept of dedication and generosity. In particular, we wish to thank Ceci Floren, Helen Iadanza, Anne Marsek, Rose Marie Martin, and Yvonne Swinton for their dedication to this project in spite of the considerable personal inconvenience this caused. The same should be said of Roberta McPheeters, formerly of Hudson, who typed most of the initial manuscript, and Chizuko Harada, Kang Chung-shin, and Sarah Loh, formerly of Hudson's Asia-Pacific Office, who labored long and hard in an effort to assist in the completion of earlier portions of the manuscript.

Special thanks also go to our editors at Praeger, Betsy Brown, Barbara Leffel, and Patty G. Sullivan, whose detailed supervision of the project contributed greatly to its completion, and to the copyeditor, Susan Badger.

We dedicate this book to the late Herman Kahn, cofounder of Hudson Institute and its dominant intellectual force until his death in 1983. Anyone who came in contact with Herman knew him to be a stimulating and engaging figure with an unfailing sense of humor. We who were privileged to have worked with him benefited greatly from his constant questioning of existing ideas and corresponding quest for new ideas.

All of these people and many others helped us to complete this book, but we alone are responsible for its contents.

Indianapolis, Indiana   Thomas Pepper
January 1985   Merit E. Janow
                                                         Jimmy W. Wheeler

CONTENTS

LIST OF ACRONYMS

AIST	Agency for Industrial Science and Technology
ANRE	Agency for Natural Resources and Energy
AT&T	American Telephone and Telegraph Company
BOJ	Bank of Japan
CAFSIS	Credit and Finance Information Switch System
CATNET	Credit Authorization Terminal Network
CDs	certificates of deposit
c.i.f.	cost, insurance, and freight
CULCON	Conference on Cultural and Educational Interchange
DARPA	Defense Advanced Research Projects Agency
DITI	Department of Trade and Industry
EEC	European Economic Community
EPA	Economic Planning Agency
ETL	Electro-Technical Laboratory
Ex-Im Bank	Export-Import Bank
f.a.s.	free alongside ship
FCC	Federal Communications Commission
FILP	Fiscal Investment and Loan Program
f.o.b.	free on board
FTC	Fair Trade Commission
FY	fiscal year
GATT	General Agreement on Tariffs and Trade
GDP	gross domestic product
GNP	gross national product
gt	gross ton
IBJ	Industrial Bank of Japan
IBM	International Business Machines Corporation
ICOT	Institute for New Generation Computer Technology
IEA	International Energy Agency
IMF	International Monetary Fund
INS	Information Network System
IPA	Information Technology Promotion Agency
ITC	International Trade Commission
ITT	ITT Corporation
JDB	Japan Development Bank
JECC	Japan Electronic Computer Corporation
JEIDA	Japan Electronic Industry Development Association

JIS	Japan Industrial Standards
JRDC	Japan Research Development Corporation
KDD	Kokusai Denshin Denwa
LDP	Liberal-Democratic party
lng	liquefied natural gas
LTCB	Long-Term Credit Bank of Japan
MCC	Microelectronics and Computer Technology Corporation
MITI	Ministry of International Trade and Industry
MOF	Ministry of Finance
MOT	Ministry of Transportation
MPT	Ministry of Posts and Telecommunications
mt	metric ton
NCB	Nippon Credit Bank
NEC	NEC Corporation
NICs	newly industrializing countries
NTT	Nippon Telegraph and Telephone Public Corporation
OECD	Organisation for Economic Co-operation and Development
OPEC	Organization of Petroleum Exporting Countries
PBXs	private branch exchanges
PFIC	Petroleum Feedstock Import Company
R & D	research and development
RCA	RCA Corporation
STA	Science and Technology Agency
SBFC	Small Business Finance Corporation
SBPC	Small Business Promotion Corporation
SRC	Semiconductor Research Corporation
USTR	U.S. Trade Representative
VANs	value-added network services
VLSIs	very large-scale integrated circuits
VRS	video response system
XDS	Xerox Data Systems

THE COMPETITION

Chapter 1

JAPAN IN PERSPECTIVE

Competing with Japan has come to symbolize difficulties that the United States faces in maintaining or improving its economic position relative to other countries. The very success of U.S. policies since the end of World War II helped create this situation. By assisting in the reconstruction and economic development of wartime allies and enemies alike, the United States helped set in motion an unprecedented period of worldwide economic growth. U.S. gross national product (GNP), despite having grown nearly threefold in real terms since 1945, has gone from approximately 50 percent of gross world product to about 23 percent of gross world product. The rest of the world, particularly Japan, has simply grown faster. Compared with the hypothetical alternative of U.S. retention of a much larger share of a smaller gross world product, this decline in the U.S. share represents an enormous gain. The United States, Japan, and the rest of the world are all economically much better off in an expanding world economy. Yet Japan, by so successfully taking advantage of a world environment favorable to economic growth, has come to represent both the costs and the benefits of the original U.S. postwar policies.

Japan—which as Japanese are fond of reminding others is only ''a small island country with no natural resources''—has seen its GNP grow 11-fold in real terms since 1950, whereas its share of gross world product has grown from roughly 4 percent to more than 10 percent. By 1990 Japan is likely to have passed the Soviet Union as the second largest economy in the world. Japan's economic achievements, challenging the United States in such visible areas as electronics, steel, automobiles, machine tools, and now computers, have raised fundamental questions about American manufacturing competitiveness. Increased competition from Japanese firms, particularly in manufactured products in which

1

U.S. firms were previously dominant, is requiring significant adjustments in the U.S. economy.

The United States is still the largest single economy in the world. For this reason alone, long-term trends in U.S. economic performance and in U.S. policy will greatly influence future global economic vitality and the degree to which economic competition occurs in a stagnant or an expanding world economy. In the broadest sense, the challenge presented to the United States by Japan's economic success is the intangible one of forcing Americans to decide what goals to seek in light of the achievements of others. Will Americans seek to insulate themselves from foreign competition and introduce still more government restrictions on trade, or will they seek to respond to increased competition by trying to become still more competitive? We think the latter is more desirable and, based on the evidence presented here, also more likely.

This book analyzes changes in Japan's economic position vis-à-vis the United States over the past 40 years. It describes how postwar Japanese economic development—particularly the role of government policy—has changed over time, suggests where the Japanese economy and Japanese government policy are heading, and outlines lessons that Americans and others might draw from the Japanese experience.

We argue that underlying economic trends in Japan are creating new and expanding opportunities for trade and investment between the United States and Japan. Chapters 2 through 6 explain, each from a different perspective, how and why this is happening. Chapter 2 shows how the Japanese economy has evolved since the midnineteenth century and describes likely U.S. and Japanese economic prospects. The chapter goes on to discuss the structure of the two economies, particularly the movement of both economies toward more specialized manufacturing activities and high growth service activities. As this is happening, the two economies are becoming more similar; by implication, many problems in bilateral relations stemming from past differences in structure are being ameliorated as a by-product of the evolution of both economies. Chapter 3 presents a detailed analysis of Japanese industrial policies, showing, as an example of evolution, that the Japanese government's use of targeted industrial policies has declined over time. Chapter 4 describes the changing structure of the Japanese financial system and how domestic and international pressure are forcing a deregulation of the traditionally segmented system. Chapters 5 and 6 cover recent and likely future trends in Japan's new and declining industries, respectively. Chapter 5 shows how government support to new indutries is becoming less important as the overall economy matures. Chapter 6 describes how Japan's basic manufacturing industries are being forced to adjust by market pressures, even as they sometimes seek increased government support. Chapter 7 presents the business and policy implications of Japan's changing economy for both the United States and Japan.

AMERICAN AND JAPANESE VIEWPOINTS

Many Americans who look back on the nearly four decades of U.S.-Japanese postwar relations recall the once tremendous disparities in per capita income, living standards, technological capabilities, and overall national strength and the support that the United States has given Japan during these years. As Japan's unprecedented record of economic development brought an increasing convergence in these various economic indexes, Americans repeatedly expressed hopes that a more prosperous Japan would gradually assume a larger share of what Americans perceived to be common burdens, either in a U.S.-Japanese alliance or in the broader sense of a community of nations. For example, U.S. officials have long urged Japan to increase its defense capabilities—still within the scope of a self-defense system limited to the home islands and the territorial waters and within the framework of the U.S.-Japan Treaty of Mutual Cooperation and Security.[1] Similarly, U.S. officials have often urged the Japanese government to initiate far-reaching trade liberalization measures aimed at bringing Japanese trade policies and practices more closely in line with those of other advanced industrial countries. Japanese responses to these pressures have been unable to offset the frustrations felt by many Americans, in and out of government, over what they consider a self-centeredness on Japan's part—its so-called free ride.

In contrast, many Japanese look back on the bleak postwar days, when even food was scarce, and feel their economic success since that time has been based primarily on their own considerable efforts. Jap-

---

1. The treaty currently in force was signed in 1960 as a successor to an earlier pact signed in conjunction with the peace treaty that ended the postwar occupation in April 1952.

anese often attribute these efforts to traits of perseverance in Japan's culture. From a Japanese perspective, U.S. criticisms of Japan's alleged unfairness in achieving an unprecedented record of economic growth are themselves unfair. Typically, Japanese feel that such criticisms stem from American frustration over declines in U.S. competitiveness generally, illustrated by declining rates of U.S. productivity growth since the mid-1960s. Japanese would generally welcome a revitalization of U.S. economic performance but see this turn of events as something that can only occur on the basis of efforts made by Americans themselves. Japanese who harbor doubts about current U.S. economic capabilities also tend to wonder whether the United States is experiencing a permanent decline in its long-term resilience and dynamism and whether the increased military power of the Soviet Union, compared with the levels of strategic and conventional forces making up the U.S.-Soviet military balance in years past, presages a further decline in either the capabilities or will of the United States to support the political goals of the Western alliance. As far as U.S.-Japanese defense cooperation is concerned, Japan's unique history as the only nation to suffer atomic bombing and to have adopted a no-war clause in its constitution makes the whole issue of national security an extremely difficult matter on which to reach a domestic consensus—let alone one that is in accord with sometimes contradictory American desires for a Japan that is both stronger than before yet still subordinate to the United States.

Over the years, numerous differences in the perceptions and expectations that Americans and Japanese have of each other have turned various bilateral economic issues into serious political problems. In the mid-1960s, Japan's concentrated export drives in various labor-intensive industries, most notably in textiles and clothing, exacerbated an already difficult adjustment process in industries that were in decline in the United States. This led the Nixon administration to suggest that Japan impose "voluntary" limits on textile shipments to the U.S. market. As negotiations over the matter dragged on for more than two years, personal feelings between government officials and political leaders of the two countries reached poisonous proportions. In the early 1970s, Japan's growing trade surpluses and an undervalued yen, combined with an unwillingness to take sufficient action to correct these problems, contributed to the collapse of the Bretton Woods fixed exchange rate system.

This period was known to Japanese for its "shocks"—for example, the "Nixon *shokku*" in July 1971 when President Richard Nixon announced, without warning to any U.S. ally, that his assistant for national security affairs, Henry Kissinger, had met with Chinese Premier Chou En-lai in Peking and that he himself would visit China early the following year. This established U.S.-Chinese ties in a single stroke, bypassing Japanese leaders who had meanwhile been tempering their own approaches to China to keep in step with the United States. A "dollar shock," or *doru shokku,* followed a month later when President Nixon announced, again without warning allies, that the United States would no longer exchange dollars for gold at a fixed price of $35 per ounce and that, in effect, the United States was demanding a realignment of major currencies against the dollar.

Subsequently, both the United States and Japan moved to ease the tensions between them. The United States sought to patch up the political damage it had caused by its unilateral actions, and Japan began to participate more actively in international economic discussions. The 1973 "oil shock" diverted both countries' attention away from bilateral trade problems. Then, beginning in the mid-1970s, Japanese exports of steel and automobiles drew fire in the United States either because of their adverse employment effects or because of their presumed strategic importance, or both. More recent export successes in semiconductors, printers, other computer components, and machine tools, coupled with a continuing high dollar (some would say undervalued yen), have raised similar questions. Generally, political relations between the United States and Japan have tended to deteriorate whenever the bilateral trade balance moved sharply against the United States, and to appear not to improve when the bilateral trade balance moved closer to equilibrium.

As a result U.S.-Japanese political friction has become a fact of life. This recurrence of political friction reflects the fundamental change in the relative positions of the two economies occasioned by Japan's postwar economic success. Throughout the postwar period, Japanese have been both willing and able to maintain a higher rate of economic growth than other advanced industrial countries. This much was understandable and acceptable to Americans for the first 20 to 25 years after the war, when the gap in per capita income was still large enough to give Americans a feeling of security vis-à-vis Japanese competition. By the late 1960s, however, the gap in per capita income had been cut in half (see Table 2.1), and Japan had begun to register significant and persistent merchandise trade surpluses with the United States. At that point the Japanese willingness to maintain a lower standard of living in the short term for the sake of a higher rate of growth over the long term became a source of subsurface conflict between the two countries.[2] The Japanese government realized full well that by providing positive incentives for investment at the expense of consumption the Japanese people would live less well in the short term than their counterparts elsewhere. Indeed, for many years Japanese consumers had virtually no access to lower-priced imports and faced artificially low interest rates on household savings.[3] Japanese planners gambled—successfully so, as events turned out—that a conscious emphasis on investment would produce a rapid enough growth rate over the long term to compensate for sacrifices made in the short term.

More specifically, and as discussed at length in Chapters 2 and 3, Japan's overriding economic goal from the early postwar years has been to catch up to Western countries through policies that promoted high levels of savings and investment generally and high levels of investment in certain specific manufacturing sectors. During the early postwar years, powerful instruments to help achieve these goals were available to the Japanese government, such as direct administrative control over foreign exchange transactions and considerable formal and informal influence over the direction of investment. Protection from import competition, based on well-accepted theories of assistance to so-called infant industries, was applied as a matter of course and, until the early 1970s, either explicitly or implicitly tolerated by the United States and other advanced industrial countries. Japan also benefited, as noted

---

2. The seeming self-sacrifice of Japanese, in the short term, doubtless contributes to the competitiveness of Japanese exports, but there is little that other countries can do in the short term to offset this kind of advantage. The difference is analogous to that between two families, one of which sacrifices to send its children to college, whereas the other neither encourages its children to attend college nor saves the money even to provide for the possibility. If, as would seem likely, the children in the first family get better jobs as a result of their better education, the second family cannot somehow blame the first family for behaving "unfairly."

3. For most of the postwar period, the consumer price index in Japan rose at roughly twice the rate of the wholesale price index, meaning that the consuming sector received less of the benefits of economic growth than the producing sector. See Herman Kahn and Thomas Pepper, *The Japanese Challenge: The Success and Failure of Economic Success* (New York: Thomas Y. Crowell, 1979), pp. 63–68.

above, from the most rapid period of world economic growth ever recorded. In this way Japanese manufacturers were able to take advantage of both a rapidly expanding and captive domestic market and rapid growth in world markets. By the early 1970s, however, many detailed controls over economic activity had been, or were about to be, abandoned—for example, most foreign exchange controls, most special tax measures designed to promote investment in specific industries, and so on. Others faced, and continue to face, increasing domestic and international pressures to be reduced further or eliminated altogether— such as remaining controls on interest rates, various barriers to entry in the financial sector, and the remaining official tariffs and quotas. All the while, Japanese economic policies have continued to provide positive incentives for investment, relative to consumption. The overall economic system remains biased toward growth.

For those other advanced industrial countries that have neither established nor retained this same growth bias and that perceive Japanese firms as continuing to benefit from considerable government support equivalent to infant-industry protection, the seemingly endless flow of competitive Japanese-manufactured exports often leads to a siege mentality. When coupled with the continuing government- and market-based difficulties associated with entering the Japanese market, the frustration sometimes seems intolerable. Frequently, business and government leaders in other countries take out their frustrations by suggesting protectionist measures of their own—almost regardless of their economic effects. For example, many U.S. business and government leaders have initiated or strengthened various measures to limit Japanese exports to, and the activities of Japan-based firms in, the United States. If this trend were to continue, the advantages of an international trading system based on free trade would be even more undermined than has already been the case.

INTERNATIONAL TRADE AND ITS DIFFICULTIES

Arguments against an unqualified reliance on free trade may at times be justifiable, but in strictly economic terms any trade restricting action has its cost. For example, infant-industry protection does allow new industries to get off the ground more quickly than they would in a competitive international market.[4] Moreover, such industries usually provide important side benefits (for example, improving the skills of the labor force) that in turn spur economic development elsewhere in the economy, creating new areas of comparative advantage that otherwise might not emerge. By most standards, Japan's use of infant-industry protection during the first 20 years after World War II was extremely successful. Too much infant-industry protection can be counterproductive, however. Many of today's developing countries have discovered this when trying to nurture new industries behind tariff walls that also prevent competitively priced exports from being developed. For this same reason, as discussed in detail in Chapter 5, Japan's telecommunications industry is now being deregulated to prevent it from falling behind a fast-deregulating U.S. telecommunications industry.

Various military or political arguments against a complete reliance on free trade may also be justifiable and sensible. A country may want to protect or subsidize a certain minimal level of, say, steel or automobile production as a base for mobilization in the event of war—or to deter war. Moreover, since shifts in the trade of goods usually occur more rapidly than shifts in the skills or location of labor, free trade brings more difficult adjustment problems for workers in industries directly affected by imports than for other workers or society as a whole. Such arguments often lead to political pressure from directly affected groups seeking to prevent, delay, or be compensated for the cost of changing comparative advantage. Yet too much protection to industries considered either infant or vital for national security, or, alternatively, too much compensation to industries or workers that face adjustment, can drain resources away from potentially more important uses—most notably the development of still newer industries seeking protection.[5]

---

4. Of the many refinements to the original argument for free trade advanced in the 200 years since Adam Smith and David Ricardo first developed their ideas, the infant-industry argument is among the most important. It is based, in turn, on the idea of economies of scale, that is, the advantages accruing to large-scale operations that lead to lower production costs per unit because of the large number of units being produced. Through infant-industry protection, the argument runs, economies of scale can be built up that then enable a new industry to stand on its own.

5. One example is in the Soviet economy, where an intense concentration on military goods and heavy industry at the expense of consumer goods and virtually all other sectors seems increasingly to be impeding the future development of both neglected and favored sectors.

For these reasons exceptions to free trade always have to be evaluated subjectively by the decision-making processes in the country making the exception. Needless to say, the subjective factors used to justify various refinements and exceptions to free trade greatly influence decisions in the real world, often straining the tolerance of other countries that have reasons of their own for seeking modifications to free trade.

A much discussed example of the kinds of strains that can arise in an international economic system based on free trade is a country's use of so-called industrial policies to promote specific patterns of economic development. As other, more explicit barriers to the free flow of goods have been reduced, the continued use (or apparently successful use) of industrial policies, especially by Japan, has become a major issue in international trade. The United States, in contrast to Japan, does not have an industrial policy in the sense of an explicit and coordinated set of government policies aimed at industrial development, and the issue of whether it should have one is currently a subject of considerable domestic debate. Meanwhile, because Japanese industrial policies have been and remain relatively more pronounced than comparable policies in the United States—and more important, because Japanese-based firms have become the major competitors to U.S.-based firms across a wide range of industrial products—U.S. allegations that Japanese industrial policies are per se unfair have become a major issue in bilateral political as well as economic relations. Indeed, discrimination against foreign firms, both explicit and implicit, has gone hand in hand with Japanese industrial policies, especially in the early postwar years. Subsequent chapters describe in detail the major characteristics of Japanese industrial policies and how these have changed over time. In particular we try to show how certain Japanese government policies and foreign tolerance of various policies and practices greatly influenced the shape of industries that evolved. It is difficult, if not impossible, however, to measure precisely what the effects of this discrimination have been and how much of an industry's success can be attributed to government policies as against the efforts of individual companies.

Disputes over industrial policies are but one manifestation of a broader problem of reconciling differences between or among countries with different social and political values. Such differences may not be reflected in approaches that countries take toward free trade per se; rather they may be reflected in approaches toward antitrust and related market-organization issues, degrees of regulation that exist in various industrial sectors, and government-business relations generally—all of which can obviously have important implications for trade. Another example of how differences in values can complicate trade among nations is the different concepts of obligation held in East Asia and the West.[6]

Until roughly the end of World War II, this issue did not arise because for the preceding 450 years European countries had colonized or otherwise dominated most of the rest of the world. Europeans and their descendants assumed that their own concepts of culture, law, and social organization, based on the granting of reciprocal rights in a horizontal relationship, were a suitable and preferable norm within and among all nations. For dealings between nations, European scholars developed the notion of sovereign equality in which each nation is deemed sovereign within its own realm and, nominally at least, equal in terms of international law. Obviously European countries applied this concept selectively. In any case the superior military and political power that European countries had in those days, vis-à-vis non-Western cultures, led international law or whatever other ''rules of the game'' existed in relations among countries to be based on European concepts of obligation.

In societies with Confucian traditions, however, concepts of obligation are generally based on unequal relationships in a vertical hierarchy. Equal rights, in the Western sense, are not part of the traditional system; rather, individuals or organizations with a higher status have a greater claim on those with a lower status than vice versa.[7] China, for example, traditionally viewed other countries, including nearby Japan and Korea, as having a lesser status. Moreover, the establishment of codes of behavior between individuals or groups with a different status is normally assumed to incorporate such status differences as a matter

---

6. Significant differences in social and political values also exist among European countries, between European countries and the United States, and among different countries in East Asia, but these are of much lesser magnitude than differences between Western culture as a whole and the Confucian-influenced societies of East Asia. For further discussion of different concepts of obligation in East Asia and the West, see Thomas Pepper, ''Obligation: East and West,'' *Worldview* 26 (May 1983): pp. 18-20.

7. Other things being equal, an older person always has a higher status in Chinese culture than a younger one. More commonly, other criteria are available, such as political power, wealth, education, or seniority within a group. Always, however, some kind of hierarchical differentiation is required for a normal relationship to ensue.

of course; the higher status unit is initially given greater weight, whereas the lower status unit has the leeway to try through various means to narrow the gap or even to change the balance completely. As these concepts of obligation have been applied to the establishment of rules for international trade, countries with a Confucian cultural tradition have begun to believe that their recent success in achieving high rates of economic growth would entitle them to have their own concepts of culture, law, and social organization accepted as international norms.[8] By this logic, Western countries can no longer expect the rules of the game, including rules of international trade, to be based solely on Western social and political values.

In general, as various nations from different cultural traditions interact with one another on the basis of greater economic equality than in the past, establishing rules for international trade will require greater understanding of different social and cultural systems. On the other hand, adherence to some set of fixed standards would probably facilitate trade, if only by reducing uncertainty. In this regard Western contract law, with its provisions for an objective review of disputes by impartial third parties, will probably prove increasingly useful in enabling individuals or groups with different social and political values to agree on the definition of obligations—and more useful than Confucian-based systems of personal responsibility in which obligations are understood only subjectively by parties operating in one culture.

Over time, Japan, China, and other East Asian nations whose economies are growing rapidly through expanded trade with other nations are likely to find Western contract law increasingly useful as a means of narrowing the scope of obligations to the performance of specific acts and thereby minimizing the differential power or influence that a stronger party might otherwise have over a weaker party. In other words, in law as well as economics some degree of convergence between the United States and Japan is probably under way. To be sure, Americans have long been frustrated by what they have felt was a tendency on the part of Japanese to want to uphold the letter of an existing agreement when the contractual obligations in such an agreement favored their interests but to appear at other times to want to "stretch" the spirit

---

8. For example, many aspects of Japanese industrial policies, such as depression cartels, joint public/private research and development (R & D) projects, and administrative guidance, are identified by Japanese as the kinds of practices they might hope would become internationally accepted.

of existing agreements on grounds that, in hierarchical terms, they were entitled to lenient treatment while catching up to the United States. Now that Japan has become so important a part of the world economy, Americans have become much less tolerant of such "younger brother" arguments. At the same time, Japanese have seen developing countries use these same arguments in their dealings with Japan; this, too, has increased Japanese interest in Western contract law as a basis for retaining a fixed set of standards in international trade. Japan's support of U.S. pleas for a new round of multilateral trade talks, focusing on services, reflects this important change in Japanese interests.

CULTURAL AND ECONOMIC CHANGE

Indeed, few differences in social and political values between the United States and Japan are likely to be as immutable as they might seem in the short term. In the broadest sense, Japan's postwar emphasis on investment, relative to consumption, has already changed to some degree. In historical terms this is hardly surprising since a long-term shift toward consumption has been a central characteristic of modern economic development. Different countries make this shift at different levels of affluence. By the same token, trade frictions reflecting such differences become less severe as economic development proceeds, even as trade friction from other causes may increase. Cultural preferences themselves can change over time. Although Japanese scholars have often argued that Japan has a unique culture, it—like other cultures—is also constantly changing, particularly as per capita income increases. In fact, discussions of Japan's alleged cultural uniqueness are as old as Japan itself, and modern Japan has seen many debates over whether some particular change in the social structure would undermine the "true essence" of the country. In 1927, for example, Mitsukoshi department store decided to change its rules and allow customers to enter in their street shoes—presumably a major change for a country whose customs had decreed for 2000 years that outside footwear was unclean and thus should be removed when entering a dwelling.[9] Similarly, immediately

---

9. At that time a tremendous public debate ensued as to whether Mitsukoshi's proposed innovation would lead to a breakdown in the "basic" character of Japanese society and the Japanese people. Those who disagreed with the breakdown theory argued that the change would be accommodated as an obvious convenience that would not prevent shoppers from feeling "basically" Japanese.

after World War II, no one could have predicted that Japan would become a significant bread-eating country within 30 years or that coffee and buttered toast would supplant the traditional combination of rice, seaweed, and fish as the standard Japanese breakfast. Given the importance of rice-growing constituencies to the fortunes of the long-ruling Liberal-Democratic party (LDP), it is hard to believe that LDP leaders would not have preferred to slow down this transformation in dietary habits.

In the past decade, Japanese attitudes toward market structure and trade itself have also begun to change. The traditional approach to market structure, favoring an oligopoly of producers with little regard for the textbook concept of "perfect competition" or the Galbraithian idea of countervailing power for labor or consumers, has given way to increased competition and to an increased regard for consumer preferences than in earlier postwar years. While barriers to entry in any major Japanese industry have usually been strict, foreign-based firms investigating the prospect of entering the Japanese market often assume, mistakenly, that strict barriers to entry were specifically designed to exclude them. In fact, Japanese newcomers have also been unwelcome—in some cases more so.[10] More recently, and as discussed at length in Chapter 4, the Japanese financial system has come to face greatly increased pressures for deregulation—not only from foreign-based financial institutions and governments but, perhaps more important, from domestic financial firms seeking to broaden the range of services they can offer customers who meanwhile have come to insist on higher rates of return or more varied instruments of investment. In this way pressures for deregulation of the financial system are building up within the Japanese financial sector itself. As this deregulation occurs—the question is not whether it will occur but at what pace—it will also provide opportunities for foreign-based firms capable of providing needed services and aggressive enough to take advantage of emerging opportunities. These kinds of changes, whether driven by domestic or international pressures or both, lead to a domestic market that, like the U.S. market, will experience many new competitive pressures and provide many new trade and investment opportunities.

Over time, as economic development proceeds, patterns of culture and of economic and industrial structure that are distinctive to one coun-

---

10. Japanese often complain that entry into the U.S. market is hampered by an excessive need for lawyers, as though this facet of American society were somehow purposely designed to exclude foreigners.

try will undergo some degree of change. Unfortunately, there is no simple way to estimate which specific patterns are likely to change most or least. Many specific aspects of the Japanese economy that once seemed immutable have already begun to change; some are changing rapidly. Correspondingly, U.S.-Japanese economic relations are also undergoing considerable change. Previously, Japan was "catching up" to a United States that was generating most of the world's new technologies and providing other countries with a large and relatively open market. Now, a pattern of two-way trade in goods and services and in investment is increasingly evident. This two-way flow (discussed in detail in subsequent chapters) is bringing greater interdependence between the two countries. This will not necessarily bring agreement on every issue or on each side's view of the terms of whatever agreements are reached. Yet the very success Japan has achieved will require Japanese to bear some increased responsibility for the smooth functioning of the global economy. Exactly how much responsibility Japanese will bear at any particular time or which particular areas naturally remain subject to considerable give-and-take.

Japanese are not responsible, however, for the revitalization of the U.S. economy. That depends on the attitudes and actions of Americans themselves. In dealing with various challenges posed by Japan, Americans must decide whether to try to make a future United States as economically dynamic as other countries in the world. If so, it is in their own interest to take actions that improve U.S. economic competitiveness, in particular the maintenance of a generally open economy. If Americans were both willing and able to reallocate capital and labor, to retrain workers, and to shift many of their economic activities to new industries, they would be little troubled by import competition. If Americans were unwilling or unable to make these adjustments, overall U.S. economic strength, vis-à-vis other more dynamic economies, would assuredly decline.

By the same token, to the degree that Japan fails to develop a more open economy to replace the infant-industry–oriented economy that has been in place through most of the postwar period, it, too, would pay a price in diminished dynamism over the long term. Japanese, both in general and in government, seem increasingly to be recognizing this point and to be changing their practices and policies accordingly. The following chapters describe and analyze such changes in the Japanese economy and in Japanese government policies, drawing out implications, opportunities, and risks for future trade and investment patterns between the United States and Japan.

Chapter 2

THE JAPANESE ECONOMY

Beginning in the midnineteenth century—and well before World War II—Japan transformed itself from an isolated, preindustrial economy to one of the world's major powers.[1] Two and a half centuries of near-total isolation from world trade had put Japan far behind other countries in the use of machinery developed during the industrial revolution in Europe and North America. As a result Japan's military power in the midnineteenth century was much weaker than that of the United States and various European countries, which, based on their superior

---

1. Some scholars argue that even during the Tokugawa era, from 1603 to 1868, Japanese society was in some respects as sophisticated as any other. See, for example, Robert N. Bellah, *Tokugawa Religion* (New York: Free Press, 1959), passim; and Kazushi Ohkawa and Henry Rosovsky, *Japanese Economic Growth: Trend Acceleration in the Twentieth Century* (Stanford, Calif.: Stanford University Press, 1973), pp. 2–8. Bellah argues that the educational system of the day, based on Buddhist-supported *terakoya* ("temple schools"), gave much of Japanese society a value system equivalent to the so-called Protestant ethic that the German sociologist Max Weber argued earlier was so important to economic development in Western countries. Ohkawa and Rosovsky note that Japan had an effective nationwide government and road system and a vigorous urban culture (Tokyo [then called Edo], Kyoto, and Osaka were among the largest cities in the world at that time) and that formal schooling covered 40 to 50 percent of all males. They also note that while nonagricultural production consisted almost entirely of labor-intensive crafts and services and was thus "unmodern," these crafts and services were in their own environment extremely sophisticated. Clearly, these various assets contributed to Japan's ability to transform itself into a modern industrial economy so quickly.

military power, seemed bent on securing trade privilege from Japan. Purposeful attempts to promote Japanese economic development and to protect the political sanctity of the country against foreign encroachment began in earnest with the Meiji Restoration in 1868. From then to the outbreak of World War II, Japan's performance in terms of growth in per capita output, the broadest single measure of economic performance, was comparable with that of other nations now characterized as advanced industrial countries (see Figure 2.1). Figure 2.1 shows what every Japanese knows as a matter of course—namely, that before World War II Japan's level of output (or income) was significantly below that of other advanced countries; Japan was doing well, but it was still poor. The big change came after World War II. Both Japan and West Germany recovered quickly from the worst effects of the war, but Japan went on to achieve higher rates of economic growth for a longer period of time than any other country. Japan's growth in total output, averaging 9.5 percent a year from 1947 to 1973, was then, and still is, unprecedented. Even in the years since 1973, when world growth rates have been much lower than the levels achieved in the preceding 25 years, Japan's growth rate has remained higher than that of other advanced industrial countries.

On the other hand, Japan did experience a greater deterioration in performance after 1973 than other countries. Where Japan's average growth from 1963 to 1973 was 10.5 percent, its growth from 1973 to 1981 averaged only 3.5 percent.[2] This weakening in Japanese performance reflected a number of strains that began to emerge within Japan and in Japan's relations with the rest of the world during the late 1960s—as well as those stemming from a general weakening of the world economy. For example, by the early 1970s, Japan's previous concentration on achieving high growth through the buildup of basic manufacturing industries began to run its course; continued growth in the medium to long term required some shift toward investment in social and physical infrastructure. At roughly the same time, public criticism of economic growth as the dominant goal of Japanese society began to mount, leading to sudden and sharply voiced calls for new policies to

---

2. Data from General Agreement on Tariffs and Trade, *International Trade 1981/82* (Geneva: GATT, 1982), table A15. Only the United Kingdom, whose growth fell from an average of 3 percent between 1963 and 1973 to 0.5 percent for 1973 to 1981, registered a greater fall proportionately.

Figure 2.1.

GROSS DOMESTIC PRODUCT PER HEAD OF POPULATION (1860–1978)

(At 1970 Prices)

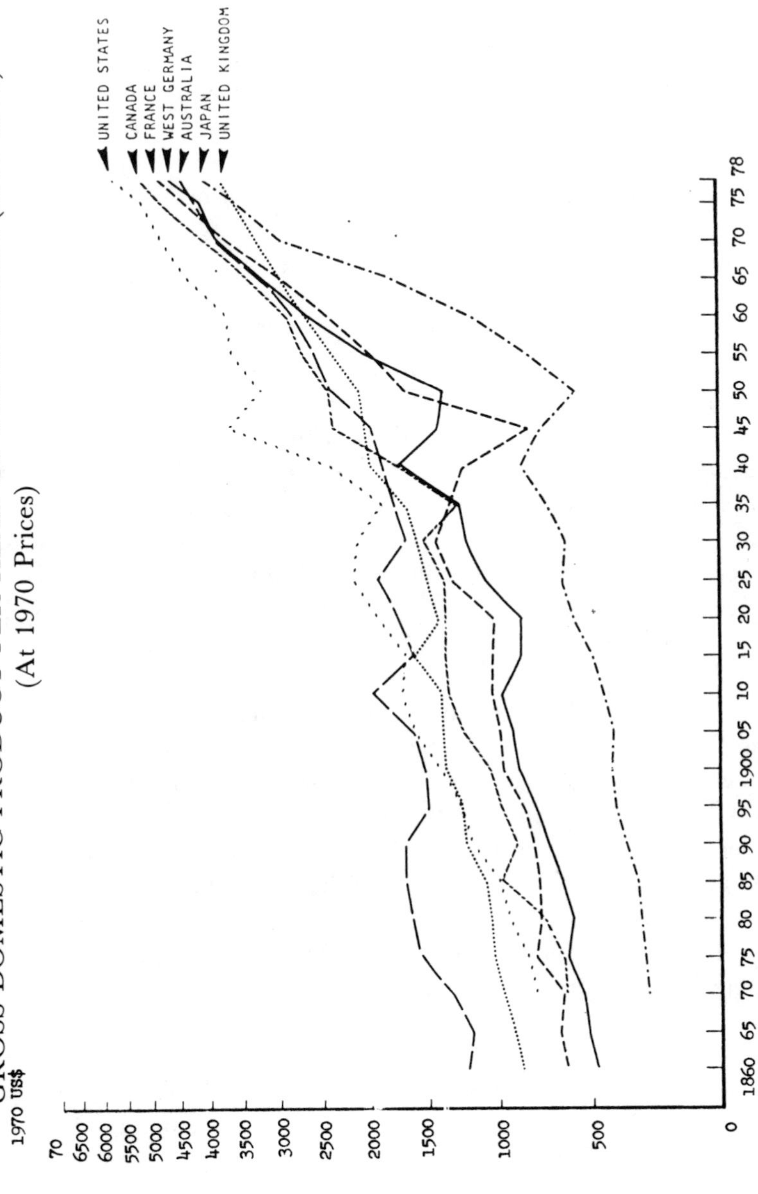

Source: Angus Maddison, "Per Capita Output in the Long Run," Kyklos 32 (1979)

deal with environmental pollution and other "quality of life" issues. Strains began to be felt with major trading partners as a series of export drives in particular commodities such as textiles, steel, and shipbuilding had their first big impacts abroad. Trade friction in particular products was intensified by perceptions, both in the United States and elsewhere, that the yen was undervalued and that the Japanese government sought as a matter of policy to maintain a relatively closed market.

Japanese authorities were slow to react to, or perhaps even to recognize, the country's increased importance in the world economy. In effect the Japanese government left it to others, notably the United States government, to force the issue and to try to convince the Japanese to shift more of their economic drive toward domestic development and less toward exports.[3] Japan's failure to react to its changed position vis-à-vis other member countries in the Organisation for Economic Co-operation and Development (OECD) contributed substantially to the collapse of fixed exchange rate system between 1971 and 1973 and to the commodity price boom of 1973. Specifically, if Japanese authorities had initiated policies before then to put more emphasis on domestic development or to raise the exchange value of the yen, or if Japanese business and government leaders had recognized the impact that Japanese commodity purchases were having on world markets, the disruptions of the mid-1970s would probably have been less serious. In the post-1973 years, Japan did face greater adjustment problems than most other OECD countries, mainly because of an excessive buildup of new capacity during the global 1971–73 boom and an unusually heavy dependence on external sources of energy and Middle East oil in particular. Nonetheless, Japan's post-1973 performance would arguably have been even better than it turned out to be if the kinds of measures mentioned above had been taken.

However one judges Japan's performance in the postwar years, its performance with respect to long-term indicators of economic progress

---

3. Writing in early 1973, Brian Beedham, foreign editor of *The Economist*, summarized Western views on this issue with the phrase: "Point the hosepipe somewhere else." See Brian Beedham, "A Special Strength: A Survey of Japan," *The Economist*, March 31, 1973, p. Survey 15.

continues to improve.[4] Gross domestic product (GDP) per capita, in terms of purchasing power parity comparisons, rose from 62 percent of that in the United States in 1970 to 76 percent in 1981, thus passing the United Kingdom while remaining below France and West Germany (see Table 2.1). Life expectancy at birth, now 77 years in Japan, surpassed the average of 75 years for advanced industrial countries during the late 1970s. The structure of production has moved steadily closer to that of other advanced industrial countries (see Table 2.2). Most notably, the share of GDP in agriculture fell to only 4 percent in 1981; however, as of 1980 some 12 percent of civilian employment remained in agriculture. Japan's level of per capita consumption in 1981 as measured in purchasing power parity terms was $4,883, compared with $8,085 for the United States, $5,485 for the European Economic Community (EEC), and $5,933 for the advanced countries as a whole.[5] In other words, by many standards the Japanese economy is gradually becoming comparable with the economies of other advanced countries. At the same time, such indices as the large difference between Japan's share of output and employment in agriculture, its higher share of GDP in manufacturing than that of other advanced industrial countries, and the gap still separating Japanese consumption levels from those other

---

4. For quantitative studies of Japanese economic development, see, in the English-language literature, Ohkawa and Rosovsky, *Japanese Economic Growth*, which includes an extensive discussion of the prewar period; Edward F. Denison and William K. Chung, *How Japan's Economy Grew So Fast* (Washington, D.C.: Brookings Institution, 1976), which focuses on the postwar period; and a condensed version of this material in chapter 2, "Economic Growth and its Sources," in the landmark Brookings Institution study of Japan's postwar economy, Hugh Patrick and Henry Rosovsky, eds., *Asia's New Giant* (Washington, D.C.: Brookings Institution, 1976). A Japanese-language study that also tries to identify sources of growth through an historical approach, now translated into English, is Takafusa Nakamura, *The Postwar Japanese Economy: Its Development and Structure* (Tokyo: University of Tokyo Press, 1981).

5. The above data not cited in accompanying tables are drawn from World Bank, *World Development Report 1983* (New York: Oxford University Press, 1983), pp. 173, 189; and OECD, *National Accounts, 1951–1981, Main Aggregates*, Vol. 1 (Paris: OECD, 1983), p. 100.

Table 2.1
RATIO OF GROSS DOMESTIC PRODUCT PER CAPITA USING PURCHASING POWER PARITY ESTIMATES OF SELECTED COUNTRIES TO THAT OF THE UNITED STATES, 1960–81

	1960	1970	1981
United States	100.0	100.0	100.0
Germany	73.3	76.3	82.2
France	61.6	71.9	79.1
Japan	31.5	63.7	76.0
United Kingdom	66.5	68.1	65.9

Sources: 1960: Irving Kravis, Alan Heston, and Robert Summers, "New Insights into the Structure of the World Economy," *Review of Income and Wealth,* December 1981, pp. 348–49, as reported in Herbert Stein, "The Industrial Economies: We Are Not Alone," *AEI Economist,* May 1982, p. 2. 1970 and 1981: OECD, *National Accounts, 1952–1981, Main Aggregates*, Vol. 1 (Paris: OECD, 1983), p. 99.

advanced countries, particularly the United States, all suggest that the Japanese economy remains at an earlier stage of devlopment than the economies of the United States and some other advanced countries.

Table 2.2
STRUCTURE OF PRODUCTION: DISTRIBUTION OF GROSS DOMESTIC PRODUCT AT FACTOR COST
(In Percent)

| | 1960 | | 1970 | | 1981* | |
	Japan	Advanced Industrial Countries	Japan	Advanced Industrial Countries	Japan	Advanced Industrial Countries
Agriculture	12.8	6.4	6.1	4.2	4	3
Manufacturing	34.3	30.6	35.8	28.4	30	25
Other industry	10.8	10.4	10.6	10.2	13	11
Services	42.1	52.5	47.5	56.1	53	61

*Reported rounded off in the source.

Sources: 1960 and 1970: World Bank, *World Tables,* 2d ed. (Washington: International Bank for Reconstruction and Development 1980), pp. 391–92, 394–95. 1981: World Bank, *World Development Report 1983* (New York: Oxford University Press, 1983), p. 153.

From a macroeconomic viewpoint, Japan's ability to continue catching up to other advanced countries even under adverse conditions was a positive contribution to the world economy; Japan's above-average performance from 1973 to 1982 helped mitigate the severity of the stagflationary conditions otherwise prevailing at that time. However (and this is perhaps the main reason Japan's superior performance has caused such problems for the rest of the world) this ability to maintain a better-than-average overall economic performance was based on exceptional export performance and no-better-than-average performance domestically—hence the intensification of trade frictions with other countries in spite of Japan's macroeconomic contributions to world prosperity.

JAPANESE TRADE AND INTERNATIONAL FINANCIAL PATTERNS

International trade has been vital to Japan's economy since the beginnings of its modern growth. Since Japan was seriously underendowed with the raw materials needed to develop basic manufacturing industries, a pattern arose early in the Meiji era of consciously limiting imports to such raw materials and to capital equipment necessary to promote industrialization. Imports of other "unessential" goods were carefully restricted, thereby husbanding foreign currency earnings for supposedly the highest priority objectives. In this way, export earnings served as a key source of growth, both for the foreign currency generated and as a means of spurring the development of higher value-added goods. This pattern of using exports as a critical instrument of overall economic development continues to this day.

During the reconstruction from World War II and the subsequent period of rapid economic growth to the early 1970s, a lack of sufficient export volume was at times an important constraint on growth. Each postwar recession, which in Japan typically meant a decline in growth rates rather than an absolute decline in GDP, stemmed from a tightening of monetary, fiscal, and other policies in direct response to an increased balance of payments deficit. Only after the mid-1960s did regular current account surpluses become the norm (see Table 2.3). A large, long-term capital outflow emerged in the early 1970s and has continued ever since, though with considerable volatility in its level from year to year.

Table 2.3
BALANCE OF PAYMENTS SUMMARY, 1967–83
(IN U.S. $ Million)

	Current Account Balance	Trade Balance	Services Balance	Long-Term Capital	Short-Term Capital	Overall Balance	Exchange Rate (Period average, ¥/$)
1961–66 cumulative	– 104	4,230	– 3,926	– 488	344	– 263	360
1967	– 190	1,160	– 1,172	– 812	506	– 571	360
1968	1,048	2,529	– 1,306	– 239	209	1,102	360
1969	2,119	3,699	– 1,399	– 155	178	2,283	360
1970	1,970	3,963	– 1,785	– 1,591	724	1,374	350
1971	5,797	7,787	– 1,738	– 1,082	2,435	7,677	350
1972	6,624	8,971	– 1,883	– 4,487	1,966	4,741	303
1973	– 136	3,688	– 3,510	– 9,750	2,407	– 10,074	271

1974	−4,693	1,436	−5,842	−3,881	1,778	−6,839	291
1975	−682	5,028	−5,354	−272	−1,138	−2,676	297
1976	3,680	9,887	−5,867	−984	111	2,924	297
1977	10,918	17,311	−6,004	−3,184	−648	7,743	266
1978	16,534	24,596	−7,387	−12,389	1,538	5,950	210
1979	−8,754	1,845	−9,472	−12,618	2,377	−16,662	219
1980	−10,746	2,125	−11,343	2,394	3,071	−8,396	227
1981	4,770	19,967	−13,573	−6,449	−958	−2,144	221
1982	6,850	18,079	−9,848	−14,969	−1,579	−4,971	249
1983*	21,024	31,649	−9,058	−17,798	176	5,177	238

*Preliminary.

Sources: 1961-66: Lawrence B. Krause and Sueo Sekiguchi, "Japan and the World Economy," in *Asia's New Giant*, ed. Hugh Patrick and Henry Rosovsky (Washington, D.C.: Brookings Institution, 1976), chap. 6. 1967-82: Bank of Japan, *Economic Statistics Monthly*, various issues; and International Monetary Fund, *International Financial Statistics*, various issues.

ALBRIGHT COLLEGE LIBRARY

199702

In only two decades, from 1950 to 1970, Japan moved from being an insignificant player on the world market to among the largest. Japan's share of free world exports doubled between 1960 and the early 1970s, reaching a rank of third largest after the United States and West Germany; it has remained relatively constant since then (see Table 2.4). In terms of manufactured exports, Japan exceeded its prewar share during the early 1960s. This share has continued to rise (see Table 2.5), where Japan is again third ranking, after West Germany and the United States. Japan's export growth, highly concentrated in a small number of industries and markets, has strained the ability of competing producers in other countries to adjust. Obviously, if Japanese imports had been larger, some of the balance of payments pressures that strained the Bretton Woods fixed exchange rate system would have been less servere, and if Japanese imports of manufactured products had been larger, some of the political pressures on the global trading system would also have been less serious. However, even if Japanese import markets had been as open as those of other advanced countries, the pace at which Japanese exports penetrated individual markets abroad would have strained the international trading system.

The structure of Japanese exports has changed dramatically since the 1950s. Between 1955 and 1973, the most notable change was a decline in the importance of labor-intensive products. The most rapidly growing category of exports was that of capital-intensive and high-wage goods—skilled labor–intensive goods such as steel and automobiles. R & D–intensive goods also showed significant growth.[6] These trends continued after 1973, although the increase in oil prices sharply curtailed growth in some of the more capital-intensive goods. Specialized machinery, office products, telecommunications equipment, automobiles, trucks, and household appliances showed particularly high export growth during this period.[7]

Relative price trends have also contributed to Japan's export growth, although these trends reflect more fundamental processes at work. With exceptions in individual years, export prices have risen more slowly than the GNP implicit price deflator. Indeed, the export price index was virtually constant through the 1960s and grew less than half

---

6. For supporting data, see Lawrence B. Krause and Sueo Sekiguchi, ''Japan and the World Economy,'' in Patrick and Rosovsky, *Asia's New Giant*, p. 409.

7. For supporting data, see General Agreement on Tariffs and Trade, International Trade, 1980/81 (Geneva: GATT, 1981), table A19.

as fast as the GNP implicit price deflator from 1970 to 1980. These price trends reflect the rapid rate of productivity growth in export industries relative to other industries. Rapid average productivity growth, compared with that in other advanced industrial countries, and conservative macroeconomic policies that kept domestic inflation relatively low permitted Japan's international competitiveness to improve sharply through the late 1960s. The Smithsonian exchange rate adjustments in late 1971 and the move to floating exchange rates in early 1973 corrected a serious undervaluation of the yen that had persisted since the mid-1960s. Except for the abnormal inflation experience in 1973/74, however, Japan continued to outperform other industrial countries in terms of relative price trends, especially for certain manufactured goods industries. As a result, Japanese firms became increasingly strong competitors on global markets. When the U.S. dollar rose dramatically in the early 1980s, largely in response to macroeconomic phenomena, the cost advantage already held by Japanese firms became that much greater.

It is difficult to argue, however, that exports have been the driving force for economic growth in the postwar years. Although exports of goods and services have grown faster than GDP in real terms, their share in GDP—and thus the stimulus they provided to aggregate demand—was relatively small, at least until the mid-1970s (see Table 2.6). The indirect stimulus from exports has been considerably more pronounced. Since exports tended to be concentrated in the more mod-

Table 2.4
SHARES OF MARKET ECONOMY EXPORTS
(In Percent)

	1960	1970	1973	1978	1980	1981	1982	1983*
United States	18.2	15.4	13.7	12.2	12.1	13.0	12.8	12.5
West Germany	10.1	12.1	13.0	12.1	10.5	9.8	10.6	10.5
Japan	3.6	6.9	7.1	8.4	7.1	8.4	8.3	8.9
France	6.0	6.4	7.0	6.8	6.3	5.9	5.8	5.8
United Kingdom	9.4	7.0	5.9	5.8	6.0	5.8	5.8	5.7
Italy	3.2	4.7	4.3	4.8	4.2	4.2	4.4	4.4
Netherlands	3.6	4.2	4.6	4.3	4.0	3.8	4.0	4.1
Canada	5.1	5.9	5.1	4.1	3.7	4.0	4.3	4.7

*Average for first three quarters.

Source: U.S. Department of Commerce, *International Economic Indicators,* various editions.

Table 2.5

SHARES OF WORLD EXPORTS OF MANUFACTURES

(In Percent)

	1960	1970	1980	1981	1982	1983*
West Germany	18.2	19.8	19.8	18.7	20.1	20.1
United States	22.8	18.4	16.4	18.1	17.3	16.4
Japan	6.5	8.9	11.9	14.5	13.9	14.5
France	9.1	9.1	10.2	9.4	9.3	9.4
Italy	4.8	7.1	8.0	7.9	8.1	8.6
United Kingdom	15.3	10.4	10.0	8.5	8.3	7.8
Netherlands	3.8	4.6	4.7	4.3	4.5	4.6
Canada	n.a.	1.8	1.2	1.2	1.2	1.1

n.a. = not available

*Average for first two quarters.

Note: World exports are defined as the sum of exports from 14 major industrial countries.

Source: U.S. Department of Commerce, *International Economic Indicators,* various editions.

Table 2.6

EXPORT OF GOODS AND SERVICES

AS A PERCENTAGE OF GNP, 1955–83

	Current Prices	Constant Prices
1955	12.8	7.6
1960	11.4	9.1
1965	11.2	11.2
1970	11.6	13.2
1973	10.8	13.9
1977	13.9	16.2
1978	11.9	15.5
1979	12.7	15.7
1980	15.2	17.9
1981	16.8	20.2
1982	16.8	19.8
1983	16.0	20.4

Sources: Lawrence B. Krause and Sueo Sekiguchi, "Japan and the World Economy," in *Asia's New Giant,* ed. Hugh Patrick and Henry Rosovsky (Washington, D.C.: Brookings Institution, 1976), chap. 6, p. 399; and Economic Planning Agency, *Japanese Economic Indicators,* various issues.

ern and highly productive industries, rapid export growth expanded still further the ability of a particular industry to take advantage of economies of scale. These industries in turn further improved productivity growth and held the prices of exported products down relative to the prices of other goods. Moreover, producers who were forced to compete in international markets aggressively sought to acquire the best technology and processes available. At the same time, the Japanese domestic market was heavily shielded from foreign competition during the 1950s and 1960s.[8]

Overall, Japan's historical trade pattern can be described as a textbook example of a simple Heckscher-Ohlin model in which one country buys or sells agricultural products and other raw materials with another that sells or buys predominantly manufactured goods. This pattern has dominated trading relations between Japan and most of its trading partners since the Meiji Restoration. As shown in Figure 2.2, Japan's imports of manufactured goods as a percentage of total imports are strikingly lower than those of other advanced industrial countries. Indeed, Japan's imports of manufactured goods are even strikingly lower than South Korea's, a country with a similar lack of natural resource

---

8. Krause and Sekiguchi specifically investigated the hypothesis that Japan's growth was driven or led by exports through the early 1970s but found little support for a measurable version of the hypothesis, while acknowledging that exports did grow at a more rapid rate than GDP. See Krause and Sekiguchi, "Japan and the World Economy," pp. 398–402. Krause and Sekiguchi also noted a commonly observed characteristic that exports tended to expand during domestic recessions. This was even more pronounced following the oil price increases of 1973/74 and 1979/80, which in turn suggests a hypothesis that Japanese industries use exports to offset depressed domestic demand. Ki-ho Kim investigated this hypothesis in a detailed analysis of trade balance changes from 1974 to 1976. Although his results are far from conclusive, the statistical tests utilized suggest that an "export drive cannot be ignored as a principal determinant of the Japanese trade balance and that the $9 billion improvement between 1974 and 1976 was due largely to such a drive during and following the 1973–75 recession in Japan." See Ki-ho Kim, "A Study of the Factors Affecting Japan's Trade Balance, 1974–76" (Ph.D. diss., Rutgers University, May 1979), p. iii. Although recession-induced export expansion can also be explained by looking at the market incentives facing firms—for example, the buildup of inventories resulting from slack domestic demand and the importance of maintaining cash flow in firms that are highly leveraged—such behavior, whatever its origins, has certainly exacerbated tensions between Japan and its major trading partners.

Figure 2.2.
MANUFACTURED PRODUCT IMPORTS
AS A PERCENTAGE OF TOTAL
MERCHANDISE IMPORTS, 1960–83
(c.i.f.)

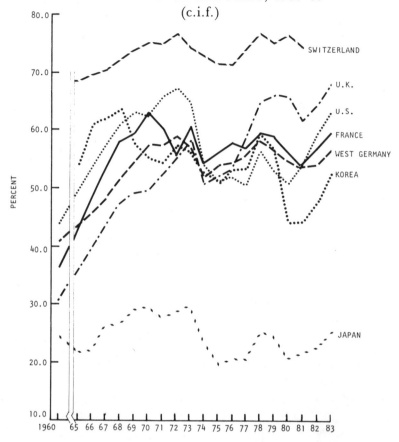

Notes: Merchandise import data for France were converted from free on-board (f.o.b.) to cost, insurance, and freight (c.i.f.) for 1960, 1967–69, and 1971–74 (also for Japan, 1960, and the U.K., 1972–74) using the factor of 1.1 as done in International Monetary Fund, *Direction of Trade*; U.S. manufactured data for 1960, 1967–69, and 1971–74 was converted from free alongside ship (f.a.s.) to c.i.f. using the factor of 1.06

Sources: Organisation for Economic Co-operation and Development, *Economic Surveys: Switzerland*, March 1973, p. 72, and October 1980, p. 59; U.S. Department of Commerce, *International Economic Indicators*, various issues; Economic Planning Board, Seoul, Korea, *Major Statistics of Korean Economy*, 1983, and *Monthly Statistics of Korea*, January 1984; United Nations Statistical Office; and Japan Tariff Association, *The Summary Report: Trade of Japan*, December 1983.

endowments and a similar culture.[9] Given Japan's lack of natural resource endowments, the distance from its major trading partners, and
thus, in the common view at least, its inordinate dependence on exports
of manufactured goods as a source of funds for the purchase of necessary raw material imports, many Japanese have always considered a
low level of imports of manufactured goods to be prima facie a necessity.

This once inviolate notion has begun to change, however, as continued economic development brings about changes in Japan's comparative advantage and in the tastes of Japanese consumers. As Figure 2.2
also shows, before the oil price increase of 1973/74 the share of manufactured imports in Japan's total merchandise imports was already increasing, if only gradually and from an extremely low base. Figure 2.3, which
adjusts the data to exclude the effects of imports of mineral fuels, lubricants, and related materials, shows this same trend even more clearly:
The slope of the trend line is more sharply upward than in Figure 2.2,
and the cyclical dips at the time of the two oil price increases are much
less pronounced. These data are too aggregative to show exactly which
manufactured products are likely to be imported into Japan in greater
volume (or percent) over some ensuing short-term time frame, but pre-

---

9. In terms of classical international trade theory, the most likely explanation of South Korea's high level of manufactured imports lies in the country's small size and its need, particularly as economic development accelerated in the 1960s, for capital goods imports.

Japan, too, has been an importer of capital goods, particularly advanced
technology products that could not yet be produced at home. But Japan's
much larger size, in terms of population, and its much higher per capita income permitted Japanese firms to develop new products for the domestic market first. Indeed, this has been the traditional Japanese pattern in the consumer
goods exports for which the country is so famous and, for that matter, in capital goods exports as well: because of the large domestic market, Japanese firms
could build up large production runs, lower their unit costs, and seek export
markets only after their products had been refined to a point, in both price
and quality, where they were very likely to be sold successfully abroad. In the
particular set of circumstances following World War II—when the shock of
Japan's first military defeat in its history was mixed with a strong consensus
to "re-catch up to the West"—the Japanese public simply did without many
finished products, especially consumer goods, that could not be manufactured
at home.

Arguably, no other country, regardless of its size, can repeat this particular postwar Japanese pattern because no other country's consumer sector will
ever again be as self-abnegating as Japan's was until recently.

Figure 2.3

MANUFACTURED PRODUCT IMPORTS AS A PERCENTAGE OF TOTAL MERCHANDISE IMPORTS, LESS IMPORTS OF MINERAL FUELS, LUBRICANTS, AND RELATED MATERIALS (c.i.f.)

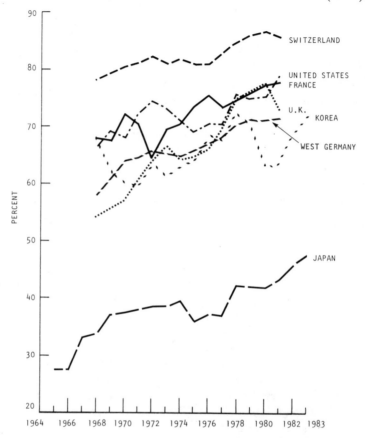

Sources: Organisation for Economic Co-operation and Development, *Economic Surveys: Japan,* July 1973 and July 1980; International Monetary Fund, *International Financial Statistics,* various issues; Japan Trade Center; Economic Planning Board, Seoul, Korea, *Major Statistics of Korean Economy,* 1983, and *Monthly Statistics of Korea,* January 1984; United Nations Statistical Yearbook, various issues; and Japan Tariff Association, *The Summary Report: Trade of Japan,* December 1983.

cisely because they are aggregative they also show an underlying trend in the direction of more imports of manufactured goods as the Japanese economy as a whole becomes still more developed. Many critics of Japanese trade policy would consider the trend shown in either figure to be rising far too slowly, but for purposes of establishing what the trend has actually been, we believe it important that the previous rate of growth for manufactured imports returned after adjustments were made for oil prices increases, and as discussed below, we expect this trend to continue and probably to accelerate.

Traditionally, Japan's international financial transactions have also been tightly controlled.[10] In the immediate aftermath of World War II, foreign exchange was allocated directly by the government, and its use was limited to what government officials considered "essential"; such restrictions continued generally in force until the late 1960s. Somewhat surprisingly, given this scarcity of foreign exchange, inward flows of capital were also strictly regulated. Some inflows were permitted before the early 1970s in order to expand investment and accelerate economic growth, but these were usually limited to loans to, or arranged by, the Japanese government and were drawn from other government organizations such as the U.S. Export-Import Bank and the International Bank for Reconstruction and Development (World Bank). The explanation usually given for such tight control on capital inflows is that the Japanese government did not want either the public or the private sectors to build up a large debt burden that could not be paid off if economic conditions turned against Japan. This does not, however, explain the maintenance of rigid controls on inward direct investment (that is, equity, not debt) until the late 1960s.[11] These controls were maintained because the government was explicitly trying to minimize foreign ownership of domestic productive assets. To achieve this goal and still promote high economic growth, the government needed to raise domestic savings, which led to the introduction of a variety of tax and other incentives to promote such savings. The fear of substantial foreign ownership apparently outweighed what would otherwise have been an intense short-term need for foreign exchange and more investment capital. Fortunately for Japan, a combination of unusual circumstances prevented

---

10. This chapter discusses Japan's international financial transactions in the context of overall, or macroeconomic, trends in the Japanese economy. Some issues mentioned in this discussion are treated in greater detail—and from an industry-specific, or microeconomic, viewpoint—in Chapter 4.

11. Control of foreign direct investment was authorized in a 1950 law concerning foreign investment.

the maintenance of tight controls on inward capital flows from seriously retarding domestic growth—most important in the 1950s, the materiel requirements for UN forces in Korea and the "special procurement" expenditures for U.S. forces in Japan. Under less fortuitous circumstances, the government might have been forced to relax capital controls or to live with a considerably lower growth rate.[12]

With Japan's development of a trade surplus from the mid-1960s and a generally persistent current account surplus from the late 1960s, many changes in the regulations governing capital flows were instituted. Most of the changes were part of a long-term liberalization policy, biased more toward permitting capital outflows than inflows. However, the Ministry of Finance (MOF) retained considerable case-by-case discretionary authority, which in turn enabled the pace of the liberalization process to vary according to economic conditions. For example, capital outflow restrictions were first eased when the trade and current account balances moved into substantial surplus in the early 1970s. When the first oil shock hit, capital outflows were once again restrained. Meanwhile, capital inflows remained highly controlled with only gradual easing, lest "too much" foreign investment come in.[13] Because of the threat that speculative pressure might cause the (previously undervalued) yen to increase further, short-term capital inflows were also kept under tight rein.

Perhaps the most important legal change affecting Japanese international transactions to date has been the Foreign Exchange and Foreign Trade Control Law that took effect in December 1980. The central assumption on which earlier legislation was based—namely that foreign exchange transactions were prohibitied except where expressly permitted—was changed to one permitting all transactions except those specifically prohibited. At the time, MOF officials regarded this as a major change—although in line with traditional practice, they were careful to leave themselves the latitude to reimpose many of the capital controls that had prevailed until then as a matter of course. Since Japanese laws are normally written with wide latitude left to bureaucratic discretion, and the system of administrative guidance based on this latitude has been an important part of the governing process, the actual impact of this change was initially expected to be less than

---

12. Such tight control of international financial transactions was matched by comparably tight controls over domestic financial transactions.

13. Beginning in 1968, a series of capital liberalizations slowly began to open the range of possibilities for foreign investors.

has in fact occurred. The greatly increased activity in foreign exchange and capital markets since the law was enacted suggests that, as also discussed below, the new law has opened the way to a whole series of interrelated changes in Japan's international financial transactions.

Looking back, it is easy to see that Japan's traditional patterns of trade and international financial transactions began to change appreciably in the late 1960s when balance of payments constraints on overall Japanese growth were clearly no longer as severe as they had been, either before World War II or during the 25 years of reconstruction and recovery from defeat. At the same time, it is also easy to see that the pace at which the remaining direct controls over trade or financial transactions have been lifted or eased—not to mention the legacy of habits and customs that run deeply through the society—would appear exceedingly slow to foreigners, particularly as the latter become increasingly aware of Japan's significance in the world econmy. The 1973/74 oil price increases and subsequent near-decade of low worldwide growth rates and high and volatile inflation rates undermined previously expected economic trends. Only in the last two years have macroeconomic trends and, more important perhaps, expectations of future macroeconomic trends become much more positive than they were in the 1970s; it is only in this recent period that changes in Japanese trade and international financial patterns have begun to be perceived by foreigners as offering significant opportunities.

U.S. AND JAPANESE ECONOMIC PROSPECTS

During the past three years, as the decline in U.S. inflation rates and the buoyancy of the U.S. economic recovery reduced previously widespread fears of an ever-continuing pattern of the low growth of the 1970s, relations between the United States and Japan have begun to be seen in both countries in distinctly more positive terms—and in spite of continued disputes over specific issues. If the current U.S. recovery is sustained to the late 1980s, as we argue below is likely, Japan will probably experience a similarly sustained upturn. In these circumstances—with both countries enjoying more buoyant economic relations than in the preceding decade—economic relations between the United States and Japan will be increasingly influenced by the common efforts of both countries to maintain high growth rates, both for themselves and others—and again, in spite of continued disputes over specific issues. Since the U.S. and Japanese economies taken together account for more than half the GNPs of the advanced industrial countries and for more than a third of gross world product,[14] their higher growth would also be likely to help pull world growth up, especially in Western Europe and various debt-burdened developing countries. The following subsections discuss U.S. and Japanese macroeconomic prospects as a basis for subsequent discussion of likely structural changes in the Japanese economy and, in later chapters, other, more detailed aspects of the Japanese economy and implications these have for U.S. policies and the U.S. economy as a whole.

The U.S. Recovery

Beginning in 1979 as the United States shifted to tight money policies in spite of rising unemployment, U.S. and global inflation rates began to fall dramatically (see Figure 2.4.). The shift in attitudes that brought about this willingness to fight inflation, even at the cost of short-term increases in unemployment, set the stage for the cyclical recovery that began in the United States in late 1982. If the positive forces that have set this cyclical recovery in motion are reinforced over the ensuing two to three years and at the same time not offset by a rekindling of inflation (or by fears of inflation manifested in rising interest rates), this cyclical recovery will gradually evolve into a sustained expansion as the remaining legacies of the 1970s stagflation are worked out and, equally important, as expectations come to reflect significantly greater opportunities for growth than in the 1970s.

The likelihood that this cyclical recovery might evolve into a sustained expansion depends first of all on the continuing strength of the underlying changes currently driving the U.S. economy in a positive direction.[15] These changes include:

---

14. Including the Soviet Union, China, and other nonmarket economies.

15. The strength of various positive forces in the economy can be seen in the strength of real nonresidential fixed investment. Contrary to the typical pattern, in which plant and equipment investment declines relative to GNP during a recession and through the first year of a recovery, such spending rose from 10.8 percent of GNP in fourth quarter 1982 (the recession trough) to 11.5 percent one year later. Moreover, at 10.8 percent, the share at the recession trough exceeded the average share from 1970 to 1979 of 10.5 percent. In other words, investment has been particularly strong in spite of recession and high real interest rates. See Federal Reserve Bank of St. Louis, *National Economic Trends*, February 1984, p. 1.

Figure 2.4.

U.S. AND WORLD INFLATION, 1955–83

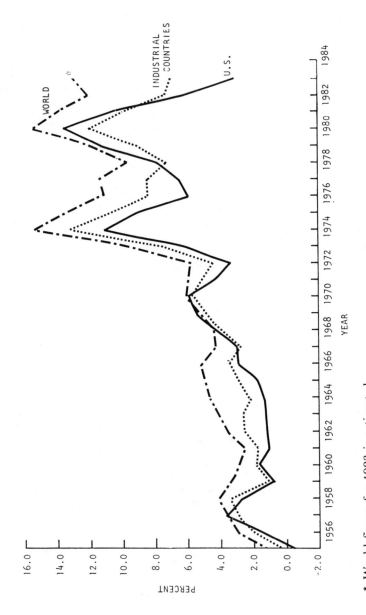

* World figure for 1983 is estimated.

Source: International Monetary Fund, *International Financial Statistics*, various issues.

1. Improvements in the labor force, particularly among the large number of people who began working for the first time in the 1970s—for example, baby boom adults, females, and minorities; as these people acquire more experience, they will also achieve greater-than-average productivity gains that will begin to show up strongly during the rest of the 1980s. 2. New technologies and many innovations stemming from these, as illustrated by developments already taking place in computers, telecommunications, energy production, and conservation, which, as they unfold, will continue to lead to large increases in productivity; similar revolutions are widely expected from biotechnologies, new materials, and space, although these fields are in earlier stages of development. 3. Modernization of services on both the supply and the demand side, as technological change and the application of modern management techniques make the provision of previously expensive services much more affordable or the services now being provided of a much higher quality (that is, new and varied financial services, privately financed job retraining, and medical diagnostics, to name a few). Both technological innovation and the modernization of services are positive long-term trends extending past the end of the century. 4. Adjustments in capital stock to the energy price changes and new environmental, health, and safety standards of the 1970s; as these adjustments are more or less being completed, an increasing share of new investment dollars can now be applied directly to productivity-increasing uses. 5. Improved government policies, such as R & D tax credits, increased incentives for saving through expanded provisions for individual retirement accounts and financial market deregulations, and a concerted effort to reduce the costs of achieving environmental, health, and safety standards; all of these policies support sustained economic growth more than the sometimes explicitly growth-inhibiting policies of the 1970s. 6. More generally, sometimes as a cause and sometimes as an effect of the above trends, new values and attitudes that promote entrepreneurship, risk taking, and self-reliance; for example, as the increasing interest in computers over the past two years suggests, the blossoming of new technologies, previously widely feared as a cause of unsettling change, is now generally welcomed as a cause of desirable change. As Figure 2.5 shows, personal computer sales are increasing rapidly in spite of fears that computerization would have adverse effects on aggregate (as well as sectoral) employment. Similarly, the significant increase in venture capital activities during the last few years shows a greater willingness to take risks.

Figure 2.5.
U.S. SALES OF MAINFRAME
AND PERSONAL COMPUTERS
(In U.S. $ Billion)

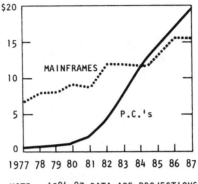

NOTE: 1984-87 DATA ARE PROJECTIONS.

Note: The 1984–87 data are projections.
Source: International Data Corporation.

Such shifts in attitudes, which if reinforced become a shift in expectations as well, have profoundly positive implications for future investment prospects. In fact, for any recovery to be sustained, attitudes toward investment have to be positive, and actual investments based on such positive attitudes have to be made. In the current U.S. situation, increased savings and investment will be required to produce a sustained recovery. Otherwise, the consumer spending on which the current cyclical recovery has largely been based would run its course, and the recovery would falter—or, if stimulated by monetary expansion, would be subject to a boom/bust cycle based on excessively speculative consumer or investment demand. Worse yet, if positive attitudes toward investment have not developed sufficiently and actual investments based on such attitudes have not been made when the economy slows down in cyclical terms, which at some point it must do in any case, the foundations for new industries needed to keep the economy on course in structural terms beyond the 1980s would not yet have been laid. Under these circumstances the "go-stop" pattern of the early 1980s would be repeated; the investments enabling the economy to maintain a sustained and more stable growth pattern than that of the 1970s would be delayed still longer.

The biggest single factor undermining the confidence needed to sustain the current recovery to the late 1980s is the fear of a return to high inflation rates. To judge by the continued high level of long-term interest rates—in real terms they remain extremely high and have been going higher (see Figure 2.6)—Americans continue to think that the dramatic decline in inflation since 1980 is only temporary and that to protect themselves against an erosion in the value of their money, lenders still need a so-called inflation premium built into (and exerting upward pressure on) interest rates. To be sure, higher corporate profits resulting from cyclical recovery and recently enacted tax law changes will enable much new investment to be financed out of retained earnings. Moreover, a number of new financing methods (for example, variable rate loans, asset-based loans, and so on) have been devised to facilitate investment in new projects in spite of high real interest rates. Nonetheless, sustained growth probably still requires that these high real interest rates steadily decline toward their historically normal levels of 2 to 3 percent. For this to happen, projected federal budget deficits will have to be brought down as a percentage of GNP and—again, equally important—perceived in the short term as likely to come down. Without such a perception, real interest rates would remain high either because expectations of renewed inflation resulting from the financing of future deficits through monetary expansion become self-perpetuating or because, with savings rates remaining low, government borrowing to finance currently projected deficits would produce a crowding out of proposed private sector borrowings.

Indeed, since the overall relationship between expectations and behavior is largely conjectural, and perhaps inherently uncertain, no one can say for sure exactly what combination of spending cuts and tax increases would be sufficient or of suitable quality to generate an expectation that future inflation rates will be kept low. Any number of proposals are currently under discussion. Some combine spending cuts with revenue increases obtained by rescinding a portion of the multiyear income tax cuts enacted in 1981. Others would keep these cuts intact but raise revenue through energy, sumptuary, or other excise taxes or through so-called consumption taxes designed to steer the tax system away from its present bias against savings and investment. Meanwhile, the continued jockeying for position between the executive and legislative branches of government—aggravated in recent years by the rivalry between a Republican administration, on the one hand, and Democratic congressional leaders and presidential candidates, on the other—has in-

Figure 2.6
REAL INTEREST RATE ON TEN-YEAR TREASURY
SECURITIES, 1955–84

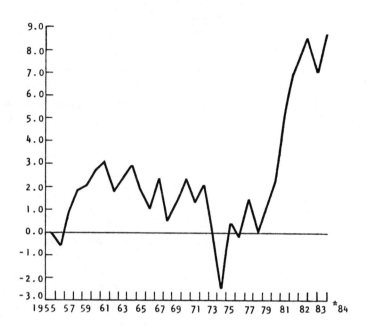

*Estimate for the first quarter of 1984.

Notes: Real Interest as defined here is the difference between the treasury security average annual rate and the fourth-quarter-to-fourth-quarter change in the GNP implicit price deflator. Economists normally define *real interest* as the difference between the nominal yield on a fixed-income security and the *expected* rate of inflation over the period of the security. Since the expected rate of inflation is necessarily a matter of judgment and often a difficult number to determine unambiguously, we prefer to use the current inflation rate, which coincides with the general usage of investors.

Sources: Executive Office of the President, *Economic Report of the President*, February 1984, p. 298; U.S. Department of Commerce, *Business Conditions Digest*, August 1983, p. 84; *New York Times*, March 21, 1984, pp. D1 and D6; Board of Governors of the Federal Reserve System, *Federal Reserve Bulletin*, various editions.

creased the risk of renewed inflation. If nothing else, the consequent delay in coming to grips with the deficit creates expectations that the government as a whole (meaning the executive and legislative branches taken together) is incapable of bringing the deficit under tighter control. With an expansionary fiscal policy even during a recovery, the burden of controlling inflation falls all the more on the monetary policy of the Federal Reserve Board, which is already overburdened and perhaps unable for technical reasons to influence the supply of money in as rational or predictable a manner as would be desired.[16] This mix of policy, besides holding market interest rates high, also adds to uncertainty; since the Federal Reserve can shift its policy stance quickly and unexpectedly, markets often react (or ''overreact'') to small and frequent changes in information (e.g., weekly money supply figures), which in turn contributes to continued volatility in interest rates.

Since 1980, large capital inflows from abroad, attracted by high U.S. interest rates and by a perceived safe-haven value to short-term investment in the United States, have made credit conditions easier than domestic policies alone would imply. These inflows also kept the exchange value of the dollar high through most of 1984, which has hurt U.S. exports, particularly of manufactured goods, and led to record deficits in the balance of merchandise trade and on the current account (encompassing goods and services). At some point this inflow of ''extra'' savings is likely to decline, as foreigners also come to see projected federal budget deficits as ''too high'' or as they simply see investment opportunities in their own or third countries as more worthwhile than those they have previously been making in the United States. When these inflows begin to decline, the exchange value of the dollar is also likely to fall, adding inflationary pressures as prices of imported goods and import-competing goods rise. As this happens, U.S. exports would begin to recover and imports would begin to slow down, and U.S. trade and current account balances would move toward surplus (or at least to less of a deficit position), thereby directly stimulating domestic growth. But with the capital inflows that previously cushioned domestic credit markets falling off and with inflation possibly on the rise at the same time (tending to raise U.S. interest rates), the net effect of these

---

16. The nature of U.S. financial markets is changing so rapidly that the various targets, indicators, and instruments of monetary policy have become increasingly difficult to measure or work with. This leads to unavoidable miscalculations in attempts to control or estimate the rate of monetary growth, which in turn leads to under- and overshooting of policy-based targets.

various cross trends, either on interest rates or on the economy as a whole, is hard to predict. Much depends on qualitative factors and expectations.

As of late-1984, with a cyclical recovery well under way, whatever benefits might have stemmed from an expansionary fiscal policy during the 1981/82 recession are by now almost certainly offset by the fears generated by large and increasing budget deficits. If—and as of this writing, it is a big "if" but one that logic suggests will happen eventually—the executive and legislative branches do fashion a package of spending cuts and tax increases in 1985, this would (or at least should) create expectations of an end to growing deficits as a percentage of GNP. In that case, whatever increases in interest rates might occur would likely be small enough to avoid nullifying the positive effects of the various underlying changes referred to above. As is often the case with "good news," the positive forces driving an economy forward tend to be undervalued simply because the offsetting negative forces—most notably, at the moment, the fear of an aborted recovery—seem all too evident. In fact, as the current cyclical recovery shows, such positive forces do exist and can have an extremely strong impact once the negative forces bottling them up are lessened or eliminated. Thus, if residual fears of inflation and resulting high interest rates are brought down, the positive forces that have been at work even while such fears existed would become even more effective. This would enable growth in the United States to average about 4 percent a year to 1988, before falling to roughly 3 percent a year to the end of the century.[17]

Under these circumstances, a sustained recovery of the U.S. economy would take place. Consumer spending, which stimulated the cyclical recovery, would be followed by new investment and exports as the main stimulants to continued growth. A virtuous cycle in which increased confidence in the future stimulates increased (and broadened) investment, leading to higher growth and improved productivity performance, would replace, at least for some years, the vicious cycle of stagflation or "go-stop" growth that lasted almost a decade following

---

17. For another version of a similar scenario, see Herman Kahn, *The Coming Boom: Economic, Political, and Social* (New York: Simon and Schuster, 1982). The 4 percent and 3 percent forecasts mentioned above should be compared with a recent consensus forecast of average annual growth of 3.1 percent for the 1984–89 and 1990–94 periods. See *Blue Chip Economic Indicators*, April 10, 1984.

the 1973/74 oil and other commodity price increases. With the cyclical recovery blending into a sustained expansion, and a generally upward trend lasting for an unusually long period, expectations for the U.S. economy even beyond the 1980s would, at the very least, be considerably more favorable than the pessimistic views characteristic of the 1970s and possibly favorable enough, as such a recovery unfolded, to create new positive expectations that would help carry the generally upward trend forward into the 1990s.

Japanese Economic Prospects

Japan's rate of economic growth, while much lower now than in the 1950s and 1960s, is still higher than the average for other OECD countries and likely to remain higher for some years hence. Having come to think that they have caught up to the previously developed, predominantly Western countries in terms of a flow of income, Japanese are now likely to want to catch up to these other countries in terms of a stock of wealth as well.[18] Simply seeking a higher rate of economic

---

18. This distinction between catching up to the West in terms of a flow of income and catching up in terms of a stock of wealth comes from a recently published "vision" in the series of such reports sponsored by the Ministry of International Trade and Industry. See Sangyō Kōzō Shingikai [Industrial Structure Council], *Hachijū nendai no tsūsan seisaku bijon* [Vision of trade and industry policy for the 1980s] (Tokyo: Ministry of International Trade and Industry, April 1980), pp. 25–27.

The possibility that Japan's rate of economic growth would remain higher than those of other countries for a longer period of time than was then generally expected, together with the specific suggestion that Japan might pass the United States in per capita income by the year 2000, were major points in Herman Kahn, *The Emerging Japanese Superstate: Challenge and Response* (Englewood Cliffs, N.J.: Prentice-Hall, 1970). For a discussion of why a several-year period of high growth would be desirable, for both Japan and other countries, and a scenario of how such growth might be attained through public and private infrastructure development, see Herman Kahn and Thomas Pepper, *The Japanese Challenge: The Success and Failure of Economic Success* (New York: Thomas Y. Crowell, 1979).

For more recent projections of why and how Japan might continue to achieve higher growth rates than other advanced industrial countries for some years hence, see Norman Macrae, "Must Japan Slow?" *The Economist*, February 23, 1980, pp. Survey 1–42; and Thomas Pepper, "The Continuing Japanese Challenge," in *Japan and the United States in a Turbulent World: Myths and Reality*, ed. Yusaku Furuhashi (West Babylon, N.Y.: KCG Productions, 1981).

growth than other advanced countries is not the same as achieving it. Still, Japan's record of growth throughout the postwar period, including the past decade when global economic performance was much weaker than the preceding 25 years, suggests that Japan is more likely than not to achieve the goals it sets for itself.

Moreover, if the current U.S. recovery is sustained to the late 1980s, which seems likely, the Japanese economy would receive a significant real and psychological lift. In terms of short-run effects (that is, another one to two years), the U.S. market would remain generally open to imports, and the volume of imports would be increasing.[19] This would stimulate Japanese exports to the United States and to other countries, particularly other countries in the Asia-Pacific region, whose own exports to the United States would also be growing rapidly.[20] More important, for the medium term (that is, three to five years), a sustained U.S. recovery would serve as an "umbrella" under which Japanese domestic demand would be able to expand more rapidly than over the past decade. Japan's pent-up demand for housing and other infrastructure needs would be freed from a seemingly ever-present and self-defeating fear of insufficient global demand or of U.S. protectionism. The growth stimulus stemming from exports to the United States would soon be outstripped by the stimulus of a domestic Japanese recovery, encompassing increased investment in infrastructure and higher-technology manufacturing and services. This would lead in turn to increased imports from the United States and other Asia-Pacific countries.

As is currently the case in the United States as well, evaluations of Japan's economic potential turn to a large extent on expectations. Since recent rates of economic growth have fallen well short of previous performance, many current expectations about future growth have been considerably scaled down. The past three years did register ex-

---

19. In a period of sustained recovery, the U.S. economy would need to remain generally open to imports as a means of containing inflation. Moreover, in such a buoyant environment, new jobs would be created quickly enough to neutralize most of the sectoral pressures for protectionism that would otherwise develop.

20. This is an important element in the upward adjustment of many recent short-term forecasts since, as one such forecast put it, "the U.S. accounts for 30 percent of Japan's total exports, and . . . Southeast Asia—the countries that receive the greatest benefit of a buisness upturn in America—accounts for 23 percent." See The Long-Term Credit Bank of Japan, Ltd., *LTCB Economic Outlook*, February 1984, p. 1.

ceptionally slow growth for Japan, at least by previous standards: growth in 1981 was 4.2 percent; in 1982 and 1983, 3.0 percent.[21] Although this poorer-than-expected performance has been used to support long-standing criticisms of various allegedly "optimistic" medium-term projections, official forecasts continue to assume that Japan will maintain a higher average growth rate than other advanced industrial countries to the end of the century.[22] Again, as in the U.S. case, weaknesses in the Japanese economy are likely to be offset by major economic strengths.

First, even in light of the lessened expectations noted above, Japanese thinking, institutions, and political processes all retain a stronger bias toward high economic growth than those of other advanced industrial countries. This preference for higher, rather than lower, growth rates is evident in the continuing drive to improve living standards, in the strong and continuing commitment by both business and government to higher-technology manufacturing, and in the continuation of a "survival" mind-set in public opinion (that is, the notion that extraordinary efforts are still needed to avoid catastrophe and consequent manifestations of this notion in various policy decisions). For example, the Japanese developed a clear commitment to move rapidly toward an information-based society in the late 1970s, earlier than either the United States or Western Europe.[23] In both policy discussions and private sector strategic planning discussions, Japanese make almost no distinction between information-intensive manufacturing activities and information-intensive service activities; both are seen as a natural continuation of the economic development that has occurred to date. Resistance to the loss of manufacturing capabilities once thought to be critical to Japan's economic health, while of course present in specific instances, has thus far largely been avoided by rapid moves into still newer manufacturing and service activities and through the use of cap-

21. Organisation for Economic Co-operation and Development, *OECD Economic Outlook 35* (Paris: OECD, July 1984), pp. 18, 152.

22. For a useful summary of existing official and semiofficial expectations of Japanese economic performance and of structural changes likely to occur between now and the end of the century, see Planning Bureau, Economic Planning Agency, *Nisennen no nippon* (Tokyo: Nihon keizai shimbun sha, 1982), translated and published in English under the title *Japan in the Year 2000* (Tokyo: Japan Times, 1983).

23. See Sangyō Kōzō Shingikai [Industrial Structure Council], *Hachijū nendai no tsūsan seisaku bijon* [Vision of trade and industry policy for the 1980s].

ital exports to establish equity stakes in older-style manufacturing capabilities located abroad. In general the broad consensus in Japan in favor of continued high economic growth provides widespread support for whatever industrial structure shifts are called for by changing technologies and changing comparative advantage vis-à-vis other countries.

Second, new sources of domestic and international demand are emerging and enabling existing major industries to show renewed vigor. Japan's past industrial successes have been built on the emergence of strong domestic markets supported subsequently by exports in an otherwise robust global economic environment. Thus industrial production growth will be particularly strong if the current U.S. recovery is sustained. Given the existing cost competitiveness of many Japanese industries and continued room for increased capacity utilization, the economy as a whole can respond rapidly to improvements in the global economic environment. For example, the Japanese automobile, shipbuilding, and consumer electronics industries are highly competitive in world markets and would all respond rapidly to an extended world recovery, meaning that Japan would be among the main beneficiaries of a sustained U.S. recovery. Such a recovery would provide a spur to domestic recovery in Japan in the short term and a basis for sustained Japanese growth through increased infrastructure development over the medium term and the enhanced development of such industries as computers and other advanced electronics, plant and equipment exports, and machine tools, among others.

Third, Japanese manufacturing firms continue to be successful in adapting new technologies and management techniques to lower-productivity sectors. This process is now spreading to small businesses and services, most notably in the distribution sector, which has long been a lagging sector in terms of productivity levels.[24] But recent innovations such as convenience stores, automated banking, fast-food chains, and the like suggest that—as has often happened in Japan's postwar economic growth—lagging sectors are turned into high-growth sectors through investment and the introduction of new technologies or managerial techniques. In fact, since the more modernized parts of the

---

24. For comparisons of U.S. and Japanese productivity levels and growth trends, see Elliot S. Grossman and George E. Sadler, *Comparative Productivity Dynamics: Japan and the United States* (Houston: American Productivity Center, 1982).

manufacturing sector grew so rapidly in the postwar years, the very differences that exist between the more modern and the more traditional sectors offer significant potential for productivity growth. More important, insofar as the future is concerned, many of the lessons to be learned in the maturation of lagging service industries can be adapted from the U.S. experience. Such adaptability is a particular Japanese strength and has the potential in the service sector to generate significant future growth for the economy as a whole.

Japan does face major economic weaknesses, although as in the U.S. case, these are often given too much weight in overall judgments. In part this stems from the predominantly short-term nature of most forecasts, which for this reason are biased against the underlying long-term factors driving the economy in a positive direction.

One major weakness in the Japanese economy stems from the constraints currently governing Japan's fiscal and monetary policies. Following a precipitous increase in government budget deficits in the 1970s, Japan now has little scope for stimulative, Keynesian-style fiscal policies. In this respect both the United States and Japan are in similar positions except that Japan's budget deficits, as a percentage of GNP, increased even earlier than the United States's, and Japan's accumulated debt is now considerably higher, as a percentage of GNP (see Figure 2.7). Because Japan's savings rate is so much higher than that of the United States—in 1982 Japan's gross savings were nearly 32 percent of GDP, as against 16 percent for the United States—its budget deficits and higher accumulated debt level can be accommodated with less immediate concern about inflation or a crowding out of private investment.[25] Nonetheless, the magnitude of the debt and the speed with which it expanded since the early 1970s have imposed a major burden on domestic financial markets and a major potential drag on future growth as investment demand for funds expands. Meanwhile, with domestic demand growing only slowly for the past several years, there is also little scope in the short term for tax increases that would reduce the government's need to finance its deficits through borrowing in domestic capital markets. Although the last two prime ministers have both made a point of saying they would reduce "unnecessary" govern-

---

25. The above data are from Organisation for Economic Co-operation and Development, *OECD Economic Outlook 34* (Paris: OECD, December 1983) p. 155.

Figure 2.7
PERCENTAGE OF GOVERNMENT DEBT
TO NOMINAL GDP, 1973–84

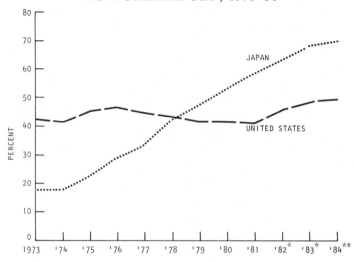

*Estimates.
**Forecast.

Source: Organisation for Economic Co-operation and Development, *OECD Economic Outlook 34* (Paris: OECD, December 1983), p. 43.

ment spending through administrative rationalization—and undertake this effort before raising taxes—the goal is still a long way from being attained as it flies in the face of the usual political resistance from entrenched special interests.[26]

Japan's monetary policy is similarly constrained. Although domestic and international forces have greatly reduced the degree to which

26. Advocates of increased stimulation not only argue that Japan's high savings rate means that its budget deficits are much less inflationary than those in other countries; they also usually see higher growth as the only way, short of supposedly infeasible (and deflationary) tax increases, of ever bringing the deficit down. By contrast, advocates of restraint argue that the deficit must be pared before increased stimulation can even be considered; otherwise, this argument runs, future deficits will become so large that even with Japan's high savings rate they would be inflationary in themselves or would crowd out private investment.

Japanese capital markets are insulated from world capital markets, the formal structure of the Japanese market remains highly regulated, segmented, and, for these reasons, relatively inflexible. When unregulated U.S. interest rates rose in 1980/81 to levels roughly double those in Japan's regulated market, Japan began to experience a substantial outflow of short-term capital, which in turn helped to weaken the value of the yen beyond all expectations. Even though the interest rate differential narrowed after 1981, it has remained a significant incentive for Japanese to continue to invest in dollar-denominated assets.[27] As long as overall domestic demand remains weak, Japanese monetary authorities cannot afford to raise interest rates significantly to strengthen the yen; and in the face of a continuing disparity between Japan's still-regulated (and artificially low) domestic interest rates and the higher rates prevailing abroad, the authorities cannot afford to stimulate domestic demand by lowering Japanese rates either.

Thus both fiscal and monetary policy are boxed in by existing conditions. Somewhat like the United States, if for different reasons, Japan has little choice, in its macroeconomic policy, but to wait out a longer-than-desirable period within which to squeeze previous excesses out of the system, that is, to work off some of its accumulated debt or at least to prevent debt levels from continuing to increase as a percentage of GNP. The deficit as a percentage of GNP did fall from 4.1 percent in 1982 to an estimated 3.4 percent in 1983 and is projected to decline to 2.5 percent in 1984.[28] Such slow but steady improvement, both before and early in a domestic recovery, suggests that the medium-term prospects for stabilizing Japan's public finance problems are encouraging and that the constraints the deficit currently imposes on macroeconomic policy will ease.

A second major weakness in the Japanese economy is the substantial pressure for disinvestment in a broad range of declining industries. The most notable examples are petrochemicals, synthetic fibers, aluminum, other nonferrous metals, and parts of the steel industry. The restructuring of these industries will obviously restrain economic growth. Japan now faces more problems in this area than in the past because

---

27. Short- and long-term interest rate differentials are discussed further in a subsequent section on likely structural changes.

28. See Organisation for Economic Co-operation and Development, *OECD Economic Outlook 34* (Paris: OECD, December 1983) p. 33.

its level of economic development has reached a point where previously well-established basic manufacturing industries are becoming uncompetitive. Nonetheless, Japan's ability to restructure declining industries has been, and seems likely to remain, superior to that of other advanced countries. Japanese firms have considerable experience in moving resources rapidly from activities with declining potential to activities with growing potential. Typically, the labor force cooperates with such restructuring plans, although the terms on which this cooperation is obtained have become tougher than in the past. Moreover, those parts of a declining sector that are retained have been, and are likely to continue to be, the more productive plants or firms in the industry. Also, as noted above, a sustained recovery in the United States, which spilled over into increased demand in Japan, would enable some of the pressure for disinvestment to be spread over several years, as producers take advantage of buoyant conditions.[29] In this environment, and with continued interest in high economic growth as an underlying motivation for investment in new industries, the deflationary aspects of restructuring away from basic manufacturing industries are likely to be offset by the stimulative effects of such new investments.

A third important weakness in the Japanese economy stems from the protectionist steps already taken by the United States and Western Europe, which do limit export growth in some key industries, notably automobiles, steel, and videotape recorders, and more important perhaps, the fear on the part of Japanese that such protectionist pressures will be intensified. In 1977 and again in 1981, exports accounted for

---

29. In fact, much of the success of any restructuring effort depends on current macroeconomic conditions. In a buoyant economic environment, companies can generate sufficient cash flow to enable industries undergoing structural change to compensate for the adjustments they must make by investing in new product lines or in new areas entirely. Through most of the postwar period, Japan was able to restructure industries relatively rapidly because aggregate growth was exceptionally high. The initial, deflationary aspects of the restructuring process could be accomplished quickly. Meanwhile, as newly released factors of production were reemployed in areas of higher productivity, the restructuring process quickly took on a positive character, stimulating rather than restraining new growth. New products with high growth potential were generated; new investments took up the slack left by declining industries.

an overwhelming share of Japanese demand growth, contributing in turn to increased friction between Japan and its major trading partners.[30] As a result the potential for continued rapid export growth is limited by a political constraint against further trade friction, particularly with regard to such important export-oriented industries as automobiles and steel where the effects on unemployment in other countries have already been strong. This political constraint against increased export growth has led to increased exports of Japanese capital, either to establish plants in the United States or to participate in portfolio investment in the United States because comparable opportunities in Japan appear less worthwhile. To this extent, protectionist steps taken by the United States so far (that is, quotas on auto imports) have been deflationary in Japan in the sense of lowering output and diverting prospective domestic investment to projects located abroad. In spite of the job-enhancing effects these protectionist steps may appear to have had in the United States in the short term, they may even have been deflationary in both the United States and Japan over the medium term because of the demand-reducing effect of higher prices in the United States. These protectionist steps have probably also deterred Japanese from investing at home in both directly affected and other industries, perhaps out of fear of even more severe protectionist restrictions in the future.[31] Much of the political pressure for protectionist measures will ease, but not disappear, as the U.S. recovery proceeds.

A fourth weakness in the Japanese economy stems from Japan's high rate of domestic savings, which, if coupled with weak investment demand and a slow rate of growth for disposable income, as has been the case in recent years, tends to restrain domestic growth. This is the so-called savings trap issue—that is, when planned savings exceed the actual demand for investment funds (both from private investment spending and government borrowing), more funds are leaking out of the aggregate flow of income than are being put back in; as a result, aggregate demand and aggregate income both fall. Given Japan's continuing high savings rate, data during the past several years might be

---

30. The role of net exports in demand growth has persisted at a high level since 1981 and is generally expected to decline only after 1984.

31. Quotas on auto imports to the United States have been self-defeating in another sense: Japan-based producers, faced with quantitative restrictions, shifted their export mix to upscale models where profit margins are higher, resulting in little or no gain in balance of payments terms and in greater competition for those segments of the market where U.S.-based producers previously were stronger.

interpreted to support fears of a savings trap. However, a persistent savings trap, lasting several more years, is unlikely. Savings rates have been declining since 1970, albeit only slowly in the wake of oil shocks that temporarily reinforced traditional Japanese fears of catastrophe. Meanwhile, the cyclical recovery in the United States and the likely subsequent recovery in Japan have expanded investment and consumer demand and thereby increase private demand for funds. Moreover, after doing without it for many years, the Japanese economy is making increasing use of consumer credit, which will significantly alter traditional spending habits and in effect stimulate consumer spending. In spite of pressures for administrative rationalization, government demand will continue to grow, especially for infrastructure investment. Private demand for infrastructure investment will grow, that is, in the housing industry, which in spite of its several-year slump has considerable potential simply because the quality of Japan's existing housing is so low compared with other advanced industrial countries. Finally, as the U.S. and Japanese recoveries continue to proceed beyond the current recovery, many industries will want to accelerate their restructuring plans to be able to take advantage of improving conditions. Thus we see the savings trap issue as a short-term problem induced mainly by the stagflationary conditions of the past decade, particularly the 1980/81 global recession and lingering fears of resource scarcity, and as an issue that is largely soluble in the course of the pickup we anticipate for the rest of the 1980s.

To summarize, Japan's economic weaknesses are mainly short term; its strengths are mainly longer term. Assuming the current U.S. recovery is sustained to the late 1980s, growth in Japanese real GNP will remain slow by earlier Japanese standards but rise from the depressed levels of the early 1980s to a 4 to 6 percent annual average through the late 1980s.

STRUCTURAL CHANGES IN THE JAPANESE ECONOMY

Any number of demographic, social, and economic changes in Japan have been widely predicted as likely before the end of the century.[32] The most assured change of all—a considerable increase in the proportion of elderly people in the total population, from 9 percent in 1980

---

32. See Planning Bureau, Economic Planning Agency, *Japan in the Year 2000*, for further details on the specific examples cited below.

to an estimated 15.6 percent in the year 2000—has been so well publicized that private and public sector planning for this contingency is well under way. Other widely expected changes include an increase in the number of one-person households; and increasing "softwarization" of economic activity (meaning an increased emphasis on intangible, rather than tangible, phenomena—that is, design, rather than fabric, in the apparel industry; or software, rather than hardware, in the computer systems); a desire for more varied life-styles, implying an ever-widening spectrum of consumer choice (and wants); a much increased acceptance of five-day workweeks and longer summer vacations than is now customary; and considerably expanded public and private pension systems to take account of the increased proportion of the elderly.

As far as trade and international financial patterns are concerned, Japan is slowly moving away from the Heckscher-Ohlin, or "vertical," trade patterns associated with the 100-plus years of economic development since the Meiji Restoration and toward the "horizontal," or intra-industry, trade patterns that have long characterized exchanges among other advanced industrial countries.[33] This pattern is most visible in intra-European trade, in which two nations buy and sell many of the same commodities—German cars are sold in France, French cars in Germany, and so on. This shift toward a horizontal pattern is occurring in spite of whatever cultural biases may have prevented it from occurring in the past or as rapidly as it might have occurred in another country moving through various stages of development. New trade patterns have already appeared in basic and various intermediate manufacturing industries (for example, petrochemicals, aluminum, and other base metals, roughly in order of their energy intensity). Japanese imports of these goods have been increasing apace and will continue to increase in percentage and volume terms in ensuing years.[34] A broader spectrum of forces will work to expand imports of other manufactured goods

---

33. For a comprehensive discussion of the post–World War II development of trade in similar products among advanced countries, see Herbert G. Grubel and P. J. Lloyd, *Intra-Industry Trade* (New York: John Wiley & Sons, 1975). For a recent evaluation of theoretical explanations of such trade, see Jagdish N. Bhagwati and T. N. Srinivasan, *Lectures on International Trade* (Cambridge and London: Massachusetts Institute of Technology Press, 1982), especially chap. 8.

34. Trends in declining industries are discussed in detail in Chapter 6.

more or less steadily in the direction of a horizontal trade pattern, but significant changes in the total volume of these imports are likely only toward the end of the 1980s.

The Japanese economy, like other advanced industrial countries, will be moving toward a more specialized manufacturing sector (that is, higher-technology manufacturing) and a more modernized service sector (that is, where services are less a residual category for underemployed persons or low-paying jobs and more a source of productivity growth comparable with the manufacturing sector). As Japan comes to manufacture higher-technology products, it will inevitably start importing more "low-end-of-the-market" manufactured goods. Indeed, it has to make this shift in order to be able to export new products competitively since various newly industrializing countries (NICs) will come to outcompete Japan and other advanced industrial countries in many basic manufacturing industries. As these shifts take place, Japanese firms will probably continue to do well in a higher-technology version of their traditionally successful methods of operation—namely, to concentrate on certain selected products, to develop a mass production capability that lowers unit costs considerably by selling in both domestic and export markets, and to do particularly well in selling to specially targeted markets.

With regard to services, Japan is likely to follow a path already laid by the United States, which is further along in a shift to more trade in services than has traditionally been thought likely. The United States may have a particular advantage over Japan in services trade because the flexibility of the U.S. social structure helps to nurture many new types of jobs and businesses. Software design, accounting, hotel management, certain kinds of financial services, and management consulting are examples of the kinds of services in which Japan may be at a relative disadvantage in part because the Japanese language is less easily transferable internationally than English. By the same token, Japanese will excel at other kinds of services, such as engineering-related consulting, freight forwarding, and wholesale trading in many bulk commodities (where Japan's famous sōgō shōsha, meaning general trading companies such as Mitsui & Company, have a commanding position worldwide).

As noted above, Japanese tastes are also changing. With further economic development, the value system of earlier postwar years no longer governs consumer preferences. Before balance of payments surpluses began to be amassed in the early 1970s (and were then temporarily, but only temporarily, interrupted by oil price increases), few Japanese consumers sought—or perhaps realized that they could seek—a wide variety of often lower-priced imported products in lieu of higher-priced, domestically produced products of more limited variety. Today the regulations governing imported products and foreign exchange have been considerably liberalized. Consumers at both the retail and the wholesale level are changing their preferences both as their incomes have risen and as they have come to expect an increased availability of foreign goods. At the retail level, the once-unquestioned idea that foreign consumer goods were simply "luxuries" is changing for various reasons—including increased travel (once foreign exchange allocations for tourism were liberalized in the early 1970s), greater efforts by foreign exporters to sell to the Japanese market, and official attempts to encourage imports or at least not discourage them.

It is at the wholesale level, however, that changing tastes (or preferences) are likely to have a more immediate impact on Japanese trade patterns. When Japanese producers find they can no longer sell goods competitively if they buy only (or mainly) higher-priced, domestically produced inputs, they are likely to purchase foreign-produced inputs—and to do so with few second thoughts. Indeed, as discussed in greater detail in Chapter 6, this shift has already occurred in various energy-intensive industries where the price differentials between domestically produced and foreign-produced inputs are so great that Japanese users of these inputs have, as they would put it, "no choice" but to buy the foreign product. Similarly, two-way U.S.-Japanese trade in semiconductors has increased as producers in both countries have decided, sometimes for quite different reasons, to purchase supplies from abroad or to establish manufacturing facilities in the other country.[35]

In time, Japan's shift to horizontal trade in manufactures and to

---

35. According to the figures compiled by the Semiconductor Industry Association, Japanese exports of semiconductors to the United States increased from $583.9 million in 1982 to $909.9 million in 1983, an increase of 56 percent. Of this total, Japanese exports of integrated circuits to the United States increased from $445.1 million to $651 million, an increase of 46 percent. U.S. exports of semiconductors to Japan increased from $184.3 million in 1982 to $243.6 million in 1983, an increase of 32 percent. Of this total, U.S. exports of integrated circuits to Japan increased from $138.6 million in 1982 to $171.4 million in 1983, an increase of 24 percent. Generally, Japanese semiconductor exports to the United States are in memory chips, and U.S. exports to Japan are in logic chips. For further discussion of high-technology trade, see Chapter 5. The figures above were supplied in private conversation.

increased trade in services will be visible in still more parts of the economy than it has been so far. For example, as technological capabilities and
wage levels in the United States and Japan converge relative to the past,
the reasons that lead various U.S.- or Japan-based companies to invest
in increased sales or manufacturing facilities in the other country, and
to specialize in producing for only certain segments of the market rather
than across the board, will stem from qualitative factors such as access
to markets, efficient production runs, facilitation of delivery, specialized proprietary knowledge, and a gradual broadening of the concept
of complementarity to more and more products (that is, a "world computer" or a "world car").[36] In services trade the by-now obvious
growth of sushi shops in New York and McDonald's-style fast-food
chains in Tokyo are two examples of how intangible concepts of taste,
industrial engineering, and marketing can cross national boundaries
with great flexibility. In general, both kinds of changes—more horizontal
trade in high-technology manufactures and more trade volume in a variety of services—are likely to characterize future Japanese trade patterns, certainly compared with the past, although the pace at which such
changes occur would clearly be greater in an environment of higher
rather than lower economic growth. At the moment the pace at which
these shifts are occurring remains a major issue between Japan and its
trading partners. But the discussion of pace is primarily a political issue and one that Japanese political leaders will have to deal with in a
political context, both domestically and in relations with other countries.
Meanwhile, the shift to a horizontal trade pattern that is gradually taking place anyway will work to ease various political tensions caused by
foreign perceptions that the pace of change is too slow.

   As with trade patterns, Japanese international financial patterns
are also gradually becoming more open to foreign participation, although here, too, the pace of change remains a major political issue,
particularly between Japan and the United States. For historical reasons the question of capital market liberalization has several distinctly
different dimensions. This means, in turn, that discussions of changes
in Japanese capital markets require an understanding of the interrela-
tionships among those different dimensions.

   First, within Japan, capital market liberalization is only one aspect

---

36. For a review of earlier trends in technological development, see Dale
Jorgensen and Mieko Nishimizu, "Closing the Technology Gap: The United
States versus Japan, With Some Inferences for Other Industrial Countries,"
New International Realities 3 (Winter 1978):1.

of the broader issue of the deregulation of Japanese financial markets in general. Many groups have conflicting interests, including the sometimes quite different concerns of the MOF and the Bank of Japan (BOJ), not to mention the commercial banks and the securities companies, the major banks (so-called city banks) and the smaller regional banks, the banks and securities companies together, and the postal savings system. For example, BOJ officials are concerned that further liberalization of Japanese financial markets would exacerbate the difficulty it already has in controlling the domestic financial system. From the traditional viewpoint of the BOJ, this concern is justified since, as discussed in Chapter 4, its ability to direct the flow of credit in a detailed manner among sectors of the economy has long since become much more difficult than it once was and since changes in global financial markets are influencing domestic conditions much more directly than in the past. However, in the MOF view much of this loosening up of Japanese financial markets is occurring anyway, as the domestic financial system becomes more integrated into the world economy. The question the MOF faces is *how*, rather than whether, to facilitate further deregulation. The problem is one of trying to mediate between and among groups that favor quick adjustments versus those that favor stretching the changes out as long as possible. In general, since the existing system imposes increasing costs on Japanese financial institutions as the overall economy becomes more internationalized, domestic pressures for further liberalization will increase.

A second dimension of the liberalization issue is the increased use of the yen as a currency in international trade and finance. Although Japan has become a major economic power, until recently the government has resisted any expansion of the role of the yen as an international currency, either for private or official purposes.[37] There are, after all, real costs as well as benefits to the internationalization of a currency. The main cost is the government's loss of an ability to intervene easily in the flow of funds affecting the exchange rate. In general, the larger the international market for yen, the more difficult it would be to pursue a monetary policy that diverges sharply from world conditions; large domestic firms could simply lend or borrow directly on international markets in yen. Over time, while the Japanese government can impede the internationalization of the yen, it cannot stop the process if traders and investors outside Japan are going to be able to deal in yen at a level required by the volume of Japanese trade

---

37. West Germany has done the same, and for similar reasons.

and overseas investment. Correspondingly, although considerable international use of the yen has begun in the past three years and continuing pressure exists through official channels (particularly, of late, from the U.S. Treasury Department) for Japan to take on greater international financial responsibilities, the degree to which this can in fact happen also depends overwhelmingly on market forces. The U.S. and Japanese governments can push for increased use of yen in international transactions, and the MOF can play a critical role in liberalizing regulations against the use of certain specific instruments, but in the final analysis the results of such moves will depend mainly on reactions in the market itself.

A third dimension of the liberalization issue is that of the efficiency of the capital market and the separate but related issue of reciprocity. Most economists would argue that freer capital markets increase the efficiency of the international financial system (that is, increase the return to ultimate savers and reduce the cost to ultimate borrowers). By extension, a greater degree of integration of the largest capital market in Asia, namely Tokyo, into the global financial market would further increase the efficiency gains already made. This raises the reciprocity issue. To date, Japanese firms have been able to take advantage of open capital markets elsewhere in the world, whereas outsiders have had only limited, though increasing, access to Japanese capital markets. Since domestic interest rates in Japan are held below those that would emerge in a freer market—domestically or internationally—the restrictions that foreigners face in obtaining access to Japanese capital markets have increasingly been perceived as an unfair trade practice. Although simple newspaper comparisons of interest rates do not give an accurate account of the gap between Japanese and world rates—since the use of compensating balances, fees, and other practices increases the real interest cost in Japan above the posted rate—an unusually large gap between world and Japanese interest rates has existed for several years. This, in turn, has exacerbated the criticism of Japan's system of administered interest rates.[38] A further internationalization

---

38. For example, the differential on money market (short-term) interest rates averaged 8.7 percent in 1981, 5.1 percent in 1982, 2.4 percent in 1983, and 3.3 percent in the first two months of 1984. Long-term rates have not converged to the same degree. Comparable differentials on government bond yields (average to maturity per annum) are 5.1 percent, 4.9 percent, 3.9 percent, and 4.9 percent (January only). These data are from the International Monetary Fund, *International Financial Statistics,* April 1984, p. 61.

of the capital market would lead as a matter of course to further deregulation of domestic interest rates. However, such internationalization would likely also lead to a lessening of the interest rate differentials that now make the idea of borrowing in Japan so attractive to foreigners.

A fourth dimension of capital market liberalization is the concern expressed by many foreign government officials and business representatives that Japanese officials are using a controlled capital market to maintain an artificially low exchange rate to promote exports. In part this concern reflects a legacy of the late 1960s and early 1970s, when such a practice was indeed the case (and was followed by European countries as well). In part the yen is seemingly undervalued at the moment because Japan's low interest rates, compared with the U.S. and Eurocurrency rates, have caused a substantial capital outflow, which has depressed the exchange rate in spite of Japan's large current account surplus. Indeed, Japanese officials have tried, without much success, to use various administrative practices to stem this flow. The capital liberalization that occurred in the wake of the new 1980 foreign exchange law released a pent-up domestic demand for foreign assets (a phenomenon likely whenever administered controls on prices are removed). This pent-up demand was then increased by the unusually high interest rates available to Japanese lenders in U.S. and European markets. Owing to interest rate differentials, borrowing abroad is not particularly attractive to Japanese firms at the moment. Moreover, despite liberalization of restrictions on foreign direct investment, Japan remains a difficult market to enter for a variety of institutional reasons. Until recently, capital investment among all the advanced countries was relatively weak for macroeconomic reasons. All these imbalances of earlier periods take time to work themselves out (for example, any expansion of incoming investment that would almost certainly occur in response to further liberalization would also not take place overnight). In the face of these trends, it is difficult to argue that the system can easily be manipulated to hold the exchange rate down. Indeed, much evidence points to a hope on the part of Japanese officials that the exchange rate would rise; the market has dictated otherwise.

At least in the short run, the interest rate differential between Japan and international markets is difficult to narrow by a significant increase in domestic interest rates; the MOF's latitude here is tightly constrained. The MOF needs to maintain generally low domestic interest rates to stimulate investment in the short term and to keep interest rates low as a means of holding down the government's debt service burden.

On the other hand, interest rates also cannot easily be lowered any further because of a fear of increased capital outflows and/or an even weaker exchange rate. The compromise policy that is currently being followed satisfies no one but cannot easily be changed. Beyond the general macroeconomic policies available to all advanced industrial countries, more detailed control of the Japanese exchange rate through monetary instruments has become less and less possible over time as the size of the foreign exchange market has grown much larger than the reserves available to the government for intervention.

Each of the four dimensions of liberalization of Japanese capital and foreign exchange markets is being driven mainly by the pace and pattern of domestic economic development. The very success of Japan's economic development to date has created an increasingly complex economic system with ever-increasing international relationships. In this environment the financial and capital controls designed for an earlier, less complex period begin to impede the efficient operation of both the financial sector and the economy as a whole. For this reason alone, even excluding protests from foreign governments, the pressures to deregulate the system domestically as well as internationally are coming increasingly to win out over the pressures to retain a highly regulated system. Given Japan's history of economic pragmatism, these pressures for liberalization can be expected to continue to prevail, with the exact nature and pace of liberalization mainly dependent on the scope of various private sector initiatives, domestic and international. These private sector initiatives will have more impact on the authorities—by forcing them more and more into accommodating such initiatives—than abstract appeals to fairness or diplomatic pressure for new ground rules.

IMPLICATIONS FOR U.S.-JAPANESE RELATIONS

Under the circumstances of sustained growth described above, the U.S. and Japanese economies would become increasingly interdependent— as has been the case even during the past ten years of sluggish growth. Such interdependence would be evident in increased cross-trade and investment between the two economies, increased trade in services, increased government-to-government consultation, and in general a much more visible involvement of one country's economic forces in the other. At the same time, any number of specific disputes, whether between the U.S. and Japanese governments or between competing *and* cooperating businesses in the two countries, will continue to arise as a matter of course. This much is built into the logic of competitive behavior and in the different national interests of the two countries. Such disputes are likely to be particularly important in policy discussions, since both governments will continue to face pressures for trade restrictions in industries or sectors subject to significant import penetration.

Still, both the U.S. and Japanese governments and businesses in both countries will share a common interest in keeping the competitive aspects of bilateral relationships within certain limits. Indeed, relationships between the U.S. and Japanese economies are already so multifaceted that interdependence would probably increase even in an adverse, go-stop environment, such as prevailed during the 1980–82 period.[39] As discussed below, a self-correcting process, similar to the concept of supply/demand equilibrium, is likely to be at work and to bring a too-sharp movement in one direction back toward an equilibrium. Even when specific economic disputes appear so intractable or fractious that they become openly politicized, U.S.-Japanese disputes are likely to be kept within limits by the common interests that both countries share in preserving the U.S.-Japan Treaty of Mutual Cooperation and Security. The continuation of a global political rivalry between the United States and the Soviet Union will serve to prevent specific economic disputes from undermining overall U.S.-Japanese relations.[40]

For example, in the well-known case of bilateral merchandise trade,

---

39. This version of increased interdependence would obviously have more negative effects, in terms of fractious exchanges between business and government leaders, intractable negotiations, mutually resented "encroachments" on sovereignty, and so on, than the interdependence arising in a buoyant economic environment—but, again, not so many that they more than offset the positive effects. Equally obviously, if overall economic performance in both countries were to weaken substantially or become extremely erratic, specific economic disputes that would inevitably be exacerbated by an uncertain economic environment could also lead to an increased divergence in U.S.-Japanese economic or even political relations. The latter case is unlikely, however.

40. The absence of such a constraint in relations between Japan and the EEC tempts both sides in that relationship to risk much more brinkmanship and confrontation in their trade and economic disputes than either party risks in the U.S.-Japanese relationship.

as Figure 2.8 shows, Japan has registered a merchandise trade surplus with the United States since 1965. But as the figure also shows, this surplus as a percentage of total bilateral trade has fluctuated widely. At the time of the two previous peaks in Japan's bilateral surplus, the yen then began to increase in value, relative to the dollar, leading in turn to a fall in Japan's trade surplus. The bilateral merchandise trade balance, although regarded by economists as a much less significant figure than the multilateral trade balance or, even more important, the multilateral current account balance, is nonetheless much more widely publicized and generally interpreted by politicians as signifying great damage if and when it becomes strongly negative. For this reason, problems in U.S.-Japanese relations arising from the bilateral trade imbalance have always stemmed less from technical disagreements over a "proper" yen/dollar exchange rate (taking account of trade and financial factors and of expectations) than from different perceptions of a "proper" Japanese political response to domestic U.S. political problems that appeared to be caused by the trade imbalance. In fact U.S.-Japanese political relations became especially testy in 1971 and in 1977/78 when the bilateral trade imbalance approached or exceeded 30 percent of total bilateral trade. However, when the yen then rose in value, and the trade imbalance, as a percentage of total bilateral trade, subsequently declined, political acrimony also declined.

In the most recent flare-up of U.S. criticism of Japan's bilateral trade surplus, the latter was actually declining from 1981 to 1982, as a percentage of total trade (refer again to Figure 2.8), but the recession then being experienced in the United States was greatly aggravating political as well as economic conditions. Correspondingly, when the U.S. economy began to experience an economic recovery beginning in late 1982, public criticism of Japan's overall trade surplus seemed, to us at least, to decline, even though this surplus, as a percentage of total bilateral trade, actually rose in 1983. Depending on how one might measure such matters, U.S. government criticism of Japanese government positions in matters under negotiation may have seemed to increase in 1983 and early 1984, compared with the recessionary days of 1981/82. In our perception of U.S. business attitudes, however, criticism of Japan's trade surplus was replaced, in the increasingly buoyant economic environment of 1983/84, by renewed attention to revived economic activity (sales increases, marketing programs, investment plans, and the like). Individual Americans and American corporations began to view the "Japanese challenge" less as a threat to the U.S.

Figure 2.8
U.S.—JAPANESE TRADE, 1961–83

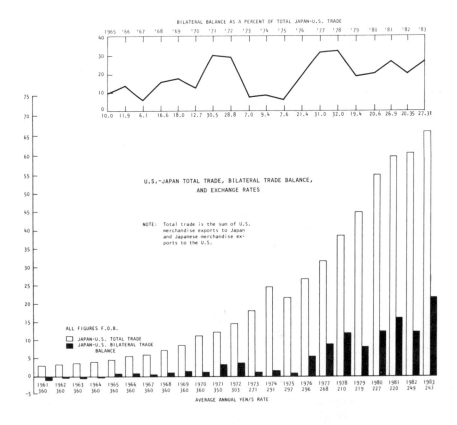

Source: International Monetary Fund, *International Financial Statistics,* various issues; and International Monetary Fund, *Direction of Trade,* various issues.

economy per se and more as a Sputnik-like spur to greater achievements on the part of the U.S. economy.

Since the United States has been recovering sooner and more vigorously than Japan and other advanced industrial countries, it will tend for macroeconomic reasons to increase imports sooner than these other countries. Inevitably, this will create a certain degree of political tension as U.S. trade and current account deficits exceed their already record levels. Nonetheless, in an expanding economy many U.S. firms have come to view competition from abroad as a normal part of doing business, rather than as necessarily a source of unfair competition. In time U.S. trade and current deficits with Japan will narrow. Japanese surpluses will cause the yen to increase in value, relative to the dollar. In addition, a cyclical slowdown in the United States and a pickup in Japan and other advanced industrial countries, combined with an increase in the exchange value of the yen and other currencies, will tend to increase U.S. exports relative to imports.

In a global environment dominated by renewed U.S. and Japanese growth, both the United States and Japan would be likely to support generally free trade policies that promote global growth in the medium to long term rather than increasingly protectionist policies that would cause long-term growth rates to slow down. In this way the United States and Japan would work together to try to minimize protectionist trends that might arise elsewhere, notably in Western Europe. This is evident, for example, in Japanese support of U.S. proposals for a formal round of negotiations, under the auspices of the General Agreement on Tariffs and Trade (GATT), on barriers to trade in services. Moreover, if the U.S. and Japanese economies experience the sustained recoveries described above as likely, this would create favorable conditions for improved economic performance in other advanced and developing countries that are prepared to take advantage of a buoyant external environment.

In Western Europe the key issue is whether the first signs of a cyclical recovery will be accompanied by long overdue structural changes within Europe, particularly greater flexibility in labor markets that, as in the United States and Japan, would enable an initial upturn to be converted into a period of sustained expansion. In general a failure on the part of European countries to continue to make significant structural changes in labor markets (that is, lower wage increases, fewer nonwage costs, more flexible job rules and hiring and firing practices) would contribute to a continuation of the sluggish growth that has prevailed in Europe since the 1974/75 recession and, in the longer term, to a continued loss of competitiveness and dynamism relative to the United States, Japan, and the rapidly growing developing countries of the Asia-Pacific region. Faced with continued low growth, Western Europe might not recover to the extent needed to lessen its serious unemployment problems. Increased protectionism would probably follow, leading in turn to further negative consequences for the nondiscriminatory structure of the world trading system as it has developed since the end of World War II. Under these circumstances both Japan and the United States would face strong pressures to work with each other to protect the gains the world economy had achieved to date and to help contain the damage to their own economies stemming from European economic failures.

The Asia-Pacific countries would benefit directly and substantially from a sustained upturn in the United States and Japan. Except for the Philippines, the Asia-Pacific countries are much less constrained by debt service burdens than Latin American countries.[41] South Korea, Taiwan, Singaport, Malaysia, and Thailand have all returned to roughly the high rates of growth they were achieving before 1973. Canada, Australia, and New Zealand, three advanced countries that are geographically outside of Europe yet retain strong social and cultural ties to Europe, are steadily shifting the focus of their economic activities to the Asia-Pacific region; because of improved U.S. and Japanese performance, Canada and Australia began to experience robust growth in early-to-mid-1983. Such high growth in the Asia-Pacific region would help pull the United States and Japan into further cooperative and competitive relationships vis-à-vis each other and other countries in the region.

To be sure, the causes of low growth and serious instability that have plagued the global economy for the past 12 to 15 years have not totally disappeared, although they do seem to be distinctly less threatening. For example, oil prices are unlikely to increase as sharply or to have as damaging effects as in the 1970s. Moreover, there is now greater understanding on the part of policymakers of the trade and financial market linkages among advanced countries and between advanced and developing countries. A monetarist commitment to resist inflationary increases in liquidity has become a more widely accepted goal among policymakers in the advanced countries, almost regardless of political party or ideology—at least relative to the 1960s and 1970s. Certainly, mistakes will still be made, either in the analysis of problems or in the willingness of political leaders to pursue unpopular or socially difficult policies. Nonetheless, policymakers and political leaders are likely to try harder than before to avoid steps that reignite inflation or that have par-

---

41. South Korea has a much higher level of debt than the Philippines but has demonstrated a considerable ability to manage its economy and thereby maintained the confidence of the international financial community.

ticularly adverse international consequences. Average cyclical movements in the world economy are therefore likely to be much less volatile than those experienced in the post-1973 decade. On the key
assumption of a generally sustained upturn in U.S. performance, world
growth is likely to increase. This higher growth and more stable pattern of economic activity would tend to extend periods of recovery and
to shorten both the lengths and depths of recessions. Increased stability in overall economic performance would almost certainly contribute
to greater willingness on the part of individuals and firms to take a
longer-term view of prospective investments—a key qualitative factor
influencing future economic performance.[42]

As noted earlier, only in the last two years, basically as a result
of the cyclical recovery in the United States, have macroeconomic trends
become positive enough to strengthen expectations about future macroeconomic trends, either in the United States itself or Japan and other
advanced industrial countries. Even this initial shift in attitudes, relative to the pessimism of the 1970s and early 1980s, is all too fragile,
depending, as it does, on the ability of the U.S. economy to experience
a sustained recovery.

In the United States a sustained recovery would mean—indeed,
it would require—increased investment as a percentage of GNP. This
would in turn require a complementary increase in savings as a percentage of GNP, whether from a decrease in government consumption
or an increase in private sector saving. (Figure 2.9 shows a comparison of U.S. and Japanese saving and investment as a percentage of
GDP.) Such increased saving and investment relative to consumption
would strengthen U.S. productivity growth and, on average, the competitiveness of U.S. firms vis-à-vis Japanese firms in any number of
manufacturing industries and services, especially in new, higher-
technology areas. In Japan the already high share of private investment

---

42. An underestimation of various interaction effects among countries has
plagued economic analysis and policy-making since the late 1960s. Such
models as the OECD Interlink and the Wharton LINK, among others, now
explicitly incorporate many direct trade and financial interactions among countries. Nevertheless, the indirect and attitudinal interactions in trade patterns,
exchange rates, interest rates, inflation rates, inflationary expectations, and
investment decisions remain highly conjectural and may well be as, or more,
important than the direct interactions.

Figure 2.9
SAVING AND INVESTMENT AS A PERCENTAGE OF GDP,
UNITED STATES AND JAPAN, 1962–82

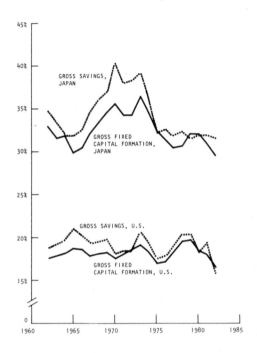

Source: Organisation for Economic Co-operation and Development,
OECD Economic Outlook 34, December 1983, pp. 154–56.

as a percentage of GNP is likely to fall somewhat, as Japanese gradually decide to reap more of the fruits of past labors than they have typically done to date. This shift toward consumption, as a percentage of
GNP, would probably be accompanied by some increase in public investment, which in this context could be interpreted as another form
of consumption. On the other hand, depending on how a program of
infrastructure investment were carried out, it might raise average
productivity growth for at least several years (that is, if improvements
in infrastructure had sufficient spillover effects to pull up the productivity growth of sectors like construction and trade more than the fall
in private investment pulled down the productivity growth of sectors
like steel, machinery, and automobile manufacturing). Either way, such
a shift away from private investment has been a normal part of the proc-

ess of economic development in other advanced industrial countries; for Japan, many people, including ourselves, would say that such a shift is overdue.[43]

This outlook implies a world environment in which the U.S. and Japanese economies continue to grow in a dynamic fashion. The United States and Japan would find even greater common interests with each other and with the rapidly developing countries of East and Southeast Asia. Under these circumstances, many aspects of U.S. and Japanese economies would gradually be converging (for example, growth rates, industrial structure, consumer tastes, financial services, and trade patterns) as Japanese imports of manufactured goods increase. Both countries would be moving along similar paths, promoting further economic development for themselves and indirectly for the world as a whole.

---

43. In time, a failure to make some sort of shift away from private investment would be self-defeating. For one thing, Japanese would continue to live less well than they otherwise might. Second, to the extent that investment continues to be concentrated in leading export-oriented sectors, trade friction with the United States and other countries would be even greater than it already is, although the trade gains to Japan would eventually be counterbalanced by increases in the exchange value of the yen.

Chapter 3

JAPANESE INDUSTRIAL POLICIES

Japan's continued economic success, in spite of two major oil price increases and the stagflationary record of the world economy for nearly a decade after 1973, has led a great number of Americans to assume that the Japanese experience must offer useful lessons for the United States. Because the Japanese government has traditionally played a more active and direct role in the management of the Japanese economy than the U.S. government has played in the management of the U.S. economy, particularly in directing or appearing to direct both public and private funds to particular sectors, industries, or firms, many Americans assume that Japan's economic success must in large measure be due to superior government policies. Moreover, since Japanese policies have at times been explicitly aimed at limiting foreign participation in the Japanese economy, many Americans assume that these government policies have also been designed to promote Japanese economic development at the expense of foreign (mainly U.S.) economic interests and to do so by taking unfair advantage of the nondiscriminatory rules of the postwar international trading system. These views have led, in turn, to suggestions that the United States adopt economic policies modeled on Japan's, either as a means of improving U.S. competitiveness or as a way of retaliating against Japan's alleged unfairness, or both. Indeed, U.S. resentment at Japanese policies or commercial practices has at times run so high that some Americans have advocated retaliation in any case—whether or not U.S. economic performance would benefit from such retaliation and whether or not such retaliation were part of a broader effort to improve U.S. competitiveness.

The record of Japanese postwar economic development, as described in the previous chapter, clearly demonstrates the success Japan has achieved during both favorable and unfavorable global eco-

nomic cnditions. But the degree to which this success can be attributed
to Japanese government policies, as against broader social and historical factors, particularly private sector initiatives, is a much more difficult question. Just to identify which government policies might be
given particular credit for Japanese economic success is itself difficult.
Indeed, many current discussions attribute Japan's economic success
to its industrial policies without necessarily defining what constitutes industrial policies against other economic policies and without attempting to measure the impact of these (often undefined) industrial policies
as against the impact of other economic policies or even broader social
and historical factors.

Accordingly, this chapter describes past and present Japanese industrial policies, assesses the impact of these policies, and suggests the
likely directions of future policies. Because the term *industrial policy* has
sometimes been used so broadly that it can encompass almost any relationship between the economic policies of a government and the economic activities of society as a whole,[1] we try to define *industrial policy*
relatively narrowly: the specific use of policy instruments to foster
growth or rationalization in particular sectors, industries, or firms. This
definition is designed to distinguish between policies that apply only to

---

1. A now-classic OECD study tried to narrow the term down by defining industrial policy with reference to its purpose: "The main purpose of industrial policy instruments is to permit the transfer of resources between the
State and industry in order to achieve specific objectives." More specifically,
"Industrial policy instruments are the means used by the public authorities
to influence the behavior of enterprises in relation to targets fixed, in some
cases, as part of a given strategy. These instruments are intended above all
to influence either the profitability prospects of investment or operating conditions in enterprises by transferring financial costs or resources." See Organisation for Economic Co-operation and Development, *Selected Industrial Policy Instruments: Objectives and Scope* (Paris: OECD, 1978), pp. 7–8. But in failing to specify
the particular objectives to which resources could be directed, this definition
is sufficiently general to permit many traditional areas of economic policy to
be classified as industrial policy—for example, (1) competition policy; (2) technology policy; (3) regional policy; (4) adjustment policy; (5) environmental
policy, health and safety regulations, and other policies aimed at improving
noneconomic aspects of life-styles; (6) other social policies; (7) commercial
policy; and (8) national security policy. Indeed, even macroeconomic policies
to stimulate investment could fit this definition.

particular sectors, industries, or firms and various broad, economywide policies and practices. Although, as we argue later, the latter are probably more important to industrial development itself, industrial policies as defined here are worth studying if only to see how much (or how little) impact they have on industrial development and to identify their trade and competitive effects.

EVOLUTION OF JAPANESE INDUSTRIAL POLICIES

There is nothing particularly mysterious about the way the Japanese government has fostered economic growth and industrial development in the postwar years. Our analysis of various specific policies the Japanese government has employed over the years, including such quantifiable measures as tax benefits and credit allocations and much broader, qualitative measures such as the formulation of future-oriented "visions" and the government's "administrative guidance" to private firms, finds the process to have been reasonably straightforward; in a word, the various policy instruments used by the Japanese government have often been used in other countries as well. That Japan's use of these policy instruments may have been more effective than other countries is a separate question. In any case the main strength of Japanese industrial policies has lain not in any particular instrument or set of instruments but in the way in which these various instruments have been used together, complementing one another directly or indirectly. In fact, to a degree that is probably unmatched anywhere, the Japanese government formulated and then held to a more or less clear commitment to economic growth as a basic national policy and for many years evaluated most important policy measures by whether they promoted this goal.

After Japan's defeat in World War II, the government and the country as a whole were intensely interested in "re-catching up" to the other industrialized countries of the West. This required an emphasis on economic growth that was not, however, based on the precise way in which this term was defined by Simon Kuznets, namely, "sustained increases in product per capita."[2] Rather, economic growth has tradi-

---

2. Simon Kuznets, *Modern Economic Growth: Rate, Structure and Spread* (New Haven: Yale University Press, 1966), p. 1.

tionally been associated in Japan with a much broader concept of "national strength," including military strength, economic strength, social stability, and, as a result, overall political strength.[3] In the early postwar years, and continuing at least through the early 1970s, the goal of economic growth was more or less synonymous with the notion of building up Japan's "national strength." This goal was then translated into policies that promoted savings and investment and, more specifically, a high level of investment in certain specified sectors deemed critical to the growth process. The key role of the government in this process, especially in the immediate postwar years, was as a catalyst to growth: Industrial policies provided specific incentives to the private sector that supported a general sense of confidence and that in turn encouraged a desired pattern of investment and high growth. The ways in which government policies interacted with general economic conditions changed markedly over time; the post–World War II history can usefully be grouped into three periods: the 1945–65 period, 1965–73 period, and 1973 to the present.

Role of MITI in Reviving
Basic Manufacturing Industries: 1945–1965

The process of promoting economic growth began as soon as the war ended and was considerably accelerated in 1948/49 when U.S. occupation policy shifted from one of trying to limit Japan's reemergence as a major power to one that deliberately favored such reemergence as a counterweight to newly perceived threats represented by the Soviet

---

3. The prewar term *kokuryoku* (literally "national strength") now has a harsh ring to it, reminding people of wartime excesses, and as such is no longer used. In effect, the notion of economic growth replaced *kokuryoku* after the war as a basic national goal. Beginning in the late 1970s, as more of the earlier postwar taboos against Japanese interest in national defense weakened, a new term that is also broader than economic growth—*sōgō anzen hoshō*, literally "comprehensive security"—has come into use. The new term incorporates the orthodox idea of national defense, but in a way that deemphasizes a traditionally military-oriented approach to defense, while emphasizing various broad-based factors affecting national security, for example, energy security, raw materials supplies, and high investment levels as a source of continued high growth and presumably thereby, domestic, social and political stability as well.

Union and the new Communist government in China. In 1949 the Ministry of International Trade and Industry (MITI) was formed as an amalgamation of the prewar-descended Ministry of Commerce and Industry and an occupation-organized Board of Trade. Since then, MITI has exercised more influence on Japanese industrial policy than any other ministry or government agency, although this influence has always been constrained by limited budgetary allocations from the MOF. MITI's actual budget remains small even today (for example, only 1.6 percent of the total government budget in 1983). Moreover, as discussed below, MITI's direct influence on industrial development has diminished as the economy itself has grown. In the early postwar years, MITI's policies adhered closely to traditional concepts of national strength, dating back to prewar and even the Meiji period. The government was expected to influence both the kinds of products to be produced and the levels of production.[4] In this regard, the main goal of the early postwar years and the main policy emphasis pursued by

---

4. Chalmers Johnson, in his extensive work on the history of MITI, characterizes this as a "plan-rational" system. He distinguishes between economies that are "market-rational," where "efficiency," in the sense of achieving a certain output with a minimum expenditure of inputs (or the maximum possible output for a fixed quantity of inputs), is the main criterion of decision making, and economies that are "plan-rational," where "effectiveness," in the sense of achieving certain specified objectives without necessarily seeking an economy of resources in achieving these objectives, is the main criterion of decision making. Johnson considers Japan and other later developing countries to be plan-rational, and he sees the government in such states as naturally taking a more active role in promoting economic development than it did or has since done in countries that developed earlier. Carrying the point a step further, Johnson argues that in a market-rational economy, the state concerns itself mainly with regulating the ground rules within which economic activities take place, without trying to direct which economic activities might be undertaken. In a plan-rational economy, on the other hand, a key role of the state is to direct what economic activities are best engaged in. Obviously, the plan-rational state is more likely to have an industrial policy—indeed, as Johnson notes, to give such policy "the greatest precedence." By contrast, "the market-rational state usually will not even have an industrial policy (or, at any rate, will not recognize it as such)." In Johnson's classification system, the United States today is a good example of a market-rational economy, Japan of a plan-rational economy. See Chalmers Johnson, *MITI and the Japanese Miracle* (Stanford, Calif.: Stanford University Press, 1983), pp. 18–19.

MITI was to revive and expand Japan's basic manufacturing industries, and to do so in a way that would also produce goods for export. In resource-poor Japan, great quantities of imported raw materials were needed to provide inputs for manufacturing industries; competitive exports were therefore required to earn the foreign exchange needed to pay for these imports. Japan's industrial development activities sought to build up economies of scale in industries facing income-elastic demand, which in turn drove down per unit prices, thereby producing goods able to compete in international markets.

The government was able to influence industrial development in the early postwar years through an elaborate system of laws and regulations governing foreign trade and international financial transactions. These gave officials direct control over the use of foreign exchange, imports of captial equipment, and, because imports of raw materials and capital equipment were so important to the development of domestic industries, the level and direction of domestic investment as well. The system carried with it the implication that government officials could and would decide, based on their own interpretation of the national interest, which particular activities (or, in some cases, which particular firms) deserved highest priority. This they did most forcefully in the early postwar years. As Lawrence Krause and Sueo Sekiguchi describe MITI's role in those days:

> The MITI had to approve, on a case-by-case basis, any foreign trade transaction that was not to be based on the standard method [of payment]. Thus, the MITI became intimately involved in business decisions from its beginning and was able to evolve into a very powerful ministry.[5]

They also note that under the "standard method of payment," export transactions were treated more generously than imports, financial resources were directed toward tradable goods and thus away from goods produced only for domestic consumption, and imports were limited to allegedly essential goods. Indeed, government policy prevented imports of almost anything except some foods, industrial raw

---

5. Lawrence B. Krause and Sueo Sekiguchi, "Japan and the World Economy," in *Asia's New Giant,* ed. Hugh Patrick and Henry Rosovsky (Washington, D.C.: Brookings Institution, 1976), p. 411.

materials, and capital goods not (yet) manufactured in Japan. Typically, intermediate goods for the producing sector were licensed for import with little difficulty; consumer imports, however, were almost nonexistent. Meanwhile, prospective exporters from other countries generally did not see a market in Japan, or if they accepted in principle that a market existed, they either did not take sufficient measures to penetrate the market or were deterred from doing so, justifiably or not, by (then) high tariffs or other trade barriers.[6]

The policy instruments available to the Japanese government during this period enabled it to influence the economy in a detailed and powerful manner, with the emphasis on a revival and expansion of basic manufacturing industries. Thus, partly by design and partly through the cooperation of the U.S. government, which led the way in setting the rules of international trade at the time, Japanese manufacturers enjoyed considerable infant-industry protection for most of the first 20 years of the postwar period. They also benefited, although clearly more as a coincidence than from any design on their part, from the most rapid period of world growth in output and trade ever recorded. In other words, Japanese manufacturers in this period enjoyed the double benefits of a rapidly expanding and captive domestic market and a large and growing world market. New Japanese products were rarely developed exclusively for export, however. In most cases a domestic market was developed first, giving producers long production runs through which they could achieve the economies of scale that enabled such goods subsequently to be exported at highly competitive prices. Japan's export successes in consumer electronics, steel, and automobiles all illustrate the point. This pattern of industrial development (and attendant policies supporting the development of basic manufacturing industries) continued without interruption until 1965, when Japan's balance on merchandise trade (that is, the value of its exports less its imports of goods) turned significantly and, to date indefinitely, positive.[7]

---

6. Some successes occurred, but the number was low because only a few foreign firms (for example, at that time, Coca-Cola) had both the high liquidity required for extensive start-up costs and the necessary long-term view that entering Japan required.

7. There were small surpluses in earlier years, but a trend was established after 1965.

A Period of Inaction: 1965–1973

Although any period might be described as one of transition, the years between 1965 and 1973 were clearly transitional for Japan's industrial policies. The kinds of government policies that were appropriate for a period of recovery from war, such as direct administrative control over the use of scarce foreign exchange earnings, quite naturally became inappropriate once economic development gradually advanced beyond a recovery stage. Similarly, trade and investment policies designed specifically for infant industries became unjustified once such industries succeeded in establishing a competitive position in world markets. In 1964, when, with U.S. sponsorship, Japan was admitted to membership in the OECD—with the specific implication that it was joining the ranks of the developed countries—the Japanese government was thereby committed to follow the same policies of relatively free trade and investment that already prevailed among other OECD countries.[8] As a result, pressures for change from trading partners, most notably the United States, became increasingly strong. On the surface, Japan did little more than fight a series of holding actions against mounting criticism of its residual trade restrictions and of the pace at which capital liberalization was scheduled to take place.[9] In fact, within the government, and

---

8. Japan had declared Article 11 status in the GATT in 1963; this involved a commitment to remove certain export subsidies and foreign exchange allocations. Japan shifted from Article 14 to Article 8 status in the International Monetary Fund (IMF) in 1964, a step that required it to end controls on foreign exchange used for current account transactions and restrictions on yen convertibility by nonresidents. These steps were followed in 1967 by a phased program of liberalization of capital account transactions.

9. In itself, the idea of a gradual liberalization of international capital transitions was completely consistent with established practice; in any developed country, immediate (that is, nongradual) changes in the regulatory environment would be deemed arbitrary. Nonetheless, heated criticism of the pace of Japan's capital liberalization program began to increase in the late 1960s in large part because Japan's trade surpluses, particularly with the United States, were also increasing. Thus the capital liberalization program became a partial scapegoat for the inability of other countries, for whatever reasons, to sell more goods to Japan. Norman Macrae, deputy editor of *The Economist,* observed as early as May 1967, before the capital liberalization program had officially been unveiled, that it would hardly constitute an opening

particularly within MITI, the period was one of great ferment. Indeed, the ferment itself probably delayed decisive action. As a result, actual changes in industrial or trade policy during these years were almost minimal.

Public discussion of any aspect of foreign trade in Japan was then—and still is—dominated by heated debates over seemingly minor matters, often made "major" by sensational treatment in the domestic press, which in turn is often encouraged to treat trade issues in a sensational manner by Japanese negotiators hoping to shore up their position. In a once-famous case from the 1965–73 period, a U.S. request that American farmers be allowed to export grapefruit to Japan was met with such counterarguments as: (1) Japanese would not like grapefruit; (2) Japanese tangerine sales (and farmers) would be drastically hurt, an event that might upset the social stability of rural constituencies, on which the ruling LDP depended, and perhaps even contribute to Communist party victories; and (3) the ever-invoked general plea that Japan was merely a "small, island country with few natural resources," making what headway it could in a cold, cruel world. Advocates of such a response did suggest at times that a few grapefruits might be admitted as a sign of "sincerity" with the understanding, of course, that for the reasons given above, no great numbers could be considered for some years hence. In retrospect, such arguments—on grapefruits and many other issues—were not based on a wide consensus

---

of the floodgates to foreign investment. As he noted at the time, when he asked a MITI official in which industries foreigners might hope to set up wholly owned subsidiaries, he was jokingly told that *geta,* or Japanese-style wooden clogs, might qualify. In a more serious vein, Macrae went on to conclude that the "first list for so-called capital liberalization is likely to be restricted to industries in which Japanese companies are already so strong, or else in which the Japanese market is already so over-supplied, that only a foreign lunatic would set up a new venture." See Norman Macrae, "The Risen Sun," *The Economist,* May 27, 1967, p. xxvii. In these years, between 1965 and 1973, foreign government officials often spoke with great bitterness about Japan's capital liberalization program, as though they had somehow been misinformed about its provisions or schedule. More likely, they had failed to understand it as well as Macrae did and were then naturally reluctant to blame themselves for problems that were more expediently blamed on the Japanese government. Of course the possibility that such a negative political reaction would arise was a risk the Japanese government took in devising the limited program it did.

of Japanese opinion, as outsiders often imagined them to be, and were probably not even a strongly supported consensus view within whatever ministry had jurisdiction over the item in question. Such arguments nonetheless were typical of discussions in those days—and still occur often.[10]

In this atmosphere, U.S. (and, to a lesser extent, other OECD) represetatives became increasingly frustrated. They saw little progress in efforts to break into the Japanese market—a task that in any event they felt Japanese should facilitate. They also had little luck—or else exhausted themselves—in various attempts to secure Japanese government support for export quotas.[11] The end to this combination of simmering friction and frustration between Japan and its trading partners was signaled by a series of external shocks to the economy described in Chapters 1 and 2 (for example, President Nixon's taking the U.S. dollar off the gold standard in August 1971 and levying an across-the-board 10 percent surcharge on all imports to the United States). This was followed, in October 1971, by an agreement limiting Japanese textile exports to the United States, which was finally reached when the Nixon administration simply threatened to impose the restrictions on

---

10. Current discussions of the prospetive further liberalization of beef, citrus, and capital markets are almost a replay of the grapefruit discussion of more than a decade ago, or indeed of the original capital liberalization program that Macrae described so well in 1967. A typical example of how trivia can become a trade "issue" arose in 1982 when, in the midst of U.S.-Japanese discussions of tobacco imports, then–Finance Minister Michio Watanabe told a group of Japanese reporters that the "reason we don't smoke foreign cigarettes isn't their high price; it's that they don't taste good." See *Asahi Shimbun,* March 4, 1982, p. 9. Under heavy criticism the following day for "substantiating" foreign claims that Japanese were biased against importing manufactured products, Watanabe was then reported to have switched his preference from a Japanese to a U.S. brand.

11. Some European countries, notably France and Italy, kept Japanese goods out altogether or held them to extremely low levels by invoking stipulated exceptions to the GATT or, in the recent cases of French restrictions on Japanese automobile shipments and videocassette recorders, simply through the sometime arbitrary administration of customs regulations. The inflationary or other anticompetitive costs of these measures were obviously deemed, in the political process of these countries, to be tolerable.

Japan unilaterally. The Smithsonian currency agreement of December 1971, reached in response to the measures the United States had taken in August, subsequently broke down in February 1973 and was followed by the establishment of a system of floating exchange rates that is still in place. These currency realignments were occurring at the same time as a global inflationary boom of unprecedented magnitude in 1972/73. Capping this sequence of shocks was the oil price explosion of late 1973.

Throughout this period, MITI was in the midst of a major debate on the future direction of the Japanese economy and its own role in that future. Already in 1970, the *Asahi Shimbun* had launched its *kutabare GNP* ("down with GNP") campaign, and the sarcastic slogan "Gross National Pollution" had gained much public appeal. The public began to criticize MITI for serving the interests of business rather than society as a whole. For a time the reaction against economic growth as a national goal (and against expanding basic manufacturing industries as an unqualified benefit to the economy) seemed to grow as rapidly as the economy itself had been growing. MITI tried to respond to these criticisms with programs to rectify complaints and to give itself a role in the suddenly important field of environmental protection.[12] MITI was also reorganized during this period to introduce so-called horizontal bureaus, covering broad policy areas, in addition to the traditionally powerful vertical, or industry-by-industry, bureaus. The aim was to promote greater consistency both within MITI and among ministries.[13] More important, for the longer term at least, were the formulation and publication of broad-based MITI plans for industrial structure shifts away from basic manufacturing and toward so-called knowledge-intensive industries, meaning those with higher capital per worker requiring (and permitting) higher skills and wages. These plans were made public in various policy papers or "visions," produced either by MITI

---

12. On the theory that environmental protection and the promotion of business interests should not be in the same ministry, an Environment Agency, with cabinet rank, was established in July 1971, with the mission of setting environmental standards and coordinating the environmental protection activities of other ministries.

13. For details, see Johnson, *MITI and the Japanese Miracle*, chap. 8.

itself or by various public/private advisory groups, notably the Industrial Structure Council.[14]

Another version of then-current ideas within MITI evolved into an openly political document when a former MITI minister, Kakuei Tanaka, borrowed heavily from in-house material to develop a plan for infrastructure development that he then used as part of a campaign for the prime ministership. This plan, *Nippon retto kaizō-ron* (literally, "An Essay on the Reconstruction of the Japanese Islands"), more commonly known as "the Tanaka Plan,"[15] stirred great interest, partly because, in contrast to the *Asahi*-led critique of past policies, it took a positive approach.[16] In terms of its scope, the Tanaka Plan was bold indeed. Among other things, it called for a vast decentralization of manufacturing away from the overcrowded Pacific coastline, aiming at a revitalization of other parts of Japan that were otherwise experiencing declining populations. The plan also called for road, school, hospital, and park construction on a scale never before imagined. Although these ideas doubtless contributed to Tanaka's popularity during his early months as prime minister, the actual results proved disappointing—or worse. Land speculation, together with alleged favoritism in contracting for the numerous infrastructure development projects called for in the plan, added to the disillusionment and brought about a dramatic inflation in land prices. A worldwide boom in commodity prices, culminating in

---

14. Such visions have been produced at various times since 1963 and have generated the usual disagreements among scholars, officials, business executives, and journalists as to their importance, either in real or symbolic terms. Yoshihisa Ojimi, then administrative vice-minister of MITI, presented what then became the most well-known such vision to a meeting of the OECD Industry Committee in Tokyo in June 1970. This statement was subsequently incorporated into an English-lanugage reference work. Organisation For Economic Co-operation and Development, *The Industrial Policy of Japan* (Paris: OECD, 1972).

15. Kakuei Tanaka, *Nippon retto kaizō-ron* (Tokyo: Nikkan kogyo shimbun, 1972), translated and published in English as *Building a New Japan* (Tokyo: Simul Press, 1973).

16. The plan appealed to Japanese who, although perhaps disillusioned with previous policies that emphasized basic manufacturing industries almost to the exclusion of anything else, were nonetheless still strongly in favor of continued economic growth.

the oil shock of late 1973 and the subsequent worldwide recession, brought this almost unprecedented political initiative to a sudden end.[17]

From the mid-1960s to the early 1970s, the earlier degree of government control over economic activities became increasingly inappropriate, given the level of prosperity achieved, and in some cases inconsistent with international agreements (but nonetheless mostly tolerated by the United States and other advanced countries). Meanwhile, as per capita income increased, a great variety of new goals emerged in addition to economic growth, for example, protection of the environment, better health care facilities for the aged, and increased leisure time activities. As a result, considerable ferment arose behind the scenes as to how to deal with this new-found heterogeneity in policy choices, com-

---

17. The idea of further infrastructure development still remains basically popular—provided, of course, that such development can be undertaken without triggering the punishing inflation rates of the post–oil shock/post–Tanaka Plan days and without resembling the pork barrel politics of the Tanaka Plan. Because Japan still needs new or improved schools, roads, parks, hospitals, and perhaps most important, housing space, the question is really not whether such infrastructure will be developed but when, how, how much, and at what cost. Because of the large debt burden now hanging over the economy, the Japanese government cannot undertake such infrastructure development through "normal" spending programs; moreover, it seems to have made an economic judgment against an expanded issuance of national bonds to finance such projects and a political judgment against appreciably increasing the net taxation burden. In principle, the government could play an important role in trying to tap the country's large pool of private savings and channel these into infrastructure projects. Various proposals for doing this have been made in recent years, including the notion of private sector financing of infrastructure development and an even broader "asset-doubling" plan unveiled in 1984 by Kiichi Miyazawa, a prominent LDP politician. Miyazawa was generally thought to have proposed this idea, which resembles the popular early 1960s "income-doubling" plan of the late Prime Minister Hayato Ikeda (with whom Miyazawa worked closely), as a means of trying to unseat Prime Minister Yasuhiro Nakasone. In any case, little progress has been made in converting these expansionary ideas into specific plans, and the overall issue of infrastructure and societal development remains one under seemingly continuing, but inconclusive, discussion. For an earlier discussion of these issues, see Herman Kahn and Thomas Pepper, *The Japanese Challenge: The Success and Failure of Economic Success* (New York: Thomas Y. Crowell, 1979), especially chap. 7.

bined with considerable paralysis in the actual implementation of new policies. Much preparatory work for new policies, both within companies and within MITI, was performed. However, perhaps because the range of choices was already too wide, Japan's much-vaunted consensus-building process failed to work as well as it had in earlier postwar years. Even in cases where certain preparatory plans were taken off the shelf and put forward as prospective courses of action—for example, in energy policy after the first oil shock—many of the detailed provisions were not actually carried out until a second oil shock six years later drove home the extent of the changes in the external environment.[18]

Post–Oil Shock Adjustments: 1973 to the Present

As they worked their way through the economy, the increases in energy prices in 1973/74 and in 1979/80 had an effect on Japanese industrial development that was far greater than the policy measures taken up to that point—and particularly greater than the combination of intellectual ferment and de facto inaction described above. For example, the initial energy price increases were passed on to users to a far greater degree than in the United States, and Japan instituted a series of sweeping energy conservation measures. Moreover, wage increases were remarkably modest, compared with the high rate of inflation that developed in 1974. However, given the five-year *decline* in oil prices in real terms between mid-1974 and mid-1979, it took a second round of price increases to bring about many of the actual changes in industrial struc-

---

18. Commenting on certain differences between a plan-rational economy such as Japan and a market-oriented economy such as the United States, Johnson notes that "when a consensus exists, the plan-rational system will outperform the market-rational system on the same benchmark, such as growth of GNP, as long as growth of GNP is the goal of the plan-rational system. But when a consensus does not exist, when there is confusion or conflict over the overarching goal in a plan-rational economy, it will appear to be quite adrift, incapable of coming to grips with basic problems and unable to place responsibility for failures." He specifically cites Japan in 1971 and 1973 as experiencing exactly this kind of drift. "Generally speaking," Johnson contends, "the great strength of the plan-rational system lies in its effectiveness in dealing with routine problems, whereas the great strength of the market-rational system lies in its effectiveness in dealing with critical problems. In the latter case, the emphasis on rules, procedures, and executive responsibility helps to promote action when problems of an unfamiliar or unknown magnitude arise." See Johnson, *MITI and the Japanese Miracle,* p. 22.

ture that had been talked about for more than a decade. Specifically, energy-intensive manufacturing, such as aluminum smelting, suddenly became much less competitive (even though the handwriting had been on the wall for some years). Nevertheless, the adjustments in energy use that had been successfully introduced after the first round of energy price increases provided a strong foundation for further adjustments in many parts of the economy when the second round of energy price increases occurred. The earlier commitment to restrain the inflationary shock of the speculative boom of 1972/73 and the energy price increases of 1973/74 set the stage for much faster adjustments to the second round of energy price increases in 1979-80. In this way, Japan's deflationary reaction to the outside shocks of the 1970s was sharp but brief. In contrast to the United States and many other advanced industrial countries, the stagflationary legacy in Japan was much less lengthy.

Looking ahead, Japan faces serious problems of industrial change. In particular, as more basic manufacturing industries continue to lose their competitiveness (whether because of higher energy costs than prevalent in other countries, because various NICs have developed to a point where their goods can compete effectively with Japanese goods or because Japanese labor costs are now comparable with other industrial countries), MITI is finding itself increasingly constrained in its ability to use industrial policy as a way of preserving (or even delaying the demise of) these industries. This much is occasionally admitted even in public.[19] Some MITI officials sometimes suggest that the government should expand its role and explicitly subsidize industries, either in the name of national security or in the name of short-term adjustment assistance to enable an industry to survive along a path of alleged long-term viability.[20] Either argument is familiar to Americans who heard and accepted virtually the same viewpoints in debates over the

---

19. For example, in a concluding section to a statement presented to the Industry Committee of the OECD in March 1981, Makoto Kuroda, then director-general of MITI's Research and Statistics Department, said, "The smooth implementation of industrial policy is becoming increasingly difficult." See Ministry of International Trade and Industry, "Japanese Industrial Policy," *Japan Reporting* series, JR-4 (Tokyo: MITI, June 1981), p. 15.

20. See Keiji Miyamoto, "What Is Happening to Japan's Industrial Structure," *Journal of Japanese Trade and Industry* I (May 1982):37–46. Miyamoto uses the term *economic security*, but the logic of his argument makes it clear that he is speaking of *national security* broadly defined, or the term referred to earlier, *national strength*.

proposed government bailouts of Lockheed and Chrysler, the institution of trigger prices for steel imports, and restrictions on imports of Japanese automobiles. The second argument is relatively new for MITI. In the past, Japanese efforts to protect industries from international competition were concentrated in newly developed, or so-called infant, industries (for example, most notably in recent years, computers and electronics).[21] Until recently, the phasing out of basic manufacturing industries had not been a central issue in Japan, primarily because its stage of development had not yet confronted Japan with the question of whether or how to phase out such industries in order to make room for newer, still higher-technology industries. Since the mid-1970s, however, the difficulties MITI has already encountered in its efforts to facilitate adjustments in mature industries such as shipbuilding, petroleum refining, petrochemicals, and aluminum suggest that the implementation of future Japanese policies is likely to become increasingly difficult.[22]

The decline in competitiveness that took place in certain Japanese manufacturing industries in the 1970s suggest that global market pressures were the decisive factor leading to economic restructuring, not government policies aimed at shifting to higher value-added production. But because the main market pressures of the decade crystallized so suddenly, especially the large-scale energy price increases brought on by exceptional supply/demand conditions and relatively unpredictable political factors, the subsequent changes that eventually took place in certain Japanese industries often seemed at first glance to have stemmed from government policies. To the degree that the energy price increases of the 1970s were in fact more sudden than most price changes in most markets, they can be likened to the political pressures imposed on Japan by the Nixon administration in the early 1970s: Both kinds of shocks originated outside Japan and both hastened the timing of many changes that would have come about eventually anyway. But the basic direction of Japan's industrial shifts has long been clear. The timing and pace at which these shifts occurred have depended all too often on the extent to which outside shocks were applied, consciously or otherwise.

---

21. Excluding, of course, the special political problems associated with agricultural imports into Japan.

22. Specific problems in a number of declining industries are discussed in Chapter 6.

Nonetheless, such shocks are hardly the only or even the major determinants of Japanese policy or private sector actions. The actual behavior of firms and consumers is determined by the overall combination of pressures on supply and demand, of which government policies or outside shocks are only one part.

In general, and as discussed in detail in subsequent chapters on the financial system, new industries, and declining industries, the Japanese government's role in promoting industrial development has declined over the course of the postwar period. On the other hand, government intervention in the economy for other reasons (for example, for environmental protection, promotion of social welfare goals, regional development, and so on) has increased over time. Japanese *industrial policies*, in the narrowly defined sense in which this term was described earlier in the chapter, have been most evident through the use of the tax system and the provision of direct government financial assistance. The following sections describe how the use of these specific instruments has changed over the course of the postwar period and what ways their impact on industrial development has declined over time.

THE TAX SYSTEM AS AN
INSTRUMENT OF INDUSTRIAL POLICY

The tax system has contributed significantly to Japan's post–World War II economic growth, although mainly as a means of promoting aggregate saving and investment rather than investment in any particular sector, industry, or firm. Moreover, the actual measures employed have not been unusual; many similar measures have been used to promote saving and investment in other countries. The creation of an overall environment favorable to saving and investment led as a matter of course to an environment favorable in the initial postwar years to basic manufacturing industries, in subsequent years to new manufacturing industries, and nowadays to services as well. The key point is the consistent use of broad-based measures to create a generally pro-investment environment for whatever industrial development would naturally follow the achievements made to date. Specific measures directed at particular industries or groups of firms have also been important, and since these measures are generally classified as industrial policy—and consistent with our own definition of *industrial policy* in the narrow sense of the term—they are the primary focus of this section. Nonetheless, because these specific measures have been less important to Japan's economic development than broad-based incentives to save and invest, the discussion focuses on these specific targeted measures in the context of the broader measures.[23]

Historical Evolution

The postwar Japanese tax system[24] was strongly influenced by allied occupation policies, in particular the stabilization policies promulgated by Joseph M. Dodge and the recommendations of a special tax mission headed by Carl S. Shoup. The latter provided the foundation for the 1950 tax reform, whose basic structure remains in effect to this day.[25] A variety of tax modifications were introduced in the early 1950s

---

23. We have found no satisfactory estimates of the general impact of the tax system on saving and investment. Macroeconomic models of the Japanese economy tend to be too aggregative to sort out the effects of specific instruments, whereas the more detailed studies of investment and consumer behavior are typically too specialized or are not structured in a way that is directly applicable to the question.

24. Details of Japan's tax system discussed below are drawn from Ministry of Finance, *An Outline of Japanese Taxes, 1983* (Tokyo: MOF, 1983); and Yuji Gomi, *Guide to Japanese Taxes, 1981–82* (Tokyo: Zaikei shoho sha, 1982). Both of these volumes are revised annually to reflect changes in legislation.

25. The key recommendations of the Shoup mission, as reflected in the system that emerged at the time, are covered in these seven points. (1) Direct taxes became the foundation of the new system—most important, progressive individual income and corporate taxes. (2) Unlike in the United States, a *corporation* was defined as an aggregation of shareholders, not as an independent taxable entity. Thus the corporate tax represented an advance payment of individual income tax by shareholders; as a result, the overall tax system was specifically designed to avoid double taxation of corporate income. (3) All income was to be taxed equally regardless of source—again, unlike the U.S. system of distinguishing between, say, capital gains and ordinary income. (4) Owing to the high inflation rates immediately after the war, a wide difference emerged between the book value and the current value of fixed assets. To make the tax structure more realistic, a reassessment of assets was undertaken. A reassessment of business assets was optional, whereas the assets of individuals were to be reassessed at the time of transfer of such assets. Income from any up-valuation was taxed at a special low and flat rate. (5) The maximum marginal income tax rate was lowered from 85 to 55 percent, while a progressive net worth tax was introduced on persons with large property incomes. (6) The extraordinarily complex prewar special tax treatment of individual sectors, industries, and firms was reduced to "a practicable minimum." The idea here was to avoid a situation in which the tax system itself might distort investment incentives. (7) Various local political entities were granted an independent right to tax.

that moved away from some of the principles on which the 1950 Tax Reform was based.[26] Proponents of these modifications argued that economic conditions—specifically a desire for high growth—warranted moving away from the earlier principles of unitary taxation of income and nondistortion of investment incentives, among others.

With rapid and continuing economic growth in the latter half of the 1950s, tax revenue gains were spectacular. Consequently, annual tax reductions became a pattern—and later an expectation. The frequency of tax rate reductions led the government to create a bureaucratic entity to review the overall tax system and recommend changes. In 1956 the Tax Commission was established as an advisory body to the Cabinet. Since then, regular tax reforms have been based primarily on reports submitted by this commission. Since the latter half of the 1970s, however, when economic growth rates fell to much lower levels than in the past while a burgeoning government deficit called for at least some *increase* in tax rates, attempts by the Tax Commission to persuade the government to raise taxes have come to naught.[27]

---

26. In 1952 the 2 percent tax surcharge on corporate-retained profits was abolished. In 1953 capital gains from securities transactions were excluded from taxable income, partly to promote development of a securities market but more importantly, perhaps, because this tax proved difficult to assess and collect. Although the effect may not have been intended, this policy shift introduced a growth-oriented bias into the tax system—at least to the extent that holders of securities influence corporate decision making. The net worth tax was abolished at the same time—again, primarily because of an inability to assess and collect it equitably. In an effort to stimulate economic growth, certain special targeted tax measures, similar to those abolished in the 1950 reform, were reintroduced. Various measures were also introduced to provide for expanded depreciation allowances, a wider application of reserves for bad debts and price fluctuations, the exemption from tax of certain income from exports, and the differential taxation of income from various sources.

27. The first major long-term review of the tax system was completed by the Tax Commission in 1959. Among other things, the commission recommended that (1) the overall tax burden of the nation should be limited to approximately 20 percent of national income; (2) as had been the case since the mid-1950s, annual tax rate reductions should return some fraction of the unanticipated revenue resulting from economic growth; (3) the indirect tax rate should in principle average some 10 percent of consumer prices or 20 percent of producer prices; and (4) a General Law of National Taxes should be enacted to bring together the general and fundamental principles of taxation; this was done in 1962. In 1964 the Tax Commission presented a new long-term plan

As noted in Chapter 2, government budget deficits and accumulated government debt grew dramatically during the 1970s (refer back to Figure 2.7). The large increase in government expenditure after the mid-1970s stemmed in part from an overdue need to build up social infrastructure and in part from the unstable economic conditions that occurred in the wake of the 1973/74 increase in oil prices. Indeed, the deficit reached 34.3 percent of national budget expenditures, or 6 percent of GNP, in fiscal 1979 before beginning to decline.[28] This has naturally resulted in continuing pressure to increase tax revenues and, correspondingly, to reduce the scope of various special tax measures granting tax relief for certain specified purposes. Moreover, as also noted in Chapter 2, the broadly conceived goal of rationalizing the functions of government and restraining its overall growth has been a major plank in the political programs put forth by Prime Ministers Suzuki and Nakasone.[29] Pent-up demand for improved infrastructure development and greater welfare spending remains strong, however. The government also faces pressure for greater defense expenditures, both for reasons of its

---

for the evolution of the tax system. It argued that income taxes should continue to allocate resources without distorting the price mechanism, redistribute income through progressive tax rates, and serve as a built-in stabilizer over the business cycle. In addition, the commission called for the eventual abolition of the special targeted tax measures that had proliferated since the mid-1950s.

This new long-term plan was followed with one important exception: reducing the importance of special taxation measures, which the commission was unable to implement during the 1960s. Later, as the revenue losses from these measures rose dramatically in the late 1960s and early 1970s, serious attention began to be paid once again to the elimination of these benefits.

28. Organisation for Economic Co-operation and Development, OECD Economic Surveys, 1982–1983, *Japan* (Paris: OECD, July 1983), p. 52.

29. Both have made a point of saying that under their administration the government would not raise tax rates until it had achieved some success in rationalizing administrative expenditures. Under Prime Minister Nakasone, the government decreased income tax rates somewhat in 1983, while simultaneously increasing various excise taxes; the two moves roughly cancelled each other out, but the income tax cut was thought to be politically popular by LDP leaders. More recent discussion suggests that net tax increases will have to be made to avoid issuing more deficit-financing government bonds; the latter have become more difficult to issue in any case because of increased international equilibration of interest rates, which makes Japanese banks reluctant to purchase government bonds carrying below-market interest rates.

own and from the United States. Thus taxes are almost certain to rise at some point, and the tax share of national income, 29.3 percent in 1981, is unlikely ever again to fall as low as the 1974–81 average of 25.6 percent and certainly not to the 1961–73 average of 20.5 percent.[30]

The Present Tax System

Japan's use of tax measures as instruments of industrial policy that we view as most significant stem mainly from various provisions in the structure of individual and corporate income taxes.[31] This section focuses on some of the detailed incentives for industrial development that grow out of these provisions.[32]

Individual income taxes in 1983 represented nearly 41 percent of Japanese government revenues.[33] The overall system is highly progressive on paper, although various exclusions, deductions, and credits significantly reduce both the progressivity and the total burden. As seen in Table 3.1, the share of income tax in national income rose from 1960 to 1973, fell through 1977, and then rose sharply through 1981. Even at its peak in 1981, income tax accounted only for 5.6 percent of national income (7.8 percent including local taxes); the decade average,

---

30. Data from Organisation for Economic Co-operation and Development, *OECD Economic Outlook 34* (Paris: OECD, December 1983), p. 160.

31. Other taxes also contribute to specific industrial policy packages, for example, the use of petroleum taxes to support energy R & D, but are of minor importance, compared with the measures associated with individual and corporate income taxes, and for this reason are not discussed in detail. The principal national and local taxes and estimated 1983 revenues are shown in Table A.1.

32. Individual and corporate income taxes contain many measures that provide benefits or impose costs, that is, incentives for certain types of activities. Most, but not all, of these measures are incorporated in a Special Taxation Measures Law. Since the law itself identifies the incentives and disincentives designed to target specific industries, and targeted tax measures are almost always temporary and directed toward specific policy goals, one can frequently relate changes in policy goals to actual implementation by reviewing the periodic revisions of the law.

33. Table A.2 provides historical data on the income tax share of total national tax revenue. The income tax is progressive, reaching a maximum marginal rate of 75 percent for incomes over ¥ 80 million ($363,636 at ¥ 220 = $1), not including prefectural and municipal income levies (see Table A.3). Prefectural and municipal tax schedules are shown in Table A.4.

Table 3.1

BURDEN OF INCOME TAX AND LOCAL INHABITANTS
TAXES, JAPAN AND THE UNITED STATES, 1950-81

Fiscal Year	Japanese Income Tax as a Percentage of National Income	Japanese Income Tax plus Local Inhabitants Taxes as a Percentage of National Income	U.S. Personal Income Tax as a Percentage of National Income
1950	7.2	8.7	—
1955	3.9	4.9	—
1960	3.2	4.1	—
1965	3.5	4.7	8.6
1970	3.8	4.9	11.8
1973	5.4	6.9	10.7
1976	4.3	6.0	10.6
1979	4.9	6.9	13.0
1981	5.6	7.8	14.0

Notes: The figures are personal income for FY 1950, 1955, and 1960 and are not consistent with successive figures. The figures of income tax for 1978 include 13 months.

Sources: Ministry of Finance, *An Outline of Japanese Taxes, 1983* (Tokyo: MOF, 1983) p. 278; OECD, *National Accounts of OECD Countries, 1962-1979*, Vol. II, table 6, p. 24, and table 6, p. 36; U.S. Department of Commerce, Bureau of the Census, *Historical Statistics of the U.S.*, p. 241, 1107; U.S. Department of Commerce, *Statistical Abstract of the United States*, various issues; and U.S. Department of Commerce, Bureau of Economic Analysis, *Business Conditions Digest,* various issues.

ending in 1981, was 4.8 percent (6.6 percent). Comparable figures for the United States have averaged more than twice those for Japan (contrast column 4 with column 2), showing that the actual individual income tax burden in Japan remains relatively low.[34]

---

34. The progressivity of the individual income tax system is significantly reduced by generous exclusions and/or deductions for income other than wages and salaries. Perhaps the most important of such benefits include the exclusion of the value of employer-subsidized housing from taxable income and the special treatment of retirement payments to employees (typically lump-sum payments). With respect to the latter, only 50 percent of retirement income beyond a generous special retirement deduction is taxable. Also important are various tax-free recreational and other benefits provided by large firms (weekend resort facilities, subsidized overseas travel, and so on). For executives, such tax-free items as expense accounts, chauffered cars, subsidized loans, and the like are added to the compensation package.

Numerous exemptions, credits, and deductions have the effect of undercutting the goal of unitary income taxation, although the principle remains on the books as an ideal to aim for. A key result of these exemptions, credits, and deductions has been to provide indirect support for economic growth through a bias in the system toward saving and investment; two examples are discussed below as particularly important indicators of this biasing.

First, interest received on "small-size" savings accounts, on certain accounts in the postal savings system, and on central and local government bonds are exempt from taxation—in all cases on principal amounts up to ¥3 million ($13,636 at ¥220 = $1)—as are various other sources of interest income.[35] This has doubtless greatly stimulated saving by the ordinary citizen, all the more so because multiple accounts under various guises have been tolerated by officials of the postal savings system, in spite of continued but ineffectual dismay on the part of tax officials in the MOF.[36] In addition, interest rates and deposit regulations are manipulated in favor of the postal savings system, thereby diverting much of the small savings that might otherwise go to banks into the postal savings system (that is, directly into government hands, for investment in favored industries or, in recent years, to fa-

35. The degree to which Japan's high propensity to save is based on an alleged culturally derived frugality, as against specific incentives to save, is a question that is frequently, if inconclusively, discussed among specialists. Many observers have noticed, for example, that Japan's savings rate before World War II was roughly the same as the prewar U.S. rate. This suggests that Japan's extremely high postwar savings rate stems from other, more proximate causes than a culturally derived proclivity for high savings, for example, an obvious and immediate economic need to rebuild capital lost during the war, and specific policies such as the above-mentioned tax exemption on small-size savings accounts designed to support this objective.

36. One indication of the degree of tax evasion permitted through the postal savings system is the number of deposits—just over twice Japan's total population! In the early 1980s, MOF officials tried to introduce a system, called a "Green Card," that would record all small-saver transactions on a single, computerized record and in this way cut down on tax evasion. The idea died when politicians of all parties and many people in the general public realized that such a system might greatly hamper their ability to conceal funds from tax authorities.

vored infrastructure projects).[37] Second, capital gains accrued from the sale of shares or other kinds of securities are also excluded from individual taxation. One of the principal effects of this exclusion is to make capital gains more atttractive to stockholders than dividends, which are taxed (either at the corporate or at the individual level).

Certain tax credits available to individuals also contribute to Japanese industrial policies. For example, a credit for dividend income, although it does not completely eliminate the tax burden as in the case of excluding capital gains income, does reduce the degree of taxation of income from corporate sources.[38] Moreover, special savings deposits for housing purchases receive a tax credit; this credit carries a variety of conditions but represents a substantial savings incentive.[39] Individuals are also permitted a tax credit for experimental and research expenditures similar to those allowed corporations; this provision benefits primarily unincorporated family businesses.[40]

The corporate tax also operates in ways that indirectly promote industrial development.[41] The system is progressive and the maximum rate is comparable with those in other advanced industrial countries.

---

37. This point is discussed in greater detail in the subsequent section on government credit policies. In effect, the government compensates for its revenue losses through the tax exemption on small savings by getting the use of these funds through manipulation of interest rates in favor of the postal savings system.

38. For individuals in tax brackets below ¥ 10 million ($45,454 at ¥ 220 = $1), a tax credit equaling 10 percent of dividend income is permitted; for individuals in tax brackets above ¥ 10 million, the credit is 5 percent. Under Japanese tax principles, this measure is justified as a means of preventing double taxation of corporate income.

39. Although the tax break to housing is reputed to be less than that given by the deductibility of interest payments in the United States, the important difference is in the effects on the system itself: in the United States the incentive is to borrow; in Japan the incentive is to save.

40. Until 1984, 20 percent of experimental and research expenditures above the largest previous amount of such expenditures (since 1966) could be credited against taxes, not to exceed 10 percent of the income tax on business income (of the individual) before the credit.

41. Effective corporate tax rates are shown in Table A.5.

In some respects, however, this comparison is misleading since many of the tax benefits discussed below apply to the computation of net taxable income. A different perspective is provided by comparing taxes to total sales (see Table 3.2). The corporate tax burden on sales is progressive, averaging 1.1 percent. Roughly comparable data for the United States (a 2.1 percent average, as shown in Table 3.3) suggest a heavior level of taxation for U.S. firms; this difference would be even more pronounced if income of U.S. firms other than sales receipts (such as dividend income and interest receipts) were excluded to bring the U.S. data more in line with Japanese data.[42] The data used here do not permit more detailed comparison since the Japanese definition of *capital* and the U.S. definition of *assets* are not analogous.

As noted previously, the Japanese system is structured to minimize double taxation of corporate income. Moreover, as also noted above, most capital gains income received by individuals is untaxed, whereas dividend income received by individuals is taxed. As far as individual owners of stock are concerned, these features bias the system in favor of higher growth through reinvested earnings and thus toward capital gains rather than dividend payments. In addition, corporate income paid out as dividends faces considerably lower corporate tax rates than retained earnings—for large companies 32 percent as against 42 percent. This feature encourages considerable cross-ownership since, with some limiting conditions, dividends received from other corporations are also excluded from corporate taxable income. Lower tax rates also apply to smaller corporations, cooperatives, and corporations in the "public interest."[43]

Certain measures within the corporate tax system are used to target specific industrial policy objectives. The most widely used of these measures fall into three categories: added depreciation, tax-free reserve funds, and tax credits.

---

42. U.S. corporate income is taxed again when realized as capital gains or distributed as dividends to shareholders.

43. Types of organizations that fit the latter two categories are too numerous to list. However, most of the special industry corporations and associations set up to undertake joint R & D, to coordinate disinvestment in declining industries, and so on, are included.

Table 3.2
CORPORATE TAX REVENUE, SALES, AND
TAX REVENUE SHARE OF SALES, BY AMOUNT OF CAPITAL, 1981

Capital (¥ million)		Corporations		Total Sales (¥ 100 million)	Tax Amount (¥ 100 million)	Tax as a Percentage of Sales
More Than	Not More Than	Number	As Percentage of Total			
	1	204,237	13.6	213,299	1,868	0.9
1	5	774,599	51.7	771,001	4,799	0.6
5	10	251,525	16.8	525,759	4,395	0.8
10	50	232,091	15.5	1,625,769	15,796	1.0
50	100	19,366	1.3	503,031	5,241	1.0
100	1,000	14,713	1.0	1,276,858	14,947	1.2
1,000	5,000	1,719	0.1	756,800	10,429	1.4
5,000	10,000	322	0.0	443,794	5,944	1.3
10,000	—	316	0.0	2,087,831	27,404	1.3
Total		1,498,888	100.0	8,204,142	90,824	1.1

Source: The 107th Annual Statistics Report of the National Tax Administration for 1981, as reported in Ministry of Finance, *An Outline of Japanese Taxes, 1983* (Tokyo: MOF, 1983), p. 292.

Table 3.3

**U.S. CORPORATION INCOME TAX RETURNS—SELECTED ITEMS,
BY ASSET-SIZE CLASS, 1979**

Asset-Size Class ($ million)		Number of Returns[a] ($ thousand)	Total Receipts ($billion)	Tax[b] ($ billion)	Tax as a Percentage of the Receipts
At Least	Less Than				
—	10[c]	2,524	1,890.1	18.1	1.0
10	25	15	264.1	4.7	1.8
25	50	7	191.0	3.8	2.0
50	100	4	211.2	4.0	1.9
100	250	3	299.0	6.3	2.1
250		3	2,743.2	83.1	3.0
Total		2,556	5,598.6	120.0	2.1

[a] Active corporations.

[b] Before deductions for foreign tax, U.S. possessions tax investment, work incentive and new jobs credits. Includes additional tax for tax preferences, taxes from recomputing prior year investment, and work incentive credits.

[c] Includes corporations with zero assets.

Source: U.S. Internal Revenue Service, *Statistics of Income, Corporation Income Tax Returns, 1979,* as reported in U.S. Department of Commerce, *Statistical Abstract of the United States: 1982–83,* 103d ed. (Washington, D.C.: Government Printing Office, 1982), p. 276.

General depreciation rules are similar to those in other advanced industrial countries but may have been applied in Japan more flexibly and with specific policy objectives in mind.[44] The Special Taxation Measures Law, however, permits a variety of special types of depreciation. The economic rationale for offering special depreciation measures is to stimulate the private sector to purchase particular types of assets. These measures are available to firms submitting a "blue return."[45] Special depreciation measures come in two broad types: increased initial depreciation and accelerated depreciation. In the former case, this simply means that in addition to the ordinary depreciation schedule the firm can deduct a specified portion of the acquisition cost of an asset during the first accounting period in which it was acquired. In the second case, firms may deduct part of the acquisition cost of the asset over and above the ordinary depreciation schedule for a designated number of consecutive accounting periods. In neither case can cumulative depreciation exceed acquisition cost. If an asset is eligible for more than one special depreciation measure, the firm can pick the most favorable choice, but such measures cannot be used in combination. The variety of policy goals embedded in these measures is considerable.[46]

---

44. These are the five main depreciation rules: (1) Both tangible fixed assets and intangible fixed assets (such as copyrights, patents, rights of business, deferred assets, and so on) are depreciable on the basis of acquisition cost and salvage value. (2) Minor assets—that is, those with a useful life of less than one year or acquisition costs of less than ¥ 100,000 ($455 at ¥ 220 = $1)—can be written off in the year purchased. (3) A firm may elect to use either a straight line or a declining balances method. Other depreciation methods may be used with special approval. (4) A corporation may apply for each item or group of properties whichever method of depreciation it prefers for that item or group. (5) Statutory useful lives for assets are determined by the government; a list is provided in Table A.6. Under certain conditions, a corporation may apply to alter the statutory life of an asset if, for example, the asset cannot live out its statutory life, or if it acquires a used asset.

45. Filing a blue return requires that a corporation or an individual follow certain designated accounting principles and provide more information to the government than on "white returns." In exchange, certain tax benefits are provdied. In practice, most special tax benefits are available only to those firms, foreign or domestic, that file a blue return.

46. Recent legislation on special depreciation measures is summarized in Table A.7.

More striking, perhaps, is the relatively narrow and specific nature of the incentives provided. Indeed, many of the measures are for designated plant and equipment. This permits detailed, discretionary government intervention for one or another policy goal. The pattern of special depreciation measures is biased toward manufacturing in general, especially by stimulating markets for types of goods that the government would like produced domestically.

Tax-free reserve funds can be created to provide tax deferral; they are initially deductible from income as expenses but must be added back into income at a later date. For example, corporations can establish a reserve for bad debts based on expected losses in the collections of receivables. With the bad debt reserve, the amount credited in each period must be added back, less actual losses, to income in the succeeding accounting period; the measure amounts, in effect, to a one-year tax postponement. Perhaps the main benefit of tax-free reserves is the provision of cash before the expense or loss is actually incurred. For highly leveraged Japanese corporations, use of this up-front cash is particularly valuable.[47]

Many types of tax-free reserve funds are permitted. One of particular interest is a reserve against losses resulting from fluctuations in the market price of inventories of items designated as especially vulnerable, such as iron ore, raw cotton, and stocks listed on the Stock Exchange. Although no empirical research has been found that estimates the impact of this incentive (or that provides good estimates of any tax incentive effects), one can well imagine that it should increase domestic price flexibility, both in the aggregate and relative senses— particularly in an era of volatile exchange rates. This reserve is scheduled to be abolished after fiscal year 1985. The current schedule drops

---

47. Japanese tax law classifies tax-free reserves in two groups: *hikiatekin* and *junbikin*. The former are roughly those justified by general accounting principles, for example, the bad debt reserve. The latter are those introduced to achieve certain economic policy goals even though they may not be fully justified by generally accepted accounting principles. Obviously, *junbikin* is the more important category for identifying specific industrial policy incentives. However, if the reserve is defined in such a way that the contingency cost for which it was designed never equals the size of the reserve (which appears to have been the case for the bad debt reserve, for example), then the distinction between *hikiatekin* and *junbikin* becomes considerably less useful.

the maximum tax-free reserve deduction from 2.5 percent of the book value of inventories and shares in FY 1983 to 1.5 percent in FY 1984 and 0.5 percent in FY 1985. Small companies may establish an overseas market development reserve. Specific conditions for this measure depend on the type of activity and registered capital.[48] This specific reserve spreads the tax postponement over five years; one fifth of the amount credited to the reserve fund in an accounting period must be added back as income in each of the five succeeding years. This clearly promotes exports by smaller companies, but the estimated tax losses from this provision have declined sharply since 1976—¥12 billion in 1976 to ¥4 billion in 1981.[49]

In addition, a specific reserve has been created to stimulate overseas investment for any size firm. An overseas investment loss reserve is permitted for acquisitions of stocks issued by, or the extension of credit to, designated types of companies under specified conditions. This reserve fund compensates for possible losses caused by a decline in stock price, among other things. It is calculated on the basis of acquisition cost and can be held in full for five years. From the sixth year, one fifth must be added back to income for five succeeding years. Although details and reserve amounts vary, the specific incentives favor investment in developing countries, foreign-sited nuclear fuel recycling facilities, and natural resources. In fact, certain natural resource investments can establish a reserve fund with a maximum of 100 percent of acquisition cost.[50]

Two reserves that are particularly important for new industries are

---

48. The greatest incentives are for those firms capitalized under ¥ 100 million ($454,000 at ¥ 220 = $1), although some benefits accrue to firms capitalized as high as ¥ 1 billion ($4.5 million at ¥ 220 = $1).

49. Data are drawn from Table A.8.

50. Besides those mentioned already, other reserves with significant industrial policy impact include: a reserve fund for investment losses in the free trade zone in Okinawa; a structural improvement project reserve for small and medium-sized enterprises; a reserve for the prevention of mineral pollution in metal mining; a depreciation reserve for specified railway construction; a depreciation reserve for the construction of atomic power plants; a depreciation reserve for the construction of specific gas distribution facilities; and a series of reserves targeted on specific types of business which meet special conditions.

(1) a reserve for losses caused by the repurchase of computers and (2) a reserve fund for the guarantee of domestically produced software programs. The reserve for repurchasing losses was created to permit computer and computer sales corporations (particularly the Japan Electronic Computer Corporation [JECC]) to deduct a certain fraction of revenue growth as an expense.[51] Since most computer sales are based on lease arrangements, a company forced to repurchase a computer ahead of schedule can realize a loss. With the reserve provisions, however, such a loss can be debited against the reserve fund and thereby have its effects mitigated. The remaining reserve is added back to income after five years. This reserve was originally designed as part of a package of measures to make Japanese based computer companies competitive with U.S.-based companies—principally International Business Machines Corporation (IBM). The reserve for software development allows companies to offset costs associated with debugging programs in the course of the industry's development. This measure—in effect, an infant-industry aid—addresses the perceived weakness of the Japanese software industry vis-à-vis foreign-based firms.[52]

Besides targeted depreciation allowances and tax-free reserves, other special tax measures address specific industrial policy goals. For example, a corporation deriving income wholly or partly from overseas sales of technical services is permitted a special deduction from taxable income. This incentive is designed to stimulate export of (1) patents and others know-how developed out of domestic research and (2) such technical services as planning, consulting, and supervision related to the construction or production of plant and equipment or to specified technical services for agriculture or fishery.[53] Firms prospecting for mineral deposits overseas are also permitted special deductions, reserves, and exemptions. An investment tax credit was introduced, initially as a tem-

---

51. The activities of the JECC are discussed in more detail in Chapter 5.

52. Despite this infant-industry bias, foreign-based firms in Japan are not excluded from using this same tax advantage.

53. These service exports must bring in foreign currency or its equivalent, and in the case of technical services, only contracts worth ¥ 2 million ($9,090 at ¥ 220 = $1) or more are eligible. The export incentive from this deduction is relatively large—a firm may deduct as an expense 28 percent of revenue in case one and 16 percent in case two—although the absolute size of this deduction cannot exceed 40 percent of corporate income.

porary measure, to encourage investment in specific industrial facilities such as those to conserve energy or reduce pollution levels. This credit was later extended in 1979 to aid only those coporations engaged in industries specified by law and Cabinet order as permanently depressed industries or certain specially defined small- and medium-sized corporations.

Tax-free reserves and other special tax measures are less obviously biased toward the manufacturing sector than the depreciation measures discussed earlier. No single sector dominates as a beneficiary of these measures. Small businesses and firms investing overseas (or otherwise exposed to certain foreign risks) receive special attention. Two explicit export subsidies remain on the books: the provision dealing with overseas sales of technical services and the overseas market development reserve for small companies. The first of these measures, with several others, reflects the broad policy goals of "knowledge intensification" and illustrates a shift in emphasis from manufacturing per se to higher-technology activities—whether in manufacturing or services.

In general, because the Japanese coporate sector is highly leveraged (that is, debt-equity ratios, though declining, are still much higher than in other advanced industrial countries), any increase in cash flow is particularly valuable, especially during periods of recession or slower growth. For this reason, accelerated depreciation, tax-free reserves, and similar general tax measures built into the Japanese corporate tax system provide strong direct benefits to any Japanese company, apart from whatever benefits might be derived from special targeting of specific industries or activities.

Recent Tax Trends

For reasons noted above, the specific benefits and incentives incorporated into the Special Tax Measures Law began to be curtailed in the late 1960s. As seen in Figure 3.1, government revenue losses (that is, tax expenditures, in the language of U.S. tax jargon) from the Special Tax Measures Law have declined dramatically since the early 1970s. The fall-off in benefits to companies has been particularly notable. Losses from special tax measures benefiting corporations declined from 9 percent of corporate tax revenues in 1972 to an estimated 2.7 per-

Figure 3.1.
REVENUE LOSSES DUE TO SPECIAL TAX MEASURES
FOR CORPORATIONS AS A PERCENTAGE OF
CORPORATE TAX REVENUE

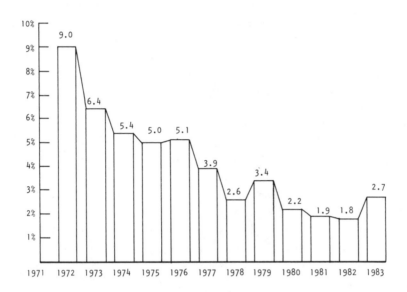

Source: Tax Bureau, Ministry of Finance, and Bradley M. Richardson, Submission to the International Trade Commission in Investigation no. 332-162, June 1983, p. A-10, as reported in U.S. Congress, House, Committee on Ways and Means, *Foreign Industrial Targeting and Its Effects on U.S. Industries Phase 1: Japan*, Report to the Subcommittee on Trade, Investigation no. 332-162 (Washington, D.C.: ITC, October 1983), p. 77.

cent in 1983.[54] When their impact was larger than it has become now, these measures unquestionably represented an important instrument

---

54. Obviously, revenue losses are only estimates. The data shown here were provided by MOF officials, but we were not provided, nor could we discover, the methodology or the assumptions used. Thus we have no basis for evaluating the quality of these estimates.

through which MITI could influence individual industries or firms. Correspondingly, the now-lessened impact of these measures represents the loss of a key instrument of MITI influence.

The rough magnitude of the revenue losses of special tax measures for enterprises in various policy areas since 1960 is shown in Table 3.4. These data are incomplete because certain incentives built into the general tax laws are not included in the compilation. However, virtually all the tax instruments that discriminate among specific activities, industries, and firms are included. Although one can quibble about the way that various items are aggregated, the data provide extremely interesting patterns. In 1960 two items dominated: those designed to strengthen the financial position of firms and those designed to promote exports. The former declined steadily in importance. The latter grew in importance until 1970 but sometime after that disappeared altogether. In part, these declines reflect an increase, in relative terms, in the importance of more selective tax measures directed at natural resource and energy development, the promotion of science and technology, and the selective targeting of small businesses and agriculture.[55] Indeed, in 1981 the single most important subsidies provided to enterprises through the tax system were directed toward small businesses and agriculture, promotion of science and technology, protection of the environment, and natural resources and energy development. It is important to note, however, that funds for items 2 to 5 in Table 3.4 were going mostly to large firms, much the same group as received funds earlier for strengthening the financial position of firms and for the promotion of exports. Even though the same group of firms received the benefit, the incentive effects of these new goals remain important. Changes in tax losses from special tax measures broadly reflect changes in policy targets expressed in various economic plans and policies as they evolved over the years and as described earlier in the chapter.[56]

---

55. Since 1975, those categories with a growing share mostly have experienced smaller absolute cuts. The main exception is the promotion of science and technology.

56. Table A.8 provides greater detail on revenue losses attributable to special taxation measures. Unfortunately, the categories in Tables 3.4 and A.8 do not correspond completely. Still, the detail in Table A.8 is useful for identifying the impact of individual tax instruments that are directly relevant to industrial policy. For example, under item III, "resource development," measure no. 10, the "overseas investment loss reserve," shows an estimated

Conclusions on the Tax System as Industrial Policy

This review of the tax system identifies several important general points about Japan's use of tax measures as instruments of industrial policy. First, the Japanese system is based on conventional taxation principles (that is, it is generally comparable with systems in other advanced industrial countries); indeed, the system remains one that is largely based on the concepts introduced by allied occupation authorities. Second, within this conventional framework, there is a specific bias in favor of saving and investment. This is achieved by avoiding double taxation of corporate income (perhaps to the point of overcompensating), by excluding from taxable income much, if not most, interest income for small savers, by favoring capital gains over dividend income, and by keeping the average tax burden low (compared with other advanced industrial countries). Third, within this bias in favor of saving and investment, there has been an additional bias in favor of the manufacturing sector, achieved by limiting many special tax benefits to designated plant and equipment. Now, however, with the value of these special tax benefits having been greatly curtailed since the early 1970s, these biases toward manufacturing will be much less important in the future.

One cannot, of course, extrapolate simply from a calculation of tax losses to the degree to which firms have been assisted as a matter of policy. One cannot even assume that the categories used by the MOF to present these data truly reflect their components and thus the policy

zero loss since 1979. This is surprising since, as noted earlier in the chapter, this measure would appear to be relatively important, given the wording of the tax law, Japan's level of economic development, its suitability as a capital exporter, and the government's expressed interest in promoting resource development overseas. Either firms are simply not taking advantage of a lucrative benefit, or there are constraints on its use that are not stated. The next measure on the list, no. 11, for atomic power plant construction, has grown rapidly in importance in recent years. Another important measure is under item IV, no. 13, for experimental and research expenditures. This is estimated to have cost the government some ¥ 27 billion ($123 million at ¥ 220 = $1) in lost revenue in 1981. Measures no. 16 and 17, the special depreciation allowances for the promotion of high-technology plant and equipment and for machinery acquisition by small enterprises, respectively, led to a revenue loss of ¥ 73 billion ($332 million at ¥ 220 = $1) in 1981.

Table 3.4
SPECIAL TAXATION MEASURES FOR ENTERPRISES: ESTIMATED REVENUE LOSSES, 1960–81

Description	1960 Revenue Losses (¥ 100 million)	1960 Share (percent)	1965 Revenue Losses (¥ 100 million)	1965 Share (percent)	1970 Revenue Losses (¥ 100 million)	1970 Share (percent)	1975 Revenue Losses (¥ 100 million)	1975 Share (percent)	1981 Revenue Losses (¥ 100 million)	1981 Share (percent)
1. Small business and agriculture, and the like	4	0.9	104	15.8	296	16.4	800	26.3	570	28.7
2. Environment	15	3.2	69	10.5	195	10.8	980	32.2	380	19.1
3. Regional development	0	0.0	6	0.9	22	1.2	120	4.0	110	5.5
4. Natural resources and energy	10	2.1	49	7.4	124	6.8	290	9.5	260	13.1
5. Promotion of science and technology	15	3.2	44	6.7	145	8.0	380	12.5	470	23.6
6. Strengthening of the financial position of firms	312	66.2	141	21.4	221	12.2	450	14.8	170	8.5
7. Promotion of exportation	115	24.4	246	37.3	759	42.0	0	0.0	0	0.0
8. Income measurement, and the like	0	0.0	0	0.0	47	2.6	20	0.7	30	1.5
Total	471	100.0	659	100.0	1,809	100.0	3,040	100.0	1,990	100.0

Source: Material provided by Tax Bureau, Ministry of Finance, Tokyo.

incentives. Recognizing the limitations of the data, one can nonetheless make ballpark estimates of the policy effects of various individual measures remain useful. For example, the Science and Technology Agency (STA) devised an extremely rough estimate of the impact of tax credits on total private expenditures on testing, research, and development through the late 1970s (see Figure 3.2). Based on the relationship between national income and research expenditures before introduction of the tax incentive, STA calculated an average elasticity figure (the percentage change in research expenditures resulting from a 1 percent change in national income). This figure was used to estimate R & D spending as if there were no tax credit for the rest of the period, after its introduction in 1967. As can be seen, the gap opens up immediately and grows continually. Crude as this procedure is, it nevertheless reveals an interest in the effectiveness of policy. STA is claiming here that the tax credit increased the average elasticity of R & D expenditures to national income by some 0.25 percentage points (from 1.06 to 1.31).

In general, Japan's promotion of savings and investment as a whole seems to us more important to economic growth and industrial development than the various special tax measures designed to aid specific industries. This seems particularly true since the early 1970s when, as noted above, the total benefits provided by special tax measures began to decline precipitously. Among the most narrowly targeted of the tax measures have been the special depreciation measures for specified plant and equipment and similar measures for machinery for small enterprises. For example, in 1981 the estimated tax losses from the former were ¥16 billion, from the latter ¥57 billion, for a total of ¥73 billion. This was less than 17 percent of the revenue losses attributable to special taxation measures.[57] Total revenue losses from special taxation measures in 1981 were only 3.3 percent of general account revenue, down from 6.6 percent in 1972.[58] These depreciation measures unquestionably bias investment toward the acquisition of targeted types of equipment by lowering their effective price. Nonetheless, the total benefits provided by such narrowly targeted measures are small compared with other, less narrowly targeted special tax measures. More-

57. This calculation is based on the incomplete list of special taxation measures shown in Table A.8.

58. Based on unpublished data provided to the authors by the Tax Bureau, Ministry of Finance.

Figure 3.2.
R & D EXPENDITURE WITH SPECIAL TAX CREDITS
COMPARED WITH ESTIMATED R & D EXPENDITURE
WITHOUT SPECIAL TAX CREDITS

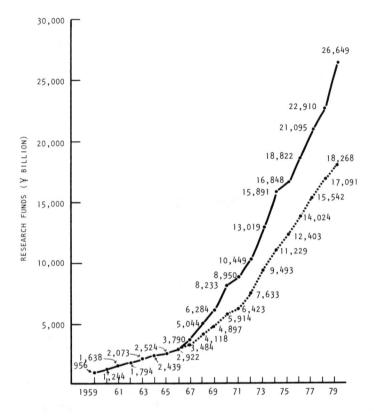

Source: Unpublished data provided by Planning Bureau, Science and Technology Agency, Tokyo, October 1981.

over, total estimated tax losses from special taxation measures are much less than comparably estimated tax losses from the promotion of saving and investment through general measures (for example, the exclusion from taxation of interest income on postal savings and of capital gains income on securities transactions). Official estimates of tax losses from general measures are unavailable—indeed, the MOF is prevented for political reasons from officially estimating (or at least releasing) tax losses from the postal savings exclusion. A simple ballpark estimate of the latter, assuming postal savings of ¥80 trillion, and a 5.0 percent interest rate, yields an annual interest income of ¥4.0 trillion.[59] Assuming that income taxes are paid on virtually none of these deposits and a marginal tax rate of 30 percent is applied, this would yield a tax loss of ¥1.2 trillion. By itself, this one general tax measure yields a tax loss larger than the total esimated tax losses from all special tax measures in 1981. By implication, the tax losses from all general tax measures would be much larger, perhaps by an order of magnitude, than those stemming from special targeted tax measures.

Two characteristics of targeted tax policy in Japan do remain important, however: (1) its general use as a carrot rather than a stick (for example, the use of special targeted tax measures to provide an improvement to cash flow or profits as a means, in turn, of inducing some positive action, rather than as a penalty against actions already taken and (2) in this same spirit, the granting of benefits to both producers and consumers of the particular sectors or goods chosen for promotion. Important "market-making" tax benefits are on the books for both frontier and declining industries.[60] During the 1950s and 1960s, special tax measures were extremely detailed, but as noted above, these have declined substantially since the early 1970s, both in terms of their absolute number and the degree of benefit allowed. Yet, as in the past, current targeted tax measures can be so narrowly focused as to benefit specific firms (for example, the special loss reserve for repurchase of computers) or specific types of activities (for example, overseas prospecting for raw materials). In the earlier postwar years, targeted tax instruments usually had the goal of stimulating economic growth and comparative advantage—mainly in basic manufacturing industries. As new social welfare goals became increasingly important during the 1970s, these, too, were promoted by special tax measures, and the overall value

---

59. In June 1983, postal savings deposits totaled ¥ 80.32 trillion (the two main types of deposits totaled ¥ 6.83 trillion in ordinary deposits and ¥ 71.65 trillion in savings certificates). The interest rate on ordinary savings effective at that time was 3.12 percent; the rates on savings certificates ranged from 4.25 percent for under one year to 6.0 percent for three years or more. See Bank of Japan, *Economic Statistics Monthly*, no. 439 (October 1983), tables 46 and 60.

60. See the discussion of incentives for computer and other advanced machinery purchases in Chapter 5 and for ship purchases in Chapter 6.

of measures directed at these new goals came to exceed the value of measures directed at basic manufacturing goals.

Partly as a matter of principle, but mostly because of the large government budget deficits of recent years, the MOF continues to fight for even further reductions in special targeted tax measures. As a result, one can expect to see a further decline in their importance. There will be exceptions for declining industries, small businesses, and new industries, but the quantitative benefits, as measured by tax losses, will remain small. Indeed, as noted above, measures to promote science and technology are the only broad category in the published statistics for which estimated tax losses continued to expand in absolute terms. While special tax measures proved useful in the past, and while new ones might again be introduced in the future if perceived as necessary to achieve a particularly important goal, in general their importance is declining.

GOVERNMENT FINANCING AS AN INSTRUMENT OF INDUSTRIAL POLICY

Japanese government financial institutions have contributed significantly to the country's postwar economic growth, although, as with the tax system, the contributions have come more through support of a general environment conducive to high rates of investment growth than through specific measures targeting industries and firms. The following chapter discusses the main characteristics of the overall Japanese financial system, as well as the pressures, both domestic and international, that are causing rapid change in financial markets and continuing pressures for deregulation. This section focuses mainly on the narrower question of the role that direct government financial assistance has played to date in promoting industrial development and the role such assistance is likely to play in the future.

Government lending has always been targeted on a variety of objectives, but different goals have received preferential treatment at different times. In the 1950s and 1960s, when economic growth was the dominant goal of Japanese policy, certain basic manufacturing industries considered essential to future growth (or to national security broadly defined) received funds directly from government financial institutions on terms that were unavailable in the private market or otherwise unavailable on any terms. In these early postwar years, when demand for loans exceeded the supply available at controlled interest rates, credit was rationed. Direct lending by government institutions naturally played an important role in implementing the industrial policy objectives of the period.[61] However, after the extraordinary growth rates that were achieved during the 1960s, the need for such direct lending declined, and the government's share of total lending also declined (see Figure 3.3). The subsequent increase in direct government lending in the 1970s stemmed from the emergence of new goals, such as environmental improvement, increased energy efficiency, and expanded social and physical infrastructure, among others. These new goals reflected changes in values that made economic growth simply one of several goals, rather than the single objective against which all other goals were measured.[62]

Most of the funds that the Japanese government lends to support various public policies are channeled through a single entity, the Fiscal Investment and Loan Program (FILP). This entity is independent of the general account budget and administered by a separate bureau in the MOF.[63] In FY 1983, the FILP budget was 41 percent as large as that of the general account budget (that is, some 29 percent of the total funds under the control of the central government were part of

---

61. For a detailed discussion of the historical importance of direct government lending to private business, see Eisuke Sakakibara, Robert Feldman, and Yuzo Harada, *The Japanese Financial System in Comparative Perspective*, a study prepared for the U.S. Congress, Joint Economic Committee (Washington, D.C.: Government Printing Office, March 17, 1982).

62. Other factors, such as slower rates of economic growth, also influenced the relative public/private shares of total lending (that is, share depends on more than policy direction alone). This shift in the importance of growth in relation to other policy goals is clearly evident in the decline in the share of loans provided by the Japan Development Bank (JDB), relative to other government entities, as shown in Figure 3.3, and in the types of loans JDB has provided, as discussed below.

63. The FILP can be thought of as roughly equivalent to the capital budget account of a private firm; like its equivalent, it is maintained separately from the government's operating budget. The analogy cannot be pushed too far, however, since significant public investment is also made out of the general account budget.

Figure 3.3.
COMPONENT RATIOS OF OUTSTANDING LOANS OF
FINANCIAL INSTITUTIONS (IN PERCENT)

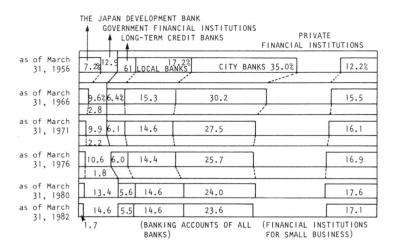

Sources: Japan Development Bank, *Facts and Figures about the Japan Develop-ment Bank,* Tokyo: JDB, 1981, p. 45; and Japan Development Bank, *JDB Fact Book 1983,* 1983, p. 37.

FILP).[64] Policy implementation financing, half of total lending under the FILP, has been divided into roughly stable shares for various pur-poses during the five years through FY 1983.[65] Small business loans (some 43 percent of such loans in FY 1983) and housing loans (26 per-

---

64. Figure A.1 shows the basic structure of the FILP and its budgeted flows for FY 1983. The Trust Fund Bureau represents the single largest part of the organization, accounting for some 87 percent of total FILP, drawn from postal savings, welfare pensions, and national pensions, among others. Use of FILP funds, by broad area, is shown in Table A.9. During the five years through 1983, funds have been distributed roughly 28 percent to public in-vestment, 22 percent to local government, and 50 percent to policy imple-mentation financing.

65. Figure A.2 shows a breakdown of policy implementation financing into broad categories.

cent) have taken some two thirds of the available funds. Loans that are typically cited as promoting targeted industrial development are usually those listed here as development loans (9.4 percent in FY 1983) and to some extent export-import loans (12.5 percent). Of course, in a functional sense, small business loans also can promote targeted industrial policy. In the context of the so-called dual structure of industry (in which a large number of small-size firms serve as subcontracting agents for a small number of large-size firms), the purposeful targeting of small business loans can reduce the costs of production to the large-size firms as well. However, since small business loans tend to be subject to less restrictive guidelines on their purposes than other types of development loans, they tend to constitute broad support for industrial development in line with the general objectives of the time (for example, basic manufacturing industries during the 1950s and 1960s and knowledge-intensive industries in the 1970s) rather than detailed targeting.

Japan Development Bank

The JDB represents perhaps the most obvious example of direct government financial support for industrial development. Established in 1951 as a successor to the occupation-founded Reconstruction Finance Corporation, its principal business has been the extension of long-term, low-interest loans for capital investment in new industries. JDB loans tend to cover between 30 and 50 percent of a project's investment costs. The government's Trust Fund Bureau (the main organization in the FILP) provides the JDB its main source of capital, although the JDB can also raise funds by issuing certain types of bonds.

In the years immediately after its formation, the JDB concentrated on loans for the reconstruction of basic manufacturing industries. Since then, the bank has diversified the range of potential loan recipients according to guidelines established by the Cabinet.[66] Each fiscal year the Cabinet prepares a basic lending policy for the JDB, and subsequent loan patterns closely reflect these broad policy guidelines. Nonetheless, the JDB operates as an autonomous financial institution, evaluating .

---

66. The basic law establishing the JDB was amended in 1972 to expand its mandate from ''economic reconstruction and industrial development'' to ''industrial development and economic and social progress.''

specific loan applications based on normal banking practices. Interest rates on JDB loans cannot drop below its cost of funds and can range up to what the JDB calls its prime rate.[67] Different categories of loans carry different interest rates, depending upon guidance from the Cabinet. For example, resource and energy projects are targeted as priority areas; loans in this category carry minimum interest rates. Loans for technology development have also typically carried minimum rates, although certain computer-related loans have recently carried higher-than-minimum rates, apparently based on the view that the industry is now too successful to justify maximum subsidization. As a declining industry qualifying for emergency assistance, ocean shipping can also now borrow from the JDB at minimum rates.[68]

Since the early 1950s, the composition of JDB lending has shown several specific trends, even as its share of total lending has declined (see Table 3.5). The share going to resources and energy, by far the largest item in the 1950s, declined sharply until the mid-1970s, when energy reemerged as a critical area. Development of technology grew in importance throughout the period, despite its more or less constant share since the mid-1960s, because some targeted new technologies (for example, energy) are listed in other categories. Policy concerns about

---

67. In early 1983 these rates were 5.5 and 8.5 percent, respectively.

68. Other examples include urban development and quality-of-life loans that range from minimum to maximum rates, depending on specific priorities and projects, and regional development loans that are issued at the prime rate. JDB loans in such areas as urban development, regional development, and improvement of the quality of life go typically to private firms working in these activities, for example, private transportation companies, construction firms actually involved in renewing urban districts, and so on. A few loans have gone to joint government-private projects.

The JDB does not typically lend money directly to declining industries. Indeed, it is prevented from extending loans to declining industries unless so designated by law. Cases of declining industry loans have included the following: in 1962 the JDB extended loans to the fertilizer industry (which principally refinanced earlier commercial bank loans); in 1963 ocean transport received loans; and in 1978 the JDB extended loans to the association established by the shipbuilding industry to purchase assets from shipyards that were reducing their capacity. The low-interest rate loans referred to in the text were provided to domestic shipping companies to enable them to purchase domestically produced vessels.

Table 3.5
PROJECT AREA SHARES OF LOANS BY THE JAPAN DEVELOPMENT BANK
(In Percent)

Fiscal Year	1951–55	1956–60	1961–65	1966–70	1971–75	1976–80	Outstanding at March 31, 1981
Resources and energy	42.8	39.0	16.8	11.5	10.6	25.6	25.5
Development of technology	0.4	4.5	8.4	11.0	11.5	11.2	7.8
Ocean shipping	23.4	27.3	30.0	35.4	17.7	7.2	10.5
Urban development	0.6	1.8	4.1	11.0	17.2	16.7	20.0
Regional development	—	3.4	18.1	15.9	15.3	14.8	12.7
Improvement of quality of life	0.3	0.2	0.5	1.3	21.7	19.7	18.7
Other development loans	32.5	23.8	22.1	13.9	6.0	4.8	4.8
Total	100.0	100.0	100.0	100.0	100.0	100.0	100.0
Total (¥ billion)	274.4	302.7	672.6	1,363.2	2,827.5	4,348.7	5,392.6*

*Equivalent to U.S. $25,557 million.

Notes: Loans in past years were classified in different ways, but they are reclassified as precisely as possible in accordance with the present way of classification. Outstanding loans at March 31, 1981, include outstanding investment of ¥ 8 billion but exclude outstanding foreign currency loans of ¥ 5.5 billion.

Source: Japan Development Bank, *Facts and Figures about the Japan Development Bank* (Tokyo: JDB, 1981), p. 10.

the development of a merchant fleet and the maintenance of shipbuilding production facilities resulted in the rising share of loans devoted to ocean shipping through the late 1960s, with the success of this effort (at that time) manifested in the subsequent drop-off.[69] Urban and regional development loans took a growing share of funds over the years, exceeding 30 percent during the 1970s. Similarly, quality-of-life loans (environmental controls, and the like) grew rapidly in the 1970s.

Some significant changes in loan distribution have emerged since the late 1970s (see Table 3.6). There was a topping out in the share of loans devoted to resources and energy, following the large increases beginning in the mid-1970s. Loan shares for ocean shipping increased dramatically in 1979 and 1980 before tapering off somewhat thereafter. The shares committed to urban development, regional development, and improvement in the quality of life also fell off after 1979, compared with earlier years. This decline was mainly due to the completion of major antipollution investment projects and cuts in redevelopment loans for large city areas. From 1976 to 1980, manufacturing received only 28 percent of JDB loans, as against 72 percent for nonmanufacturing sectors.[70] To be sure, many nonmanufacturing loans suppport the manufacturing sector indirectly through the provision of infrastructure or increased demand for manufactured goods. One example, discussed in detail in Chapter 5, is the high level of loans to JECC for the leasing of computers produced by Japanese manufacturers. Another example, referred to above, is the loans to shipping companies for the purchase of domestically built ships. Nevertheless, manufacturing activities per se have been receiving significantly less direct lending than services and infrastructure (especially transportation, communication, and energy development).

Technology support is often cited as one of Japan's policy strengths. In JDB lending, the specific category for "development of technology" is ambiguous simply because a large percentage of all JDB loans focus on new or improved technology. The loan procedures established for this category characterize the technology-lending practices of other JDB

---

69. The recent designation of shipbuilding as a declining industry produced a policy package including lending measures that have increased the ocean shipping share since 1979.

70. A breakdown of JDB loans by industry for the 1976–80 period is provided in Table A.10.

Table 3.6
PROJECT AREA SHARES OF NEW LOANS BY THE JAPAN DEVELOPMENT BANK, BY FISCAL YEAR
(In Percent)

	1977	1978	1979	1980	1981	1982	1983
Resources and energy	17.0	27.6	29.9	36.3	37.2	44.9	41.8
Development of technology	10.5	13.0	11.4	9.9	8.9	9.5	10.0
Ocean shipping	3.0	3.3	8.6	13.4	11.9	11.6	10.4
Urban development	20.2	17.7	18.7	10.9	13.4	12.0	12.0
Regional development	20.2	15.1	13.2	11.0	14.5	12.1	13.2
Improvement of quality of life	22.8	18.0	12.6	15.2	10.9	7.7	8.6
Others	6.3	5.3	5.6	3.3	3.2	2.2	4.0
Total	100.0	100.0	100.0	100.0	100.0	100.0	100.0
Total (¥ billion)	673.2	992.4	948.9	973.4	1,077.5	1,161.5	1,134.0

Notes: New loans in FY 1978 include ¥ 152.2 billion of loans that were approved in FY 1977 but extended in FY 1978. FY 1978 includes an investment of ¥ 8 billion.

Source: Japan Development Bank, *Facts and Figures about the Japan Development Bank* (Tokyo: JDB, 1981), p. 16; Japan Development Bank, *JDB Fact Book 1983* (Tokyo: JDB, 1983), p. 11.

loan categories. The following discussion of "development technology" helps to illustrate the process of targeted support and the way specific decisions are made on allocation of funds among various areas.

There are three JDB loan programs for technology development, one focusing specifically on the computer industry and two general programs.[71] Of the latter, one is set up under a 1978 law and provided some ¥13 billion ($59.1 million at ¥220 = $1) in FY 1982.[72] Loans from this program must be directed toward specific project areas designated by Cabinet order. Should a designated project area be oversubscribed, the JDB can force larger firms that have better access to private financial markets to utilize those markets while preserving JDB loans for the smaller firms. The other general technology development loan program is established by the bank itself and not designated by specific law, although it still falls within the broad policy guidelines of the government. This part of the JDB budget totaled some ¥46 billion ($209 million at ¥220 = $1) in 1982. These loans are devoted to new domestic technologies, initial manufacturing efforts for commercialization, development of heavy industry, and so on.

Firms that believe they have developed a process or technology falling within the broad parameters established by the Cabinet must apply for loans; JDB does not solicit customers. The firm's proposal is submitted to a council of scientific advisers, which evaluates the proposal from a technical viewpoint.[73] If the technology passes review, the loan applicant then faces an evaluation of credit worthiness and of the financial characteristics of its loan application. If the applicant is large, with well-established financial links, it must concurrently seek private financing since the JDB will provide only partial funding. If the appli-

---

71. Table A.11 provides a breakdown of JDB loans for the specific category "development of technology" from FY 1977 through FY 1982. The computer industry has been the largest single recipient of technology development funds. In some years the category known as "development of domestic technology" has been as large or larger but spread over many more industries. Most of the computer funds, as a matter of policy, have gone to JECC, although some software firms have also been targeted recently.

72. See Chapter 5 for more details on this law.

73. This step in the process is sometimes alleged to restrain certain highly competitive firms from applying for new loans since detailed proprietary information must be submitted to the advisory council for evaluation.

cant is small and has relatively weak financial links, or if the project is very large-scale and viewed as a high priority for the country, the JDB may take a lead manager's role in putting together a consortium to finance the project. Finally, by general agreement the JDB only finances the first plant in a new area. Its mandate is to help launch a new technology, not to provide low-cost financing for the expansion of industry.

There are specific advantages to JDB loans as against straight commercial loans. First, interest rates tend to be lower, as discussed above. Second, loans may be extended for a longer period of time than commercial loans. Third, compensating balances are typically not required.[74] However, a recent study on industrial targeting measures in Japan by the U.S. International Trade Commission (ITC) produced some ballpark estimates of the subsidy effects of JDB loans, showing these to be small.[75] This study concluded that the subsidy effects, based on an estimate of the savings due to lower interest rates and the lack of compensating balances, averaged from 1.6 percent to 2.0 percent of the value of the loan;[76] this estimate is necessarily rough since limited industry-specific data are available. Moreover, JDB lending as a share of total bank lending has been insignificant in most manufacturing industries (see Table 3.7). Only in shipping (not shipbuilding), electric power, coal, and, to a limited extent in the 1970s, petroleum refining has JDB lending constituted a large enough source of funds for the implicit interest rate subsidy to be significant.

In recent years the JDB has actively sought to provide capital to foreign firms investing in Japan. Loans to foreign-owned companies (that is, companies in which foreign-based equity is 50 percent or more) increased from ¥5 billion in FY 1979 to roughly ¥15 billion in FY 1982 ($22.7 million to $68.1 million at ¥220 = $1). Such JDB funds have been specifically provided for investments in land, buildings, and ma-

---

74. Compensating balances are funds that firms must leave on deposit with a bank as a condition for receiving a loan. Typically, such balances average some 10 percent of the value of long-term loans from private banks.

75. See U.S. International Trade Commission, *Foreign Industrial Targeting and Its Effects on U.S. Industries Phase 1: Japan* (Washington, D.C.: ITC Publication no. 1437, October 1983), p. 94.

76. Ibid., p. 94.

Table 3.7

JDB LENDING AS A SHARE OF TOTAL BANK LENDING
TO INDUSTRIES, SELECTED PERIODS, 1953–80

(In Percent)

Industry	1953–60	1961–70	1971–80
Shipping	48.6	59.9	44.3
Electric power	55.4	52.2	n.a.
Coal	24.6	38.8	n.a.
Petroleum refining	0.1	0.6	11.5
Iron and steel	12.2	1.4	3.8
Machinery[a]	1.5	1.6	0.7
Electric Machinery[b]	0.3	0.6	0.8
Transportation machinery[c]	1.3	1.8	0.9
Precision machinery[d]	1.5	1.0	0.4
Textiles	0.8	1.0	1.3

n.a. = not available

[a]Machinery includes processing machinery, general industrial use machinery, and textile machinery.

[b]Electric machinery includes electronics and computers.

[c]Transportation machinery includes automobiles, ships, and railway machinery.

[d]Precision machinery includes optical measuring devices.

Sources: Submission of Bradley M. Richardson to the U.S. International Trade Commission in Investigation no. 332-162, 1983, p. A-6, based on Bank of Japan, *Economic Statistics Yearbook*, as cited in U.S. International Trade Commission, *Foreign Industrial Targeting and Its Effects on U.S. Industries Phase 1: Japan* (Washington, D.C.: ITC Publication no. 1437, October 1983), p. 99.

chinery and equipment purchases. Following typical domestic practices, these loans normally cover between 30 to 50 percent of investment costs. Although loans to foreign-owned companies remain a small portion of overall JDB lending, the bank expects such lending to grow significantly in the years ahead and has officially committed itself to "actively assist" foreign-based companies in this effort.[77]

---

77. See Japan Development Bank, *Introducing the JDB: A Guide for Borrowers* (Tokyo: JDB 1982), p. 4.

Export-Import Bank of Japan[78]

Like the JDB, the Export-Import Bank of Japan (Ex-Im Bank) receives its funds primarily from the MOF Trust Fund Bureau and at roughly the same level as the JDB (and therefore roughly the same low share of total public and private loans). Loan applications for Ex-Im Bank financing typically come through commercial banks. Much of the negotiation about the viability of a project occurs between the private firm and the commercial bank before the Ex-Im Bank is approached. However, as in lending from other government financial institutions, approval for Ex-Im Bank financing is widely thought to be as important, if not more important, than the actual funding level since such approval tends to provide an implicit guarantee to commercial bank loans. Under the interest rate guidelines in effect since July 1982, minimum allowable interest rates are 10 percent to 14 percent—depending on the financial conditions of the recipient country. The minimum rate for official yen export credits is 0.3 percent above the long-term Japanese prime rate. Also like the JDB, the Ex-Im Bank's primary loan policies and priorities have gradually been expanded as the Japanese economy itself has become more developed. The bank's emphasis first broadened away from export promotion per se to loans to developing countries and loans in support of Japanese overseas investment. These policies then broadened further to include the financing of imports, the facilitation of technology transfer to developing countries, and development financing for natural resources.[79]

Initially, loan policies and priorities reflected a bias toward exports of heavy and chemical industries. From 1950 to 1955, 100 percent of the Ex-Im Bank's financing was for exports, with ships and manufacturing receiving the bulk of available funds—65 percent and 35 percent, respectively. From 1956 to 1967, export credits to Japanese firms accounted for 77 percent of the bank's credit commitments—with ships receiving the bulk of this, 50 percent, and manufacturing receiving about 27 percent. Loans to foreign governments, which also supported

---

78. Much of this section is drawn from material provided by Yukinori Ito, formerly the Ex-Im Bank's representative in Washington, D.C.

79. Recent Ex-Im Bank financing has even supported Japanese automobile manufacturing investments in the United States.

Japanese exports, totaled 16 precent. Loans for Japanese overseas investments and a small amount for import financing accounted for the remainder. From 1968 to 1973, there was a rapid increase in import and overseas investment financing—to some 39 percent for the two categories together for the period as a whole. Export financing absorbed the remaining 61 percent of total bank commitments during this period. After the first oil crisis, and ostensibly in an effort to offset large deficits that developed in Japan's current account, financial support for imports and overseas investments as a share of total bank commitments declined from 52 percent in FY 1973 to 17 to 18 percent in FY 1976/77. When the current account deficit declined, the FY 1978 share of total bank financing in the areas of imports and overseas investment went up to 61 percent. As of the end of fiscal 1981, loans outstanding were distributed as follows: 35 percent export credits, 21 percent import credits, 15 percent overseas investment credits, and 29 percent overseas direct loans.[80] As in other countries, Ex-Im Bank export credits support primarily the export of manufactured goods. In recent years the emphasis has been on ship machinery for heavy and chemical industries and on exports for non-Japanese projects. Ex-Im Bank import credits have been used almost exclusively to support the import of natural resources by domestic manufacturing firms.

Conclusions on Government Financing for Industrial Policy

The Japanese government has traditionally provided direct financial support to priority sectors and industries. The share of such direct support, as a percentage of total financing, was only 13 percent in the mid-1950s and gradually declined through the late 1960s. This share then rose to its present level of nearly 15 percent, but the composition changed considerably, with infrastructure and other broad social goals receiving almost all of the increased government share of lending in recent years.

As noted above, since the official imprimatur of a government financial institution is often interpreted by private lending institutions as an implicit guarantee of the credit worthiness of a project, the willingness of the JDB, the Ex-Im Bank, and other government financial

---

80. Export-Import Bank of Japan, *Annual Report for Fiscal Year 1981* (Tokyo: Export-Import Bank of Japan, 1981), p. 11.

institutions to lend money to a particular sector, industry, or firm has probably been more important than the actual amount of money involved. JDB lending accounts for only about 3 percent of total private capital formation in industries receiving JDB loans. In areas such as energy, resource development, and technology promotion, JDB loans are closer to 1 percent of total capital formation.[81] In this sense the role of the JDB, the Ex-Im Bank, and other government financial institutions is analogous to that of the World Bank, whose approval of a country's macroeconomic policies or of a particular project in a country can often constitute a "green light" to commercial banks for their participation in lending to a country or a project. Participation by the JDB or the Ex-Im Bank implicity reduces, although it does not eliminate, the risk to participating private sector institutions.[82] In contrast to efforts in other countries that might seem at first glance to be similar, the record of financial support by the Japanese government to date shows that it usually has not supported projects with low expected returns but rather projects with extremely high expected returns, albeit with associated high risks.[83]

In spite of the high debt level hanging over from the past, the Japanese government will continue to provide some level of financial assistance to selected sectors of the economy for the foreseeable future. Although there is considerable debate in Japan about the continued need for, and effectiveness of, the JDB and other public financial institutions whose original purposes have in some people's eyes long since been met, opposition has not yet reached the point of seriously threatening the continuation of the existing system—the institutions themselves go on, while modifying their goals and activities to take account of new priorities.

---

81. U.S. International Trade Commission, *Foreign Industrial Targeting*, p. 99.

82. In private discussions with the authors, commercial bankers and officials from the JDB and the Ex-Im Bank have also argued that the once-close relationship between government support of a project and the implicit backing of commercial banks has greatly attenuated in recent years.

83. Recently, the JDB and MITI have started discussing a new loan program aimed at financing what they are calling high-risk research and new venture projects. At this point no real elaboration of this idea has been made public, and it is not clear that what the JDB and MITI might call high-risk projects are necessarily what other countries might call high-risk projects.

The various goals of these financial institutions will certainly continue to change. Direct government financing for infrastructure development will probably continue to increase. The need for government promotion of higher value-added industries has lessened as the country has become wealthier, and other goals will continue to draw the predominant share of funds. However, in light of the substantial pressures for adjustment that have emerged in a number of basic industries, financing for declining industries could also take a growing share of government lending over the next several years, although not necessarily a growing share of JDB or Ex-Im funds.

INCREASED IMPORTANCE OF OTHER
MINISTRIES AND NEW PRESSURE GROUPS

The above discussion of the use of tax and direct financial assistance as instruments of Japanese industrial policy, as well as the more general discussion at the beginning of the chapter on the overall direction of Japanese industrial policies, points up the profound changes in the Japanese economy that have occurred since the end of World War II. As the economy has matured and grown more affluent, Japanese society itself has become more pluralistic. A much larger number of distinct interest groups, inside and outside of government, compete for resources and influence than in earlier postwar years. The proliferation of these diverse interests and the new priorities they represent have reduced the ability of the Japanese government to target sectors, industries, or firms for narrowly defined pruposes. Such once seemingly all-powerful ministries as MITI and the MOF are now much less able to assume that the private sector will let the traditional scope of their powers go unchallenged. Moreover, several ministries are caught up in turf battles among themselves that are also likely to continue and in some cases to intensify well into the future.

Although industrial policy has been primarily the province of MITI, other ministries have always had specific areas of influence. The most important of these has been the MOF simply because its budgetary power over tax and spending policies automatically gives it some influence over all other ministries. As noted earlier, Japan's high level of accumulated debt will significantly limit the MOF's ability to provide direct or indirect financial support for industrial policy purposes; a proliferation of requests for spending on defense, infrastructure development, and various other quality-of-life goals, while contributing indirectly to industrial development, will also limit the scope that the MOF will have for tax or spending programs directly related to future industrial policy goals. In effect, the MOF's budgetary stringency, whether expressed in continued pressure to reduce revenue losses from special taxation measures or in increased disagreement over which policy goals will receive whatever direct government financial assistance is provided, will continue to put de facto limits on those industrial policies that require expenditures.[84] The increasing complexity of the Japanese economy has also meant that various ministries, even the MOF, have faced market pressures that challenge their established domains. For example, the MOF has found it increasingly difficult to maintain its traditional regulatory role over the banking and securities industries as international pressures make this previously tight control costly for these industries.[85] Because of this continued tight control, Japanese financial institutions have had to cede various new markets in offshore financing to counterparts in Singapore and Hong Kong.[86] Stringent administrative requirements have also impeded the development of many new innovations in financial services that have recently been introduced in the United States—such as the explosion in money market funds and other retail and wholesale financial services. The MOF's impulse to try to supervise the pricing and diversification activities of commercial banks has come into conflict not only with the banks' own interest in developing an international capital market but also with the desire of manufacturing and other nonfinancial companies to raise or issue capital abroad freely. In general, the stronger the drive toward internationalization of the economy, the more costly the traditional MOF position has become.

Market-based pressures have greatly increased the degree of inter-

---

84. Moreover, the chief source of FILP funds used to provide direct government financial assistance, the Postal Savings System, will come under increasing pressure from the deregulation of the financial structure.

85. This and other developments in the Japanese financial system are discussed in greater detail in Chapter 4.

86. The MOF appears now to be increasingly willing to discuss the implications of, and the policies required to prepare for, the development of a Tokyo capital market comparable with London or New York.

ministerial conflict. For example, MITI and the Ministry of Posts and Telecommunications (MPT) are in the midst of an intense struggle for influence over information processing—the rapidly expanding combination of computing and data transmission. Increased competition from U.S.-based information-processing companies, which have been much less burdened by regulatory constraints, has recently led to significant changes in Japan's regulatory system and to a partial dismantling of the Nippon Telegraph and Telephone Public Corporation (NTT).[87] The MPT, with a tradition of working through monopoly corporations like NTT, has allowed or encouraged the latter to proceed with advances in communications and data transmission technology at a much slower pace than the computer industry. Computer manufacturers, which are under MITI's jurisdiction, have from the outset been encouraged to compete vigorously with each other. MITI officials believe that competition has helped to foster a more dynamic industry than would have evolved without competition—and the rapid growth and strong competitiveness of the Japanese computer industry supports this view. For this reason, MITI is now seeking jurisdiction over all data-based communications; it argues that the national interest requires a faster rate of innovation, based more on its own traditional formula of oligopolistic competition than the MPT's traditions of monopoly and direct administration would be likely to permit. Indeed, negotiations on the future structure of NTT itself, on regulations governing newly developed value-added network services (VANs), and other data-processing and data transmission systems are in process. These negotiations are likely to continue for some time both among different domestic interests and between the Japanese and foreign governments (principally the United States). Where MITI and the MPT continue to disagree, LDP politicians are called in to try to "umpire" the dispute. This struggle is likely to continue for some years, especially since the issue has important implications for the future competitiveness of many higher-technology industries.

International factors have also increased the importance of other ministries relative to MITI. The Ministry of Agriculture, Forestry, and Fisheries, which has always kept a tight hold over agricultural imports, can now do so only with considerably greater visibility—and thus at considerably greater cost. In earlier years the ministry could maintain the

---

87. This development is discussed in detail in Chapter 5.

status quo simply by taking a low profile. Nowadays, this is no longer possible, and its typical insistence on few or no concessions to prospective exporters has led to continuing grief for MITI, the MOF, and the Ministry of Foreign Affairs. All of these institutions have had to bear the brunt of foreign criticism of Japan's continuing barriers to agricultural imports. Even the Ministry of Education, through its jurisdiction over copyrights, became entangled in an international industrial policy wrangle over proposed software legislation. MITI sought administrative responsibility for software on grounds that it was an industrial product, whereas the Ministry of Education contended that software should remain within the province of authorship, which by international convention is covered by copyright statutes.

The increasing pluralism of Japanese society in general has contributed to a proliferation of competing interests in areas once overwhelmingly dominated by producers. In tourism, for example, the traditional preference of Japan Air Lines (and its advocates in the Ministry of Transportation) for cartelized pricing on international tickets to and from Japan is coming under increased pressure, separately and together, from consumers and competing airlines. Members of the general public have sought to reduce the influence of medical doctors and the Japan Medical Association over decisions on insurance coverage for different kinds of care. Consumer safety and antipollution groups that blossomed in the early 1970s have continued to press for greater consideration of their views, and some of these demands, especially regarding environmental measures, have been met.[88]

---

88. For more details on environmental issues, see Margaret A. McKean, "Pollution and Policymaking," in *Policymaking in Contemporary Japan*, ed. T. J. Pempel (Ithaca and London: Cornell University Press, 1977), pp. 201–39. There has been considerable disagreement among scholars about the degree to which Japanese decision making has been characterized either by consensus or conflict. Those who subscribe to a consensus model tend to argue that decision making occurs in a supposedly harmonious environment. They usually stress the alleged commonality of interests among Japanese government officials, business executives, and politicians. On the other hand, those who see Japan decision making as fraught with conflict naturally emphasize examples of such conflict as a way of invalidating the consensus model. This second group tends to see Japanese decision-making conflicts as generally similar to decision-making conflicts in other developed and/or democratic countries. For an example of the first group, see Robert E. Ward, "Japan: The Continuity

Another force bringing new interests to bear on Japanese society generally is the rise of entrepreneurship, especially in new or higher-technology–related areas. As in the United States, Japan is experiencing an explosion of new companies producing software programs, computer-related publications, new peripheral equipment, and the like. In the past, the term *small-and medium-size enterprises* was usually synonymous with capital-short, subcontracting firms that depended for their survival on the more highly capitalized large firms. In the future, small- and medium-sized firms are likely to seek considerable deregulation of administrative barriers between industries and to prefer such deregulation even at the price of receiving less subsidization from MITI than

---

of Modernization," in *Political Culture and Political Development*, ed. Lucian Pye (Princeton, N.J.: Princeton University Press, 1965); and of the second group, see Gerald L. Curtis, "Big Business and Political Influence," in *Modern Japanese Organization and Decision-Making*, ed. Ezra F. Vogel (Berkeley and Los Angeles: University of California Press, 1975). Still other scholars fall somewhere between these two approaches. See, for example, John C. Campbell, "Policy Conflict and Conflict Resolution within the Governmental System," in *Conflict in Japan*, ed. Thomas Rohlen, Ellis S. Krauss, and Patricia G. Steinhoff (Honolulu: University of Hawaii Press, 1984). Scholars of whatever school have noted that it is relatively easy to imagine how a consensus could be reached among ministries and/or business groups on such broad policy goals as a desired rate of economic growth but much more difficult to see how a consensus-based system might work if the objective is to deal with more specific problems, for example, capacity reductions in a dying industry, investment priorities in a frontier industry, or subsidy and loan programs of government agencies. For an illuminating discussion of one aspect of policy-making in this second, more complex sense, see Chalmers Johnson, *Japan's Public Policy Companies* (Washington, D.C., and Stanford, Calif.: American Enterprise Institute for Public Policy Research and Hoover Institution on War, Revolution and Peace, 1978). In general, in our view at least, the more developed the economy, the more pluralistic the society and the more important the specific interests of various groups in prospective decision making. By implication, consensus-based models of Japanese decision making are becoming less accurate over time.

might otherwise be possible if the traditional structures were to continue unchanged.[89]

For these reasons, coordination of Japan's future industrial policy efforts is likely to be more difficult than in the past. The Economic Planning Agency (EPA), founded in 1955 as a coordinating body, has often been able to forge a consensus of views of different ministries even though it lacks operational responsibility. However, its actual influence on specific decisions has been occasional at best. Its success has stemmed from its ability to summarize existing views and to prepare medium- and long-range plans and annual white papers that serve as reference documents upon which further discussions can be based. This ability stems in turn from EPA's being staffed by a combination of economists who make their career in the EPA itself and officials on detail from MITI, the MOF, and other ministries. Like the President's Council of Economic Advisors in the United States, the EPA's intellectual standards are high. But it has not been able—nor has it tried that hard—to play a stronger role in the sense of trying to force through changes in government policy in one direction or another.

The EPA's role is analogous to, and sometimes part of, the process of developing various government-sponsored "visions" of future economic or industrial development. These visions are designed to be a coherent but purposely sketchy outline of likely future trends. They have been drawn up regularly over the postwar years, serving both as public relations ventures, officially promulgating a party line, and as a sum-

---

89. The several years–long dispute between the previously established department stores and the newly established chain store conglomerates is an excellent example of this phenomenon. The latter's combination of distribution outlets includes U.S.-style supermarkets and franchised convenience stores (for example, 7–11 stores, licensed to Ito-Yokado by the Southland Corporation of Dallas) and so-called *super-stores*, a specifically hybrid term designed by Ito-Yokado to describe stores that fit into a loophole between MITI's specifications, in terms of size and product mix, for department stores and those governing supermarkets. In fact, to be able to establish themselves in the market, such new entrants often prefer—and sometimes even depend upon—their independence from MITI, from both its subsidies and its regulations.

mary of a genuine consensus of expectations among those groups most directly concerned with the problem at hand. In the case of visions of industrial policy, MITI officials usually take charge of the writing process but always in consultation with various representatives of industry, labor, political parties, the media, and certain pressure groups. Drafting of the more detailed sectoral or industrial visions is commonly under the direction of an official advisory body such as the Industrial Structure Council and its various subcommittees or some comparable organization drawing upon similar, broad-based private sector views.[90] Although these visions are invariably too general to serve as an operational document for a specific firm, they still provide an important planning tool insofar as they successfully articulate what spokesmen for major relevant interests agree to be a consensus of future trends.[91] They are clearly no substitute for the normal determinants of market behavior; neither, however, are they so rigid as to distort the likely chain of events that would occur in the absence of their publication. Indeed, the broad-based discussions among the major interested parties that take place in the preparation of a vision document have helped avoid inconsistent planning among various sectors. On the other hand, there is always the danger, as in any indicative system, that all participants can be wrong at once.[92]

In general, as pluralistic interests, domestic and international, have come to exert influence on the allocation of government resources and even government priorities, interministerial coordination is becoming both more important and more difficult. Before 1965 the consensus in favor of economic growth (and, as the main engine of growth, the de-

---

90. Recently, in response to claims by U.S. trade negotiators that deliberations of the Industrial Structure Council and similar bodies responsible for drafting visions have significant trade effects, representatives of U.S.-based firms have begun to be included in such deliberations. The vision-drafting process in Japan has often been likened to the congressional hearing process in the United States.

91. In this sense, they resemble any system of indicative planning.

92. For example, the decision to expand steel capacity in the early 1970s was accompanied by reasonably consistent capacity plans in firms both up- and downstream; none expected the events of the mid-1970s that completely undermined such plans, and thus all faced trouble concurrently.

velopment of basic manufacturing industries) was sufficiently strong that specific policies in such areas as tax policy and direct government financial assistance worked more or less in tandem with MITI's explicit industrial development goals. In the years of intellectual ferment but policy inaction from 1965 to 1973, this consensus weakened significantly, and the coordination or coincidence of policies among ministries grew weaker still. Since 1973, market pressures, particularly shifts in competitiveness of some manufacturing sectors, have forced an increased degree of industrial restructuring and deregulation.

THE ROLE OF ADMINISTRATIVE GUIDANCE

As the continued development of the Japanese economy has brought an end to various direct government controls over the economy, and the increased importance of other ministries and new interest groups has led to a decline in MITI's position as an overwhelmingly important determinant of Japanese industrial policy, MITI has had to exercise influence more through the use of a wide range of informal measures, usually grouped under the category of "administrative guidance." Administrative guidance has a long tradition in Japanese law. It refers, in a technical sense, to a recognized degree of discretionary authority that the executive has in implementing the goals of specific legislation. Japanese tradition since the Meiji era, when Japan's first parliament was constituted, has always been to draft extremely general language in the body of legislation, thereby leaving the bureaucracy wide latitude within which to exercise discretion depending on circumstances prevailing at the time.[93] *Administrative guidance* also refers, in a more informal sense, to any suggestion that bureaucrats might make to private parties, whether or not they have specific legislative authority to make the suggestions. Again, the tradition in Japan is to heed such suggestions either because enabling legislation might be assumed to exist that would in turn justify the latitude a particular bureaucrat was seeking

---

93. Western political theory has been debating the desirable mix between legislative specificity and executive discretion since Montesquieu. For a twentieth century discussion with particular relevance to foreign policy, see Walter Lippmann, *Essays in the Public Philosophy* (Boston: Little, Brown, 1955).

to take or because the practice of judicial review has been sufficiently weak that private parties are reluctant to challenge a bureaucrat's authority, or both.

Even before trade and capital liberalization was begun in the mid-1960s and continuing to this day, industry and government representatives have often favored the use of administrative guidance because it gives *both* sides a high degree of flexibility compared with more formal measures that would require legal authorization or, worse yet, public scrutiny. One of the most common forms of administrative guidance is in the area of so-called voluntary production cutbacks in industries specified by law as exempt from antimonopoly legislation. As Chalmers Johnson notes, industry executives prefer administrative guidance in dealing with the always delicate problem of capacity reductions because they have more confidence in MITI (that is, in the bargaining process with MITI) than in any available alternative.[94] With the use of administrative guidance, companies do not have to open their books for review by the Fair Trade Commission (FTC), as would be the case if they were to establish a formal depression cartel under the provisions of the Anti-Monopoly Law.[95] As Johnson also notes, MITI and an affected industry use administrative guidance procedures to help arrange for agreements among companies on production and export allocations when foreign governments seek supposedly voluntary export restraints.[96]

As more basic manufacturing industries face the prospect of difficult capacity reductions or other pressures for structural adjustment, and as Japan is forced to negotiate new trade agreements with foreign countries, attempts by both MITI and the affected industries to use administrative guidance procedures are likely to increase. But MITI's net

---

94. See Chalmers Johnson, "MITI and Japanese International Economic Policy," in *The Foreign Policy of Modern Japan*, ed. Robert Scalapino (Berkeley: University of California Press, 1977), p. 254.

95. The Anti-Monopoly Law, formally called the Law Relating to the Prohibition of Private Monopoly and to the Methods of Preserving Free Trade, is aimed at prohibiting collusive activities among firms with regard to price fixing and production and sales volume. It was passed by the Diet during the occupation and is modeled on U.S. antitrust laws. For an account of this history and of the founding of the FTC, see Eleanor M. Hadley, *Antitrust in Japan* (Princeton, N.J.: Princeton University Press, 1970).

96. Johnson, "MITI and Japanese International Economic Policy," p. 254.

influence will not necessarily increase. Johnson describes how MITI officials themselves have long recognized that the success of Japan's continuing economic development would mean a decrease in MITI's direct influence on economic activity; he notes that when Japan started down the path of liberalizing its economy in 1964, a bureaucratic "crisis" erupted in MITI over what its future role would be without the authority to exercise direct control over the economy.[97] Administrative guidance may be a better means of giving MITI some continuing influence over the economy than would exist in the absence of this tradition. The long-term trend, however, is still in the direction of less MITI influence than in the past. MITI does remain responsible for trade negotiations with foreign governments—at least in those industries within its jurisdiction. Since it must be able to implement whatever agreements are reached, some degree of industry-government cooperation is essential. When administrative guidance procedures are used to reach agreements acceptable to foreign governments, an affected industry has implicitly more leeway in bargaining with MITI over capacity reductions or export restraints than in the past, when MITI's authority over foreign exchange allocations gave it extraordinary powers over the private sector. By the same token, as MITI's formal mechanisms to exercise control over the economy have waned, industry compliance has become correspondingly harder to obtain. Thus, MITI is likely to remain in the middle of continuing crossfire between what it perceives as the interests of the country as a whole, vis-à-vis foreign governments, and the interests of some of its constituents—not to mention its own institutional interest in keeping some sort of bureaucratic influence over the economy.[98]

---

97. Ibid.

98. The career path of a MITI official normally leads to an executive position in the private sector upon retirement from the government at age 55 or thereabouts. Since government salaries and tangible perquisites are smaller than in the private sector—and the gap is growing—MITI officials are slowly becoming increasingly dependent, for their life-cycle income, on their ability to work out their post-retirement employment arrangements. While this system has sometimes been praised as a means of promoting smooth working relationships between business and government, it also creates an obviously symbiotic relationship that can all too easily be directed against, as well as for, the *public interest*, broadly defined. The discretionary authority that is an inherent part of administrataive guidance procedures makes the leeway in this symbiotic relationship that much broader.

A more general debate on the utility or desirability of administrative guidance has long underlain the tug-of-war between MITI and the FTC on what constitutes a proper competition policy for Japan. MITI has traditionally taken a mediator's role between companies in cases when major industrial mergers are in the making, especially those precipitated by economic downturns. This self-appointed role as guardian of its view of competition policy has at times precipitated open conflict between MITI and the FTC, usually centering on the latter's claim that either industry or MITI itself is violating the spirit, if not the letter, of the Anti-Monopoly Law.

The FTC, which administers the Anti-Monopoly Law, has had an anomalous position in Japanese society since its inception in 1947. In the early postwar years, there was so much opposition to its very existence that few analysts expected the FTC ever to gain real authority or legitimacy. Gradually, it has indeed gained some of both, relative to the past, but the degree has fluctuated over the years, often depending on the personal dynamism of its chairman. MITI, for its part, has always favored (1) more, rather than less, control over industry even though MITI officials could see their degree of control slowly declining over time and (2) less, rather than more, public accountability than the FTC has sought. The FTC has repeatedly argued that MITI also favors and, directly or indirectly, fosters a high degree of cartelization of industry, including, where necessary, collaboration among companies on prices, production levels, and the like. MITI's typical defense against such allegations, when it has felt obliged to respond, has been either that the Anti-Monopoly Law if followed too closely would lead to excessive fragmentation of industry or that whatever actions it has taken were done through formal measures, such as administrative guidance, and therefore not subject to any official breach of the law. Both of these arguments have typically also been grouped under the more general argument that MITI was acting in the "national interest," with the overall health of the economy uppermost in mind.

This institutional tension between the FTC and MITI erupted into open hostility in two famous cases: the merger of Yawata and Fuji Steel in 1969 and the allegations by the FTC in 1974 that member companies in the Petroleum Industry Association had illegally restricted supply even when doing so at MITI's behest. In the steel case, the FTC argued that it did not oppose mergers per se if the resulting corporation would not be too powerful by standards that it, on its own authority, would issue. Thus, with regard to the proposed Yawata-Fuji merger, the FTC offered its seal of approval if both companies would divest themselves of certain subsidiaries. The companies initially resisted these requests, which led in turn to a formal restraining order issued by the FTC and, eventually, to a court judgment in the fall of 1969 that the merger could go through if both firms rid themselves of a small number of facilities. Both companies then complied with the court decision, albeit with widely advertised reluctance, and in 1970 a new company, Nippon Steel Corporation, came into existence with more than a 30 percent market share in Japan. The case was important insofar as the FTC was able to establish the principle that it, not just MITI, had a right to pass judgment on the desirability of proposed mergers. However, since the actual outcome of the case saw the creation of a company with a more than 30 percent share of the domestic market, which in those days was generally regarded by economists as constituting de facto conditions for an oligopolistic market structure, the Yawata-Fuji case can hardly be called a model of antimonopoly law by the standards of other advanced industrial countries.[99]

In the oil case, the FTC filed charges in 1974 of illegal activity to restrict production and fix prices; oil executives contended that their actions were legitimate because they were based on administrative guidance from MITI. A court judgment in 1980 ruled that MITI lacked the authority to use administrative guidance to induce firms to take actions that were otherwise illegal. Thus the case became the first in postwar Japan in which criminal proceedings involving cartelization were carried through to an adverse court ruling. However, the decision left many unanswered questions about the degree of latitude MITI could in fact take—in the exercise of its view of the national interest, in inducing firms to reduce capacity and concurrently fix prices. As in the steel case a decade earlier, the oil case did establish the principle that some limits, at least, could be set on MITI's discretionary powers. In addition, in both the steel and oil price cases, much criticism was brought to bear against MITI's behavior. Social critics and opposition politicans denounced MITI for representing only the interests of big

---

99. As discussed below, the use of a domestic market standard of bigness has since been viewed by an increasing number of economists as inadequate, given the degree to which imports or exports affect the share of a domestic market going to domestically based producers or the number of competitors facing even a large-size producer in a worldwide market.

business, not those of the economy as a whole. In neither case, however, was MITI formally sanctioned, and its influence does not seemed to have diminished significantly because of these cases per se.[100]

Moreover, the criticism that MITI received over these cases has lessened neither its nor industry's desire to continue using administrative guidance procedures rather than more formal (or more public) procedures of the sort favored by the FTC. As MITI's direct influence over industry wanes, it is likely both to want to rely on administrative guidance even more than in the past and to have little choice but to try to use these procedures if it also wants to exercise influence in a manner similar to earlier postwar years.[101] Where the problems and issues at hand are seemingly intractable, MITI's intervention is still considered useful, again in part because of the flexibility provided by the administrative guidance system. For example, as more basic manufacturing processes lose their competitiveness, these industries will be forced to scale down or even close domestic production facilities. Such adjustment is difficult and painful in any country, including Japan. In some of these cases, MITI's advice and assistance appears to have been actively sought. As discussed in greater detail in Chapter 6, those indus-

---

100. Parts of the above discussion of the FTC are drawn from Johnson, *MITI and the Japanese Miracle*, especially pp. 221, 245–47, 298–300; Frank K. Upham, "Administrative Guidance in Japan: In Decline or Evolution?" in *U.S.-Japan Relations in the 1980s: Towards Burden Sharing*, Annual Report 1981/82, Program in U.S.-Japan Relations (Cambridge, Mass.: Center for International Affairs, Harvard University 1982), pp. 121–127; and J. Mark Ramseyer, "Japanese Antitrust Enforcement after the Oil Embargo," *American Journal of Comparative Law* 31 (Summer 1982): 395–430. For a further discussion of the petroleum case, see Chapter 6.

101. Interestingly, some business executives have told us privately that even administrative guidance is "dead," meaning that many more firms than in the past are willing to ignore or minimize MITI suggestions if these go against the company's own desires at the time. This trend is not brand-new—most firms in the automobile industry successfully resisted MITI's ideas for reorganization more than a decade ago—and in this form the reported trend is probably overdrawn. But the decline of MITI's influence over economic activity, even in terms of its inability to influence economic activity through administrative guidance, is being talked about much more readily than in the past, which in itself is a sign of MITI's decline.

tries designated by law as structurally depressed are eligible for direct guidance by MITI and, under certain conditions, direct financial assistance. Even industries such as petrochemicals, which have yet to be designated structurally depressed, have both sought and accepted MITI advice and mediation with regard to production levels and capacity reductions. Thus, in hard-hit sectors, MITI retains considerable influence and will probably seek to exercise this influence through an increased use of administrative guidance, compared with the days when direct intervention was the dominant pattern. On the other hand, the record of late suggests that MITI's influence is no longer strong enough to be able to force an industry to comply with administrative guidance if an affected industry strongly opposes the particular measures suggested by MITI.[102] Moreover, the internationalization and the increased pluralism of the Japanese economy means that increased demands for transparency (that is, publicly accountable procedures rather than the behind-the-scenes deliberations characteristic of administrative guidance procedures) are likely to be sought by foreign governments, by the FTC, by opposition parties, and by other Japanese representing consumer interests and various additional sectors of the general public.

FUTURE TRENDS IN JAPANESE INDUSTRIAL POLICIES

Continuing changes in world market conditions—from the high global growth rates of the 1950s and 1960s to the sharp increases in energy prices in 1973/74 and again in 1979/80 and now to the growing importance of the NICs—have each contributed to significant changes in Japan's comparative advantage. Correspondingly, Japan's industrial policies have in turn changed with new conditions and continue to evolve to this day. This chapter defined *industrial policy* narrowly in order to differentiate between specific and economy-wide measures. It then examined how two major instruments of Japanese industrial policy, tax policies and direct government financial assistance, had changed over the course of the postwar period. Such an examination has limited meaning, however, in the absence of an accompanying analysis of the

---

102. Concrete examples are discussed in Chapter 6.

broader macroeconomic and international context influencing the effectiveness of these specific industrial policy instruments. Neither purely quantitative analyses nor purely institutional analyses seem able to produce a satisfactory assessment of the role of the government in Japan's industrial development. For this reason, we have explicitly analyzed those aspects of industrial policy that can be quantified, such as the specific instruments discussed above, in light of broader, qualitative factors.

In general, whether one is simply trying to identify the effects of industrial policies on the Japanese economy itself or trying also to identify implications these policies might have for the trade and investment patterns of other countries, problems of definition and measurement seem to us to be critical to a full understanding of these policies. Existing quantitative estimates of policy effects seem to us to be incomplete—at least to the degree they suggest that a precise measurement of overall policy effects is possible.[103] Similarly, qualitative (that

---

103. Studies that have directly sought to identify and measure the sources of Japan's economic development contribute greatly to an understanding of *how* this process worked without necessarily explaining *why* it came to work this way. Even the extensive quantitative work by Edward Denison and William Chung concluded that the explanation for Japan's extraordinary postwar growth "is not to be found in any single determinant of output. Rather, changes in almost all important determinants were highly favorable in comparison with other countries, and in none was the change particularly unfavorable." See Edward F. Denison and William K. Chung, *How Japan's Economy Grew So Fast* (Washington, D.C.: Brookings Institution, 1976), p. 46. Moreover, in their view Japan's growth was comparable with that of other developed countries in terms of the relative importance of the various sources of growth they were able to measure, using a standard growth accounting framework. But since this framework seeks specifically to quantify those aspects of economic analysis that can reasonably be quantified and treats other factors as a residual, it leaves open many questions about the nonquantifiable factors, which may in fact be more important in understanding "fundamental" causes of Japanese economic growth than the quantifiable factors.

For example, in their discussion of capital stock, Denison and Chung argue that the increase in Japan's capital stock can be attributed to three major developments: a rapid increase in national output, an increase in the proportion of income saved, and declines in the price of capital goods relative to the price of other components of GNP. Yet the question remains, Should the increase in capital stock be in turn attributed to government policies? In other words, did the selective application of a then-detailed system

is, institutional) analyses of, say, MITI or the MOF alone, although valuable as such, also tend to be incomplete since they often ignore or at least underemphasize the impact of other aspects of the Japanese economy. This becomes all the more true as the Japanese economy itself has become more developed. If methodologies existed that could clearly measure or even clearly distinguish the influence of the government from the influence of purely market forces, an understanding of the Japanese economy—or any economy, for that matter—would obviously be improved.[104]

In practical terms the issue for policymakers and business executives in the United States and other countries that trade heavily with Japan is mainly one of trying to understand how the Japanese economy is changing over time and in what direction. Johnson himself argues, at least by implication, that as an economy becomes more developed, it becomes, in his terms, more "market-rational" and less

---

of trade and foreign exchange controls enable the Japanese government to use international competition to hold down the price of capital goods while providing a protected, high-priced domestic market for consumer goods produced primarily at home? Such questions admittedly cannot easily be dealt with in a growth accounting framework.

Hugh Patrick, among others, has suggested that economists need to look beyond orthodox economic methodologies—and to incorporate political science, sociology, anthropology, and psychology—in order to understand not simply that Japan's high savings and investment rates have contributed to high rates of economic growth but also how these high savings and investment rates might have come about. This was a major point in a presentation Patrick made to the 1982 United States-Japan Conference on Cultural and Educational Interchange (CULCON), sponsored by the U.S. Information Agency and the Japanese Ministry of Foreign Affairs.

104. Johnson emphasizes the role of government in economic development particularly for countries such as Japan that were trying to catch up to others for basically political reasons—that is, they did not want to be poorer or less powerful than countries that had already industrialized. In Johnson's view, Japan's modern economic history can be explained by the role of the "developmental state," an institution he traces to a German school of thought "sometimes labeled 'economic nationalism,' *Handelspolitik*, or neomercantilism." He argues that "in states that were late to industrialize, the state itself led the industrialization drive, that is, it took on *developmental* functions." Thus, he distinguishes Japan from countries like the United States where the state performs regulatory functions. Moreover, "in the developmental state

"plan-rational," meaning that the role of the "developmental state" diminishes over time relative to the role of the private sector. This is certainly our reading of postwar Japanese economic history and of the evolution of targeted tax policy instruments whose utility and impact diminished as the economy became more developed.[105] As also noted above, even the use of administrative guidance, which in the absence of more direct controls has been MITI's obvious hope as a means of trying to continue to exercise influence over the country, is facing increased opposition.

Earlier sections of this chapter sought to identify and where possible to quantify the specific effects of various industrial policies. Chapters 5 and 6 identify and where possible quantify such effects in two areas that have received particular attention from MITI: new industries and declining industries. However, as should be clear from the

---

economic interests are explicitly subordinated to political objectives. The very idea of the developmental state originated in the situational nationalism of the late industrializers, and the goals of the developmental state were invariably derived from comparisons with external reference economies." See Johnson, *MITI and the Japanese Miracle*, pp. 17, 19, 24, and chap. 1 passim.

By contrast, most of the scholars who contributed to the Brookings Institution study referred to in Chapter 2 give the government a subordinate role, relative to the normal workings of a market economy—as such economies have been understood in the United States. Hugh Patrick and Henry Rosovsky, coeditors of the Brookings volume and coauthors of the introductory and concluding chapters, take this view, although they do not address the question of why various specific sources of growth might have been brought into play by the market. To the degree that they discuss how this process worked, they do so as part of a discussion of the role of government policy *versus* the role of the market. "The main impetus to growth," they write,

> has come from the private sector, both in business initiative and in private demand. The government's role has been supportive, mainly by providing an environment well suited to economic growth....
> ....Government intervention generally has tended (and intended) to accelerate trends already put in motion by private market forces—the development of infant industries, the structural adjustment of declining industries, and the like....
> ....Thus, while government policy may have been important, its impact on economic performance was not "uniquely Japanese."

above discussion, any consideration of the net effects of specific industrial policies is necessarily speculative since the degree of economic growth or industrial development that would have occurred in the absence of such policies is itself uncertain. In other words, it is actually not possible to develop a quantitatively precise methodology for measuring the overall impact of Japanese industrial policies, as against the impact of market forces and more general macroeconomic policies, on industrial development itself. Moreover, even when considering the extent to which the growth of a particular industry has been promoted by specific Japanese government policies, such as the infant-industry protection enjoyed by many basic manufacturing industries in the 1950s and 1960s, one can still make only the most general statements as to how effective (or ineffective) such policies would have been if the international environment of the day had been less "tolerant" of these

---

See Hugh Patrick and Henry Rosovsky, "Japan's Economic Performance: An Overview," in *Asia's New Giant*, ed. Hugh Patrick and Henry Rosovsky (Washington, D.C.: Brookings Institution, 1976), pp. 20, 47, 48, and chap. 1, passim.

In our view—and this much may seem obvious—both the government and the market contributed to Japanese economic development; thus both Johnson and the Brookings scholars are correct, up to a point. However, neither has measured exactly what the role of the government or the role of the market has been, to the exclusion of the other. Johnson emphasizes the role of government in Japanese economic development without systematically comparing Japan's pattern of development with other already developed countries that have had a similarly activist government—or with those. like the United States, that seemingly developed without benefit of a comparably activist government but that surely benefited from some government intervention, for example, land-grant colleges, agricultural extension services, and the like. On the other side of the argument, most of the Brookings scholars are correspondingly assertive in their notion that the market has been "the main impetus to growth." Having no methodology to measure such qualitative factors as the role of government, but a well-defined methodology to measure various quantitative factors, the Brookings scholars tend to generalize from these quantitative measurements to a theory of causation they also do not explicitly outline. Two of the Brookings scholars, Krause and Sekiguchi, recognize this problem and prudently note that "the many faceted participation of the government in the operations of the Japanese economy presents a difficult analytical problem." See Krause and Sekiguchi, "Japan and the World Economy," p. 385.

measures or, alternatively, if foreign (for example, mainly U.S.) firms had made more vigorous efforts to enter the Japanese market earlier and/or with greater force. In several industry areas discussed in Chapter 6 (for example, petroleum refining), government policies *and* foreign tolerance of these policies and related practices greatly influenced the eventual shape of the industry. Discrimination against foreign firms, both explicit and implicit, has clearly gone hand in hand with Japanese industrial policies, but here, too, it is difficult, if not impossible, to measure in precise terms what the overall competitive effects of this discrimination have been.

Generally, this chapter has shown that the Japanese government's role in promoting industrial development through the specific application of narrowly targeted measures has declined over time. In the early postwar years, MITI's authority to allocate foreign exchange gave it

---

105. Unfortunately, Johnson seems to contradict himself on this point when, in his concluding chapter, he seems to suggest (without explicitly advocating) that a Japanese model might be suitable for the United States and/or other countries seeking rapid growth. Johnson does note that the United States, because its traditions and current situation are different from postwar Japan, might do well "to build on its own strengths and to unleash the private, competitive impulses of its citizens rather than add still another layer to its already burdensome regulatory bureaucracy." But without particular elaboration, Johnson goes on in the next (and final) paragraph to suggest that such a reliance on private economic activity may "be unrealistic for the longer term" and that "Americans should perhaps also be thinking seriously about their own 'pilot agency,'" comparable with MITI, to coordinate economic policies. See Johnson, *MITI and the Japanese Miracle*, p. 323. The difficulty here is that if, as Johnson himself argues, a plan-rational economy is characteristic of later developing countries and a market-rational economy is characteristic of already developed countries, there is no logical progression from a market-rational to a plan-rational system. Moreover, there would logically also be a separate set of issues relevant to the transition from a developing to a developed economy. Indeed, we believe the key issues in Japanese policy-making today belong to this transition stage—for example, how much investment versus how much consumption Japanese should seek as they become more affluent than before and roughly as affluent as Americans and Europeans. Johnson, on the other hand, seems to be suggesting that the United States adopt a Japanese model at a time when, in our view at least, Japan is moving away from that very model and toward a more market-rational economy characteristic of the United States and other already developed countries.

considerable leverage over the private sector. Over the years, as domestic industries prospered, they came not only to rely less on MITI (whether for foreign exchange, tax breaks, preferential financing, or other direct supports) but also to resent continued attempts by MITI to guide their further development. All along, MITI's role has been especially significant in the early stages of the development of new industries, the most prominent recent examples being computers and electronics, as discussed in Chapter 5. In such case, MITI's ability to provide subsidies, tax credits, and other forms of direct support, together with various forms of indirect support that promote private sector confidence, gives it more leverage than in the middle stages of an industry's development. Once into a sustained growth phase, companies typically become more reluctant to share information, have less need for government funds, and are less willing to comply with outside suggestions.

Nowadays, as the Japanese economy is no longer in as much of a "catch-up" phase vis-à-vis other advanced industrial countries, Japan is beginning to face a situation in which previously successful basic manufacturing industries have beome uncompetitive. In this environment, MITI's role has recently become significant in facilitating the compromises necessary to bring about capacity cutbacks or in negotiating agreements with foreign governments to restrain exports.[106] In other words, changes in Japan's comparative advantage have meant that MITI's role has become more explicitly related to influencing or supporting industries mainly at the beginning and the end of an industry's cycle. In this regard, MITI is now targeting the development of new

---

106. The increasing tendency to seek government-to-government orderly marketing agreements also affects the sometimes separate field of competition policy, which is itself in considerable flux. Through policies promulgated by William F. Baxter, former U.S. assistant attorney general for Antitrust, the Reagan administration began to incorporate concepts of a world market test of competition that had been under discussion in academic circles for some years. One effect of these new policies was to contribute to the breakdown of regulatory barriers in the United States between computing and data transmission, which because of the sheer size of the U.S. market then spilled over to Japan and Europe. Meanwhile, Japanese interest groups, in both the public and private sector and within the public sector (for example, between MITI and the FTC), have found it necessary to reexamine previous Japanese concepts of competiton policy in light of changes going on in the United States. This reevaluation is still in its early stages.

service industries such as leisure and information processing and various new technologies, materials, and production processes, all of which received considerable attention in the latest "vision" document.[107] MITI's importance in the development of these industries, although greater than the role it currently plays in the "middle years" of an industry cycle, is not as all-powerful as the role it formerly played in stimulating the development of earlier industries. In this sense, MITI's role in influencing Japanese industrial development is in a long-term, secular decline.

Perhaps the most important single implication to be drawn from this review of postwar Japanese industrial policies is their declining importance, compared with other factors, as the Japanese economy itself has matured. This decline is certain to continue as the economy develops further. Regardless of how effective Japanese industrial policy instruments have been in the catch-up era or how effective they remain compared with those in other advanced industrial countries, a combination of market forces, budgetary constraints, and political pressures have already required, and will continue to require, a reevaluation of the goals and methods of industrial policy. Barring an outbreak of global protectionism, the vestiges of Japan's once-detailed trade, investment, capital, and foreign exchange controls will become increasingly costly to the domestic economy. This effect is becoming increasingly apparent to new and heterogeneous interests, as well as becoming increasingly irksome to Japan's trading partners. Moreover, the tremendous accumulation of government debt will severely limit the use of policy instruments requiring large budgetary expenditures or tax breaks. This decline in the importance of industrial policy is relative to Japan's own history; relative to other countries with a more limited history of detailed industrial development policies—or less success in making use of such policies—Japanese industrial policies appear formidable indeed. Moreover, in the absence of serious efforts on the part of foreign firms to compete with Japanese firms at home and abroad, some Japanese industrial policies give some industries competitive advantages they would not otherwise have. Subsequent chapters will show how, in specific sectors, this decline in the importance of industrial policy has come about.

---

107. Sangyō Kōzō Shingikai [Industrial Structure Council], *Hachijū nendai no tsūsan seisaku bijon* [Visions of trade and industry policy for the 1980s] (Tokyo: Ministry of International Trade and Industry, April 1980).

Chapter 4

THE JAPANESE FINANCIAL SYSTEM

Japan's financial system is in the midst of a dramatic transformation. Beginning in the 1970s, the segmented and highly regulated system in existence since World War II (and before) began to face much increased pressures for change from both internal and external causes. Many of the changes that occurred are typical of those previously observed in other advanced industrial countries as they became wealthier.[1] The higher and more volatile world inflation rates of the 1970s (refer back to Figure 2.4) led Japanese as well as Americans to begin to reexamine traditional means of saving and investing. As in the United States, major nonfinancial corporations in Japan began to seek more sophisticated cash management services, which Japanese banks concurrently began to provide. Individual depositors became more sensitive to rates of return, leading Japanese financial institutions to begin offering them new services as well. Japanese financial institutions also began moving into international markets—often offering services they were prohibited from offering at home—and foreign-based institutions began to offer financial services in the Japanese market that had previously been unavailable. Large secondary bond markets began to develop when government budget deficits increased after the mid-1970s. Partly as a result of this and partly in response to international market forces, some Japanese interest rates began to be deregulated. Meanwhile, as the cost of data processing and data transmission continued to fall during the decade and financial transactions came to be made "on-line," cus-

---

1. See Raymond W. Goldsmith, *The Financial Development of Japan, 1868-1977* (New Haven and London: Yale University Press, 1983), especially chapt. 7 for a discussion of the broad patterns of change after World War II.

tomary requirements for face-to-face contact became increasingly unnecessary. With all these developments, the traditional segmentation in the Japanese financial system became increasingly costly.

Today, for the first time in Japan's modern history, public and private financial institutions and their corresponding regulatory bodies are in fierce competition with each other. An extended shakeout in the financial sector is under way. Institutions that once "knew their place" in a tradition-based hierarchy are making dramatic changes in their attitudes toward profits, market share, and rules of the game, and the changes currently taking place will almost certainly stimulate still further changes. Financial transactions are the lubricants on which an economy runs. Because changes in the financial sector and the so-called real sector of an economy are highly intertwined, neither can be viewed in isolation. Accordingly, this chapter first describes the Japanese financial system that evolved after the Meiji Restoration and continued more or less intact through the 1960s. It then describes how this system began to change in the 1970s and again in the 1980s and the impact these changes began to have on the economy as a whole. It concludes with a projection of likely future changes.[2]

EVOLUTION OF THE FINANCIAL SYSTEM[3]

Major elements of the modern Japanese financial system can be traced

---

2. Chapter 2 discusses some aspects of the financial system, particularly international financial transactions, as these have affected (or been affected by) the overall economy, for example, through trade policy, relations with the United States, and Japan's role in the world economy. This chapter discusses the internal structure of the financial system, particularly changes in this structure during the past 15 years.

3. This discussion draws upon T. F. M. Adams and Iwao Hoshii, *A Financial History of the New Japan* (Tokyo: Kodansha International, 1972); L. S. Pressnell, ed., *Money and Banking in Japan* (London: Macmillan, 1973), chaps. 1–10; Henry C. Wallich and Mable I. Wallich, "Banking and Finance," in *Asia's New Giant*, ed. Hugh Patrick and Henry Rosovsky (Washington, D.C.: Brookings Institution, 1976); G. C. Allen, *The Japanese Economy* (New York: St. Martin's Press, 1981), chap. 4; Andreas R. Prindl, *Japanese Finance: A Guide to Banking in Japan* (New York: John Wiley & Sons, 1981), chaps. 1–3; Yoshio Suzuki, *Money and Banking in Contemporary Japan* (New Haven and London: Yale University Press, 1980); and Goldsmith, *Financial Development of Japan*.

to the early days of the Meiji Restoration. In 1880 the Yokohama Specie
Bank, which later became the Bank of Tokyo, was founded as a foreign exchange arm of the Japanese government. A banking act created
the Bank of Japan (BOJ) as a central bank in 1882. In 1900 the Industrial Bank of Japan was founded with a charter to finance new industrial companies. During this same period, a variety of semigovernmental
institutions, such as various agricultural cooperative banks, were also
set up to service different sectors of the economy, thereby complementing the then-budding commercial bank networks but also explicitly reinforcing a segmented financial system in which different groups of financial institutions would draw on different sources of funds and make these
funds available to different sectors of the economy. As they proliferated,
these semigovernment institutions also formalized an already-established
practice of using public monies to support private activites perceived
to be in the national interest.[4] Much later, under impetus of colonial
expansion and war in the 1930s, the Japanese financial system became
much more centralized, in part because of the growth of so-called
zaibatsu, or "financial groups" (in effect, holding companies that included a commercial bank), and in part through even greater government involvement in financial activities than had previously existed.
World War II and the occupation changed some characteristics of the
system but left some of the most important intact.

Major Institutions in the Financial System

The primary official institutions in the financial system are the MOF
and the BOJ. The MOF is responsible for the typical government treasury functions, such as preparation of a budget and allocation of
resources among government agencies and the design, implementation,
and collection of taxes, as well as having administrative responsibility
for the licensing and regulation of Japanese financial institutions. The
MOF is the most powerful ministry in the Japanese government, although it has almost always limited its efforts to influence the policies
of other ministries to the indirect device of vetoing or circumscribing
their budget requests. The BOJ is the sole bank of issue. It serves as
the government's own bank, as manager of the government securities
market, as a lender of last resort for the commercial banks, as the im-

---

4. See Adams and Hoshii, *Financial History,* p. 12 and passim. They identify this practice as an important element in the prewar Japanese financial system that continued into the postwar period.

plementing agency for monetary policy, and as the regulator of the monetary system on a day-to-day basis. The BOJ also carries out interventions in foreign exchange markets. In implementing monetary and foreign exchange policies, the BOJ works in concert with and under a framework set by the MOF. Banks, securities houses, and almost all other financial institutions act under MOF/BOJ guidance, whether or not this role is specified in law. Given the day-to-day interaction between private institutions and the MOF/BOJ and the strong discretionary authority vested in the government, a significant degree of self-regulation exists.

Although the BOJ's legal powers are more limited than those of the MOF and the latter is clearly dominant on matters involving overall macroeconomic policy, in practice the BOJ shares authority on economic and financial issues with the MOF.[5] Implementation of monetary policy is clearly up to the BOJ, which handles detailed aspects of money supply growth, credit and financial conditions, and the smoothing of frictions among competitors for funds and in international financial flows. Nevertheless, the two institutions do take differing policy positions, for example, on the timing of changes in the discount rate or the pace of liberalization of international financial transactions.

World War II and the postwar financial difficulties virtually destroyed private accumulations of capital in Japan. Initially, the occupation authorities concentrated on moves to dissolve the *zaibatsu*, which at the time were thought to have contributed to Japan's going to war, and to loosen the government's highly centralized control over the economy. This had three immediate implications for the financial sector.

---

5. The legal division of authority is relatively clear. Article 42 of the Bank of Japan Law (implemented in 1942) states that the BOJ is "under the supervision of the competent Minister [of Finance]"; Article 43 gives the minister of finance full power to "order the Bank to undertake any necessary business or order alternatives in the by-laws." Nevertheless, BOJ officials question whether the MOF is the primary determinant of financial policy. A BOJ publication states: "In practice, active mutual contacts and cooperation are always maintained between the Bank of Japan and the government authorities with regard to the actual business and policy operations of the Bank, and this power to issue orders with regard to the Bank's business has never been invoked." See Economic Research Department, Bank of Japan, *The Japanese Financial System* (Tokyo: Bank of Japan, 1978).

First, the dissolution of the *zaibatsu* broke the formal, organizational ties between banks and various manufacturing and commercial enterprises, although relationships of lender to borrower were of course retained.[6] Second, the once-powerful special-purpose government banks were either dissolved or had their functions dramatically altered. Those banks with special roles abroad—that is, the government banks in former colonial areas and the Yokohama Specie Bank, which had a special role in foreign exchange transactions—were closed outright.[7] Three of the major debenture-issuing government banks specializing in long-term financing were made private, reorganized as commercial banks, and in 1952 given the choice of confining their business to deposit banking and short-term lending or long-term financing; the Nippon Kangyo Bank and the Hokkaido Takushoku Bank chose to remain commercial banks, and the Industrial Bank of Japan chose to undertake long-term financing. Third, banking and securities activities were separated along lines of the U.S. Glass-Steagall legislation, with the apparent intention of further weakening the interlocking ownership ties associated with the *zaibatsu*.

In the capital-short environment of the early postwar years, the central government was almost the only source of investment funds, and much of its money came initially from U.S. aid. The government, by

---

6. After the occupation, the main *zaibatsu* banks, which had changed their names during the occupation as a means of deemphasizing their prewar history, took back their former names and integrated themselves into the large industrial and commercial conglomerates that were also reconsolidating based largely on previous *zaibatsu* ties. However, relationships among these new groupings, now called *keiretsu,* have been less exclusive than in prewar days and are becoming less so over time.

7. Subsequently, the Bank of Tokyo was created as a successor to the Yokohama Specie Bank, also with a view toward specializing in foreign exchange. However, its purview was made much less exclusive, as other commercial banks were also permitted to deal in foreign exchange. The Bank of Tokyo retains certain exclusive privileges over other commercial banks such as the right to issue debentures and to create yen from dollar swaps, higher lending limits to any single borrower, and easier access to borrowed reserves. On the other hand, it is more restricted than other banks in the scope of its lending activities, which must be concerned with foreign trade or foreign financial flows, and in its ability to establish domestic branches.

this time with support from the occupation authorities (whose own goals had shifted from attempts to eliminate the alleged causes of the war to attempts to hasten Japan's recovery as a means of forestalling communist influence within Japan and elsewhere in Asia), began to allocate funds in great detail for reconstruction and recovery. A new financial institution, the Reconstruction Finance Corporation (Fukkō Kinyū Kinkō), was created to distribute much of the money made available by the government. The corporation derived its funds directly from the BOJ (and in turn from U.S. aid). The Industrial Bank of Japan increasingly resumed its former role as a major lender to basic manufacturing industries (although it remained independent of the government). Several new government-based long-term credit banks were established for similar purposes or assumed such functions—that is, the JDB; the Agricultural, Forestry, and Fishery Corporation; the Small Business Finance Corporation; the Ex-Im Bank; and the Long-Term Credit Bank of Japan.[8] These banks raised funds by issuing debentures that were purchased partially by commercial banks and partially by the Government Trust Fund Bureau. The JDB inherited the functions of the Reconstruction Finance Corporation when the latter was disbanded in 1947 and, as noted in Chapter 3, focused its activities on infrastructure projects and basic manufacturing industries. Initally, the JDB received most of its capital from U.S. counterpart funds; later, from the Trust Fund Bureau and other government accounts.

Japan's current financial system continues to be dominated by banks (see Table 4.1), preeminently the 13 so-called city banks (*toshi ginkō*).[9] These handle the bulk of the country's short-term and trade financing. Four of the six largest city banks are direct descendants of prewar *zaibatsu* banks (now called *keiretsu*, or group, banks), although each of these has since developed significant business outside their respective groups. City banks control slightly less than one third of the

---

8. The Long-Term Credit Bank of Japan was formed in 1952 with 50 percent backing from a consortium of financial institutions and industrial corporations, but subsequently it became fully private.

9. These are Japan's main institutions for day-to-day banking operations. The 13 city banks today, as listed by the size of their assets, are: Daiichi Kangyo, Fuji, Sumitomo, Mitsubishi, Sanwa, Mitsui, Bank of Tokyo, Tokai, Taiyo Kobe, Daiwa, Kyowa, Saitama, and Hokkaido Takushoku.

financial resources of all financial institutions (down from one half in the early 1950s) and 60 percent of the funds of all commercial banks. All large enterprises are clients of one or more city banks. Although the number of individual depositors is considerable, city banks focus primarily on large-scale enterprises and large-scale transactions. The high dependence of large enterprises on bank financing throughout the postwar years has made them virtual partners with the city banks in long-term business relations. The close relationship between city banks and their principal clients has meant that much of their short-term credits are almost automatically rolled over, giving the borrower what amounts to long-term credit. The heavy dependence on bank lending as a source of finance began to decline somewhat in the 1970s, although it remains much greater than in the United States.

Local banks (*chihō ginkō*) are permitted the same range of activities as city banks, but their business is usually concentrated in one prefecture. In practice the activities of local banks fall between those of U.S. commerical banks and U.S. savings and loan associations. Although some local banks are as big as the smaller city banks in the amount of deposits, most are small institutions. Their loan customers tend to be small- or medium-size local enterprises, with more than half of their loans given to businesses with a capital base of less than ¥10 million (or $45,454 at ¥220 = $1). Almost half of their balances represent individual deposits, and some three fourths are time deposits. They are active lenders in the call market, channeling liquidity to the city banks.[10] Only rarely would a local bank be forced to rely on borrowings from the BOJ. In periods of monetary stringency, larger enterprises have been known to turn to local banks to supplement the funds they can borrow from city banks.[11]

The primary business of the three long-term credit banks—the Industrial Bank of Japan, the Long-Term Credit Bank of Japan, and Nip-

---

10. The *call market* is an interbank money market in which banks can lend and borrow to meet short-term liquidity needs (for as short a period as overnight). This market is analogous to the U.S. Federal Funds market and until the 1970s was the only major financial market in Japan that was largely free of controls over interest rates.

11. Local banks also have lost share to other private institutions since the 1950s.

Table 4.1
ASSETS AND ASSET SHARES OF PRIVATE FINANCIAL INSTITUTIONS,
1953, 1963, 1973, AND 1983

Institution	ASSETS IN 1953[a]		ASSETS IN 1963[a]		ASSETS IN 1973[a]		ASSETS IN 1983[a]	
	Amount (¥ billion)	Percent of Total	Amount (¥ billion)	Percent of Total	Amount (¥ billion)	Percent of Total	Amount (¥ billion)	Percent of Total
City banks	2,641	50.5	14,416	41.8	64,917	36.1	155,707	30.6
Local ("regional") banks	1,065	20.4	6,361	18.4	30,828	17.1	89,005	17.5
Trust banks (banking accounts)	97	1.9	754	2.2	5,562	3.1	19,684	3.9
Long-term-credit banks	250	4.8	2,061	6.0	12,214	6.8	35,111	6.9
Mutual loan and savings banks	342	6.5	2,648	7.7	14,608	8.1	40,909	8.0
Credit associations	243	4.6	2,667	7.7	18,111	10.1	51,390	10.1
Credit cooperatives[b]	20	0.4	519	1.5	3,757	2.1	12,225	2.4
Labor credit associations[b]	10[c]	0.2	88	0.2	790	0.4	4,362	0.9
Agricultural								

cooperatives[b]	347	6.6	1,847	5.3	12,852	7.1	38,149	7.5
Fishery cooperatives[b]	24[c]	0.5	131	0.4	876	0.5	2,622	0.5
Subtotal	5,039	96.4	31,492	91.2	164,515	91.4	449,164	88.1[d]
Trust accounts of all banks	189	3.6	3,029	8.8	15,486	8.6	60,490	11.9
Total[e]	5,228	100.0	34,521	100.0	180,001	100.0	509,654	100.0

Notes: [a]An institution is associated with each of the groups serving small business, agriculture, and fisheries that in greater or lesser degree acts as a central bank, accepting surplus funds and lending them out to members or investing them in other forms. While there are specialized credit facilities serving each of the major producers' groups—the degree of specialization varies considerably—there are no institutions specifically designed to serve the consumer in his or her role as homeowner or personal borrower. Some amount of credit is available to households, of course, through the commercial banking system and the banks serving principally small business.

[a]End of calendar year.

[b]Assets = sum of liabilities (deposits plus capital and borrowings).

[c]Data for 1954.

[d]The subtotals of the percentage does not equal 88.1 because of rounding.

[e]Does not include government-financed institutions or the funds of the central institutions of credit associations and cooperatives that are partly derived from deposits by their member institutions.

Sources: Bank of Japan, *Economic Statistics Annual*, 1954, 1963, and 1973, as reported in Henry C. Wallich and Mable I. Wallich, "Banking and Finance," in *Asia's New Giant*, ed. Hugh Patrick and Henry Rosovsky (Washington, D.C.: Brookings Institution, 1976), p. 281; and Bank of Japan, *Economic Statistics Monthly*, no. 416 (November 1981), pp. 41–66.

pon Credit Bank—has been to provide explicitly long-term loans for corporate expansion. Although these banks can accept deposits from borrowers and from the government, their funding comes mostly from the issuance of debentures. They cannot accept deposits from the general public. Loans have traditionally been made to Japanese industry for plant expansion on a mortgage basis. By establishing foreign branches and joining leading international lending syndicates during the last ten years, the long-term credit banks have become heavily involved in international markets. Long-term credit banks also perform investment banking functions, except for the underwriting of corporate bonds.[12]

The seven "trust" banks fall roughly into the same category as the long-term credit banks.[13] In their present form, the trust banks are descendants of trust companies that flourished in the 1920s. In those days, such companies had trust management and investment banking functions but could not conduct commercial banking activities. A series of financial difficulties led to a reduction in the number of trust companies from 422 in 1921 to 39 in 1927. The prewar and wartime centralization of the financial system reduced this number to seven during the war.[14] After the separation of banking and securities activities in 1948, the trust companies were stripped of their investment banking functions and reorganized as commercial banks (that is, they were given broadly the same authority as city and local banks) with a special charter to manage trusts. They operate now as commercial banks but must keep their trust and commercial banking activities separate. Their financing comes largely from so-called money trusts, of which the largest are loan trusts in which certificates are sold to the public and become, in effect, long-term deposits. Trust banks share with insurance companies the

---

12. Long-term credit banks can, among other securities activities, (1) act as trustee for the issue of government and local bonds, industrial debentures, and so on; (2) act as trustee for mortgages of secured debentures; and (3) serve as registration agents of debentures.

13. The seven trust banks, as listed by the size of their assets, are Mitsubishi Trust, Sumitomo Trust, Mitsui Trust, Yasuda Trust, Toyo Trust, Chuo Trust, and Nippon Trust. Daiwa Bank also operates a trust bank.

14. Adams and Hoshii, *Financial History*, pp. 108–109. The seven organizations of that period only partially overlap with the seven trust banks that currently exist.

authority to manage pension funds; these account for some 14 percent of the trust banks' liabilities.[15] Their investment activities have been mainly in lending for industrial plant expansion and, more recently, in the purchase of bonds, especially those of the central government.

The Japanese Postal Savings System is the world's largest financial institution other than central banks; its assets are close to $400 billion.[16] Through its access to post offices throughout the country, the Postal Savings System has more than 22,000 branches. In addition to the advantages of proximity to customers, the Postal Savings System normally offers slightly higher interest rates than commercial banks and benefits from a special income tax exclusion on the interest income on deposits of ¥3 million or less ($13,636 at ¥220 = $1). This tax advantage is also available on small deposits in commercial banks, but the availability of additional exclusions for deposits in the Postal Savings System, coupled with the usually higher interest rates available, makes the latter an attractive option for millions of individual depositors.[17] The government Trust Fund Bureau, which administers postal savings deposits, is empowered to invest those only in (1) government loans or bonds, (2) local government bonds, (3) government-related institutions, and (4) a limited amount of bank debentures. Commercial banks complain regularly about the advantages given to the Postal Savings System, but the institution is so popular as a source of "off-the-books" income that these complaints have been ineffective so far. Moreover, the system's ability to capture private savings that can then be directly allocated by the government makes the bureaucracy in general, and the MOF in particular, obviously reluctant to alter the status quo. Through this role it plays as an important financial intermediary, the Postal Sav-

---

15. Data from Bank of Japan, *Economic Statistics Monthly,* no. 442 (January 1984), pp. 45–46. In May 1984 the MOF agreed to give qualifying foreign banks the right to manage pension funds but not the city or local banks or securities companies.

16. In November 1983, assets totaled $379 billion, calculated at ¥220 = $1. See Bank of Japan, *Economic Statistics Monthly,* no. 445 (April 1984), p. 75.

17. As noted in Chapter 3, the number of accounts under false names is so large that the total number of postal savings deposits is more than twice the population of the country.

ings System and its parent agency, the Ministry of Posts and Telecommunications, also play a role in setting interest rate policy.

Many other specialized public and private financial institutions came into being over the years; these are summarized in Table 4.2. Of these, government institutions besides the Postal Savings System continue to play a role as financial intermediaries (among other activities, they allocate funds collected by the Postal Savings System). As noted in Chapter 3, this role declined from the mid-1950s to the late 1960s and then increased significantly to meet demands for increased infrastructure investment and other goals; such direct lending remains less than 14 percent of total lending, however. Miscellaneous private financial institutions (including those serving small business) grew rapidly, in terms of share of assets, from the 1950s through the 1960s but then leveled off.

Among the private institutions that developed as the overall economy grew were a variety associated with securities markets (that is, securities companies, securities finance companies, and investment trusts). However, the share of assets of all securities market-related institutions remained small through the mid-1970s, reaching only 1.6 percent in 1977.[18] Four securities houses—Nomura, Nikko, Daiwa, and Yamaichi—dominate the market; these four and another ten exert the major influence in the Security Dealers Association. Although these major securities firms closely follow guidelines specified by the MOF, they nevertheless are generally considered to operate with less reliability, in the fiduciary sense, than the banks. Securities firms in Japan are widely believed to manipulate share prices for their own profit or as means of generating funds for political contributions. Whether or not such a belief is based on fact, it is held widely enough to influence perceptions of the securities market by both specialists and the general public.

The growth of equity and bond markets was held back by a number of institutional factors. Perhaps the most important of these is cross-ownership of equity shares. Within each business grouping (the so-called *keiretsu*), each company normally owns a certain percentage of the other members' stock. Group banks act as treasurers of the group. Since the *keiretsu* banks also provide a high percentage of the group's trade financ-

---

18. Calculated from data in Goldsmith, *Financial Development of Japan,* table 7-7, p. 161.

Table 4.2

JAPANESE FINANCIAL INSTITUTIONS

	Example	Number
Private		
Commercial banks	City banks	13
	Regional banks	63
	Foreign banks	54
	Foreign Exchange Bank (Bank of Tokyo)	
Long-term credit banks	Industrial Bank of Japan	
	Long-Term Credit Bank of Japan	
	Nippon Credit Bank	
	Trust banks	7
Financial institutions for small businesses	Mutual loan and savings banks	71
	Credit associations	470
	Credit corporations	489
	Labor credit associations	47
	Central Bank for Commercial and Industrial Co-operatives	
Financial institutions for agriculture, forestry, and fisheries	Central Cooperative Bank for Agriculture and Forestry	
	Agricultural cooperatives	4,738
	Fishery cooperatives	1,695
	Forestry cooperatives	2,139
Insurance companies and securities companies		
Government		
Central bank	The Bank of Japan	
Banks	Japan Development Bank	
	Export-Import Bank of Japan	
Public corporations	People's Finance Corporation	
	Housing Loan Corporation	
	Agricultural, Forestry and Fishery Finance Corporation	
	Small Business Finance Corporation	

	Hokkaido and Tohoku Development Corporation
	Finance Corporation for Local Public Enterprise
Other	Trust Fund Bureau (formerly Treasury Deposits Bureau)
	Overseas Economic Co-operation Fund
	Post Office Life Insurance
	Postal Annuity Special Account

Source: G. C. ALLEN, *The Japanese Economy* (New York: St. Martin's Press, 1981), pp. 45, 57.

ing and exchange transactions, they can offset differential cash needs and move liquidity where it is most needed within the group; this reduces the need to seek funds from sources outside the group. In effect, the various groups operate their own internal money markets. An important aspect of cross-ownership relates to the very concept of equity in Japan. Unlike in the United States, where equity generally represents an arms-length investment calculation, equity in Japan is often equivalent to a kind of insurance policy, through which a stake in one firm is held by another known to be "friendly" and expected to provide new capital to avert bankruptcies and/or to preserve the independence of the existing management and its successors. Since expectations of support under the cross-ownership system are mutual, depending of course on the degree of ownership that exists, each party can take comfort from the insurance (and assurance) it is receiving—although bankruptcies naturally occur and situations also naturally arise where one company's ownership of another becomes suffocating. In general, dilution of ownership to firms or individuals outside the group reduces the certainty of the safety-net aspects of cross-ownership.[19] The existence of intragroup financial markets managed by a group bank also held back the development of bond markets; the group banks naturally

---

19. Dividends on shares held by corporations are not taxed, making cross-ownership even more attractive. Until recently, new stock issues had to be offered at book value to existing stockholders first, which had the effect of making capital raised by new equity issues much more expensive than borrowing.

sought to promote debt financing through loans rather than bonds.[20] Moreover, the administered interest rate structure kept demand for bonds low relative to long-term deposits. Thus, until the large government budget deficits of the 1970s forced a partial deregulation of interest rates, both private and public bond markets remained thin and shallow.

As noted above, corporate expansion has been financed largely by debt rather than equity and by debt composed mainly of bank loans and trade credit rather than bonds. In the early 1950s, 60 percent of new industrial investment came from bank advances, 25 percent from internal sources, and the remaining 15 percent from equity and bond issues and direct government loans. By the mid-1970s, reliance on external sources had declined to roughly 50 percent (from the earlier 75 percent), most of which still came from banks.[21] Loans and discounts from banks still represent some 40 percent (1978–81 average) of external funds for industry.[22] On the other hand, many factors prevent a sharp drop in the heavy reliance on debt, that is, continuing high growth (compared with other OECD countries), tax deductibility of interest payments, and a higher implicit cost of capital from issuing equity. The heavy reliance on debt stems directly from the extraordinary levels of investment that Japanese have maintained since 1945. Since the war and the postwar inflation had all but eliminated accumulated private and public savings, debt was a logical pattern of finance to which to turn. The direct and indirect support provided by the government and the cross-ownership of shares within business groups made high debt-equity ratios considerably less risky than such ratio might seem in other countries. As noted above, a high share of outstanding debt is short term but almost automatically rolled over at maturity, making such loans more or less equivalent to long-term debt in the United States. Moreover, many assets carried on Japanese corporate balance sheets, especially land, are significantly undervalued. Hidden reserves exist in fixed

---

20. This situation is similar to that prevailing between the so-called universal banks in West Germany and Switzerland and their customers.

21. Data from Allen, *Japanese Economy*, pp. 58–59.

22. Ministry of International Trade and Industry, *Statistics on Japanese Industries, 1982* (Tokyo: Ministry of International Trade and Industry), pp. 106–7.

assets carried at cost, in securities carried at purchase price, and so on. In addition, Japan has been lucky; the high growth registered by the world economy from 1947 to 1973 supported Japanese attempts to achieve high growth and minimized the risks inherent in highly leveraged financing. As might be expected of an economy as it becomes more developed, there has been in recent years a slow movement away from the traditionally heavy reliance on bank loans and trade credit and toward internal financing and share issues.

Government Influence on Lending Activities

As discussed above and in Chapter 3, government influence on the financial system was considerable in the early postwar years, when capital was extremely scarce and the government had direct control over a significant share of loanable funds and over foreign exchange, as well as considerable indirect control through its strong influence over credit creation. During these early postwar years, direct lending by government institutions was a more effective instrument through which to influence investment flows than the indirect influence available through various monetary instruments. Even now, the Japanese government continues to act as a financial intermediary, although, as also noted in Chapter 3, the goals of its lending policies have changed over time, away from industrial development and toward infrastructure development and other social priorities.

As the economy began to grow rapidly during the late 1950s and 1960s, private demand for funds expanded sharply, far exceeding the supply available from internally generated funds and securities issues. The gap was filled mainly by the private banking system, supplemented by official financial institutions and aided indirectly by government policies on credit creation. Despite already high and still rising domestic savings rates, the banking system lacked the deposit base to meet investment demand on its own. As a result, and in line with their efforts to provide most of the external funds required by the private sector, the commercial banks became heavily dependent on the BOJ as a source of reserves. Since the financial system was based on well-defined categories of institutional specialization and had only limited access to funds from the rest of the world, the use of monetary instruments to influence credit flows was relatively easy. In addition to the normal loosening and tightening of the level of credit that any central bank would seek for macroeconomic reasons, the BOJ had enough leverage in the 1950s and

1960s to influence the directions in which credit would flow and to enable these directions to be more or less consistent with the industrial
policy objectives of the day.

In those days the main beneficiaries of the government's industrial
policy were large companies specializing in the various basic manufacturing
industries targeted by MITI, that is, steel, shipbuilding, chemicals, and
the like. These firms relied heavily on debt financing from city banks.
The city banks, in turn, relied heavily on the BOJ for reserves. Since
the monetary authorities maintained detailed oversight of bank operations, and since the banks also maintained their own detailed oversight
of the manufacturing companies (frequently through ownership links),
the whole credit system was subject to detailed policy guidance from
the BOJ—again, with regard both to the volume of lending and to the
direction in which investment funds would flow. This influence was un-
derstandably most evident near business cycle peaks, when the macroeconomic requirement to cool down the economy fell most heavily
on those sectors considered at the time to be less important in terms
of overall economic development goals.

Yet there is no definitive support for the notion that the monetary
instruments of the BOJ's credit control system were purposefully and
continuously used in a detailed way for purposes of industrial development. More likely, BOJ officials simply had no particular reason to oppose MITI's industrial policy goals in the 1950s and 1960s and every
reason to support them, implicitly as well as explicitly. Henry Wallich
and Mable Wallich, in their discussion of the operation of Japanese
monetary instruments at that time, note that large firms—the main ve-
hicles through which MITI sought to implement its industrial policy
goals—had a dominant position in the market:

> These firms represented the best risks; they had the closest relation
> to the large banks and were their best depositors. Thus to the ex-
> tent that the city banks had funds—and this depended importantly
> on the will of the authorities—large firms were likely to have pre-
> ferred access to financing.[23]

Indeed, the coincidence or correlation between the way in which monetary and industrial policies were implemented up to the early 1970s sug-

---

23. Wallich and Wallich, "Banking and Finance," p. 266.

gests that the two complemented each other easily, whether or not different ministries or agencies of the government set about to coordinate these two strands of overall government policy. In other words, whether MITI, MOF, and BOJ officials ever explicitly agreed that monetary instruments could be extremely useful for purposes of industrial policy—and there is no evidence of a formal agreement or even of a formal mechanism for agreement—the bureaucracy as a whole acted at the time as if it agreed on the importance of high economic growth as a basic national policy and, within the general goal, on the importance of basic manufacturing industries as a critical ingredient in the growth process. In effect, the BOJ's implementation of monetary policy simply reinforced what MITI was attempting to promote at the time in terms of industrial policy, and, as Wallich and Wallich point out, such public policy was also reinforcing the preferences of the market.[24]

This system of more or less indirect, or coincident, influence on the direction of investment as a result of the heavy role the monetary authorities played in the generation of aggregate investment flows remained in place until the early 1970s. Subsequently, as Japanese firms themselves became more multinational—and more important, as balance of payments surpluses continually weakened the control that monetary authorities had over the details of the lending practices of commercial banks—the BOJ became much less able to use monetary instruments for purposes of industrial policy.

The postwar decision to retain considerable segmentation in the system was a deliberate policy aimed at facilitating government influence over financial activities within the country, particularly the direction of financial flows, as well as financial activities between Japan and other countries. This policy almost certainly enhanced reconstruction and economic growth until the mid-1960s. By preserving a "greenhouse" environment, segmentation probably contributed more to economic growth through stability and predictability than it took away in inefficiencies caused by restrictions (or subsidies) on investment and consumption choices. Because a large fraction of Japan's wealth had been destroyed by World War II or by the postwar inflation, the overall economy experienced what amounted to a massive market failure. The postwar financial system, by continuing the segmentation of prewar days, was able to build relatively easily on the experience of the population; the

---

24. Ibid., p. 252.

transition was smooth enough to enable a functioning financial system to be rebuilt in spite of the scarcity of capital prevalent in those days. By limiting the use of funds to specified, high priority areas (as suggested by the government, acting as coordinator or catalyst of a national consensus), a segmented financial system was able to establish financial markets serving these specified sectors of the economy. In this sense, segmentation clearly subsidized broad sectors of the economy, especially certain subsectors of manufacturing, at the expense of others. The cost of this segmentation was borne mainly by consumers, who had access only to low rates of return on their savings.[25] The latter tended to carry low interest rates compared with the average return on investments in the economy as a whole. In other words, by keeping the rate of return to savers low relative to real rates of return in the economy as a whole, government policy subsidized investment at the expense of consumption and corporations at the expense of individuals.[26]

In general, the two main characteristics of the postwar financial system during the first 25 years after World War II were the maintenance of regulated interest rates and the channeling of savings toward high priority sectors of the economy. As noted above, the government also manipulated interest rates in favor of the Postal Savings System,

---

25. On the other hand, Japan's high rates of growth produced comparably rapid growth in wages, which, given the public acceptance at that time of a preference for long-term over short-term gains, more than offset costs otherwise built into the system. Indeed, the broad policy of imposing what are technically called static losses on certain groups (for example, consumers) in hopes of promoting longer-term dynamic gains that more than offset such static losses appeared in the Japanese context to prove overwhelmingly successful. Both political and governmental elites were able to justify the costs of existing policies in terms of prospective longer-term gains. A similar trade-off between short- and long-term gains (with certain important differences in the effects on consumers) has subsequently been followed by governments in South Korea, Taiwan, and Singapore.

26. As noted above, this trade-off was apparently accepted by a majority of the population until perhaps the late-1970s, when Japan's rapid recovery from the oil price increases of 1973/74 began to make people question, more than ever before, traditional appeals for austerity that were often used to justify the maintenance of historical advantages to certain institutions in the face of increasing demands for change.

thereby making a substantial share of household savings directly available for intermediation by government financial institutions. Given the extraordinary rates of economic growth that Japan achieved in the 1950s and 1960s, the government's policy of regulating interest rates and channeling savings toward high priority sectors greatly reduced the risks otherwise inherent in the high rates of borrowing undertaken by major corporations. Since the government also tried to moderate sharp changes in interest rates (preferring to use vaious nonprice measures as a way of rationing credit), the cash flow burden on large corporations did not seriously impede their long-term growth prospects—even when short-term financing proved difficult to obtain. Regulated interest rates in Japan were not always low, relative to interest rates prevailing in other countries.[27] Rather, the real cost of funds for corporations was kept substantially below real rates of return on investment, thus providing an indirect subsidy to major corporations with heavy borrowing commitments while also stimulating investment. This subsidization was paid for by ultimate savers and by small borrowers who did not have access to comparably generous credit.

PRESSURES FOR CHANGE IN THE 1970s

The 1970s saw the emergence of many important new pressures for change in the Japanese economy and more specifically in the Japanese financial sector. Any one of these pressures would have caused some change in Japanese financial activities and in established institutional relationships, if only gradually. Taken together, these various pressures greatly accelerated change and created a situation in which both the regulatory authorities and the private institutions with a strong stake in the status quo were forced to give ground. The major pressures for change included a permanent slowdown in the rate of growth of the economy; an accumulation of foreign exchange reserves; the emergence of massive government deficits; and in part because of these factors, a

---

27. Again, interest rates in Japan *were* low relative to rates of return on real investment. Relative to interest rates elsewhere, Japan's nominal interest rates were for many years higher than those prevailing in the United States. Only in recent years, as U.S. interest rates rose to extraordinary levels, have these conditions been reversed.

shift in the behavior of large corporations and a comparable shift in the behavior of consumers.

The slowdown in Japanese economic growth after 1973 exacerbated major structural pressures on the financial system as well as the economy as a whole. Most important, investment demand declined with slower economic growth rates after 1974, whereas high personal savings rates continued (see Table 4.3).[28] The use of funds by the corporate sector, as a share of GNP, declined dramatically, whereas the public sector's financial deficit as a share of GNP tripled between the first and second half of the 1970s and has been consistently and significantly higher than the corporate sector's since 1975 (see Table 4.4). This new set of circumstances required the financial system, which had been concentrating for 25 years on channeling funds into private investment, to change gears and channel funds elsewhere, that is, into support for government deficits, overseas investment, consumer borrowing, portfolio management, and so on. Given the competitive strength already achieved by Japanese industry and Japan's success relative to its trading partners' in controlling inflation, the economy no longer faced so-called structural deficits on either the trade or the current accounts, even after the oil shock. As a result, capital outflows increased and were accelerated by the slowdown in overall growth. This in turn made Japan's traditionally tight controls over foreign exchange difficult to justify—or to enforce. Meanwhile, the accumulation of foreign exchange reserves and the growth in the share of Japanese business activity overseas, coupled with the slowdown in domestic growth, forced Japanese financial institutions to shift their own activities to in-

---

28. As shown in Figure 2.9, Japanese gross savings and investment rates have been generally declining since the mid-1970s but remain much higher than corresponding U.S. rates and, as Table 4.3 shows for savings rates, much higher than the average for the seven leading advanced industrial countries. Average personal savings of 21.4 percent of disposable income for 1974–81 in part reflects a spurt to 24 percent triggered by the 1974 recession. This atypically high rate somewhat masks a generally declining trend since the early 1970s. Some of the causes of Japan's high personal savings rate have doubtless weakened in recent years, as individual Japanese have become more affluent and less fearful of pending catastrophes than in years past. Other motives to save, such as fears of price fluctuations and of slow growth in real after-tax income, have probably strengthened, however.

Table 4.3

SAVINGS RATES, BIG SEVEN ADVANCED INDUSTRIAL
COUNTRIES

	1960–66			1967–73			1974–81		
	I	II	III	I	II	III	I	II	III
Japan	33.2	20.7	17.2	37.7	24.0	18.1	32.6	19.3	21.4
United States	19.6	9.5	7.2	19.2	8.9	8.4	18.9	6.5	7.4
Germany (F.R.)	27.5	18.6	16.0	26.9	16.7	16.1	22.3	11.0	12.2
France	24.8	15.0	12.2	25.6	15.9	12.8	22.5	11.2	13.1
United Kingdom	18.2	10.1	5.6	19.9	11.2	5.7	18.2	6.9	9.2
Italy	24.6	16.4	17.5	23.2	15.1	19.2	21.7	11.8	21.8
Canada	21.2	9.2	5.5	22.0	10.9	6.9	21.6	10.6	11.2
Total for the big seven	21.9	11.9	9.4	23.0	12.6	11.0	22.2	10.1	12.0

I = Gross savings as a percentage of GDP

II = Net savings as a percentage of GDP

III = Net household savings as a percentage of disposable household income

Source: Organisation for Economic Co-operation and Development, *OECD Economic Outlook, Historical Statistics, 1960–1981* (Paris: OECD, 1983), pp. 69–70.

ternational markets in order to expand profits, market share, and their customer base.

Goverment budget deficits increased when tax revenue expansion slowed with economic growth after 1973 and long-term social and infrastructure needs were meanwhile creating increasing demands for government expenditures. With wages growing at a slower rate than in the past, the government felt unable to raise taxes. The budget deficits that followed were financed by issuing domestic bonds, which led in turn (and as implied in the flow-of-funds accounts summarized in Table 4.4) to a significant shift in the share of the country's total debt burden toward the public sector (see Table 4.5).[29] Following traditional practices, the major banks were required to purchase these bonds at administra-

---

29. Chapter 2 discusses this problem from the viewpoint of its effect on the economy as a whole.

Table 4.4

SECTORAL FINANCIAL SURPLUSES AND DEFICITS,
1955–83

(In Percent of GNP)

	Public	Personal	Corporate Business	Financial Institutions[a]	Rest of the World
1955–59	– 0.5	7.7	– 7.0	—	– 0.3
1960–64	– 0.6	8.9	– 9.0	—	0.7
1965–69	– 2.8	8.6	– 5.0	—	– 0.8
1970–74	– 2.4	9.6	– 7.4	1.2	– 0.9
1975–79	– 7.8	10.6	– 2.9	0.7	– 0.6
1980–83:III[b]	– 6.7	9.6	– 3.3	0.8	– 0.4

[a]For 1954–69 no surplus or deficit is shown in the flow-of-funds accounts.

[b]The three-quarter average for 1983 is given proportionately less weight in the period average.

Note: Each entry is the average of the annual percentages for the period indicated. Thus each row may not sum to zero.

Sources: 1955–77: Bank of Japan, *Flow of Funds Accounts,* as reported in Raymond W. Goldsmith, *The Financial Development of Japan, 1868–1977* (New Haven and London: Yale University Press, 1983), p. 158. 1978–83:III: Bank of Japan, *Economic Statistics Monthly,* no. 430 (January 1983), pp. 201–2; Bank of Japan, *Economic Statistics Monthly,* no. 442 (January 1984), pp. 201–2; and Bank of Japan, *Economic Statistics Monthly,* no. 445 (April 1984), p. 197.

tively determined interest rates, which in the economic environment after the mid-1970s were well below the banks' costs of new funds and thus increasingly unsupportable. The major financial institutions voiced understandable objections about increasing bond purchases on these terms. To offset the strain somewhat, the MOF was forced to liberalize various restrictions on primary and secondary securities markets that were an integral part of the traditionally segmented financial system. For example, it reduced the holding time before bonds could be resold, which in turn facilitated the growth of the secondary bond market. Interest rate in this market then began to reflect demand and supply conditions. Since new government bond issues faced increasing resistance unless they carried interest rates that were reasonably competitive with alternative uses of funds, interest rates on primary issues began to rise

Table 4.5
PRIMARY ISSUE VOLUME:
JAPAN DOMESTIC BOND MARKET, 1970–83
(In Million)

	Private Sector[a]	Public Sector[b]	Total	Public Sector as a Percentage of Total
1970	36,400	22,250	58,650	37.9
1971	49,479	35,711	85,190	41.9
1972	58,085	46,933	105,018	44.7
1973	68,337	59,266	127,603	46.4
1974	74,823	73,650	148,473	49.6
1975	97,641	107,030	204,671	52.3
1976	103,057	136,279	239,336	56.9
1977	116,381	170,579	286,960	59.4
1978	127,681	191,419	319,100	60.0
1979	135,222	212,870	348,092	61.2
1980	147,452	218,115	365,567	59.7
1981	155,374	211,020	366,394	57.6
1982	179,565	264,440	444,005	59.6
1983	198,469	303,000[c]	501,469	60.4

[a]Does not include convertible bonds from 1970 to 1977.
[b]Does not include short-term government securities.
[c]Preliminary.
Sources: Bank of Japan, *Economic Statistics Monthly*, various issues; Bank of Japan, *Economic Statistics Annual*, various issues.

to reflect market conditions. To compensate banks for continuing to purchase deficit-financing bonds (by then carrying improved but still below market rates), the government relaxed other rules such as permitting the issuance of certificates of deposit and easing restrictions on participation in the so-called *gensaki*, or "repurchase," market. A more or less free secondary bond market, operating alongside a still-administered primary market, weakened the segmentation of the system—and the government's ability to maintain such segmentation.

Meanwhile, partly in response to changes in the structure of the overall economy and partly in response to changes in their own capabilities and desires, Japanese corporations began to seek new methods of dealing with financial aspects of their operations. For one thing, the emergence of trade and current account surpluses gave large corporations (both financial and nonfinancial) an increasing degree of latitude in their use of foreign exchange; neither MITI nor the MOF could claim that foreign exchange was so scarce that corporations needed government approval to import goods or services. Full-scale regulation of foreign exchange had been eliminated in principle in 1964, but various exceptions and informal legacies of government authority remained—much to the annoyance of prospective foreign extrants and increasingly to Japanese firms as well. As in the case of the step-by-step deregulation of the secondary bond market referred to above, a number of gradual changes were implemented—that is, so-called automatic approval of foreign exchange use up to a certain amount, but with registration of the transaction required; the latter step left government officials with enough intelligence on business activity to enable them to discourage prospectively unwanted transactions through administrative guidance, or at least a recurrence of such transactions.

Second, many large nonfinancial corporations began to find the traditionally close relationships with their main banks stifling. This stemmed mainly from the sheer size and diversity of the interests of the major firms, as well as the movement of Japanese manufacturing companies into offshore operations. Thus, large firms started to behave more independently of both the government and their major banks almost as a matter of course.

Third, the structure of the financial needs of corporations changed markedly. In the high-growth period before 1973, companies needed operating and investment funds on terms and conditions suitable to rapid growth; in the credit-constrained environment that prevailed during those years, access to funds, to take advantage of high growth, was more important than variations in the terms. After 1974, slower growth meant that access to funds became much easier, but in an environment of high and volatile inflation rates, the need to manage funds carefully, balancing their cost against their prospective use in line with increasingly sophisticated ways of measuring the cost and use of funds, became much more important than in the past. Slower growth also meant that corporations diverted a smaller share of profits into fixed investment, leaving more funds to be managed. This shift in the needs of major corporate customers forced Japanese financial institutions to begin offering a wider range of instruments that in turn permitted corporations to be more sophisticated in the management of their own assets and liabilities. The rapidly developing art of asset and liability management in other advanced industrial countries, especially the United States, accelerated the shift. Indeed, since foreign-based financial services firms were eagerly offering to develop such capabilities for the overseas subsidiaries of Japanese firms and increasingly for domestic companies as well, Japanese financial institutions soon began to try to emulate and perhaps even leapfrog the services being offered abroad.

Japanese consumers have also been changing traditional behavioral patterns in response to long-term structural trends. Most important, they have become much more affluent, producing a growing diversity of interests and tastes. Among other effects, affluence has created a demand for more diverse savings instruments and more extensive consumer credit. In the past, consumer credit was neglected as a matter of policy in an effort to stimulate household savings (which could then be funneled through public and private financial institutions into business investment). As long as real wage growth was extremely high, neither the low rate of return on savings nor the absence of consumer credit hurt individual life-styles that much—at least by the standards prevailing at the time. But with the slowdown in economic growth after 1973 and consequently low wage growth, rates of return on savings became much more important than in the past. Here, again, behavioral changes forced the MOF into policy changes. Actually, Japanese consumers had already been responding positively to opportunities for increased rates of return on alternative instruments of saving, as evidenced by the widespread use of multiple deposits in the Postal Savings System. Slower rates of overall economic growth strengthened this inclination, intensifying the search for a higher return on savings. The rising age structure of the population added to the pressures for higher rates of return on savings. As a result the government, major corporations, and individuals all began to focus much more than in the past on issues of social security, pension funds, life insurance, and the like. Social security payments increased sharply in the 1970s. Pension and insurance funds accumulated additional assets at a dramatically increased rate. The traditionally low rates of return earned by these funds then began to come under pressure from beneficiaries and subsequently from prospective rivals seeking to break into the fund management market. Competition for the management of this large and growing pot of money constituted a direct challenge to the staid ways in which trust funds had been managed in the past.

In other words, the traditional segmentation in the Japanese financial system, which kept different savers and investors in separate categories and thereby facilitated the maintenance of artificially low interest rates, began to unravel in the 1970s for a variety of reasons. The slowdown in the rate of growth of the overall economy made obsolete many previous assumptions about the means used to compensate for various administrative barriers to a free flow of funds. Balance of payments surpluses were providing companies with funds outside the BOJ's control. Capital began to flow abroad because rates of return there were higher. Large firms began to seek nonbank sources of funds—from bond and equity issues and foreign financial markets. Meanwhile, with large budget deficits the government was forced to raise funds in competition with the private sector. New instruments and activities emerged to begin to respond to these changes. As a result the MOF and the BOJ began to face increasing pressure to deregulate financial markets and, indeed, even to change the way in which their primary macroeconomic policy objectives are achieved.

A further look at the operation of monetary and credit policies during the 1970s is a useful way to see in greater detail the kinds of changes that have taken place in the Japanese financial system. At first glance, Japanese monetary and credit policies might appear to operate much as they do in other advanced industrial countries. In fact, they have operated considerably differently.[30] For example, Japan did not even have *open market operations*, defined as the central bank's purchase or sale of government securities on the private market to constrain or expand money supply, until the 1970s.[31] With other policies and practices preventing the development of a mature domestic bond market, open market operations could not operate since, to function properly, such operations require a market deep enough to prevent official purchases and sales undertaken to adjust overall liquidity from creating massive disruption in the market. Moreover, the market must permit free competition among different maturities and issues and, indeed, between new issues and bonds outstanding. In this way, buyers and sellers can respond to interest rate movements, based on their respective best guesses about the future. The growth of budget deficits has, as noted above,

---

30. This general statement would receive wide agreement among analysts. Exactly how monetary policies have operated has been the source of much debate, however. Refer to the issues raised in Allen, *Japanese Economy*, chap. 4; Gardner Ackley and Hiromitsu Ishi, "Fiscal, Monetary, and Related Policies," in *Asia's New Giant,* ed. Hugh Patrick and Henry Rosovsky (Washington, D.C.: Brookings Institution, 1976); Wallich and Wallich, "Banking and Finance"; and Eisuke Sakakibara, Robert Feldman, and Yuzo Harada, *The Japanese Financial System in Comparative Perspective,* a study prepared for the U.S. Congress, Joint Economic Committee (Washington, D.C.: Government Printing Office, March 17, 1982).

31. Open market operations are the major U.S. monetary policy tool.

forced liberalization of some aspects of the interest rate structure and the rules governing bank participation in primary and secondary bond markets, while also creating a larger bond market.[32] These changes have since begun to permit open market operations to function in Japan, although they have not yet been able to work as effectively as in the United States.

Similarly, although the BOJ introduced a system of required reserves held against deposits as early as 1958, it seldom put the system to use; and even when put to use, it had little effect until the 1970s. Because credit was basically rationed, the banking system simply operated with little regard to liquidity, and the BOJ regularly legitimized this behavior by providing reserves to support an overloan position.[33] Since the early 1970s, reserve requirements have been changed more frequently—although they remain low in absolute terms. The greater use of reserve requirements stemmed in part from a desire by the BOJ to contain the growth in bank reserves caused by balance of payments surpluses and to influence the exchange rate. Because balance of payments surpluses increased bank deposits relative to loan demand, the banks could then lend money without going to the BOJ for additional reserves. This enabled the banks to act more independently of the authorities. By increasing its use of reserve requirements as a means of regulating monetary growth, the BOJ was in effect trying to make use of a new regulatory instrument to replace the now less effective and more direct means it had previously employed.[34]

The discount or *rediscount rate* (the rate at which banks can borrow

---

32. Japanese banks had traiditonally been forced to absorb some quantities of low-interest government bonds. But as long as deficits were small and inflation remained low, the profit squeeze from these purchases was small enough to be tolerable. Moreover, in earlier years the banks were much more dependent on the BOJ for reserves than in the mid-1970s and therefore more willing to comply with administrative pressure to absorb government bonds.

33. This was a situation in which loans exceeded deposits of major banks.

34. It is important to note that the most used reserve requirement has been that on nonresident-held (so-called free) yen deposits and on borrowings from abroad. The former served primarily as a tool for defense of the yen, reaching 100 percent during periods of extreme inward speculation. The latter serves as a means of controlling the pace by which the yen is internationalized and raises the cost to firms (and others) of attempting to bypass domestic monetary stringency by seeking funds overseas.

reserves from, or "rediscount" assets with, the central bank) has had little direct impact in Japan in terms of the actual cost of the borrowed reserves since, on average, the rate itself has usually been low. But as a signal it has indeed been important. The banks that borrowed from the BOJ were typically in relatively heavy debt to the central bank, often suffering from an overloan position. Such borrowers were subject to detailed oversight, and borrowing at all was considered a privilege rather than a right. As a result, variations in the rediscount rate had a strong influence well beyond the simple volume of borrowing. Moreover, because interest rates were set by administrative fiat rather than by the market, the BOJ's control over the rediscount rate traditionally translated into—and to a decreasing degree, still translates into—control over virtually the entire interest rate structure.[35] All interest rates, including the rediscount rate, continue to be subject to the additional policy desire of keeping the nominal rate low—even in the face of high credit demands from the private sector. This naturally results in demand for credit that exceeds the supply available (that is, the market fails to clear at an equilibrium price); therefore, credit must be rationed (allocated by nonprice mechanisms).[36] With increasing deregulation, the ability

---

35. Interest rate control is over nominal rates. Such devices as fees, compensating balances, and the like, make the effective interest rate reflect market conditions more closely. Since the early 1970s a growing array of instruments have been released from direct control; those interest rates generally free from control now are on certificates of deposit, bills, *gensaki* issues, call money, certain limited medium-term government bonds, and the secondary bond market.

36. A low interest rate policy also lowered the cost of government borrowing. However, this was a relatively unimportant factor until balanced budget policies were abandoned in the mid-1960s and inflation rates surged in the 1970s. At this point the Budget Bureau of the MOF has a vested interest in sticking to low and administered interest rates (even if this leads to increased nonprice methods of allocating credit); because the level of accumulated government debt is so high, the Budget Bureau has a narrowly defined interest in holding down interest payments required by this high debt level. But the Banking and Securities Bureaus, faced with increased market-based pressures to deregulate interest rates, are being forced to "insist" on further deregulation simply to keep up with the interests of their constituencies. The considerable intra-MOF conflicts implied by these cross pressures have meant that the minister of finance himself as well as the career vice-minister are being forced to resolve such issues rather than, in the preferred pattern, simply ratifying decisions made lower down.

to manage interest rates has become correspondingly more difficult and with it the main objective of monetary control—that of controlling the volume of credit.

All governments retain at least residual rights to impose credit controls, but Japan's extensive system of controls has been much greater than those of many other countries and, naturally enough, has required special circumstances to operate effectively. During periods when inflation surged or balance of payments deficits threatened banks' reserves, a standard BOJ practice was to set limits on the amount of credit that could be extended by each banking unit. This rediscount/credit control mechanism worked reasonably well as long as the segmentation of the financial system and the almost continually strong demand for credit gave the BOJ the leverage it needed to direct the lending that would be made almost in spite of many supply and demand forces. In recent years, however, as the boundaries between different segments of the domestic financial system and between the Japanese and other countries' financial systems have broken down, the rediscount/credit control mechanism has worked less well. As in the relationships between MITI and the industrial sector, the BOJ has been forced to rely more on its own version of administrative guidance, known in the financial system by the more technical phrase "window guidance" *(madoguchi shidō)*. Through almost daily contact between relevant BOJ sections and the commercial banks, the composition and magnitude of bank lending have long been shaped by a form of moral suasion that is, in effect, the legacy of an earlier era.[37] But with less need for central bank reserves and an increasingly internationalized environment, the banks are increasingly resisting this informal attempt to maintain control. As a result, market-based methods of implementing regulatory policies, such as open market operations and changes in reserve requirements, are slowly becoming more important (where, in earlier years, they played little or no role), and direct controls such as the rediscount mechanism are becoming less important. The shift from direct and detailed to indirect and general policy intervention almost certainly represents

---

37. Any lack of adherence on the part of the banks to BOJ window guidance risked the imposition of tighter credit ceilings or restricted access to the rediscount window. In Japan's capital-short environment of the 1950s and 1960s, the commercial banks had virtually no choice but to adhere to such guidance.

a major improvement in economic efficiency. By the same token, it also forces the authorities to rely more on market forces and weakens their ability to control the system in detail.

Japan's financial system as it evolved in the 1970s reflects an increasing degree of tension between detailed official regulation of economic activities and the drive of private institutions toward larger markets and more deversified activities that inevitably lead to decentralization. To a large extent, earlier official efforts to require institutional specialization remain enshrined in practice, although, among other policies, attempts to separate rigidly short- and long-term financing failed, and both commercial banks and security companies are exerting continuing pressure to break down the "Chinese wall" separating banking and securities activities. While such segmentation may have been extremely useful in the past, when Japan was trying to mobilize scarce financial resources for reconstruction and economic development, it is much less useful and even counterproductive once a country becomes developed and manageable only through complex and decentralized methods.

FURTHER PRESSURES FOR CHANGE IN THE 1980s

The simultaneous emergence of powerful external and internal pressures for change in the Japanese financial system during the 1970s led to so many step-by-step changes that by 1980 these amounted to a change in kind rather than degree. Partial liberalization measures had major unintended side effects; these then had to be offset by other partial liberalization measures designed to compensate temporarily those hurt by the initial liberalization.[38] Two major legislative actions, the 1980 For-

---

38. The dynamics of pressures for future change emerging from past partial liberalizations is the central theme of Ronald Napier, "Japanese Capital Markets in Transition," in *U.S.-Japan Relations: Towards a New Equilibrium*, Annual Review, 1982–83, The Program on U.S.-Japan Relations (Cambridge, MA,.: Center for International Affairs, Harvard University, 1983), pp. 69–84. For a recently published summary of changes in the Japanese financial structure in the 1970s and early 1980s, see Organisation for Economic Co-operation and Development, *Japan*, OECD Economic Surveys (Paris: OECD July 1984) pp. 42–65.

eign Exchange and Foreign Trade Control Law and the 1981 Banking Act, ratified in a de jure sense many de facto changes that had already occurred. They also set the stage for still further changes to come. In other words, these new laws represented no radical departure from the past; rather they were consistent with previous efforts by MOF and BOJ officials to permit marginal changes in the system. Increasingly, however, commercial banks, trust banks, securities firms, insurance companies, and foreign financial institutions and governments have all pushed for still further changes beyond what officials had previously claimed was "possible." As in the United States, the changes in Japanese regulatory policy have usually lagged behind private sector initiatives based on new technologies, new marketing concepts, or both. Several examples show the cumulative power of the seemingly marginal changes that have already occurred.

First, as noted above, the large increase in government deficits that began to be incurred in the mid-1970s has been financed primarily by the issuance of ten-year government bonds. The first group of these are now reaching maturity and are being traded on secondary markets as short-term paper—with interest rates that are competitive with two-year fixed-rate bank deposits (and with the latter rate fixed at roughly this same level in order to try to preserve the competitiveness of the rate on government bonds). Since two-year bank deposits have traditionally been an important savings vehicle for Japanese consumers and a correspondingly important instrument by which Japanese banks acquired stable sources of liquid funds, competition from so-called seasoned government bonds has contributed to a significant drop in the net inflow of long-term deposits to the city banks.[39] This decline in the growth of new long-term deposits constrains the banks' ability to lend. For this reason, it has led the banks themselves to push for a liberalization of deposit rates and of other constraints on their access to new sources of funds.

The authorities initially responded to the banks' pressures for liberalization with measures that created pressures for still further change. Again as in the United States, deposit rate liberalization has proved politically difficult. For this reason, liberalization initially came in the form

---

39. Such a pattern is familiar to students of recent U.S. financial history in which depository institutions constrained by controls on interest rates (so-called Regulation Q) found themselves at a severe disadvantage when market rates rose to levels higher than the controlled rates.

of grants of authority permitting the banks to offer new or broadened financial instruments, that is, reductions in official controls on the operation of the call (interbank) money market in the 1978–81 period, establishment of a market for large bank certificates of deposit (CDs) in 1979, and the removal of restrictions on bank participation in the *gensaki* market in that same year. Major changes in regulations governing deposit rates themselves were delayed until other financial institutions, partly in response to encroachments the banks had made into what they perceived as their markets, began to offer instruments that drew deposits away from city banks. In 1980 major securities firms started to sell government security trust funds, so-called *chukoku* funds, that are essentially a money market fund based on medium-term government bonds.[40] The minimum investment was only ¥100,000 ($455 at ¥200 = $1) and was easier to cash in than long-term deposits and trust accounts. Beginning in late 1982, asset growth in these funds exploded, from ¥1 trillion ($4.5 billion at ¥220 = $1) in October 1982 to ¥3.5 trillion ($15.9 billion at ¥220 = $1) by the middle of 1983.[41] The trust banks tried to counter the securities' firms with their own comparable instruments, which they labeled a "big" loan trust, and the long-term credit banks offered a similar product, a so-called wide debenture;[42] both of these offered higher interest rates than conventional two-year time deposits. The *chukoku* funds, the big trusts, and the wide debentures not only took in most of the new savings being generated but also drained savings out of cash and city bank deposits.[43]

---

40. Smaller securities firms were not permitted to issue these until April 1982.

41. Donald Curtin, "A Better Lubricant than Oil," *Euromoney*, March 1984, p. 162.

42. The terms *big loan trust* and *wide debenture* are translations of the advertising terms used to describe these instruments in contemporary Japanese.

43. Until August 1983, the best alternative the city banks could offer was a three-year deposit. At that point, Mitsubishi Bank introduced its Mitsubishi Money Capsule, which combines a ten-year bond fund (60 percent of the package) and a ten-year time deposit (a three-year deposit to be rolled over three times). On the first day of sale it took in ¥15 billion ($68.2 million at ¥220 = $1). In September 1983 other city banks introduced similar instruments and took in ¥70 billion ($318.2 million at ¥220 = $1) in that month. See, Curtain, "A Better Lubricant than Oil," p. 162.

Pressures mounted until early 1984 when a further surge in the liberalization of bank deposits occurred. As of January the minimum denomination for large bank CDs was reduced from ¥500 million to ¥300 million. In April the MOF allowed banks to set their own deposit rates on three-month deposits of ¥20 million or more within a ceiling under the controlled six-month rate. Then in May, as part of a major announcement resulting from negotiations with U.S. Treasury representatives, Japanese authorities announced that over a two- to three-year period all interest rate ceilings and restrictions on new deposit instruments would be relaxed or removed.[44] As an example of these further moves, in April 1985 the minimum CD denomination is scheduled to be lowered from ¥300 million to ¥100 million, and the minimum CD maturities are scheduled to be reduced from three months to one month; meanwhile, banks will also be permitted to issue large denomination deposit instruments with market-related interest rates. As these steps take place, they will represent important relaxations of restrictions in the operation of Japanese financial markets. Although many foreign observers remain skeptical of the authorities' now-stated commitment to full liberalization of interest rates, the overriding necessity to permit a more-or-less free secondary market for maturing government bonds has clearly forced through dramatic changes that Japanese authorities otherwise prone to favor controlled markets have been unable to prevent.

The partial liberalization of deposit rates in response to the emergence of competing assets for long-term deposit funds represents only one example of the changes under way in the Japanese financial system. Indeed, compared with the even greater degree of change seen in capital markets, the banking sector remains highly compartmentalized and regulated. Capital markets, on the other hand, have expanded greatly, both in the size and in the variety of the instruments being offered—again, in response to new conditions created by the great increase in government bonds issued since the mid-1970s. Between 1975 and early 1984, the volume of bond trading in Japan increased some sixfold, making Tokyo, after New York, the second largest domestic

---

44. For further discussion, see Robert D. Hershey, Jr., "U.S. Financial Accord with Japan Announced," *New York Times,* May 30, 1984, pp. D1, D7; and "Relaxation of Japanese Capital Restrictions Announced by U.S. and Japanese Authorities," *IMF Survey,* June 4, 1984, p. 161.

securities market in the world. Banks as well as securities firms sought to build up the bond market. The banks were given greater latitude to participate in capital markets as a way of compensating them for the massive losses they suffered when being forced to absorb below-market government bond issues. In April 1981 the required minimum holding time by commercial banks for new government bonds was reduced from one year to 100 days, enabling these bonds to be resold on the secondary market much sooner. From April 1983 commercial banks were allowed to sell new ten-year bonds over the counter to their customers. From October 1983 they were also allowed to sell new medium-term (two-to four-year maturity) government bonds and five-year discount bonds. From June 1984 they were permitted to deal in seasoned bonds. Thus in less than 18 months three major Glass-Steagall-like barriers separating the banking and securities industries were eliminated.

The barrier jumping has also worked the other way as securities firms seek to take business away from banks. For example, in June 1983 brokerage houses were given the authority to lend up to ¥5 million ($22,727 at ¥220 = $1) to borrowers who used holdings of government bonds as collateral. A consensus has also been building to permit both banks and brokerage houses to sell foreign commercial paper and foreign CDs denominated in yen. This would represent an important first step toward the issuance of domestic commercial paper, which would give the securities firms an instrument through which to compete with short-term bank financing comparable with those available in other advanced industrial countries.

Two other major changes appear likely in the area of corporate finance. First, there is considerable pressure to change the traditional mechanisms by which the prime and other lending rates are linked to the official discount rate and the yield on long-term credit bank debentures. With deposit rates increasingly deregulated but lending rates still controlled, the profit squeeze on banks has naturally increased. More important, the custom of tying interest rates to government borrowing costs, rather than to demand and supply conditions for credit in the economy as a whole, makes it virtually impossible to balance the needs of lenders and borrowers through marker-based adjustments. As a result, financial institutions (primarily the long-term credit and trust banks) have become increasingly vocal advocates of letting market forces play a larger role—at least of breaking the link between government borrowing costs and interest rates. Second, as Japan's financial markets mature, interest rates have gradually moved closer to levels the market would have dictated in the absence of controls. For example, as corporations have lessened their dependence on their main banks and concurrently sought greater freedom to borrow abroad, the desire to bypass banks altogether and to borrow directly from other lenders has also increased. For short-term funds, Japanese corporations appear to prefer commercial paper. For long-term funds, borrowers are seeking greater flexibility in issuing bonds, which historically have had to be approved on an issue-by-issue basis by the MOF (and have carried terms that effectively nullified their use by requiring that they not compete with the issuance of government bonds). Now, with the continuing corporate interest in greater freedom for bond issuance, the MOF is trying to retain the authority to approve domestic issues but easing up on regulations governing foreign issues.

Dramatic changes are also under way in the management of trust and pension funds—again, largely as a result of changes in the market to which the authorities have responded, rather than because of changes initiated by the regulatory authorities. With the aging of the Japanese population, the resulting accumulation of assets by pension funds and life insurance companies, and growing political and personal concerns about social security issues (including dissatisfaction with the traditionally low rates of return achieved by existing institutions), trust and pension fund management has become a major growth sector in Japanese financial services. As a result, various Japanese and foreign-based institutions have sought to enter the field, and competition is heating up. For a time the most notable efforts to enter the market were made by proposed joint ventures of U.S. banks and Japanese securities firms. Together they hoped to leap over the legal barriers previously restricting the market to Japanese trust banks and insurance companies; the idea was to combine the expertise in return-conscious fund management possessed by the U.S. banks with the access to major corporate customers possessed by the Japanese securities firms. The proposed joint ventures involved Morgan Guaranty and Nomura Securities, Citicorp and Daiwa Securities, Chemical Bank and Yamaichi Securities, and Bank of America and Nikko Securities. After nearly a year of intense negotiations between the proposed joint venture partners and the MOF and then between the MOF and U.S. Treasury representatives, a bilateral U.S.-Japanese agreement was reached in May 1984 allowing U.S. banks to enter the market, provided they did not tie up with Japanese securities firms; the MOF continued to restrict access to pension fund management by Japanese institutions to the trust banks and insurance companies on grounds that the previous segmentation entitled them to, at worst, a phasing in of new competition.

Here again, the MOF was caught in a bind of its own making: To deregulate one part of a segmented financial system is to disrupt relationships based on the previous segmentation while being unable to use the flexibility of a price system to adjust to this disruption smoothly and efficiently. Consequently, the ad hoc changes that are made create new forms of segmentation that in turn require further modification, either through further regulatory change, or as is increasingly the case with the internationalization of the Japanese economy as a whole, further changes in market forces that cause the system to change in a de facto sense almost regardless of the aims of the regulatory authorities. In the particular example of pension fund management, the regulatory changes to date have necessarily been unable to deal with the international pressures for change in a wholly satisfactory manner. When a U.S.-based bank like Morgan Guaranty, which in the United States is engaged in services that under the Japanese system would fall into the province of both the city banks and the trust banks, is allowed to engage in pension fund management in Japan, it is in this way getting better treatment than the Japanese city or trust banks themselves, which are prohibited from engaging in activities designated only for the other. In fact, the Japanese trust banks fear competition from Japanese city banks much more than from foreign-based banks, which recognize the difficulties they face in trying to market pension management services without some assistance in gaining access to customers that could presumably be provided by Japanese institutions. Hence Japanese trust banks have sought to preserve a legacy of the segmentation they were nurtured on in the past and perhaps to use this continued grant of authority as a basis for establishing joint ventures with foreign-based banks seeking to enter the market. The latter, of course, are trying to get a share of a fast-growing business. Rather than making some abstract case for market entry on the basis of principle, they are concerned mainly with finding ways of doing business in the pension management market, even if this requires joining with a Japanese institution to gain better access to potential customers.

Another major factor influencing pension fund management in Japan is the newly developed ability of institutional investors to diversify into foreign securities. Since 1981, Japanese institutional investors have been purchasing overseas securities, primarily bonds, at an accelerating rate.[45] To date, institutional buying of foreign securities has focused on high-quality foreign bonds, particularly U.S. Treasuries. As Japanese buyers become more accustomed to foreign markets, they will naturally diversify toward higher-return, higher-risk instruments. Along with other large financial institutions, Japanese trust banks and insurance companies have been major purchasers of government primary bond issues. Increasingly, the low rates of return provided by these bonds are becoming unacceptable to institutional and even individual customers. Hence the trust banks and insurance companies, which had previously been able to pass these low rates of return on to their customers, are on this question allied with the city and long-term credit banks in wanting the government to issue deficit-financing bonds at rates closer to market levels.

Meanwhile, international pressures on the economy as a whole, from both private and official sources, have exerted continuing pressure on the structure of the financial sector.[46] This generalized pressure was the main single reason for the 1980 foreign exchange law revising the basic principle of Japanese foreign exchange transactions; in contrast to the previous law, which prohibited all foreign exchange transactions except those explicitly permitted, the new law permits all transactions not explicitly prohibited. Some of the specific changes permitted (or ratified) by the 1980 law include the following: Overseas subsidiaries of Japanese city banks could begin to float local currency bonds for local use, and in 1981 they could float dollar bonds for local use; in April 1983 this authority was expanded to enable overseas branches to float dollar bonds for their parents' use. Japanese banks could also set up new investment banking entities to deal in Eurobonds and syndicated loans. From April 1984 Japanese banks were permitted to take

---

45. As of March 1983, life insurance companies had acquired about a third of their total holdings of foreign securities during the preceding 12 months. Purchases of foreign securities were large enough during the rest of the year to bring them close to an MOF-decreed limit of 10 percent of total assets.

46. As noted in Chapter 2, this general pressure for change, especially for increased capital outflows, had begun to be felt as far back as the late 1960s. The large petrodollar inflows to Japan after the oil price increases of the 1970s greatly strengthened these pressures, leading to the codification of various changes that had already come into use during the 1970s in the 1980 Foreign Exchange and Foreign Trade Control Act.

out foreign currency swaps, a privilege previously restricted to government-guaranteed issues. In June 1984 swap limits were abolished, and Japanese banks were given authority to issue yen-linked and Euroyen bonds. Meanwhile, foreign-based securities firms were given the right to seek seats on the Tokyo Stock Exchange (a right that the MOF pledged to support further in the U.S.-Japanese bilateral agreement of May 1984).

Foreigners had already been allowed to participate in the long-term bond and equities markets in the mid-1970s.[47] The actual level of participation has been limited, however, by macroeconomic factors and by domestic Japanese regulations that made Japanese assets unattractive. Since 1979, when foreigners were given free access to both the *gensaki* and CD markets, foreign banks have been given increasing freedom to operate in the domestic market—approaching equal treatment with Japanese banks. At the same time, Japanese banks have been allowed to begin making foreign currency loans to domestic companies (formerly a privilege restricted to foreign banks). In other words, gaining greater access to the Japanese market has also meant that foreign banks have had to give up some areas previously reserved for them. The trade-off is not always positive in the short term but is clearly unavoidable if the considerable structural and institutional differences between the Japanese financial system and those of other advanced industrial countries are to be lessened.[48] Perhaps the newest area that foreign banks are

---

47. This was temporarily halted in 1978 for balance of payments reasons.

48. For example, because of their small domestic asset base, foreign banks are classified by the MOF as small banks, which face more stringent control on day-to-day operations than larger-size banks. Although some have entered certain nontraditional fields in search of profits, the long-term profitability and growth potential of foreign banks in Japan will remain in question until they develop a deposit base in yen or some other yen-funding base. Acquisition is one possibility. New banking legislation permits the acquisition of domestic banks by foreigners, although no actual cases have arisen as yet. The improved ability of foreign banks to make swaps and to participate in European markets will slowly make yen financing easier. For example, as of June 1984, Japanese and foreign banks were allowed to make Euroyen loans one year or less to domestic residents and as of the end of 1984, to issue yen-denominated CDs with maturities of six months or less (provided these are issued by bank offices outside Japan and sold outside Japan). Moreover, foreign insitutions can now lead manage any Euroyen bond issue without being required to have a branch or representative office in Japan to do so.

seeking to enter is the underwriting of government bonds. This is currently a money-losing business for new issues, as Japanese banks realize all too well. Citibank, Bank of America, and Chase Manhattan Bank have expressed interest in joining bank syndicates for such issues, whereas Jardine Fleming and Smith Barney have been seeking to join the securities firms syndicates. The sheer size of the government's deficit financing needs, coupled with the growing secondary market, promises to provide enough potential fee income to make the handling of government bonds profitable at some point.[49]

FUTURE IMPLICATIONS

In only a few years, the Japanese financial system has been transformed from a tightly administered set of institutions and procedures to a system that provides considerable and increasing scope for market forces. The combination of domestic and foreign pressures discussed above has initiated a series of changes that will in turn continue for some years. The exact configuration of Japan's future financial system will of course depend on the give-and-take of the various cross pressures discussed above. Clearly, however, market forces have played an increasingly important role, relative to government regulations, in determining the ground rules of the system. As the Japanese economy has grown in sheer

---

49. A Treasury bill market is also likely to emerge once policy differences are resolved between the BOJ, which wants to introduce Treasury bills as new instruments of monetary control in open market operations, and the MOF, which sees Treasury bills as a more expensive instrument than long-term bonds; Treasury bills must be issued at market values, whereas, as noted earlier, bonds are still issued in Japan at below-market rates. A more interesting development, from a foreign perspective, is the possibility of a yen-dominated bankers' acceptance market. MITI has been promoting this idea for some time to facilitate and lower the costs of trade finance, although the BOJ has resisted it since bankers' acceptances would dilute BOJ control over bank lending and bypass traditional trade finance lines. New short-term instruments will also be needed to support the volume growth of foreign exchange trading. In late 1983 the so-called real demand rule—requiring that forward market transactions be based on some underlying transaction—was abolished. This opens the possibility for a wide range of financial transactions not directly related to trade.

size and become more affluent, and concurrently more internationally oriented, the previous degree of government control over the financial system has become counterproductive. Looking ahead, even if further deregulation is resisted by the authorities, it cannot be stopped indefinitely. If, for example, a coalition of government bureaucrats and domestic financial institutions were to try to block changes in the financial system in a way that would be extremely costly to nonfinancial sectors of the economy, pressures for change from these other sectors would naturally increase—and eventually prevail.

Further changes in the financial sector, besides involving a greater role for market forces domestically, will also bring about greater integration of Japanese financial markets with the global financial market. For example, the increasing internationalization of the financial sector will make Japan's previously favored methods of managing monetary policy, through credit rationing or credit manipulation, much more difficult. Existing pressures that force the monetary authorities to utilize more general instruments of monetary control applying across the whole economy, as against selective instruments applying only to certain industries, sectors, or firms, will continue to be felt. Moreover, the authorities will lose still more of the autonomy they have been accustomed to in the formulation of domestic monetary policy as international capital flows increasingly offset whatever actions they might take that would differ significantly from those taken in other advanced industrial countries.

In the private sector, because the number, variety, and scope of new financial services are increasing constantly, Japanese nonfinancial firms are increasingly able to loosen the links they maintained with major city banks and to seek financing from many other sources—securities issues, pension funds, foreign financial institutions, and internally generated funds. Over the medium term, the growing diversity of financial instruments and financial management practices that will evolve as deregulation proceeds will also provide new and probably profitable opportunities for both financial and nonfinancial firms. Financial firms will be able to offer instruments and services that respond more precisely to the increasingly diversified needs of their customers; nonfinancial firms will be able to tap sources of funds that fit their investment and financing needs more appropriately than has been the case in the highly segmented financial system of the past. Both kinds of firms will be able to earn higher rates of return on liquid assets and to balance risk and maturity requirements more easily than in the past.

In the short term, however, continuing deregulation of the financial system will create serious transitional problems, including increased competition among a more diverse group of Japan-based firms as well as increased competition from foreign-based firms. This increased competition, from whatever source, will strain the traditional relationships among business groups, the so-called *keiretsu*, and permanently change the "rules of the game"—since "outsiders," whether foreign or Japanese, are rarely able or willing to play by the same rules as "insiders." A more specific transitional problem, which may prove less important in the long term but has particularly obvious short-term costs, is the vulnerability of Japanese corporations to increases in interest rates that are a likely by-product of deregulation.[50]

As noted above, Japanese corporations have traditionally been highly leveraged, with debt-equity ratios that are (or to date have been) inconceivable in the United States. The risks otherwise inherent in highly leveraged positions have been much reduced in Japan by government policies that prevented rapid increases in real and nominal interest rates through administrative fiat. Arguably, these government actions thereby provided an explicit safety net for the large, highly leveraged firms in a high-growth economy.[51] In the future, interest rates will almost certainly follow more closely the rates prevailing elsewhere in the world. Depending on the magnitude of the financing and refinancing needs of the government, the rate of growth and of inflation in the domestic economy, and the level of world (that is, mainly U.S.) interest rates, this equilibration of Japanese and world interest rates could lead to a credit crunch—in spite of domestic savings rates that are proba-

---

50. Obviously, interest rates in Japan can and do rise and fall in line with macroeconomic conditions. Deregulation of the financial system, by explicitly loosening the government's administrative control over interest rates, makes changes in interest rates more likely than they would be under the previously more administered system in which supply and demand pressures are balanced off by nonprice adjustments.

51. See Napier, "Japanese Capital Markets in Transition," for further discussion of this point. On the other hand, and as mentioned earlier in the chapter, the degree of leverage implied by simple numerical comparisons of debt-equity ratios overstates the degree of risk actually carried by Japanese firms.

bly high enough to support the anticipated borrowing requirements of the government and the private sector. A credit crunch could occur if the process of deregulation led to significantly higher and more volatile real interest rates for highly leveraged firms. In effect, the cost of borrowing for such firms might become unsustainable. As mentioned earlier in the chapter, in the past Japan's highly leveraged firms were indirectly subsidized by a government policy mandating low nominal interest rates. Even when interest rates rose for macroeconomic reasons, a more-than-proportionate share of the increase was borne by other sectors of the economy, notably small businesses (which, when interest rates rose, had less access to credit than large firms) and households (which had access only to low interest rates on their savings). Now that small businesses and households are actively seeking easier access to credit or higher rates of return on their savings, they, too, along with commercial banks, securities firms, and foreign financial institutions and government, will pressure the government to deregulate interest rates still further. In other words, although it might want to maintain a low interest rate policy to keep down its own nominal cost of borrowing (with the real cost being borne elsewhere in the economy) or to subsidize large firms at the expense of other sectors of the economy, the government will almost certainly be forced at some point to deregulate interest rates completely. When this happens, corporations large and small will be forced to control their borrowing costs more carefully than in the past. Although a credit crunch of serious proportions may not occur, the mere possibility of such a turn of events is one indication of the fundamental changes that the Japanese financial system is likely to experience as deregulation proceeds.

Chapter 5
JAPAN'S NEW INDUSTRIES

Although industries using new technologies are sometimes assumed to be a recent phenomenon, they have been a central part of economic development since the industrial revolution. The steam engine, the railroad, the harnessing of electric power, the internal combustion engine—all these were once new technologies, all have contributed to economic development, and all are now taken as a matter of course. By the 1950s, technological progress had become similarly obvious in a myriad of everyday products: frozen orange juice and polyester apparel, for example. In the 1980s, biotechnologies and composite materials are two new technologies that show considerable promise. Far from applying only to one or two sectors of an economy, new technologies almost always have secondary and tertiary effects throughout an economy and usually on the social structure as well.[1] In general, all countries that have achieved sustained increases in per capita income have done so because of the continuing and widespread applications of new scientific and technological developments.

Japan is no exception in this regard. If anything, Japan's success in developing a continuing stream of internationally competitive products over the past 30 years has led many people—in the United

---

1. Joseph A. DeRose, a program director at International Business Machines Corporation (IBM), argues that the most "high-tech" industry in the United States is agriculture, the oldest industry on earth but one that in the United States has been completely transformed by scientific and technological advances to enable it to produce increasing volumes of output with decreasing amounts of labor input.

States, Japan, and elsewhere-to assume that Japanese are particularly skillful in applying new technologies to productive uses. Indeed, the nature of Japan's technological successes during this period has shifted increasingly from innovations based on technologies originally developed elsewhere toward state-of-the-art developments originating in Japan. Examples of this progression are particularly conspicuous in electronics industries: In consumer electronics, the progression from transistor radios to black-and-white and later color televisions, through several generations of audio and tape recording equipment, to the commercialization of the world's most advanced video recorders; in information processing, the progression from mainframe computer prototypes derived from foreign technology to the mass production of semiconductors and other computer components and plug-compatible peripheral equipment, to personal as well as mainframe computers, and now to a wide variety of telecommunications and other data transmission and office automation equipment; and in industrial electronics, the progression from desktop and pocket calculators to numerically controlled machine tools and robots. The strong positions taken by Japanese firms in domestic and international markets for these products have clearly benefited from considerable investments in new technologies.

This record of success has also led many people outside Japan to wonder whether Japanese companies might soon be the world's leading producers of future electronic products. Since current Japanese capabilities in electronic products were developed during a period when exports of such products to the Japanese market were either restricted as a matter of policy or assumed by potential exporters to be of little potential value, attempts now to break into a well-developed Japanese computer and electronics market often appear—at best—extremely difficult. For many foreign-based computer and electronics firms, the current competitiveness of various Japan-based manufacturers often appears to stem from Japanese government support to domestic industries, whether through subsidies or preferential loans to help defray start-up costs, explicit or implicit barriers to import competition, or officially sanctioned cartel-like arrangements among prospective buyers as well as manufacturers. Such government support is also often thought likely to continue and thereby to impede still further the progress of foreign-based electronics firms in their own and third-country markets as well as in Japan.

Accordingly, this chapter describes the system of Japanese government support to new industries that has operated in the post-World War II years. It then assesses the degree to which such support has contributed to the development of these industries to date. Finally, the chapter suggests how future patterns of government support are likely to affect the further development of new industries in Japan. The discussion focuses primarily on computers and related electronics industries because they are the clearest single example of how government support for new technologies has operated in the postwar years and how such support has been changing in recent years.

GOVERNMENT INVOLVEMENT

As discussed in Chapter 3, Japanese government actions throughout the postwar period have continually sought to spur or assist the private sector in attempts to develop an ever-more sophisticated economic base—meaning, in turn, an ever-more sophisticated scientific and technological base. The support the Japanese government has given to scientific and technological development continues today, although, as also discussed in general terms in Chapter 3, the impact of government support on any particular industry, sector, or firm is gradually becoming less decisive than in the past. As Japanese companies have acquired scientific and technological capabilities that are independent of government support, their need for such support is less critical than it was in the past. Meanwhile, the government's traditional emphasis on applied research has slowly been changing toward a greater emphasis on basic research. This gradual shift reflects a recognition that in an increasing number of areas Japanese technology has become state of the art. For this reason, future Japanese research efforts, public and private, are likely to be forced by the logic of technological development itself to focus more on long-term, high-risk research programs while continuing, of course, to support applied research.[2]

As far back as the late 1940s, when Japan was still in the midst of reconstructing the physical damage of the war, various government science and technology institutions were created on the assumption that

---

2. For a succinct presentation of this viewpoint, see Yujiro Hayashi, *Atarashii kenkyū kaihatsu ni mukete* [Towards a new R & D] (Tokyo: Sangyō gijutsu kaihatsu chōki keikaku sakutei kenkyū kai [Study Group on Long-Term Plans for Industrial Technology Development], October 1981).

they could accelerate the country's economic recovery.[3] Government histories on science and technology policy consider the period of recovery from the war to have ended by the early 1950s; subsequently, science and technology began to be seen as a positive future-oriented process, rather than simply a means of repairing the damage of the war.[4] This positive view of the importance of new technology led to the creation of still other institutions, such as the Science and Technology Agency (STA) in 1956, which was specifically charged with a mission to promote and coordinate government science and technology efforts in pursuit of further economic growth. This nearly exclusive focus of science and technology policies on the promotion of economic growth continued into the early 1970s. Then, as economic growth became one of several national objectives, science and technology policy shifted from the promotion of "efficiency first" to the promotion of "environmental integrity, safety, and resource saving," in addition to efficiency.[5] Indeed, by the early 1970s, "knowledge intensiveness" was being promoted in official documents, not only as the most logical means of developing new industries with a comparative advantage appropriate to Japan's continuing development but also as the most suitable means of developing a "mature, welfare-oriented society." This phrase, like its frequent companion, "stable growth," served as a metaphor that the government used both to rationalize the slower rates of growth that were occurring anyway and to give this slower growth a positive, rather than

---

3. These included the Science Council, the Science Technical Administration Committee, various public and private research institutions and laboratories, and new bureaucratic procedures to facilitate the introduction of foreign technology.

4. For a typical example of this view, see Science and Technology Agency, *Outline of the White Paper on Science and Technology* (Tokyo: STA, February 1977).

5. Ibid., p. 16. Some 87 percent of the technology developments selected for commendation by the STA in the first half of the 1960s were aimed at contributing to economic growth and/or efficiency; the comparable figure for the 1970s was 69 percent. There was a concomitant rise in the preference for environmental integrity, growing from 3 percent in the early 1960s to 13 percent in the mid-1970s. See ibid., p. 17.

Figure 5.1.
TRENDS IN TECHNOLOGY TRADE

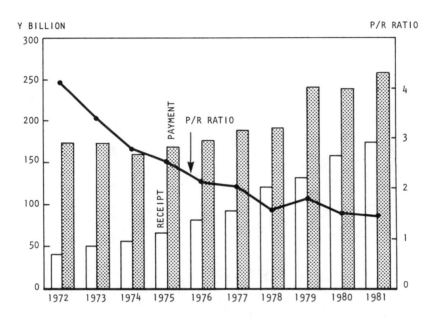

Source: Science and Technology Agency, *Kagaku gijutsu hakusho 1983*
[Science and technology white paper 1983] (Tokyo: STA, 1983).

negative, tone. In any case, a shift toward "knowledge intensiveness"
was reflected in concrete changes in Japan's industrial structure and
technological achievements.

The improvement in Japan's level of technological development
is clearly evident in technology trade data for the postwar period. Figure 5.1 shows payments and receipts for technology, in value and ratio terms, from 1972 through 1981. Japanese exports of technology (that
is, receipts from royalties) rose steadily from ¥42 billion in 1972 ($191
million at ¥220 = $1) to almost ¥170 billion in 1981 ($773 million).
Imports of technology (that is, payments of royalties) also increased,
from ¥175 billion in 1972 ($795 million at ¥220 = $1) to roughly ¥260
billion in 1981 ($1.2 billion). But the ratio of payments to receipts stead-
ily declined—from approximately 4:1 in 1972 to approximately 1.5:1
in 1981, reflecting the marked increase in Japanese technology exports

Figure 5.2.

RESEARCH EXPENDITURE OF MAJOR COUNTRIES

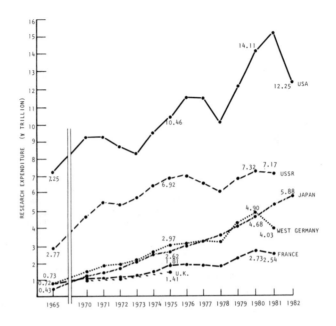

Note: Data for the US, USSR and France include social sciences and humanities.

Source: Science and Technology Agency, *Kagaku gijutsu hakusho 1983* [Science and technology white paper 1983] (Tokyo: STA, 1983).

over the last decade. More important, receipts from royalties for "new" technological processes have risen markedly.[6]

This improvement in Japanese technological independence cannot be attributed simply to the Japanese government's support of science and technology. Quantitatively, this support has been greater than that

---

6. See James C. Abegglen and Akio Etori, "Japanese Technology To-day," *Scientific American,* November 1983, pp. J10–J11, Special Advertisement Section.

of some other advanced industrial countries such as West Germany and France but less than that of others such as the United States and the Soviet Union. Comparisons of aggregate research expenditures (Figure 5.2) show that Japan ranks third in absolute amounts of research expenditures (approximately $26.7 billion in FY 1982, compared with approximately $55.7 billion for the United States, $32.6 billion for the Soviet Union, $18.3 billion for West Germany, and $11.5 billion for France).[7] In terms of research expenditures as a percentage of national income (Figure 5.3), Japan ranks fourth, at 2.78 percent in FY 1982, as against 4.86 percent for the Soviet Union in 1981, 3.04 percent for West Germany in 1981, 2.86 percent for the United States in FY 1982, and 2.28 percent for France in 1980. Japan's figure represents an increase from 2.4 percent in FY 1980, bringing its overall research expenditures, in percentage terms, roughly on par with those of the United States. Moreover, 69.2 percent of total research expenditures in 1981 (by industry, government, and universities) was provided by industry. Understandably, almost all of industry's expenditures went to activities within industry (Figure 5.4). Government funds were approximately 25 percent of total research funds, with less than 2 percent of total research expenditures going from government to industry. Comparable data on the government share of funds and allocation to industry for the United States, West Germany, France, and the United Kingdom were considerably higher—for example, 47.3 percent of total research funds in the United States coming from government and 22.8 percent of industrial expenditures going from government to industry; in West Germany in 1979, government funds accounted for 46.8 percent of total available funds, with 13.8 percent of research expenditures going from government to industry. These comparisons show that Japanese government support for R & D expenditures, at least at this level of aggregation, has been modest indeed.

As mentioned previously, however, Japan's overall research expenditures have focused mainly on applied research and prototype development—a bias reflected both in government-supported R & D and private sector research expenditure (see Table 5.1). This bias is also reflected in the government's institutional structure for scientific and technological development. The STA, which is the major Japanese

---

7. Dollar figures are approximations, converting yen figures provided by the STA at ¥ 220 = $1.

Figure 5.3.

RESEARCH EXPENDITURE TO NATIONAL INCOME IN
MAJOR COUNTRIES

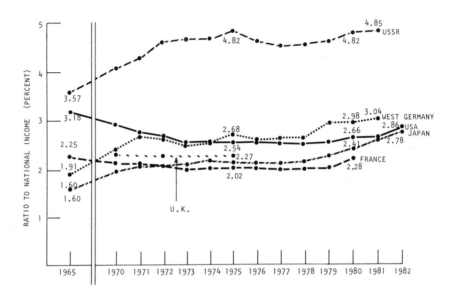

Source: Science and Technology Agency, *Kagaku gijutsu hakusho 1983*
[Science and technology white paper 1983] (Tokyo: STA, 1983)

government institution responsible for promotion of science and technology, supports various basic research activities while also monitoring the applied research activities undertaken elsewhere in the government.[8] Most government-supported basic research is conducted at STA laboratories or affiliated institutions.[9] Examples of the STA's areas of

---

8. The STA also supports its own applied research activities, discussed below.

9. Examples of STA's basic research programs include the Institute of Physical and Chemical Research, a public corporation reporting to the STA that conducts advanced research in physics, chemistry, agriculture, and biology, and the Creative Scientific and Technology Promotion Program, initiated by STA in 1981 with a capitalization of ¥10 billion ($45.5 million at ¥ 220 = $1). The latter's mission is to concentrate on fine polymers, special structure materials, crystallization, and super minute particles.

Figure 5.4.
FLOW OF R & D FUNDS IN MAJOR COUNTRIES

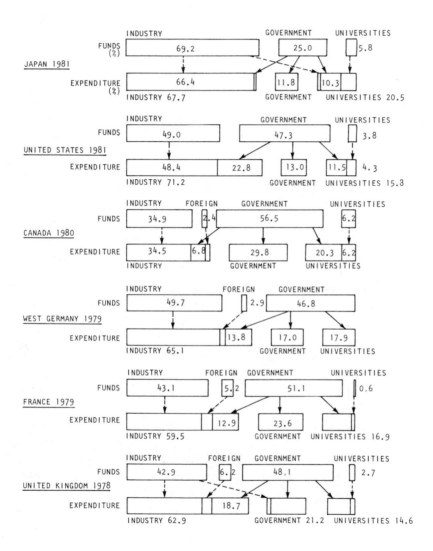

Note: Figures for the United States and France include social and humanistic sciences.

Source: Science and Technology Agency, *Kagaku gijutsu hakusho* [White paper on science and technology] (Tokyo: STA, 1983).

Table 5.1
TOTAL R & D EXPENDITURE BY TYPE OF ACTIVITY
(In Percent)

	Basic	Applied	Development
1970	18.9	28.2	52.9
1974	15.0	21.7	63.3
1975	14.2	21.5	64.3
1977	16.2	25.1	58.7
1978	16.6	25.1	58.4
1979	15.6	25.9	58.5
1980	14.5	25.4	60.0
1981	13.9	25.7	60.4
1982	14.1	25.9	60.1

Note: Expenditures for a given year may not add to 100.0 owing to rounding.

Source: Science and Technology Agency, *Kagaku gijutsu hakushō* [white paper on science and technology] (Tokyo: STA, 1983).

responsibilities include the promotion of health and safety–related technology such as disaster prevention and the promotion of pioneer work in such fields as nuclear energy, space and ocean development, aviation technology, remote sensing technology, laser technology, and material sciences. In general, the STA provides grants, conducts surveys on the research activities of private companies, and controls the administration of nine advisory groups to the STA and the office of the Prime Minister.[10]

The STA also directs a small commercially oriented organization—the Japan Research Development Corporation (JRDC), which acts as the agency's vehicle for disseminating new technologies. The JRDC operates on a formula through which private companies are given inducements, usually in the form of financial aid, to undertake

10. These groups, made up of government and industry representatives, are the Council for Science and Technology; the Resources Council; the Council for Aeronautics, Electronics, and Other Advanced Technologies; the Space Activities Commission; the Council for Ocean Development; the Consulting Engineering Council; the Atomic Energy Commission; the Nuclear Safety Commission; and the Radiation Council.

further technological developments for the express purpose of commercialization. Separately, the JRDC disseminates the achievements made under such development projects and makes arrangements for the industrial application of new technologies, largely through licensing. Companies that cooperate in the development phase often have an inside track of obtaining benefits once commercialization has proven viable, if only because they have developed additional know-how and methodological experience in the course of the development process. At the same time, the JRDC receives royalty payments from successful projects, thereby building its own capital base much like a private company. Although the JRDC is clearly an important means of promoting commercialization, its total spending on an annual basis has been small, that is, for fiscal 1981, about ¥5 billion ($22.7 million at ¥220 = $1). Once a project reaches the prototype stage, it may be eligible for preferential financing by the JDB or the Small Business Finance Corporation (SBFC). Moreover, as noted in Chapter 3, companies utilizing the JRDC or engaging in other R & D-related programs that have government priority are then eligible for certain tax deductions and accelerated depreciation allowances.

The other major body responsible for science and technology-related activities—and the organization with primary responsibility for applied research—is the Agency for Industrial Science and Technology (AIST), which is part of MITI. The AIST is explicitly oriented toward R & D of technology with industrial applications, as against basic research, although its activities can, and do, include financing for infrastructure technology and other indirect support for industries such as medical equipment technology. The AIST, like the STA and MITI itself, has various means at its disposal to provide assistance to the private sector; these are discussed in detail below. The AIST also undertakes activities that are wholly within the public sector, including the operation of 16 laboratories.[11] Overall, AIST's activities are designed

---

11. AIST's activities center around its 16 laboratories. The largest of these is the Electro-Technical Laboratory (ETL), which specializes in electricity and electronics-related projects. A major AIST project is the R & D Project on Basic Technology for New Industries; the major research areas and participating companies in this project are described in Appendix B, and the funding structure is described later in this chapter. The R & D Project on Basic Technologies for New Industries, inaugurated in 1981, concentrates on new

to develop technology (1) to improve the quality of life or (2) to provide Japanese society as a whole with needed industrial technology.

The AIST also has an explicit mission to conduct collaborative research with affiliated laboratories and private companies. Japanese government officials frequently argue that a collaborative approach to technological development has proven especially useful as a means of solving problems that arise at the boundary between applied research and commercialization. By spreading the recognizably high costs of the initial commercialization of new technologies among several companies as well as the government, the argument runs, new measures can be brought on stream more quickly for the benefit of society, as well as for the companies undertaking the work.[12] The AIST also administers the industrial standardization program, known by its initials, JIS (Japan Industrial Standards). This program sets industrial standards, in-

---

materials, biotechnology, and new types of semiconductor elements; this project is jointly financed by public and private funds, with a majority of the research conducted at corporate laboratories.

Two blue-ribbon programs, the Sunshine and Moonlight projects, are wholly financed by the AIST. These projects, which are in the demonstration phase of development, are designed to promote alternative sources of energy. The Sunshine Project, begun in 1974, was designed to develop stable, long-term energy supplies and to prevent (or lessen) environmental pollution. Specific activities in this project are listed in Table B.1. These have tended to be in risky, long lead-time areas such as solar energy, coal liquefaction, and ocean thermal and wind conversion. The Moonlight Project, established in 1978, was designed to develop new technologies for energy conservation. (See Table B.2 for details.) The so-called Large Scale Project is an extremely broad category encompassing such diverse activities as jet engines, optical measurement systems, undersea resource recovery technology, and other capital-intensive long lead-time projects. It also is government-financed, although the degree of government funding varies according to the particular project. (A list of current and completed projects under the Large Scale Project is shown in Table B.3.) The Subsidy System for the Development of Important Technologies, also operating out of the AIST, is a means of providing low-interest loans for major R & D activities in the private sector. The actual amounts of these subsidies have been small.

12. Ministry of International Trade and Industry, *AIST 1981* (Tokyo: MITI, 1981), p. 42; and private discussions.

cluding the designation of categories of goods or processing techniques qualified to bear a JIS mark.[13]

A number of additional practices have also worked to promote science and technology policies that are consistent with the goals of continued industrial development. Numerous advisory councils (*shingikai*) and study groups (*kenkyūkai*) have been formed under government auspices, for example, the Electronics Industry Deliberation Council, the Council on Biotechnology, and the Study Group on Long Term Plans for Industrial Technology Development. These meet regularly, and although they have no legal authority, they provide a means of discussing new developments and engaging in "consensus building" among business executives, academics, journalists, scientists, and government officials. Moreover, the custom, referred to in Chapter 3, that encourages government officials to retire at around age 55 and then to enter senior management positions in business (known as *amakudari*, or "descent from heaven") is common in almost all sectors of the economy. The gains to business from the *amakudari* system obviously vary from case to case, but at the very least the practice gives Japanese firms a strong in-house lobby through which to influence government policies and decisions.[14]

Thus, although Japanese government support of R & D activities is lower than that of some other countries in terms of the amount of money available, various consultative programs and institutions greatly enhance the effectiveness of the funds that are provided. Japanese government support of the computer and electronics industries has been especially pronounced, although not necessarily more than equivalent

---

13. The JIS system has been severely criticized by would-be importers as a method of preventing competition from imports. Unlike the U.S. system, in which the certification organizations such as Underwriters' Laboratory maintain testing facilities in Japan to facilitate Japanese exports to the United States, the JIS mark was until recently unobtainable for products manufactured abroad.

14. The custom of *amakudari* is not limited to Japanese firms; Japan-based subsidiaries of American computer manufacturers have employed a former director of the AIST's Electro-Technical Laboratory and a former MITI vice-minister.

efforts made by the private sector.[15] The Japanese government has
tried to foster a favorable environment for investment in new industries in general and computers in particular and then to provide specific incentives for investment at the industry and project level (for example, computers, software, new materials, and so on). Both general and
specific policies and incentives have been employed. At the same time,
both Japanese society as a whole and the world economic environment
have also worked generally to foster the development of new industries.
Except in the once critically important area of providing infant-industry
restrictions on imports, Japanese government policies have not tried to
replace the market mechanism.

THE JAPANESE COMPUTER INDUSTRY

From the founding of a domestic computer industry in the late 1950s,
the Japanese government, especially MITI as the major government
ministry responsible for the manufacturing sector, has supported the
development of the industry as something it considered particularly important.[16] Computers and computer components were considered ''strategic industries'' because of their presumed importance for many future manufacturing activities, their relatively low labor requirements,
their relatively high added value, and their own high demand growth.
Government support was aimed at developing a group of companies
capable of competing with major foreign producers, notably IBM. This
support facilitated the rapid development of a domestic computer industry, although the structure of this industry is now changing as an
increasing number of smaller firms are being established and an increasing number of foreign-based firms are entering the Japanese market
through sales or manufacturing activities.[17]

---

15. MITI's definition of the electronics industries includes consumer electronics, communications, computers, components, and electronic test and
measuring equipment.

16. Merton Peck and Shuji Tamura, in their chapter in *Asia's New Giant*, argue that computers illustrate the most extensive Japanese government
involvement in a particular industry in the postwar period. See Merton J. Peck
and Shuji Tamura, "Technology," in *Asia's New Giant*, ed. Hugh Patrick and
Henry Rosovsky (Washington, D.C.:1 Brookings Institution, 1976), p. 571.

17. At the moment, six Japan-based firms—Fujitsu, Hitachi, NEC Corporation, Oki, Mitsubishi, and Toshiba—together with IBM-Japan dominate
the domestic market.

Evolution of Government Support

In the early years, essentially through the 1960s, the Japanese government made concerted and largely successful efforts to enable Japan-based firms to gain access to foreign technology and, specifically, to IBM technology through IBM-Japan. The latter, a wholly owned subsidiary of U.S.-based International Business Machines Corporation, had been established before World War II and resumed its activities after the war. In 1960, with the production of its 7000 series, IBM-Japan became the first foreign-based computer manufacturer in Japan. In these early years, IBM-Japan enjoyed considerable competitive advantages over domestic firms in all areas—hardware, software, support services, and so on. Concurrently, it cooperated with MITI requests to license computer manufacturing technology to Japan-based producers.[18]

With the fourth stage of capital liberalization in 1971 and the freeing of imports of peripheral equipment in 1972, the Japanese government then initiated a further liberalization program for the domestic computer industry—largely through phased reductions in import duties. In part in response to this phased liberalization and in part because of Japanese government pressure *and* assistance, Japanese computer manufacturers organized themselves into three groups in the early

---

18. Meanwhile, Japanese firms made conscious efforts to avoid head-to-head competition with IBM-Japan. Instead, they followed a fourfold strategy. First, they actively sought technology imports through licensing arrangements with other foreign producers as well. For example, by 1970 Hitachi had established a licensing arrangement with RCA, Mitsubishi with XDS (Xerox Data Systems), NEC with Honeywell, Oki with Univac, and Toshiba with General Electric. Although such licensing agreements have changed substantially since 1970, as has the structure of the industry as a whole in both Japan and the United States, technology licensing, as against joint venturing or establishing wholly owned subsidiaries, remains the most prevalent form of foreign participation in the Japanese computer industry. Second, the Japan-based firms concentrated on lower end-of-the-market activities, both as a means of improving technological capabilities on a step-by-step basis and as a means of increasing sales in markets where they could readily build on previous experience in other manufacturing processes. Third, Japanese firms invested heavily in R & D and plant and equipment expenditures, building up their own service organizations and gradually developing economies of scale through larger production volumes. Finally, they pursued these strategies with explicit government support, including protection from imports and a buy-Japanese policy in government procurement.

1970s: Fujitsu-Hitachi, NEC-Toshiba, and Mitsubishi-Oki.[19] This overall strategy was sufficiently successful to enable several Japanese vendors to introduce IBM-compatible systems by 1974 and then to start encroaching on IBM-Japan's up-scale markets, such as the banking system, by moving into peripherals, terminals, and other equipment that amounted to add-on sales to IBM equipment. Then, in December 1976, imports of mainframe units and foreign investment in the computer industry were made completely free of restrictions—at least in principle.[20]

Shortly thereafter, however, the Cabinet issued a resolution that seemed to imply the opposite belief: "In view of the high expectations of independence and continued growth of Japan's computer industry, the government is resolved to keep careful watch on trends on the computer market with the aim of preventing adverse effects on domestic firms which could lead to confusion in the electronic computer market."[21] Toshio Komoto, then minister, later added:

> It is the opinion of the Ministry of International Trade and Industry that the independence and future growth of Japan's computer industry, following liberalization, will hinge on the industry's ability to secure an appropriate share of the domestic market. While keeping a close watch on the trends of computer import and installation, the Ministry will put into effect strong measures for the promotion of the domestic industry which will include, and not be limited to, encouraging the development of VLSIs [very large-scale integrated circuits] for use and next generation computers, as well as the securing of sufficient rental funds for domestic machines.[22]

---

19. According to Japanese government publications, the results of this consolidation of efforts in the Japanese computer industry were, by 1974, the ACOS and COSMOS series (May 1974), the M series (November 1974), and subsequently machines compatible with IBM's 3.5 generation computers, the 370 series. See Japan Information Processing Development Center, *Computer White Paper* (Tokyo: JIPDEC, 1980), p. 4.

20. Toshio Komoto, MITI minister at the time, stated that the decision to liberalize computer imports was based on the government's belief that— partly because of previous government support—Japan's computer industry would be able to stand on its own and continue to grow, even after liberalization.

21. Japan Information Processing Development Center, *Computer White Paper* (Tokyo: JIPDEC, 1978)

22. Ibid.

In fact, Japanese government support to the computer industry has been considerably more extensive than suggested here by Komoto. Such support is grounded in law, implemented through loans, subsidies, and tax measures, and facilitated by the creation of various institutions, both advisory and operational. The statutory basis [23] for government support of the computer and related electronic industries is embodied in a series of laws:

1. June 1957. *Law on Extraordinary Measures for the Promotion of Electronic Industries. (Denshinhō)* This law gave MITI authority to formulate overall plans for a reorganization of the then-nascent computer industry as well as authority to design specific support packages for the industry.
2. April 1971. *Law on Extraordinary Measures for the Promotion of Electronics and Machinery Industry. (Kidenhō)* This law was designed to respond to a new set of conditions in which foreign investment, if not countered, might lead to more foreign ownership of the computer industry than either government policymakers or domestic producers thought desirable. It specifically covered 37 types of machinery in the electronics industry and 58 types in the machinery industry itself. Later, for each machine indicated, specifically designed promotion programs were outlined. The major purpose of this law was to raise the technological level in both the machinery and the electronics industry; hence, the machinery and information industries were combined, in an effort to increase the range of applications of electronic industries. Specifically the law covered prototype R & D promotion of commercial production and manufacturing improvements. Government subsidies were provided to prototype R & D in a variety of specific areas, discussed below.
3. June 1978. *Law on Extraordinary Measures for the Promotion of Specific*

---

23. For a more detailed discussion of this legislation, as well as earlier computer-related support measures during the period before foreign investment in the industry was permitted, see U.S. Congress, House, Subcommittee on Trade, Committee on Ways and Means *High Technology and Japanese Industrial Policy: A Strategy for U.S. Policy Makers* (Washington, D.C.: Government Printing Office, October 1, 1980); Comptroller General of the United States, *United States/Japan Trade: Issues and Problems* (Washington, D.C.: General Accounting Office, September 21, 1979); and Japan Information Processing Development Center, *Government Policy* (Tokyo: JIPDEC, Summer 1978).

Machinery and Information Industry. (Kijōhō) The *Kijōhō* replaced and extended the functions of the *Kidenhō*, especially in the area of software. It was initially intended to be terminated in 1982 but was then extended for an additional three years. It is structured much like its predecessor in that it also designates plans for specified industries, provides for tax measures to facilitate the availability of investment funds, and can also be used to initiate large-scale undertakings. MITI officials and legal specialists explain the need for this continued and expanded support for the industry as an outgrowth of continuing need to develop domestic software and other advanced components of an overall information processing system. This law is being used specifically, although not exclusively, to promote software production.

The government has also fostered, in part through financing and legislation and in part simply through encouragement and persuasion, an institutional infrastructure for computers and electronics. This has included the creation of a Machinery and Information Bureau within MITI that has several divisions closely monitoring and, in some cases, directly supervising various computer-related programs.[24] The bureau has administrative responsibility over all government computer projects. It exerts strong influence over AIST's activities and aims to improve, develop, and regulate the machinery and information industries. In addition, a number of advisory councils, such as the Electronics Industry Council and the Information Industry Committee of the Industrial Structure Council, have been formed. The government has also encouraged the formation of trade associations, such as the Japan Electronic Industry Development Association (JEIDA), and the pooling of financial resources among computer manufacturers.

Perhaps the bast example of the latter phenomenon is the Japan Electronic Computer Company (JECC), founded in 1961 to purchase hardware and software from shareholder companies and lease them to

---

24. For example, the Electronics Policy Division and the Data Processing Promotion Division are responsible for supervising software development programs; the Industrial Electronics Division is responsible for new computers.

users.[25] The JECC is financed largely by the computer manufacturers themselves (minus IBM-Japan, which was excluded when JECC was formed); with this pooled capital and its ability to leverage special low-interest loans from the JDB, the JECC can greatly ease the financial burden for participating companies, compared with the costs of each company's operating an independent leasing program. According to the 1981 *JECC Annual Report*:

> As a result of the establishment of JECC, indigenous computer manufacturers in Japan have freed themselves from the otherwise tremendous task involved in the procurement of the very substantial amount of operating capital required, and the work of attracting investment capital. This has allowed them to concentrate on further research and development for computer hardware and software and on expanding the computer market.... In order to meet the rapidly growing need for funds, JECC has also put considerable effort into raising loans. These consist mainly of long-term low-interest loans provided through the Japan Development Bank from the funds for public financing, and the various credit arrangements granted by a wide range of private financial institutions such as city banks, trust banks, local banks, and life and other insurance companies, even including foreign banks.[26]

Such achievements are not the whole story, of course. One disadvantage of the leasing system became apparent when new models were rapidly introduced and old models were then returned to the JECC, which in turn required the manufacturers to buy these back. To respond to these rapid changes in the market, a new tax measure was adopted

---

25. Shareholding companies in JECC are NEC, Fujitsu, Hitachi, Toshiba, Oki, Mitsubishi Electric, and NEC-Toshiba Information Systems. Leasing is a major marketing mechanism for large computer manufacturers, especially IBM. Smaller companies are less able to bear the up-front costs of a major leasing program than larger companies; thus, the competitive logic behind the JECC was to pool resources to support a leasing program.

26. Japan Electronic Computer Company, *JECC Annual Report*, Tokyo: JECC, 1981, pp. 2–3. The foreign bank referred to above is Morgan Guaranty Trust Company of New York.

in the 1960s allowing manufacturers to create a tax-free reserve of up to 15 percent of the value of sales to the JECC. This was aimed at covering losses that might accrue when models were bought back from the JECC.[27] This tax-free reserve has contributed to the continued viability of the JECC even in the face of a rapidly growing and changing market. By allowing money to be put aside in the form of a tax-free reserve, this system permitted companies to take a tax write-off sooner rather than later, thereby providing them additional cash up front. In highly leveraged firms with high fixed costs—which Japanese computer manufacturers were, especially in their early growth period—such predictable cash up front was extremely useful. Moreover, the subsequent need to increase the amounts that could be set aside in a reserve suggests that at least until 1978 the buy-back requirements were sufficiently burdensome that the initial reserve allotments were not an egregious subsidy. Nonetheless, the system had obvious advantages.

In time, the very success of the JECC contributed to a lessening of its importance in the further development of the computer industry. Table 5.2 shows that the value of Japanese computers leased through the JECC, as a percentage of domestic sales, has declined from an average of 36.8 percent of domestic sales from 1960 through 1971 to an average of 19.8 percent from 1972 through 1981. In 1976 MITI and the JECC sought to increase the latter's net worth and asked the major computer manufacturers to increase their capital participation by a total of ¥5 billion ($22.7 million at ¥220 = $1). Because Hitachi had by then established its own rental program aimed at providing lower credit terms that would presumably lead to increased business, it rejected the proposal. Toshiba, Mitsubishi, and Oki also refused. The proposal was eventually accepted when Fujitsu agreed to pay 80 percent of the proposed increase (¥4 billion), and NEC agreed to pay the remaining 20 percent (¥1 billion). The JECC continues to exist, and the JDB continues to provide loans to private firms through the JECC, even as individual companies build up their own programs. Thus, although the usefulness of the JECC to the major computer manufacturers has diminished, it remains one of the best examples of a task-oriented, government-supported technology organization in Japan.

---

27. The reserve amount was later raised to 20 percent; and in 1978 companies were allowed to put aside even greater reserves if they could demonstrate larger buy-back obligations.

Table 5.2
ROLE OF THE JECC IN FINANCING COMPUTERS
(In ¥ Billion)

	Total Production in Japan	Exports	JECC Purchases	JECC Share in Japanese Sales (percent)
1961	5	0	1	23.4
1962	9	0	3	34.4
1963	19	0	6	31.6
1964	25	1	12	47.2
1965	38	1	21	57.3
1966	66	3	21	33.1
1967	106	5	37	36.3
1968	164	4	67	41.8
1969	196	7	82	43.7
1970	310	6	92	30.2
1971	346	9	87	25.9
1972	421	12	89	21.7
1973	472	16	108	23.7
1974	589	24	124	21.9
1975	541	32	126	24.8
1976	619	60	134	24.0
1977	719	67	134	20.6
1978	910	105	131	16.2
1979	1,124	129	144	14.5
1980	1,293	168	178	15.8
1981	1,498	266	184	15.3

Sources: Japan Electronic Computer Company, *Konputa Nōto* [Computer Notes] (Tokyo: JECC, 1983); and Japan Computer Usage Development Institute, *Computer White Paper*, as reported in Edward J. Lincoln, *Japan's Industrial Policies* (Washington, D.C.: Japan Economic Institute of America, April 1984).

Another important government organization aimed at developing and disseminating information and computer systems is the Information Technology Promotion Agency (IPA), established in 1970. Its aim is to promote the use of computers, encourage the development and use of programs, and help software firms. Financing for the IPA comes from government subsidies, private corporations, three long-term credit banks (the JDB, the Industrial Bank of Japan, and the Long-Term Credit

Bank of Japan), and revenues earned by the association itself.[28] Total annual IPA revenues, from both government and private sector sources, have been declining in recent years, from a peak of ¥3.46 billion ($15.7 million at ¥220 = $1) in 1982 to ¥2.68 billion ($12.2 million) in 1984.[29] Among the more important of the IPA's activities are its credit guarantee programs. Information processing firms and software houses are often in need of funds to develop software programs but have limited property that can be used as collateral. The IPA has a system for guaranteeing such obligations, as long as they are registered with the IPA; this system is illustrated in Figures 5.5 and 5.6.[30] Loans for specific projects funded by the IPA are under the scrutiny of the Machinery and Information Industries Bureau of MITI.[31] To enhance the usefulness of the IPA, the tax system was amended in 1979 to institute a tax-free reserve fund for software programs resembling that established for repurchasing computers, discussed above. Yet, in contrast to the 20

---

28. The impact of IPA subsidies is sufficiently diffuse to appear unclear even to IPA officials. As one IPA official told the authors in 1981, "Consignment payments of ¥10 billion have been allocated to the information processing industry, software houses, and even end users over the last 12 years. . . . These must have had some investment effects, but we have no way of measuring these effects."

29. Japan Electronic Computer Company, *JECC Konputa Nōtō* [JECC Computer Notes] (Tokyo: JECC, 1984), p. 98.

30. In order to promote the development of software and raise the technological level of program development in Japan, the IPA is consigning to the private sector the task of developing programs related to upgrading. Each of these programs must satisfy the following conditions: (1) there must be a special need for its development, (2) the fruits of such development must be seen as widely usable in business activities, and (3) independent development by companies is difficult. In the ten-year period ending in FY 1979, 97 such programs had been developed. Japan Information Processing Development Center, *Computer White Paper*, 1980, p. 235.

31. An IPA-style credit guarantee system is not uncommon in the United States. However, the American credit guarantee systems tend to be aimed at broad industries, such as housing, rather than at narrowly targeted sectors.

Figure 5.5.
IPA SYSTEM, FY 1983

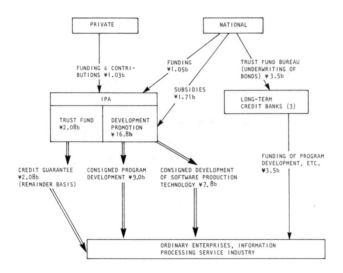

Note: b = billion

Source: Japan Electronic Computer Company, *Konputa Nōtō* [Computer Notes] (Tokyo: JECC, 1984).

percent commonly put aside for computer buy-backs, as much as 50 percent of the income from software programs developed and registered with the IPA can be put into the tax reserve.[32]

---

32. In order to be eligible for the tax break, programs have to be registered with the IPA. Since the IPA was specifically designed to encourage the development of domestic software programs, until recently only those programs "domestically developed by Japan" were eligible for registration. The system in effect until 1980 is explained in the Japan Information Processing Development Center, *Computer White Paper*, 1980, p. 47. Tax credits for software development since 1981 have become available to foreign-based computer firms with manufacturing facilities in Japan.

Figure 5.6.
IPA CREDIT GUARANTEE SYSTEM

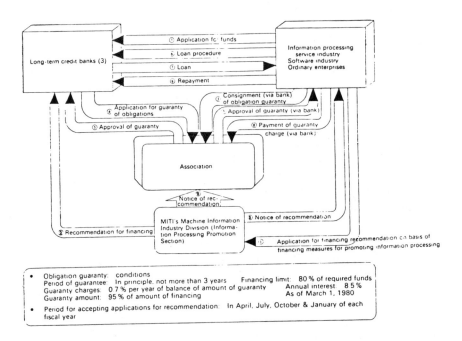

Source: Japan Information Processing Development Center, *Computer White Paper,* (Tokyo: JIPDEC, 1980).

Structure and Degree of Financial Support

Figures 5.7, 5.8, and 5.9 show schematically the major subsidies, loans, and tax measures that have been applied to the computer industry during the last two decades.[33] This is followed by a brief description of

---

33. Numerous organizations other than those discussed here have been formed to facilitate the development of an information infrastructure in general and a computer infrastructure in particular. For example, there are a number of programs tailored to small- and medium-sized firms. The SBPC, a subagency of the Small- and Medium-Sized Enterprise Agency of MITI, was established as a means of diffusing information to small- and medium-sized enterprises, which in recent years have come to include computer and computer-related firms. The discussion here concentrates on the major organizations and programs.

Figure 5.7.

SUBSIDIES TO THE COMPUTER INDUSTRY

SUBSIDIES TO THE COMPUTER INDUSTRY

1960 1961 1962 1963 1964 1965 1966 1967 1968 1969 1970 1971 1972 1973 1974 1975 1976 1977 1978 1979 1980 1981 1982 1983 1984 1985 1986 1987

(1) 4/50 ————————————— 3/68
Subsidy for R&D for Mining (10)

(2) 66 ————————————————— 71
Super High Performance Electronic
Computer (10)
(3)

(4) 4/68 ——————————————————————————— (3)
Subsidy for R&D for Important Technologies
(5) 4/71 —————————
Subsidy for IPA Operation

(4) 4/62 ——— 3/66
Fontac Subsidy

(6) 71 ———————————————————— 80
Pattern Information Processing System (22)

(7) 4/72 ——— 3/77
Subsidy for Promotion of Developing
New Types of Computers (57.1)

(8) 72 —————— 76
Subsidy for Promotion of Developing
Computer Peripherals (8.7)

(9) 4/73 ——— 3/75
Subsidy for Promotion and Development

(10) 4/73 ——— 3/76
Subsidy for Promotion of
Information Processing Industry (3.0)

81 ——— (6.6) Software Production
Development Program

(11) 4/77 ——— 3/80
Subsidy for Promotion of
Developing VLSI For Next
Generation Computers (30)

(12) 7/79 ——————— 83
Subsidy for Developing Basic
Technologies for Next Generation
Computer (47)

(13) 79 ——————— 87
Optical Measurement and Control System (18)

(14) 81 ———————— 89
High Speed Computer System for Scientific and Technological Uses (22)

(15) 81 ————————— 90
Next Generation Basic Technology (104)

(16) 81 ————————— 90

Figures in () on right represent subsidy amount
where available in billions of ¥

Figures in () on left are reference numbers

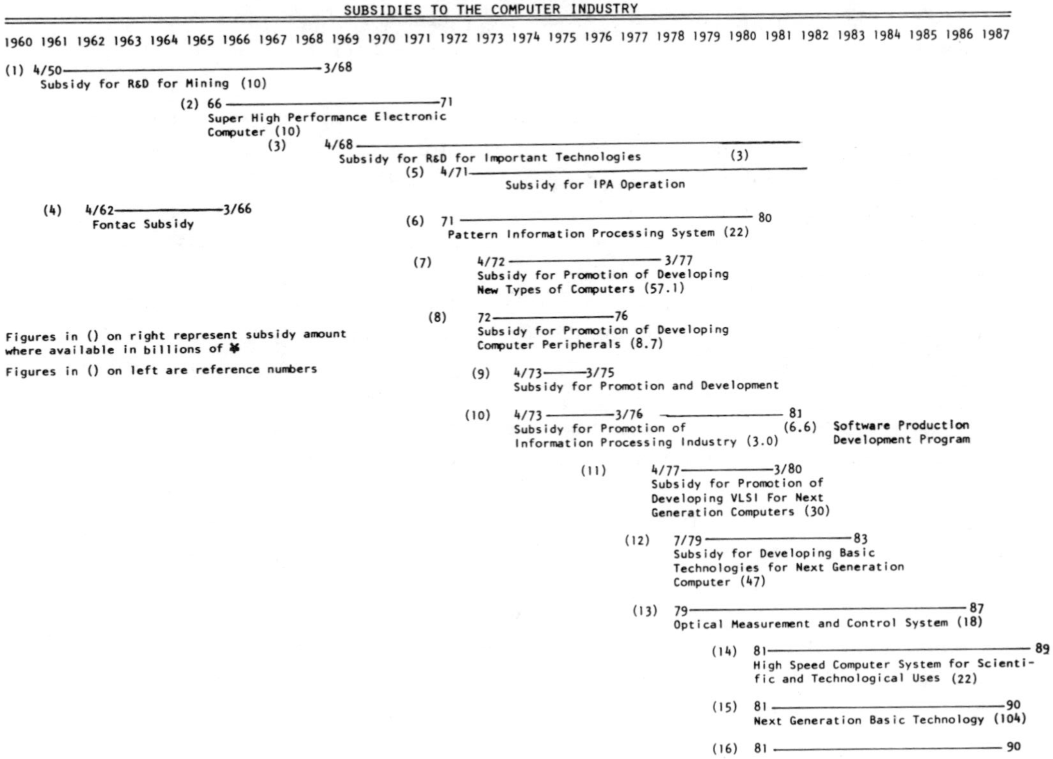

(1) &
(3): These are combined because (3) is a continuation of (1). *Sponsors*: AIST, MITI. *Funding*: all government funding through consignment payments.

(2): *Sponsors:* AIST, Large Scale Project; MITI. *Funding:* all government funding through consignment payments.

(4): FONTAC was aimed at developing a large-size computer competitive with IBM systems. *Corporate participation:* Fujitsu, Oki, NEC.

(5): The IPA was established by law in 1970 to encourage the development of software by direct and indirect financing. IPA operations are reviewed by MITI. Three long-term credit banks provide loans to software houses and data services through IPA's guarantee fund. Total government support unclear, but subsidies totaled ¥14.9 million for FY 1972 through 1980 (see text for additional material).

(6): Continuation of (2). *Sponsors:* AIST and Electro-Technical Laboratory. *Corporate participation:* Toshiba, Hitachi, Fujitsu, NEC, Mitsubishi Electric, Sanyo, Matsushita Research Institute, Konishiroku, and Hoya Glass.

(7): Subsidy aimed at developing a new series of computers competitive with IBM's 370 series. *Funding:* a 50 percent subsidy to three computer manufacturer groups. *Corporate participation:* Fujitsu-Hitachi (produced M series), NEC-Toshiba (produced ACOM), and Mitsubishi-Oki (produced MELCOM).

(8): *Sponsor:* MITI. *Participation:* 31 companies. *Funding:* 50/50 (government/private). *Goal:* develop high-efficiency input-output units and terminals.

(9): *Sponsor:* MITI. *Participation:* MITI. *Funding:* 50/50 (government/private).

(10): *Sponsors:* Machinery and Information Industries Bureau and Data Processing Division, MITI. *Corporate participation:* 17 large Japanese software companies belonging to an IPA subsidiary, the Joint Systems Development Corp.; in addition, a number of unspecified smaller firms. *Goal:* to increase the production and use of software programs. This constitutes IPA's most active software development program to date. Results unclear.

(11): &

(12): Combined, as (12) seen as a continuation of (11). *Sponsors:* Machinery and Information Industries Bureau and Industrial Electronics Division, MITI. *Corporate participation:* two phases: (1) Fujitsu, Hitachi, Mitsubishi, NEC, Toshiba, OKI, Sharp, Matsushita; (11) above, plus NTT and AIST's Electro-Technical laboratory staff. *Association formed:* Phase 1: VLSI Research Association formed; Phase II: Electronic Computer Basic Technology Research Association formed (July 1979). *Funding:* (government) conditional loan, repayable if profits are generated from technologies; Phase I: ¥ 30 billion from the government; ¥ 42 billion from the private sector; Phase II: ¥ 22.5 billion from the government; ¥ 24.5 billion from the private sector.

(13): *Sponsors:* AIST, National Research and Development Program, MITI. *Corporate participation:* Fujitsu, Hitachi, NEC, Toshiba, Mitsubishi Denki, Matsushita Furukawa, Oki, Sumitomo Electric. *Association formed:* Engineering Research Association of Optoelectronics Applied Systems (January 1981). Laboratory formed by association: Optoelectronics Joint Research Laboratory within the Fujitsu Kawasaki Plant. *Funding:* all government funding through consignment payments.

(14): *Sponsors:* AIST, National Research and Development Program, MITI. *Corporate participation:* Fujitsu, Hitachi, NEC, Toshiba, Mitsubishi Denki, Oki. *Government laboratory assistance:* Electro-Technical Laboratory, AIST. *Association formed:* the Association for the Development of High Speed Scientific Computers (December 1981); MITI's Electrotechnical Laboratory is also involved, although majority of work will be conducted at companies' own research facilities. *Funding:* all government funding through consignment payments.

(15): *Sponsors:* Next Generation Basic Technology Planning Office, AIST, MITI. *Corporate participation:* 48 companies in three areas; numbers in ( ) indicate number of firms; Area I: New Materials (33); Area II: Biotechnology (14); Area III: Semiconductor Function Elements (10). *Association formed:* five associations formed, three for Area I, one for Area II, and one for Area III. *Funding:* all government funding through consignment payments.

(16): *Sponsors:* Machinery and Information Bureau, MITI. *Corporate participation:* Fujitsu, Hitachi, NEC, Toshiba, Mitsubishi Denki, Oki. *Government laboratory assistance:* Electro-Technical Laboratory, AIST. *NTT personnel participation:* primarily at preparatory stages. *Association formed:* the Institute for New Generation Computer Technology, an endowed research foundation (April 1982). *Funding:* total funding yet to be determined.

each of these projects. Table 5.3 shows subsidy amounts, financing methods, and patent control practices for eight major computer-related programs that have been operating since 1976.[34]

The center of Table 5.3 shows the financing method. Although all of these funds can be subsumed in English under the term *subsidy*, this terminology is something of a misnomer. In fact, subsidies are either grants, including conditional loans (*hojōkin*, or government-contracted work, in the form of consignment payments (*itakuhi*). Conditional loans tend to have low, and in some cases no, interest rates. Repayment in basic research projects is not required. Repayment in applied research depends on the success of the project: if no successful technologies result, these loans tend not to have to be repaid. Even when the research is successful, a seven-year grace period is allowed before the loan must be repaid.[35] Typically, these loans represent up to 45 percent of the total expenditure of the project, with the remainder provided by the firms. (For specific project details, see Figure 5.7 and accompanying references.) Allocations of conditional loans are at MITI's discretion—with the usual budgetary and other political constraints. As far as we know, the conditional loans listed in Table 5.3 have yet to be repaid.[36] Drawing on Table 5.3 one can see that approximately ¥79.6 billion (or $361.8 million at ¥220 = $1) was allotted in the form of conditional loans in the 1976–81 period, as against approximately ¥13.2 billion (or $59 million) in consignment payments.[37]

---

34. As far as we know, these data on government support programs are the first of their kind in English. They represent, to the best of our knowledge, all major government projects and support measures. Abbreviations, changes in project titles, changes in accounting procedures, termination of projects midway, and other such developments are plentiful. Some small projects or programs have been intentionally omitted because they were so minor. At the same time, the possibility of error by omission remains.

35. Until 1983, this grace period was five years.

36. In discussions with the authors, a MITI official said that some of these loans had been repaid, specifically item 8 in Figure 5.6; however, no supporting documentation or verification was available.

37. These dollar figures are also somewhat inflated since currency fluctuations were considerable during this period. According to BOJ figures, the exchange went from 297 in 1976 to 221 in 1981; thus, using these exchange rates, the dollar amounts would be smaller.

Table 5.3

MAJOR JAPANESE GOVERNMENT PROJECT SUBSIDIES FOR R & D, 1976–81, FINANCING
METHOD AND PATENT CONTROL

	Government (¥ billion)	Subsidies ($ million at ¥ 220 = $1)		Financing Method	Patent Control
Subsidy for R & D for important technologies	13.4		61	Grant in the form of conditional loans between 26 to 40 percent of total expenditure, depending on type of research (*hojōkin*).* Repayment according to success of project.	Technologies go to subsidy recipients, except environmental control and safety.
Software Development Production Program	6.6		30	Total funding provided by MITI; no repayment obligation.	All resulting software technologies belong to IPA.
Subsidy for promotion of developing VLSI, for next-generation computers	30.0	Phase I	136.4	Conditional loans (*hojōkin*) provided to VLSI Research Association. Repay-	Majority of patents belong to association (over 90 percent); remaining be-

	22.5	Phase II	102.2	ment linked to profit levels. No interest payment due. (Some 42 percent of total expenditure provided by government.)	long to MITI. Patents owned by the association are available to association members and other firms (that is, cross licensing to foreign firms allowed) after MITI review. Access to MITI-owned patents is through AIST subsidiary, Industrial Technology Promotion Agency.
				Conditional loans (*hojōkin*) provided to Electronic Computer Basic Technology Research Association. (Half of total expenditure provided by the government.)	All patents will be owned by the government.
Subsidy for developing basic technologies	13.7		62.3	Conditional loans (*hojōkin*). (Some 45 percent of total ex-	Contract basis; all resulting patents belong to MITI.

			penditure provided by government.)	
Optical Measure and Control System	3.4	15.4	Total government funding, in the form of consignment payments (*itakuhi*); no repayment necessary.	Contract basis; all resulting patents belong to MITI.
High-Speed computer system for scientific and technological use	0.30	1.4	Total government funding; consignment payments (*itakuhi*); no repayment necessary.	Contract basis; all resulting patents belong to MITI.
Next-generation basic technology	2.7	12.3	Total government funding; consignment payments (*itakuhi*); no repayment necessary.	Contract basis; all resulting patents belong to MITI.
Fifth-generation basic computer	0.15	.682	Initial monies from JIPDEC. Total amount to be allocated undetermined.	Undetermined.

*For the rest of this chart, "Grants in the form of conditional loans" is abbreviated.
Source: Discussions with government officials, various documents: JDB, IBJ, LTCB, MITI, STA, and AIST.

Figure 5.8.
TREASURY INVESTMENT AND LOANS FOR INFORMATION INDUSTRIES

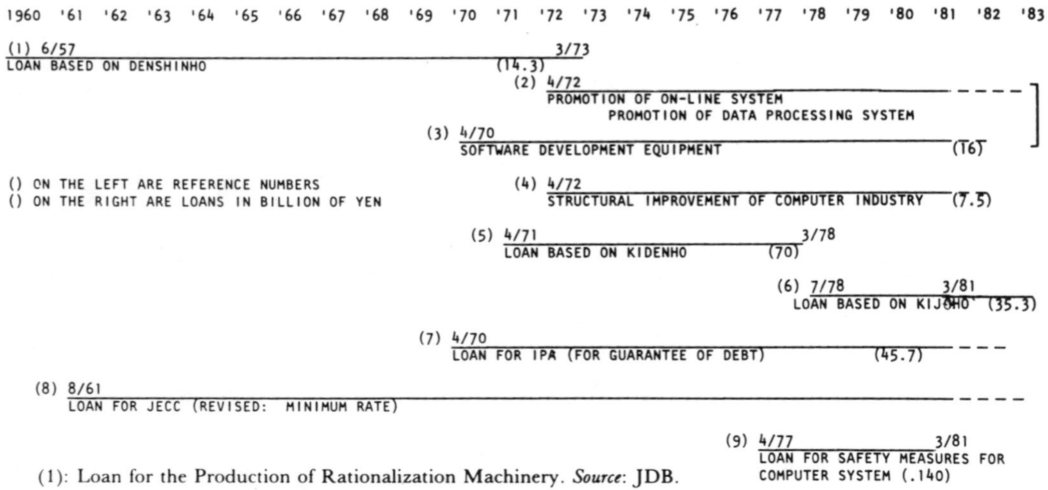

1960 '61 '62 '63 '64 '65 '66 '67 '68 '69 '70 '71 '72 '73 '74 '75 '76 '77 '78 '79 '80 '81 '82 '83

(1) 6/57
LOAN BASED ON DENSHINHO

(2) 4/72 3/73 (14.3)
PROMOTION OF ON-LINE SYSTEM
PROMOTION OF DATA PROCESSING SYSTEM

(3) 4/70
SOFTWARE DEVELOPMENT EQUIPMENT (16)

(4) 4/72
STRUCTURAL IMPROVEMENT OF COMPUTER INDUSTRY (7.5)

(5) 4/71 3/78
LOAN BASED ON KIDENHO (70)

(6) 7/78 3/81
LOAN BASED ON KIJOHO (35.3)

(7) 4/70
LOAN FOR IPA (FOR GUARANTEE OF DEBT) (45.7)

(8) 8/61
LOAN FOR JECC (REVISED: MINIMUM RATE)

(9) 4/77
LOAN FOR SAFETY MEASURES FOR
COMPUTER SYSTEM (.140)

( ) ON THE LEFT ARE REFERENCE NUMBERS
( ) ON THE RIGHT ARE LOANS IN BILLION OF YEN

(1): Loan for the Production of Rationalization Machinery. *Source:* JDB.

(2): &

(3): Software development and data processing systems are combined under the JDB's classification of "promotion of data processing." Both are ongoing loans, the total to date reported at ¥16 billion.

(4): This is an ongoing JDB loan.

(5): This is provided by the JDB and the Small Business Finance Corporation (SBFC). JDB loan totals ¥61.8 billion; SBFC totals ¥9.0 billion.

(6): Ongoing. This is provided by the JDB and SBFC, with JDB loans totaling ¥32.5 billion and SBFC totaling ¥2.8 billion.

(7): IPA loan is through the Industrial Bank of Japan, the Long-Term Credit Bank, and the Nippon Credit Bank. As of FY 1980, total loan amount was ¥45.7 billion.

(8): An accumulated JDB balance to date of ¥156.6 billion. With loans from other financial institutions, the total accumulated loan balance is ¥288.2 billion.

(9): This is a SBFC loan.

Sources: Various documents and discussions: IDB, IBI, LTCB, SBFC, MITI, and STA

Figure 5.9.

TAX MEASURES RELEVANT TO INFORMATION INDUSTRIES IN JAPAN

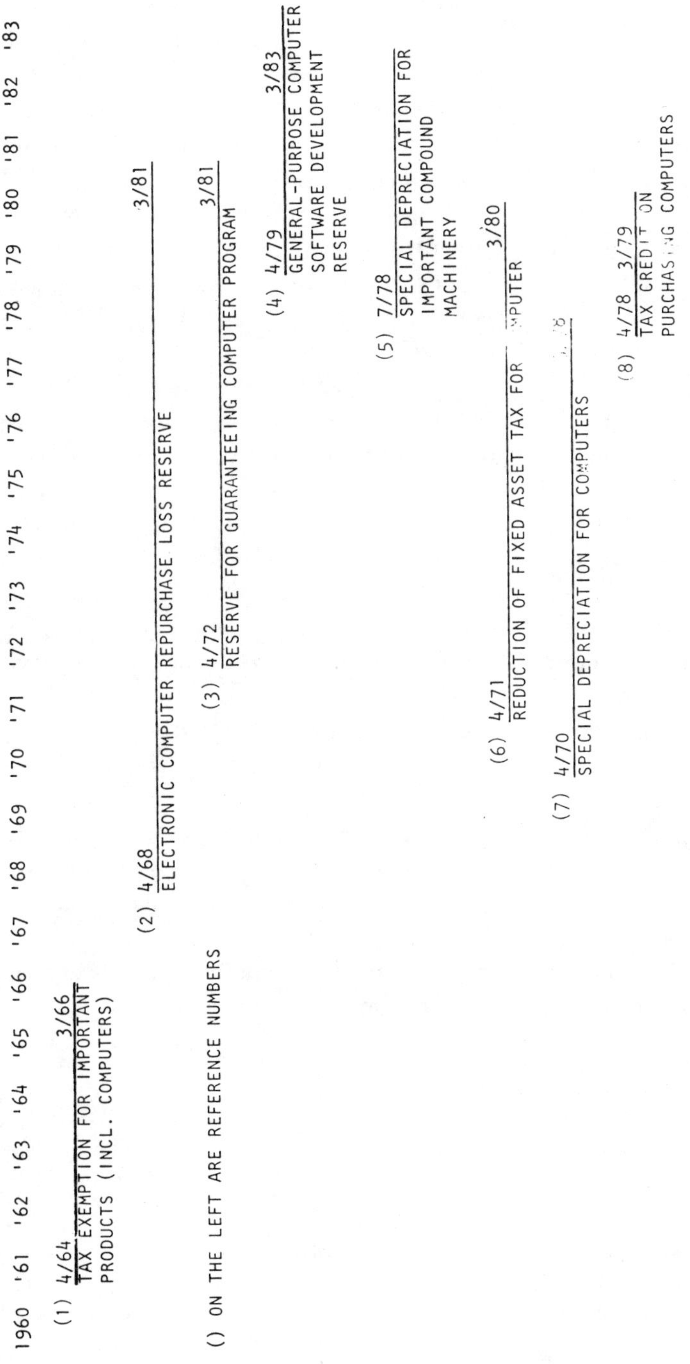

1960 '61 '62 '63 '64 '65 '66 '67 '68 '69 '70 '71 '72 '73 '74 '75 '76 '77 '78 '79 '80 '81 '82 '83

(1) 4/64 — 3/66
TAX EXEMPTION FOR IMPORTANT
PRODUCTS (INCL. COMPUTERS)

( ) ON THE LEFT ARE REFERENCE NUMBERS

(2) 4/68 — 3/81
ELECTRONIC COMPUTER REPURCHASE LOSS RESERVE

(3) 4/72 — 3/81
RESERVE FOR GUARANTEEING COMPUTER PROGRAM

(4) 4/79 — 3/83
GENERAL-PURPOSE COMPUTER
SOFTWARE DEVELOPMENT
RESERVE

(5) 7/78 —
SPECIAL DEPRECIATION FOR
IMPORTANT COMPOUND
MACHINERY

(6) 4/71 — 3/80
REDUCTION OF FIXED ASSET TAX FOR COMPUTER

(7) 4/70 —
SPECIAL DEPRECIATION FOR COMPUTERS

(8) 4/78 — 3/79
TAX CREDIT ON
PURCHASING COMPUTERS

To be eligible for conditional loans or consignment payments, private companies have to belong to a legally constituted nonprofit entity, either a research association (*kenkyū kumiai*) or a more generally defined nonprofit group (*zaidan hōjin*). Typically, the process works as follows: The government announces that it wants research conducted in a given area; in the case of the computer industry, the responsible agency is MITI. Interested firms submit proposals for review. Simultaneously, or sometimes consecutively, the individual firms try to agree among themselves on how they might work together. Once they achieve a working agreement, they announce that they want to form a research association. At that point, MITI officials select those firms that appear most able to contribute to the research under discussion, which in principle would be those that officials considered the most competitive in the field. The selected firms submit a proposal requesting authorization as a research association. After further negotiations with prospective members and verification of their financial solvency, the government grants authorization under the Industrial Technology Association Law (*Kōk-ōgyō gijutsu kumiai ho*).[38] The private sector can also initiate this process, in which case an industry's request serves as an impetus for government action. *Zaidan hōjin*, the more general category of nonprofit organizations that can also receive consignment payments for government-contracted research, are not restricted to doing only government work. They must remain nonprofit, however. These organizations are also under no obligation to divide revenue proportionately among participating companies; such allocations can be made at their discretion.[39] The extensive preliminary discussions involved in organizing joint public/private research projects through *kenkyū kumiai* or *zaidan hōjin*, together with an absence of published criteria and open bidding, carry the strong implication that by the time the government announces its intention to support a particular research project, the negotiation

---

38. For useful source material on the Industrial Technology Association Law, see Agency for Industrial Science and Technology, *Kenkyū kaihatsu josei seido riyō no tebiki* [*Guidebook on assistance measures for R & D*] (Tokyo: Kōgyō Gijutsuin [Agency for Industrial Science and Technology], 1980).

39. Like many recently established public lotteries in the United States, which raise funds that are then directed toward specific public purposes such as education, *zaidan hōjin* in Japan can receive money from such sources as motorcycle- or boat-racing funds.

process and selection of participating companies will more or less have been determined—at least in the sense that the most competitive firms already know they have a better-than-even chance of being selected for membership in the not-yet-sanctioned research association.[40]

Although this method of operation is a characteristic of Japanese government-supported projects, and can even be called a basic pattern under which public/private research projects are undertaken, the particular conditions governing which Japanese firms will participate, and under what terms, vary considerably. For this reason, apart from noting the obvious exclusion of foreign-based firms from public/private research projects in the past, only the most general comments can be made about the ground rules for current research projects. Nowadays, as attempts to insulate Japanese computer manufacturers from international competition come into conflict with domestic and international pressures for change, the ground rules for public/private research projects are also undergoing considerable change.[41]

Impact of Government Support to the Computer Industry

Even if one were able to separate the domestic conditions facing the Japanese computer industry from world market conditions, the sheer complexity of government support to the computer industry makes it difficult to measure the impact of this support. For one thing, as discussed in general terms in Chapter 3, the effects of government support can-

---

40. In a recent case involving the Biotechnology Association, for example, the process worked as follows: In November 1980, a Biotechnology Roundtable (*kondankai*) was held, at the industry's behest, in which five firms participated. They suggested that an association be formed. In July 1981, the five firms in the original round table, together with additional firms, officially announced that they wanted to form an association. In August, MITI announced that it wanted various biotechnology firms to submit proposals to undertake the biotechnology portion of the newly established New Materials Project. Shortly thereafter, the not-yet-officially-recognized Biotechnology Association, then composed of 14 companies, "won" a contract to undertake this research. In September the association was officially registered by MITI and officially awarded responsibility for the biotechnology portion of the New Materials Project.

41. Specific examples are discussed later in the chapter.

Table 5.4

LOANS BASED ON THE LAW ON TEMPORARY MEASURES FOR PROMOTION OF SPECIFIC MACHINERY AND INFORMATION INDUSTRIES AGAINST THE TOTAL FACILITY INVESTMENT IN MACHINERY INDUSTRIES

(In ¥ Billion)

	Investment Amount of Machinery Industry (annual average) (A)	Loan Amount Based on the Law by the Development Bank (annual average) (B)	B/A (percent)
1961–65	299	7.5	2.5
1966–70	588	8.4	1.4
1971–75	866	8.9	1.0
1976–79	1,146	9.2	0.8

Notes: Investment amount is on payment basis. The loan based on the law includes the loans made by *Kijōhō, Kidenhō*, and *Denshinhō*.

Source: Questionnaire on ''Plant and Equipment Investment Plans of Key Industries'' by the MITI, Japan Development Bank, 1980.

not readily be separated from the effects of other nonquantifiable factors whose effects may also be considerable; some government effects can be explicitly valued, whereas others are implied or indirect. More specifically, although the monetary value of various subsidies, loans, and tax benefits can be quantified, this would not reflect the full value of government support. In the case of the computer industry, as Table 5.4 shows, recent JDB loans to the machinery and information industries, based on the *Kijōhō, Kidenhō*, and *Denshinhō*, have been extremely small as a percentage of total investment (roughly 0.8 percent) and no more than 2.5 percent of total investment even at the height of infant-industry encouragement in the early 1960s.[42] Yet the total impact of government support has surely been greater than these numbers suggest. Certainly in the early years of the industry's development,

---

42. Data for Table 5.4 were supplied by MITI from an internal document and could not be independently verified. However, even if the percentage figures considerably understate the value of direct government support, the amount of such support would still be small, relative to total investment.

such loans and other direct support were widely interpreted as a signal that still broader, indirect support would also be forthcoming; these indirect effects cannot be quantified.

Indeed, if it were possible to evaluate the relative value of direct and indirect effects of government support, the latter would likely be just as advantageous as the former. In the case of JDB loans, for example, the amount of the loan itself is by most accounts a less important aid to industry than the implications that JDB approval will enable a firm to obtain more sizable commercial loans quickly and on generally favorable terms. Typically, once the JDB has analyzed and approved loans to a particular company producing a given new technology or process, that company is then "cleared" for commercial lending simply because the JDB's technical and credit review procedures are considered highly rigorous. Moreover, JDB support is often assumed to imply that further government financial backing would be forthcoming in the event the new technology or process in question were to encounter unexpected difficulties—although this assumption has never been tested on a large scale.

The kind of signaling implied by Japanese government support to the computer industry worked particularly well when economy and industry were in a catch-up phase. Such signals could be clearly formulated because the future direction of the industry was more or less clear. But the investor confidence that such signals seek to inspire is much more difficult to generate after an economy has reached the frontier of industrial development and its future direction is therefore inherently less clear than before. Moreover, during Japan's catch-up phase—roughly the first 25 to 30 years after World War II—both foreign-based competitors and the governments of Japan's major trading partners were willing to tolerate Japanese government support to domestic industries in general and to the infant computer industry in particular. Once the Japanese economy and computer industry became noticeably more competitive, such international tolerance obviously waned.

In retrospect, by explicitly linking scientific and technological development with industrial development, the Japanese government helped to create a political and economic environment that has encouraged investment and research in new technologies. This general commitment to scientific and technological development has been supported by more specific policies aimed at fostering priority areas. For more than a decade now, the government has sought to foster an environment that promotes continued economic growth through "knowledge-intensive industries.'' The government has also seen its own role as that of a facilitator, encouraging collaborative research among otherwise competitive firms and providing inducements in the form of matching grants, loans, or indirect financial support to encourage such collaboration. This pattern of government involvement in technological development—as a supplement to, rather than determinant of, private sector efforts—is almost certain to continue in some form. MITI officials have suggested, for example, that a new overall basis for government support of a variety of new technologies (including biotechnologies and new materials, as well as computers and electronics) will be drawn up in 1985 and presented to the Diet as a bill to replace the *Kijōhō*, which expires in July 1985. They have also broached the idea of a so-called Small Business New Technology Promotion Law, designed specifically to promote high-technology ventures through provisions for targeted tax-free reserves similar to those discussed in Chapter 3. But, again, such support is likely to be less important than it was in the past, in part because much new R & D is being undertaken by companies themselves whether or not the government provides special support.

DISCRIMINATION AGAINST FOREIGN COMPANIES

Japanese government support for new industries, and particularly for the computer industry, has included explicit as well as implicit discrimination against foreign-based computer manufacturers. Here, too, however, no overall measurement of the degree of discrimination is possible. Explicit discrimination against foreign firms, stipulated in law, has declined in recent years. But vestiges of Japan's earlier system of infant-industry protection for the computer industry remain strong.

The process by which a firm or a group of firms become eligible for government support, either through conditional loans, contract work, or selection for participation in research associations, continues to have at least an implicit antiforeign bias. The high degree of ''off-the-record'' communication among Japanese firms seeking to participate in collaborative public/private research projects makes it difficult for foreign firms to engage in this process. Unless—and in some cases even when—foreign-based firms have a strong presence in Japan, years of experience building channels of communication, and a recognized competitive capability, it is still difficult to fit into long-established patterns of treating foreign-based firms as outsiders.

Many questions about both explicit and implicit discrimination in Japanese government support for the computer industry arose in the landmark project to develop VLSIs in the mid-1970s. Here the specific issue concerned the ways in which patent rights were to be distributed. A report published by the Ways and Means Committee of the U.S. House of Representatives described the VLSI project as follows:

> The most famous and controversial project since liberalization has been NTT's and MITI's collaboration in large-scale integrated circuits [VLSI]. In April 1975, NTT formed a LSI group with Hitachi, Fujitsu, and NEC at a cost of ¥20 billion to maintain telecommunications at a high level. Once the project was underway, MITI proposed consolidating NTT's efforts with MITI's own research, which was then conducted jointly with five major manufacturers at MITI's Electro-Technical Laboratory. Initially, NTT rejected the idea, primarily because it was reluctant to alter its telecommunications research to suit the more general needs of computer development. Nevertheless, on July 15, 1975, MITI and NTT agreed that part of the two efforts could be joined. In March 1976, the VLSI Technology Research Association was formed and commenced a four-year program with a budget of ¥70 billion. Basic research was conducted at the joint laboratory of the association, while the Joint Computer Development Laboratory and the Information Systems Laboratory took responsibility for applied research.[43]

By most standards, the VLSI program can be considered a success, producing more than 600 patents and processes and demonstrating that private corporations could work under the umbrella of a research association and with the technical and financial support of the government. As this success became evident, U.S. officials began to argue that the VLSI program was giving unfair advantages to Japanese computer manufacturers since (1) patents were distributed, at least initially, only to those companies participating in the research association and (2) foreign-based firms were excluded from participating in such associations and thereby gaining access to their patents.[44] Perhaps out of fear

---

43. Subcommittee on Trade, *High Technology and Japanese Industrial Policy*, p. 14.

44. IBM-Japan was also excluded, even though by law it is a Japanese company and maintains manufacturing facilities in Japan.

of U.S. retaliation, MITI altered its position in 1979 and indicated that it would license patents developed by government researchers to foreign as well as domestic firms and that patents owned by the VLSI Technology Association would also be made available to foreign firms. In late 1982, MITI announced that it would review the entire subsidy system and study how and under what conditions foreign firms could be eligible for consignment payments and how in practical terms a foreign firm could join a research association. Nonetheless, considerable ambiguity remains about the access actually available to foreign-based firms—if not in the specific joint R & D projects cited above, at least in other computer-related activities.[45]

---

45. One example of explicit discrimination against foreign firms that remains on the books is the Subsidy for R & D for Important Technologies (see Figure 5.7 and Table 5.3). Because the subsidy amounts are small, we will discuss it only briefly. Unlike other subsidies, funds in this program go directly to individual firms, and the statutes for the program expressly discriminate against foreign firms. The program dates back to 1950, when it was called the Subsidy for R & D for Manufacturing and Mining. Funds under this program have covered between 26 and 40 percent of the cost of a given project. As of FY 1980, ¥ 46.4 billion ($211 million at ¥ 220 = $1) had been allocated to 4,284 applicants, or an average of ¥10.8 million per applicant ($49,090 at ¥ 220 = $1). Funding is provided under the following five general categories: (1) "virgin" and innovative research, (2) applied research, (3) industrial research, (4) prototype machinery, and (5) research for commercialization. All resulting patents belong to the individual applicant (that is, the firm) except in category 5, which, because it applies only to research on environmental control and safety, is considered in the public interest. In all categories, the company must repay some or all of the funds it receives, depending on the degree of success of the project. The statute notes (in Section 2.4.2) that "anyone" is eligible for support except:

1. A company that is in the process of reorganization, and whose reorganization has not been officially accepted by a court of justice;

2. A person who does not have Japanese residence or a person who does not have Japanese citizenship:

3. A corporation or organization whose by-laws are based on foreign laws, or whose headquarters are located outside of Japan;

As recently as December 1983, proposals for new legislation on software development, prepared by a subcommittee of the Industrial Structure Council, led U.S. business representatives and government officials to protest vigorously against what they considered unfair treatment. The draft legislation sought to alter Japanese copyright law (1) to reduce the ownership rights of software authors from 75 years to 15 years; (2) to establish a registration system, similar to one that exists for patents, that would also require compulsory licensing to other software firms when MITI officials judged this to be in the "public interest"; and (3) to require additional disclosure of the details in software programs, ostensibly to assist customers in understanding the capabilities of the product. Because Japanese software is widely considered to be behind that produced in the United States, IBM and other U.S.-based firms objected to the proposed new law, particularly to the compulsory licensing clause, arguing that it would provide MITI officials with wide discretionary powers to order licensing if they decided that the development of a particular item of software had too much of a competitive advantage. In other words, U.S.-based firms feared that the proposed new law would be used to strip them of software rights whenever comparable Japanese software programs did not exist. U.S. officials also argued that the draft law, if passed by the Diet, would violate two international agreements that Japan had signed—the Berne and the Universal Copyright conventions. Meanwhile, the Cultural Affairs Bureau of the Ministry of Education also objected to the draft legislation, contending that it, not MITI, had administrative responsibility for the protection of copyrights; it saw the Industrial Structure Council's proposal as an attempt by MITI to encroach on its turf. Accordingly, Ministry of Education officials prepared alternative legislation and opened negotiations with MITI that proved unsuccessful, at which point various LDP politicians interceded to try to defuse the issue. In the spring of 1984, under pressure of the U.S. government, U.S.-based firms, and the Ministry of Education, MITI decided to shelve the pro-

---

4. A corporation or organization that is controlled by persons or organizations mentioned in (2) or (3) above.

See Agency for Industrial Development and Technology, *Kenkyū kaihatsu josei seidō* [Subsidy system for research and development of important technologies](Tokyo: AIST, 1980).

posed legislation. For the time being, software-related legislation is on hold.

While recent changes in government policy in the wake of the VLSI case have provided for some degree of liberalization of the ground rules affecting the treatment of foreign-based firms in computers and related new technologies, the system of government-industry cooperation appears to retain significant discriminatory biases. The recurrence of proposals such as those made in the recent software case contributes to a perception in the United States that despite Japanese claims that the economy is now open to foreigners, the Japanese government will continue to try to introduce discriminatory policies whenever it can get away with them.[46]

To date there has been no direct foreign participation in any completed public/private R & D project. Historically, the obvious reason for this is that such government-financed projects as FONTAC, VLSI, and the Fourth Generation Computer Subsidy were specifically designed to help domestic firms compete with foreign manufacturers, notably IBM. At the same time, from the foreign firms' perspective, depending on who was sharing what with whom, participation in such projects and/or other technology-sharing arrangements could prove more disadvantageous than advantageous. Although some foreign firms have at times been vociferous in their criticism of Japanese government support for high-technology industries, it is not clear how much of a head start Japanese companies receive from participating in joint public/private research projects. On the one hand, all firms—Japanese or foreign—want government support for the development of new technologies if such support would improve their competitiveness. On the other hand, foreign firms naturally wonder whether participation in Japanese government–supported R & D projects would actually be disadvantageous if it required them to "share" technologies or production processes with Japanese competitors in much the same way that Japanese firms have shared technologies or collaborated in joint projects.

---

46. As discussed below, at the same time that MITI was being criticized for the discriminatory nature of the proposed software legislation, it was criticizing the Ministry of Posts and Telecommunications for trying to preserve a telecommunications system that discriminates against some Japanese as well as foreign-based telecommunications manufacturers.

However, the degree to which such sharing occurs even among Japanese firms is itself unclear.

For these reasons, only the most general conclusions are possible about either the technological advantages of participation in joint public/private projects or the "true" desires of foreign firms with regard to participation in such projects. It is not at all clear, on an *a priori* basis, that the most competitive U.S.-based firms actually want to participate in Japanese joint public/private projects. It is clear (1) that U.S.-based firms do not know the extent to which technology sharing actually occurs among participating Japanese firms, (2) that they do want to be allowed to participate in joint public/private R & D projects if they decide they would gain from doing so, and (3) that they feel they are entitled to participate as a matter of right under the letter and spirit of agreements governing the international trading system since World War II. Moreover, U.S.-based firms also feel they are entitled to access to the technologies and processes that result from Japanese public/private R & D projects.

In concrete terms, decisions on whether to participate in joint R & D projects depend on the quality of the research design, the diffusion of technology and know-how that is likely to occur as a result of such research, and the extent to which collaborative efforts would improve on individual efforts.[47] Japanese-style collaborative research was designed mainly to develop new technologies or processes for Japan-based firms. Until recently, this process was clearly part of a larger effort to catch up to technological levels previously achieved in other advanced industrial countries. Yet it must be left to technical experts and to the top management of individual firms to decide, on a case-by-case basis, whether participation in collaborative projects would likely yield technical know-how and hands-on experience that in turn would give

---

47. The technological benefits of collaborative research in frontier areas, not to mention the economic benefits for an individual firm, are highly uncertain in both the United States and Japan. Six major U.S.-based information processing manufacturers—American Telephone and Telegraph (AT&T), IBM, ITT, Texas Instruments, Xerox, and Burroughs—have declined to participate in a new U.S.-based collaborative R & D consortium, the Microelectronics and Computer Technology Corporation (MCC); 18 firms, including United Technologies, RCA, Control Data, and Motorola, are participating.

participants distinct advantages. In some cases, participation may provide a competitive advantage; in other cases, it may well not.

As Japanese firms reach a technological frontier, foreign participation in various activities involving new technologies in Japan, particularly a much increased level of manufacturing activity, an intensified search for joint venture arrangements, and a concurrent increase in cross licensing of new technologies, is likely to become much more attractive than in the past to *both* Japan-based and foreign-based firms. Japan-based firms are increasingly likely to recognize their need to sell new products abroad as well as at home and a corresponding need to avoid stimulating protectionist policies among Japan's trading partners. To do this, Japan-based firms specializing in new technologies will need to permit, and even encourage, foreign-based firms to participate in the Japanese domestic market in various ways. To some degree such changes are already discernible. For example, since 1981 the Japanese government has indicated that foreign-based firms can be included in most government-sponsored R & D projects if they wish and if they meet otherwise objective eligibility criteria. As an indication of this change in policy, the government sought foreign participation in the Fifth Generation Computer Project, begun in 1981.[48] In the early stages of the project, MITI sponsored a Fifth Generation Computer Conference in October 1981, which brought together more than 300 participants from seven countries.[49] However, the extent to which foreign-based fims will come to participate in the project—or want to participate—is still unclear.

Japanese government support to the computer industry has clearly facilitated its development to date. As argued above, the government created a policy environment that encouraged private sector investment,

---

48. The much-publicized Fifth Generation Computer Project has been organized around the following themes: basic application systems, basic software systems, new advanced architecture, distributed function architecture, VLSI technology, systemization technology, and development of supporting technology. Total capitalization for the project is expected to exceed ¥100 billion ($454 million at ¥ 220 = $1) over a period of ten years. See Tohru Motooka, "Challenge for Knowledge Information Processing Systems" (Keynote speech at the Fifth Generation Computer Conference, Toyko, October 1981).

49. A follow-up conference was held in November 1984 to report on results to date, and solicit still newer ideas.

both in general and in specific areas. In many areas, government support for further investment in new technologies has been narrowly targeted, with clear and positive incentives in favor of Japan-based firms and a discriminatory bias against foreign-based firms. It is also clear, however, that the actual amount of government funds allocated to the development of new technologies has, on average, been small, relative to the total amount of funds invested. Moreover, as the above discussion of discriminatory practices suggests, while Japanese government support for technological development could once be considered a domestic issue, this is no longer the case. Now that Japan-based firms are competitive with foreign-based firms in many areas of the computer and related electronics industries, foreign governments and foreign corporations are watching developments in Japan closely. In this sense, the Japanese market and the policy environment in Japan have become more open without any changes in Japanese laws, and the costs to the Japanese government and Japanese firms of practices that violate either the letter or the spirit of established international commercial norms have clearly increased.[50]

An important implication of these developments, and one that we discuss at greater length in Chapter 7, is that over time and relative to Japan's own past the Japanese government has become less able by itself to call the shots as to the kinds of technologies that will be developed and the degree to which new technologies can be developed by Japan-based firms at the expense of foreign-based firms. As the following section shows, competitive pressures, not government industrial policies, are increasingly important in determining the future structure of the Japanese economy and future developments in Japan's computer and related electronics industries.

MARKET PRESSURES ON NEW INDUSTRIES

As in the United States and in part because of developments there, tech-

---

50. The out-of-court settlements reached in suits filed in 1982 by IBM against Hitachi, Mitsubishi, and US-based National Semiconductor Corporation over the alleged theft of IBM software illustrate the increased costs of practices that may go against international commercial norms, whatever the nationality of a firm's head office.

nological change is both blurring distinctions between and among traditional industries and calling into question the traditional distinction
between basic and applied research. The computer and telecommunications industries, for example, are rapidly merging into a new and
much broader information processing industry.[51] The many changes
now taking place in the information processing industry also illustrate a more general point: Innovations come almost by definition
from a multitude of sources, and some decentralization of efforts is a
necessary (though of course not sufficient) condition for successful innovation. A central body, whether in the public or the private sector,
can play an important role in scientific and technological development.
By establishing long-range goals and marshaling large-scale resources,
it can channel individual efforts toward these larger objectives. It cannot, however, ensure the success of any particular R & D effort in advance even when commiting more money to one or another effort.
"Picking winners," to use a phrase that is often suggested as a goal for
a government's industrial policy, is at best difficult and normally impossible to do in a precise way—even for profit-seeking firms, let alone
for policymakers or legislators. Indeed, in an era of rapid technological change, even people directly involved in R & D are reluctant to
"predict" which products are likely to prove decisive in the marketplace. Consequently, the once-considerable emphasis on the importance
of basic research, relative to applied research, as a means of ensuring
competitiveness is being widely questioned. As discussed below, government officials, industry executives, and academics in both Japan and
the United States are intensively reexamining various factors usually

---

51. Nowadays, computers can be adapted to transmit the information
they process across vast distances, thereby incorporating capabilities that traditionally lay in telecommunications; the latter, meanwhile, rely increasingly on
computer-based technologies. Thus, information processing includes, besides
the processing of data within a single computer: (1) data transmission (that is,
the movement of information processed in a computer or telecommunications
device in one location to a computer, terminal, or telecommunications device
in another location); (2) the application of artificial intelligence capabilities
(that is, the incorporation of pattern recognition and logical reasoning in
machines, such as some robotics and expert systems); and (3) interactive en-
tertainment and educational systems (for example, video games and teaching
machines).

thought to contribute to long-term productivity growth and trying to assess which of these contribute most to international competitiveness.

The effects of technological change and market pressure on information processing are clearly evident in recent moves to reorganize the Japanese telecommunications industry. Where telecommunications has been seen—and until recently correctly so—as an "essential" product for which demand was relatively inelastic (that is, rising steadily with income but not spectacularly), sophisticated forms of information processing are rapidly becoming discretionary products or services for which demand is increasingly elastic. Because the development and marketing of telecommunications systems is increasingly being driven by entrepreneurial factors, the pace of change has become so rapid that firms must adapt more quickly than traditional regulatory processes have encouraged or allowed.

The Example of NTT

The Nippon Telegraph and Telephone (NTT) Public Corporation, a quasi-public monopoly nominally controlled by the Ministry of Posts and Telecommunications (MPT), is in the process of becoming privately owned and concurrently divided into a number of companies operating in different parts of the overall information processing market. With annual purchases of approximately $3 billion, NTT in its current or future configuration is likely to continue to be a major force in the development of Japan's information processing industry.

Because of its monopoly position in domestic telecommunications, NTT became the second largest telephone company in the world, after the American Telephone & Telegraph Company (AT&T). Yet in contrast to the pre-1983 configuration at AT&T, NTT has no shareholders to whom it is responsible, and the MPT, while establishing areas of business within which NTT could operate, has not regulated its activities as strictly as the U.S. Federal Communications Commission (FCC) has regulated AT&T and the rest of the U.S. telecommunications industry. Also in contrast to the "old" AT&T, which manufactured most U.S. telecommunications equipment as well as providing telecommunications services, NTT has not had its own manufacturing facilities. Instead it has contracted for equipment purchases from major Japanese electronic companies, mainly Fujitsu, Hitachi, NEC, and Oki, known collectively as the "NTT family." NTT has operated four research laboratories, which have a considerable R & D budget ($390 million in 1983) and employ approximately 3,000 engineers.[52] Numerous NTT officials have "retired" into senior management positions in these companies. NTT scientists and engineers have worked with various private firms on a number of major joint public/private computer projects—such as the early phase of the VLSI project and the Fourth Generation Computer Project.

After World War II, NTT officials saw their primary mission as one of establishing a telecommunications infrastructure throughout the country. Toward this end, telephone subscribers, both business and residential, were required to pay a substantial one-time fee, in the form of "telephone bonds," to establish service; revenue from the sale of these bonds was then used to finance the expansion of the system. Installation charges were set at a higher rate for residences than for businesses on grounds that a home phone was a "luxury," whereas telephoning from a business location contributed more to overall economic development. Slowly but steadily, the desired infrastructure, including a nationwide direct dialing network, was put in place, and the number of telephones per capita reached levels comparable with other advanced industrial countries.

Procurement of telecomunications equipment was entirely from domestic sources until the late 1970s, when international (notably U.S.) pressure for liberalization led to significant revisions in NTT policies—as seen in the Government Procurement Code under the Tokyo Round of the Multilateral Trade Negotiations and in a bilateral U.S.-Japan NTT agreement.[53] As NTT began to implement its obligations under

---

52. See U.S. International Trade Commission, *Foreign Industrial Targeting and its Effects on U.S. Industries, Phase I* (Washington, D.C., ITC Publication no. 1437, October 1983), p. 111.

53. As part of the Tokyo Round agreement, procurement of off-line telecommunications equipment such as private branch exchanges (PBXs), facsimilies, and off-line computers was liberalized. In the U.S.-Japan Agreement, a three-track criteria for liberalization of procurement practices was established. Track I applies to all NTT purchases of off-line telecommunications equipment, and this provision will be made available to all signatories of the Tokyo Round Government Procurement Code. Track II refers to mainline telecommunications equipment available in the market and suitable to NTT requirements. Track III refers to mainline equipment that in NTT's opinion is not viable in the marketplace and requires development specifically for, or in

the latter agreement in January 1981, purchases from U.S.-based firms amounted to $15 million in 1981 and increased to $40 million in 1982 and $140 million in 1983. More than 30 foreign-based companies, including ITT, Rolm, General Electric, Northern Telecom, Memorex, and Motorola, among others, became designated equipment suppliers for NTT.[54] NTT has taken various additional measures to open NTT procurement to foreigners—that is, applications are now accepted in English and through the New York as well as Tokyo office.

Beginning in late 1981, some NTT officials began to argue that the sheer size of NTT was making it too unwieldy for the new conditions influencing the information processing industry. Many came to feel that NTT's monopoly position in data transmission had contributed to Japan's being considerably behind the United States in this particular aspect of information processing. Innovation was admittedly being impeded by the regulated environment; the close ties between NTT personnel, on the one hand, and both the manufacturing companies and the MPT, on the other hand, meant that few contrary views surfaced to challenge established plans. With the achievement of considerable reduction in waiting lists for telephone installation and concomitant growth in demand for leased circuits capable of handling new data transmission services, the underlying rationale for a monopoly structure in telecommunications became increasingly mechanistic and obsolete.

---

cooperation with, NTT. Among foreign-based companies, only U.S.-based firms are allowed to bid on contracts in Tracks II and III. For further details on the Government Procurement Code and the U.S.-Japan NTT Agreement, see U.S. Congress, Subcommittee on Trade of the Committee on Ways and Means and the United States–Japan Trade Task Force, *Report on United States-Japan Trade 26,* Committee Print no. 96–68, 96th Cong., 2d sess., 1980; *Agreement on Government Procurement,* April 12, 1979, reprinted in U.S. Congress, House, *Agreements Reached in the Tokyo Round of Multilateral Trade Negotiations,* 96th Cong., 1st sess., 1979, H. Rept. 153, pt. 1:167–189; *Agreement on Procurement in Telecommunications,* December 19, 1980, United States–Japan, T.I.A.S. no. 9961; U.S., General Accounting Office, *Assessment of Bilateral Communications Agreements with Japan* (Washington, D.C.: GAO, October 7, 1983); and Chalmers Johnson, *Japan's Public Policy Companies* (Washington, D.C., and Stanford, Calif.: American Enterprise Institute for Public Policy Research and Hoover Institution on War, Revolution and Peace, 1978).

54. "Japan's Telecommunications Industry—Present and Future," *Prudential Bache Securities,* May 1983, p. 21.

In response to these developments, the Public Electric Communications Law was revised in 1982 to allow private companies to lease telephone lines for use in providing some data transmission services. This constituted a major step in the direction of relaxing restrictions on joint usage of communications circuits previously monopolized by NTT. Message switching by common carriers (that is, public communications circuits) remained restricted to NTT, but interconnections between public and leased circuits were also deregulated.[55]

Additional changes in the industry were accelerated by the recommendations of the Ad Hoc Commission on Administrative Reform in July 1982. This commission proposed that NTT be reorganized into a private company—astually into a central company and several independent regional companies. Essentially, it argued that the time had come for Japan to allow more competition in telecommunications, if only because it had little choice if it wanted to keep up with new developments in the world market. The commission, headed by Toshio Doko, a former chairman of Keidanren (the Federation of Economic Organizations), had been set up as part of then Prime Minister Zenko Suzuki's campaign to reduce government's administrative expenses as a way of lessening the debt burden. For different reasons, its proposals on NTT had the strong support of both the MOF and MITI—support that had the effect of forcing the hand of the MPT. As noted above, world market pressures, particularly deregulation of the U.S. telecommunications market, were causing Japanese as well as foreign-based firms to push for deregulation in Japan. Requests for liberalization by Japanese as well as foreign-based firms also created pressures for privatization. For its part, the MOF supported the commission's proposal for privatization because this course of action offered a way to raise significant new revenue for the treasury through the sale of NTT stock to private investors. MITI had two reasons to favor the commission's

---

55. For a useful summary of these and earlier developments, see Tetsuro Tomita, ''Japan's Experience of Monopoly and Competition in the Field of Telecommunications Policy'' (Presentation to the Committee for Information, Computer and Communication Policy, Special Session on the International Implications of Changing Market Structures in Telecommunication Services, Organisation for Economic Co-operation and Development, Paris, December 13–15, 1982). Tomita spoke in his capacity as deputy director general of the Telecommunications Policy Bureau, MPT.

proposals on NTT: it had long believed that competition among domestic computer manufacturers accelerated the development of the computer industry and that such competition was now needed in telecommunications; moreover, MITI was then, and is still, seeking administrative responsibility for all of information processing, including telecommunications.

Since 1982, various Japanese and foreign-based firms have been clamoring to introduce new data services to the Japanese market. Among the first was IBM-Japan. In July 1983 it made known a plan to provide value-added network services (so-called VANs) (that is, on-line data transmission services through a computer network) to small- and medium-sized companies. The idea was to process, on *its* own network, data transactions between a large retailer (the Tokyu supermarket chain, with 75 stores nationwide) and some 200 wholesalers and manufacturers. This move startled other companies, both the Japan-based computer and electronics manufacturers and Tokyu's retailing competitors. Many Japanese were suddenly fearful that the sophisticated capabilities and experiences of foreign-based firms like IBM, which had a already developed large-scale data networks outside of Japan, would in turn lead to foreign domination of VANs within Japan. Doubtless under pressure from the Japanese government (especially the MPT), IBM-Japan decided against pursuing this particular venture until the MPT had completed the drafting of, and the Diet had approved, a new law on VANs.

IBM-Japan's aggressive efforts in other areas continued, however. Also in the summer of 1983, it revealed a plan to launch a credit data communications service, called Credit Authorization Terminal Network (CATNET), designed to serve independent consumer credit companies. NTT officials were apparently dismayed by this initiative, seeing in it the capability to compete directly with a similar service, called Credit and Finance Information Switch System (CAFSIS), planned by NTT. As in the VANs case, NTT argued that IBM-Japan's credit network would produce "confusion" in the industry and threaten Japan's "telecommunications sovereignty." A compromise ensued under which IBM-Japan's proposed system would be connected, as an individual network, to the overall NTT system. In the fall of 1983, IBM-Japan concluded a partnership with Mitsubishi Corporation, Japan's largest trading company, and COSMO 80, a newly established software developer and distributor. Two joint ventures, a marketing company and an R & D firm, were formed to provide future data services linked to a new

NTT project, called Information Network System (INS). The INS project seeks to provide digital interactive videotext services, a video response system (VRS), a digital facsimile storage capability, and a voice storage service, among other things, through new nationwide optical fiber trunk lines. In response to these IBM-based initiatives, major Japan-based computer and electronics companies are actively trying to introduce competitive alternatives. In April 1984, Fujitsu announced that it was planning to introduce a large-scale VANs capability in 1985. As a first step, it will build a ¥20 billion intracompany integrated digital network. Meanwhile, NEC and Hitachi announced similar plans. A group led by Kyocera (and including Sony, Mitsubishi, and Ushio Electric) announced plans to enter the market from scratch by forming a so-called Daini Dendensha (literally "second telephone/telegraph company") specializing in VANs. The deficit-ridden Japan National Railways is considering plans to lay optical fiber cables along its track bed in hopes thereby of operating a new and profitable VAN service. The Japan Highway Corporation, which builds and maintains express highways, has similar plans.

These various competitive pressures on NTT and the MPT are forcing both to redefine their activities. As of now, NTT remains Japan's common carrier, and message switching remains under NTT's jurisdiction. However, VANs, videotext receivers, and other telecommunication services are subject to continuing controversy, both within Japan and between Japan and its trading partners, especially the United States. The international controversy stimulated by the MPT's draft legislation on VANs in late 1983 illustrates the kinds of ambiguity that can easily arise in an environment in which technological change is outpacing regulatory change. In late 1983 the MPT revealed draft legislation that barred companies with 50 percent or more foreign ownership from offering nationwide, large-scale data networks—that is, VANs. Japanese government officials hinted that such measures were needed to prevent IBM-Japan and AT&T from taking over this lucrative and still developing market in Japan.[56] U.S. government officials and U.S. computer and telecommunications manufacturers were quick to object to this draft legislation, arguing that such moves

---

56. See Christopher J. Chipello, "Japan Ministers Clash Over NTT's Future," *Asian Wall Street Journal*, March 2-3, 1984, p. 1.

by the MPT were protectionist, discriminatory, and contrary to the spirit of the U.S.-Japan NTT agreement and Japan's overall trade policies in the direction of increased openness. These arguments were supported by MITI, which, as discussed above, had long felt that competition would spur the further development of the information processing industry. MITI officials argued that enhanced data transmission services, such as those provided in VANs, should be considered outside the scope of existing regulations on basic transmission services. Not surprisingly, the MPT took the opposite approach, consistent with its own desire to retain control over as much of the burgeoning information processing industry as possible. MITI, at a time when its own Industrial Structure Council was recommending restrictive legislation on the ownership of software, was in this case favoring more openness— doubtless because it involved an area under the jurisdiction of another ministry. In April 1984, after much internal negotiation and considerable foreign pressure, compromise legislation was put forth that proposed a reorganization of NTT itself as well as new regulations governing VANs.

Under this compromise, NTT will remain government owned for the time being. In 1985 it will become a private company whose shares will be owned by the government, similar to Japan's international telecommunication monopoly, Kokusai Denshin Denwa (KDD). After several years—exactly how many is unspecified—as much as 49 percent of NTT's stock will be offered for sale to the public, although foreign investors will probably be prevented from purchasing these. Japan's telecommunications industry will then be divided into two main categories: common carriers (that is, companies that own public communication circuits) and companies that provide leased circuits. This latter category will be further divided into those companies that provide services in specified geographical areas and those firms that offer nationwide services. The geographically restricted firms will theoretically be unregulated, whereas firms that seek to provide nationwide services will have to register with the MPT—a process that some fear will amount to licensing. The draft legislation eliminates all mention of restrictions on foreign capital participation; in this sense, it eliminates explicit discrimination. It does not, however, spell out the procedures by which companies register with the MPT. These will be delineated later in ordinances drawn up by the Cabinet and the MPT.

Clearly, future patterns in Japan's telecommunications system will differ radically from past patterns. Technological changes—specifically the bringing together of computers and telecommunications—have already forced NTT to yield its previous monopoly position over domestic data transmission. International data transmission by definition involves more than one supplier. Foreign-based information processing firms and foreign telecommunications authorities are certain to seek a larger share of Japan's international communications market than they have either sought or been granted in the past. The ground rules under which such competition will occur are clearly still evolving, with many of the specific terms subject to case-by-case negotiation. In the recent U.S.-Japan controversies involving ownership of software and the provision of VANs, U.S. government officials added their voices to what U.S.-based firms saw as discriminatory measures governing future competition—at one point even making presentations before an LDP Subcommittee on Commerce and Industry, roughly comparable with appearances before congressional hearings in the U.S. system but previously a venue thought to be out of bounds to foreigners. The forceful presentation of U.S. government views doubtless influenced the terms of the revised draft legislation in both the software and VANs areas, although worldwide market pressures for further deregulation of information processing were weighted on the side of the U.S. arguments.

R & D and Innovation in New Industries

Now that Japanese firms have developed scientific and technological capabilities that in many areas have caught up with (or surpassed) those of other advanced industrial countries, speculation abounds—both in Japan and elsewhere—about whether Japanese will now be able to move into so-called original scientific and technological work, going beyond existing achievements. Actually, this question is as old as Japan's emergence from the isolation of the Tokugawa era. Since the late nineteenth century, Westerners and Japanese viewing Japan's success at industrialization and its unprecedented post–World War II growth rates have asked themselves whether Japanese are simply extremely skillful copiers, capable of catching up to almost any achievement of others, or whether they are also "original," meaning capable of contributing supposedly new ideas to the stock of human knowledge. Many Japanese as well as Western intellectuals, building on a Western-based distinction between *invention* and *innovation*, have argued that Japanese do best when operating within a given set of parameters, that is, innovating (or simply coping). Japanese do poorly, the argument runs, when they have to pick the parameters within which to operate, that is, inventing "entirely" new things or concepts.[57] Those who have applied or accepted a sharp distinction between *invention* and *innovation* also tend to argue that Japanese are much less skillful than Westerners at abstract conceptualization.[58] In short, the most generally accepted view of Japanese original-

---

57. The late Hideki Yukawa, Japan's first Nobel Prize winner, has been quoted by colleagues as having said that he did his best work while thinking in English, since the Japanese language, with its penchant for shadings rather than sharp distinctions, made it difficult to conduct scientific inquiry through hypothesis testing. Leo Esaki, a Japanese Nobelist who has subsequently worked for IBM and lived in the United States for more than 20 years, contends that Japanese society is too conformist to encourage true creativity. "Japanese culture," Esaki wrote in a *Yomiuri Shimbun* article, "is overly sentimental, too aesthetic, too intuitive and irrational. My fellow Japanese are obsessed with form and peripheral behavior without being able to get to the heart of the matter." See "Notable and Quotable," an excerpt from the original *Yomiuri* article as reprinted in the *Asian Wall Street Journal,* January 27, 1983. Makoto Kikuchi, director of the Sony Research Center, has written in a similar vein: "We Japanese are very strong in learning and understanding when we have a clear target in view, but perhaps not quite so strong when it comes to setting a new target or finding a new direction." For this reason, he went on, "papers by Western authors show a preference for a way of thinking and analysis related to fundamental principles, and Japanese researchers concentrate more on sophisticated, detailed approaches to existing problems." See Makoto Kikuchi, "Creativity and Ways of Thinking: The Japanese Style," *Physics Today,* September 1981, pp. 42–51

58. See, for example, observations made by Yukawa at a 1959 conference at the University of Hawaii and quoted in *Philosophy and Culture East and West* (1960), as cited in Richard W. Rabinowitz, "Law and the Social Process in Japan," in *Transactions of the Asiatic Society of Japan,* 3rd series, Vol. 10 (Tokyo, 1968), pp. 74–75. Rabinowitz, an American lawyer with many years of experience in Japan, has traced what he believes to be Japan's rejection of a legal system to Japanese methods of perception. He considers these basically aesthetic rather than cognitive. In his view, the reading of Chinese characters is more a matter of seeing their beauty on the page than the substance behind the thought itself. Rabinowitz argues that this characteristic of Japanese behavior gets in the way of the objectivity required in a Western-style legal system in which impersonal judgments are derived through abstract reasoning rather than through references to the experience at hand. See Rabinowitz, "Law," pp. 79–80.

ity, as articulated by Japanese and Westerners with varying degrees of argumentation and supporting evidence, accepts a sharp distinction between *parameters* and *variables* and between *invention* and *innovation*.

A newer view of Japanese capabilities for "original" achievements that is gaining support in Japan asserts that creativity can exist within the process of innovation.[59] Those who hold this view argue that there is considerable value in avoiding the rigidities of Western-style, black-and-white distinctions.[60] The notion that the potential for originality exists both in the process of inventing something "entirely new" and in the process of innovating from an existing base does seem to us a more useful way to think about the issue of originality as it affects business decisions than the traditionally sharp distinction between *invention* and *innovation*.

More concretely, the now-unquestioned ability of Japanese firms to become internationally competitive largely through innovations in applied research and product development has led many people to try to consider specifically the importance of basic versus applied research in the development of competitive advantages for individual firms. As discussed earlier in the chapter, the postwar Japanese emphasis on applied research continues to this day—albeit with some increase in both the level and share of basic research and a stated desire on the part of government officials and business executives for still further increases. There is, of course, no automatic relationship between the amount of funds allocated to basic research and the technological breakthroughs

---

59. Kikuchi distinguishes between "independent creativity," by which he refers to the traditional (that is, Western-based) ideas of a sudden inspiration of genius that provides a brand-new insight into the problem at hand, and "adaptive creativity," by which he refers to improvements on an already established base. "While I will always reject the argument that Japan only imitates other countries," Kikuchi writes, "it is nonetheless clear that Japanese creativity differs somewhat from the Western mode." See Makoto Kikuchi, *Japanese Electronics* (Tokyo: Simul Press, 1983), pp. 183, 185–186.

60. Kikuchi, for example, suggests that Japanese may be well-suited to work in future computer-related innovations precisely because they tend to avoid Western-style "yes-no" categories. He argues that Japanese methods of pattern recognition deemphasize logical, or sequential, thinking, which he sees as advantageous in going beyond the yes-no logic built into previous concepts of computer design. See Kikuchi, "Creativity and Ways of Thinking."

that can in turn give developers a dramatic competitive advantage. In other words, one cannot say that simply because aggregate figures show Japanese R & D to be concentrated more in applied than basic reasearch, Japanese firms will be either less or more successful over the long term than foreign-based firms that place greater emphasis on basic research. Nor can one conclude from this emphasis on applied versus basic research that Japan-based firms will necessarily be more or less able to achieve commercially valuable technological breakthroughs over the long term.

Nonetheless, future developments in new industries, both in Japan and the United States, will differ from past patterns in a number of important ways. Whether because of inventions or innovations, many Japan-based firms are now producing state-of-the-art technologies and products, particularly in computer and associated electronics industries. Foreign-based firms and foreign governments are now watching developments in Japan much more closely than before, not only because of a widely held view that Japanese firms still enjoy preferential government support and pursue discriminatory practices but, more important, because in many areas foreign firms and governments recognize that to remain competitive they must know much more about Japanese capabilities than they did in the past. In this sense, knowing what Japanese firms are trying to accomplish in their domestic market as well as abroad has become essential for U.S. business planning. By the same token, the ''splendid isolation'' within which Japanese firms were able to make their plans is becoming a thing of the past.

Previously, most Japanese firms in export-oriented industries, including computers and electronics, achieved their successes in large measure through the application of the so-called learning or experience curve, meaning the process of developing economies of scale and driving down unit prices. This strategy worked extremely well for Japanese manufacturing firms when cost advantages were the most important variable affecting competitiveness. It could also be successfully pursued when the international environment tolerated the infant-industry protection that usually accompanied this approach. Nowadays, the international environment is far less tolerant of infant-industry policies pursued by advanced countries. More important, in some growth sectors of the computer and electronics industries, especially in software development, *knowledge*, not cost of production, is the single most important variable affecting competitiveness. The challenge is to think creatively and to design new products and systems.

All executives in new industries are wrestling with the difficult problems associated with maintaining competitive advantage in an era of rapid technological change. In this context the importance of basic research, the kind of originality needed in both basic and applied research, and the scope of product development, as well as the role of government support for R & D, are the issues of the day. As should be evident in the discussion of the deregulation of NTT in an environment of rapid technological changes, both Japan- and U.S.-based information processing firms are trying to capitalize on their respective strengths and offset or compensate for their weaknesses. This has come to mean expanded cross trade and investment between the two countries. Japan-based firms are no longer simply following their traditional pattern of manufacturing only in Japan and then exporting products to the United States and other countries. Rather, such firms as Sony, NEC, and Fujitsu have established plants in the United States, not only as a base from which to expand production in the future in the event that protectionist barriers increase but also for the more positive reason of wanting to serve the U.S. market and absorb U.S.-based technological developments close at hand. These moves are a logical development in light of Japan's having caught up or surpassed other advanced industrial countries in terms of per capita income, productivity growth, technological levels, and so on. As noted in Chapter 2, when technological capabilities and wage levels between countries converge, relative to the past, the reasons for a firm based in one country to increase its sales and manufacturing capabilities in another stem increasingly from qualitative factors such as knowledge of and access to markets, specialization of production, and facilitation of delivery. For similar reasons, U.S.-based computer and electronics firms such as Intel, Motorola, Fairchild, and Cincinnati Milicron have bejun to establish or expand production facilities in Japan.[61]

In this environment of rapid technological change, increased competition from Japan-based firms, and increasing incentives for cross

---

61. Many U.S.-based firms appear to feel, with the wisdom of hindsight, that in the past they sold or licensed technologies to Japanese manufacturers too cheaply. Having realized this, they are now trying to be more careful about preserving whatever competitive advantages they may have or to build future advantages by investing in increased sales, distribution, and manufacturing facilities in Japan.

trade and investment between the United States and Japan, U.S.-based firms and the U.S. government also seem to be trying to identify various domestic barriers to competitiveness, whether found in the tax system, the regulatory environment, government support for R & D (or the lack of it), short-time horizons in investment planning, or wherever. Just as Japanese government and business leaders are asking whether Japan needs to put more emphasis on basic research, their American counterparts are asking whether the United States needs to put more emphasis on applied research and product development in addition to, or possibly in lieu of, the traditional U.S. emphasis on basic research. This desire to reduce impediments to competitiveness in new industries has stimulated interest in U.S.-based cooperative R & D programs, as well as various efforts to reduce the antitrust liabilities associated with such collaboration.[62] Broad-based efforts are under way to convince the Justice Department and the Federal Trade Commission that collaboration among firms need not, by definition, be anticompetitive. Rather, the argument runs, U.S. firms are no longer so likely to dominate world markets, either in terms of market share or technological leadership, that they can remain competitive in the absence of collaborative R & D programs.

As discussed in greater length in Chapter 7, there may well be lessons for U.S. business executives and government officials in Japan's experience in the development of new industries. As the above discussion on Japanese cooperative R & D suggests, collaboration per se is no panacea; it is only as good as the specific research design, the scientists involved in the project, the manageability of the efforts, and so on.

---

62. The Semiconductor Research Corporation (SRC), supported by a consortium of U.S.-based firms, was set up in 1982 to underwrite long-term "basic research" primarily through contracts with universities. The MCC, mentioned above, was established in 1983 to support long-term "applied research" that is specific enough to be marketable but not so specific as to constitute product development. That function was left to individual companies. (The Institute for New Generation Computer Technology [ICOT], the official name of the Japanese Fifth Generation Computer Project, operates with a charter similar to MCC's.) The U.S. Defense Advanced Research Projects Agency (DARPA) has also established a project to develop a computer system based on artificial intelligence. Meanwhile, other Reagan administration officials have been promoting the concept of R & D–limited partnerships as a means of conducting jointly funded research in new technologies.

Overall, the Japanese government has succeeded in fostering an environment that encouraged (and still encourages) investments in new areas of economic activity. As discussed in previous chapters, Japan's macroeconomic *and* its industrial policies have encouraged savings and investment, and it has been in this favorable overall environment that incentives in certain key areas, such as computers and electronics, have been particularly effective. Yet it is Japanese firms themselves that have taken advantage of this environment, made the necessary investments, and developed competitive products. This is perhaps the single most important lesson from the Japanese experience with new industries.

Chapter 6
JAPAN'S DECLINING INDUSTRIES

Since 1973, a number of basic manufacturing industries in Japan have experienced serious declines in competitiveness. This signals a fundamental change in the structure of the Japanese economy from one in which new growth has come primarily in manufacturing industries to one in which new growth is beginning to come primarily in services. To the extent that all economic progress requires growth in new industries and a corresponding decline of older industries, this turn of events is both inevitable and desirable. Yet the phenomenon of declining competitiveness requires painful adjustments on the part of both management and labor. Japan's success in making these adjustments has been due in large part to a strong underlying commitment to economic growth that existed throughout the society during the first 25 years after World War II.

Even in the last 15 years, as economic growth became one of several goals rather than a single, all-encompassing goal of Japanese society, both the Japanese government and the private sector have recognized that as new industries come on stream, the resources used by older, less advanced industries are too valuable to permit them to remain locked in lower productivity uses indefinitely. On balance, this willingness of Japanese society as a whole to support structural change in the economy has continued to hold and to underlie government policies that have in turn facilitated such change. The thrust of these policies has been to encourage the contraction or phasing out of declining industries with tax, financial, or other assistance. Moreover, the government has encouraged such changes whether the reasons for declining competitiveness stemmed from domestic or international forces. To be sure, new forms of protection for hard-hit industries have often been considered by business and government representatives in hopes of offsetting a decline in competitiveness, but once a decline has been clearly seen as permanent, both the industries themselves and the government have generally shifted gears and begun making the necessary adjustments.

Although Japanese government policies have facilitated the adjustment process, world market conditions have been the main determinant of whether and at what pace Japan's declining industries have carried out various adjustments. In general, the combined efforts of the private and public sectors to deal with declining industries have been at least as effective as comparable practices and policies in other advanced industrial countries—and probably more so. However, the continued development of the Japanese economy means that many existing manufacturing industries will become less competitive than they have been in the postwar years to date. Thus the adjustment burdens that are likely to be placed on these industries and on government policy will almost certainly increase.

All advanced industrial countries pay at least nominal attention to the need for structural adjustments in the face of major economic changes, as evidenced by the basic principles of "positive adjustment policies" agreed upon by the OECD Council of Ministers.[1] In reality, most advanced industrial countries have been unwilling to bear the costs associated with such adjustments (for example, temporary unemployment, the need for retraining and reemploying of workers, and the scaling down of certain industries). Many so-called positive adjustment measures have actually served to subsidize continued production in otherwise declining sectors (that is, to amount to negative adjustment, or nonadjustment, policies). Japan's experience with structural adjustment has been more successful than other countries' in part because it began to face major adjustment problems only in the past few years. Before 1973, a few sectors that had emerged as important shortly after World War II—for example, plastic toys, flowers, and Christmas tree lights—did give way to newer, higher-technology activities, but such adjustments were hardly controversial since these simple, labor-intensive activities were perceived from the start as no more than a way station to more advanced industries. At MITI's behest, coal mining was also phased out, largely because domestic supplies were clearly insufficient

---

1. The key documents are collected in Organisation for Economic Co-operation and Development, *The Case for Positive Adjustment Policies* (Paris: OECD, June 1979).

for Japan's future growth and imported oil seemed likely to be (and for many years turned out to be) cheaper than imported coal. Moreover, amidst the extraordinarily high growth rates and mild recessions characteristic of the world economy from 1947 to 1973, it was relatively easy to phase out less advanced sectors or industries. Demand for labor was growing so rapidly that reemployment was not an issue, and the transfer of capital to higher-growth areas enabled the costs of adjustments to be absorbed relatively quickly.

Since 1973, however, the industries that have experienced a decline in competitiveness have been more important to the overall economy than the earlier examples cited above; moreover, the environment in which structural adjustments needed to be made has become a more difficult one in which to manage such change. In this context, the Japanese began to want—and in the late 1970s established—a systematic process to facilitate the phasing out of old industries. Accordingly, this chapter describes the framework of government support for declining industries that developed in the late 1970s. It looks at three examples of adjustment that have take place since 1973: shipbuilding, petrochemicals and petroleum refining, and aluminum and other nonferrous metals.[2] Each case illustrates different aspects of the problems associated

---

2. The textile industry is not discussed in detail partly because much has been written on it already and partly because it does not seem to us to be a likely precedent for the future. Except for agriculture, the ability of Japan's otherwise declining industries to prosper in future years is likely to depend more on their own efforts than on the kind of government assistance the textile industry received. For useful summaries of the textile case, see Brian Ike, "The Japanese Textile Industry: Structural Adjustment and Government Policy," *Asian Survey* 20 (1980): 532–52; and I. M. Destler, Haruhiro Fukui, and Hideo Sato, *The Textile Wrangle: Conflict in Japanese-American Relations, 1969–1971* (Ithaca and London: Cornell University Press, 1979). Ike argues that the Japanese textile industry has been declining since the 1950s and by rights should no longer exist in its current fragmented form. But industry representatives had sufficient political power in the late 1960s and early 1970s to induce the government to try to keep it alive through various assistance programs. These failed, however, to prevent imports from increasing, and the textile firms that continued to prosper did so because they switched to new product lines. Large firms with access to capital, such as Toray Industries, have developed new technologies and highly innovative product lines, such as carbon fiber, reverse osmosis membranes (used in water desalinization and purification), and zirconia ceramics (used in industrial tools).

with declining industries, as well as various types of government and industry responses. The chapter concludes by discussing some of the difficulties Japan is likely to face in implementing structural adjustments in the future.

GOVERNMENT SUPPORT FOR DECLINING INDUSTRIES

A variety of measures are available to the Japanese government to promote rationalization or adjustment in declining sectors of the economy.[3] These can be applied to industries, workers, and communities.[4] Measures directed toward an industry have typically been grouped together as a policy package, tailored for the particular industry in trouble, and reinforced by other national policy programs. For example, as discussed in detail later in the chapter, an adustment plan was specifically designed for the shipbuilding industry. Government support was available—but only on condition that the industry actually reduce capacity. This plan was reinforced by direct support to workers through the National Employment Insurance Law. Benefits were disbursed to workers only if they agreed to participate in retraining and placement programs. As noted above and perhaps more important, Japanese adjustment policies make no distinction between whether the cause of a competitive decline is due to domestic or to international factors. By contrast, the U.S. system only provides adjustment assistance once it has been determined that competition from imports has been the ma-

---

3. The usual English translation of the basic Japanese law on declining industries is misleading in American usage. The Japanese wording is *Tokutei fukyō sangyō antei rinji sochihō*—the Law on Temporary Measures for the Stabilization of Specific Depressed Industries. The phrase *fukyō sangyō* is normally translated as "depressed industry." But the law as a whole is specifically designed to deal with structural, rather than cyclical, problems, and the word *depressed industry* in English normally carries the connotation of a cyclical downturn. Thus we prefer to use phrase *declining industry* to refer to those industries thought to be suffering from long-term, or structural, problems. But the law itself is normally referred to in English as the Depressed Industries Law. We ask the reader to remember that the problems being discussed are of a predominantly structural, rather than cyclical, nature.

4. The discussion below focuses on industry measures.

jor cause of the competitive decline.[5] Despite this generally result-oriented framework, Japanese policies for declining industries have to be judged, on an absolute scale, as no more than partially successful. As discussed in various cases below, the policy packages designed to deal with a particular industry have been put together later rather than sooner.

The basic legislative framweork governing programs for declining industries, the Depressed Industries Law, was enacted in 1978.[6] The law identified four sectors—shipbuilding, aluminum refining, synthetic-fiber manufacturing, and open-hearth steel—as candidates for government support and gave MITI discretion to specify other industries as eligible for support within one year.[7] For an industry to be eligible for help, the following conditions must apply:

1. The industry must have severe overcapacity (with little likelihood of a turnabout in economic conditions);
2. More than one half of the firms in the industry must be in dire financial condition;
3. Firms representing two thirds of the industry must sign a petition seeking designation under the law; and

---

5. Compare Japan's Depressed Industries Law or the National Employment Insurance Law with the trade adjustment assistance program in the 1974 U.S. Trade Act. For further details, see U.S., Comptroller General, General Accounting Office, *Report to the Congress: Worker Adjustment Assistance under the Trade Act of 1974 to New England Workers Has Been Primarily Income Maintenance*, HRD-78-153, 20, 1978; and idem, *Report to the Congress: Adjustment Assistance to Firms under the Trade Act of 1974—Income Maintenance or Successful Adjustment?*, ID-78-53, 25, 1978.

6. For a Japanese government commentary on this law, see Tsūshō Sangyōshō, [Ministry of International Trade and Industry], Tsūshō Sangyō Seikaku Kyoku, [Trade and Industry Policy Bureau], ed., *Kōzō fukyō hō no kaisetsu* [A commentary on the Structurally Depressed Industries Law] (Tokyo: Ministry of International Trade and Industry, 1978). See also Frank K. Upham, "Legal Framework of Structurally Depressed Industry Policy," in *U.S.-Japan Relations: Towards a New Equilibrium*, Annual Review 1982/83 (Cambridge, MA.: The Program on U.S.-Japan Relations, Center for International Affairs, Harvard University, 1983), pp. 143–55.

7. In all, 14 different industries, including, in addition to those listed above, cotton and worsted yarn spinning, three chemical industries (urea, ammonia, and phosphate), corrugated paper, and ferro-silicon, were covered.

4. There must be broad agreement that some scrapping of facilities is necessary to overcome the situation.[8]

Once an industry is so designated, the ministry with responsibility for overseeing its activities (usually MITI) drafts a stabilization plan outlining possible plant reductions, reemployment measures, and other adjustment measures. This plan may be highly specific or general, depending on circumstances, and consultation with industry and union representatives is required in drawing it up. The plan lacks the force of law, and an industry is not compelled to go along with all aspects of it. Nonetheless, the antitrust immunity and loan guarantees and other financial support provide powerful incentives for troubled industries to seek designation under the law and to cooperate with the government. On completion of the plan, negotiations over specific measures begin in earnest.[9] These inevitably lead to considerable disagreement over prospective "voluntary" actions by firms in return for the prospective government support they are seeking. No individual firm is anxious to have its capacity reduced if holding out for a better deal might somehow improve its market share or its competitive position generally.

Since declining industries are by definition a relatively high-risk category, one goal of the government's support measures is to induce private banks to lend firms in the industry sufficient funds to facilitate the adjustment process. For industries in extremely weak financial condition, the loan guarantee measures authorized by the Depressed Industries Law for the disposition of facilities are channeled through a special Depressed Industries Credit Fund. The initial capitalization is provided from a pooling of funds by the government and private companies in a particular industry; this pool serves as a basis for subsequent loans from the JDB and/or commercial banks. If competitive and other conditions prevent the voluntary actions of the companies or the policy measures of the government from achieving the goals of the basic plan, industry representatives can be directed to meet as a group with the relevant ministry in an effort to hammer out joint actions for capacity reduc-

---

8. Detailed provisions of the law are outlined in Figure C.1.

9. The law does give the ministry in charge of a particular industry the right to prohibit construction of new facilities once an industry has been designated as depressed, which, as noted above, is only after firms in the industry have requested help. Thus, the law gives the ministry some degree of direct control over an industry, though not an unlimited amount.

tion. In general, actions under the 1978 law are exempt from antitrust laws. However, the FTC has the right to review all joint plans. Should it find these excessively anticompetitive, the FTC can call for their alteration or withdrawal.[10]

The law was extended in 1983 for another five years; its name was changed to the Law on Temporary Measures for the Structural Improvement of Specific Industries, and its mandate was broadened to cover additional sectors and functions going beyond facilitating capacity reductions. Since the original law came into effect in 1978, several additional sectors, such as petrochemicals and additional ferro-alloys, appeared to have become declining industries. The new version of the law gave the government the authority to designate still other industries by the end of 1984. Some MITI officials have indicated that they would like the new law to permit a more active pursuit of mergers and other steps for the revitalization of specific industries. As with the original law, FTC officials have indicated their wariness toward such moves. MITI is apparently also trying to use the extended law as a means of providing a new legal basis for dealing with cyclical downturns. If this emphasis is pursued in practice—and at this point it is still too soon to tell—it would bring about an important change in the thrust of Japan's adjustment policy generally: away from capacity reductions in support of structural change and toward a variety of measures to support industries during a cyclical downturn. Specifically, this can include establishing joint sales companies, promoting technology and servicing tie-ups, and various new tax incentives.[11] Parenthetically, this change

---

10. The FTC cannot force such alteration or withdrawal, however. MITI's initial draft of the law proposed that MITI be empowered to control investment and to exempt from antitrust laws mergers and acquisitions involving even those firms in an industry that had not petitioned for support under the Depressed Industries Law. This generated such criticism on constitutional, economic, and philosophical grounds from the FTC, consumer groups, legal scholars, economists, and even some firms that MITI redrafted the law, eliminating this provision. For further details, see J. Mark Ramseyer, "Japanese Antitrust Enforcement after the Oil Embargo," *American Journal of Comparative Law* 31 (Summer 1982): 395–430. Upham, "Legal Framework"; and Gary R. Saxonhouse, "Industrial Restructuring in Japan," *Journal of Japanese Studies* 5 (Summer 1979): 273–320.

11. For a useful discussion of the new law, see *Nihon Keizai Shimbun*, February 3, 1983, p. 1.

of focus would also augment MITI's otherwise declining powers vis-à-vis Japanese industry generally.[12]

Besides these two laws, a variety of other measures can and have been taken to facilitate adjustment in declining industries. Industry-specific laws, such as the Cotton Textile Industry Law and the Petroleum Industry Law, have been commonplace, and these can serve as a basis for government actions to further structural adjustment, even if the law was not initially drafted to address competitive declines. Additional steps to lessen the pain of unemployment caused by structural adjustment have also been established. These include an extension of the eligibility time for unemployment benefits, increases in unemployment allowances for displaced workers in designated industries and communities, and direct assistance, via a computer bank, in the placement of workers in new locations. Correspondingly, workers who refuse government offers of retraining or relocation cannot receive the incremental benefits flowing from laws specifically addressed to structural problems.[13]

The government (again, usually MITI) can also promote structural adjustment informally through its use of administrative guidance. As noted in Chapter 3, although the government cannot force industries to comply with requests made through administrative guidance, its de facto power has always exceeded those specifically outlined in legislation. In MITI's case, this additional influence stemmed from its once-extensive authority over foreign exchange required for imports, its power of suggestion in the granting of preferential loans from government-affiliated financial institutions, as well as direct support for special tax breaks and other industry assistance measures. However, as also noted

---

12. In much the same manner as in the disputes over the proposed 1978 law, the FTC was highly critical of the proposed 1983 law, fearing that its broadened scope would enable MITI to sanction much greater concentration in the affected industries than the FTC would consider reasonable. After much negotiation between MITI and the FTC, a compromise was reached in which MITI officials agreed to discuss any proposed merger with the FTC in advance.

13. For community assistance measures, see Ramseyer, "Japanese Antitrust Enforcement," especially p. 608. An outline of major unemployment measures under these laws is shown in Figure C.2. The Law on Temporary Measures for Unemployed of Specific Depressed Industries is summarized in Figure C.3.

in Chapter 3, MITI's foreign exchange powers have disappeared altogether, and the importance of preferential government financing has declined considerably.[14] In the cases described below, the interplay between government and business was complex, and the outcome of efforts as structural adjustment depended primarily on world market conditions as well as on the visions of individual business executives, the skill of individual government officials, and the overall framework of government policies.

EXAMPLES OF ADJUSTMENT

Shipbuilding

Shipbuilding represents perhaps the most successful example to date of an industry in Japan that has been forced to adjust to changed economic conditions—initially in response to the collapse of the World tanker market in the mid-1970s and more recently to increased competition from shipbuilding firms in South Korea, Taiwan, and other NICs. In the 1950s the Japanese government designated ocean shipping (both shipbuilding and the merchant marine) as a "strategic industry," partly because of its heavy utilization of labor, steel, and other domestically produced manufactured goods and partly because of its presumed na-

---

14. Even when MITI's influence was greater than it is now, many industries have resisted MITI's rationalization and stabilization plans. The famous case of automobile manufacturing is the most dramatic example on record. In the mid-1960s, MITI officials concluded that domestic auto manufacturers would probably be unable to compete in world markets and perhaps even in the domestic market once foreign-based manufacturers began efforts to sell in Japan in earnest. MITI then sought to consolidate all domestic manufacturers into two major firms, Toyota and Nissan. The effort failed completely: Isuzu and Toyo Kogyo, which were in weak financial condition at the time, stayed alive by seeking new capital from foreign-based manufacturers, in Isuzu's case from General Motors and Toyo Kogyo's from Ford. Meanwhile, Mitsubishi Motors established a tie-up with Chrysler. Honda, previously a manufacturer only of motorcycles and motorbikes, expanded into automobiles, thereby increasing the number of Japanese auto manufacturers and eventually becoming the first Japan-based auto manufacturer to establish a manufacturing plant in the United States.

tional security value for a trade-dependent island country. Consequently, both in the initial stages and as the industry evolved, the government extended various kinds of support in the form of tax benefits, low-interest and deferred loans, financing through the JDB and the Export-Import Bank, and, in an unusual move, a special subsidy based on a grant of industry control of the licensing of raw sugar imports.

When the boom in shipbuilding induced by the 1956 Suez crisis collapsed in the early 1960s, the Japanese shipping industry suffered serious stagnation. Special legislation—specifically, the Law for Temporary Measures for Reconstruction and Integration of the Shipping Industry—was passed in July 1963 to help the industry get through this downturn. Key provisions of the law included a consolidation of the industry into six groups and a rescheduling of outstanding loans. By the end of a five-year "reconstruction period," the stagnation problems stemming from the post-Suez collapse had been largely resolved, but various forms of industry support continued. Loans were extended under the Government Shipbuilding Program, administered by the Ministry of Transportation (MOT), which has jurisdiction over shipbuilding (except when exports are involved, in which case MITI also has partial jurisdiction). Shipping companies continued to receive subsidies for a portion of the interest payments they incurred in shipbuilding loans, and various other measures were continued in altered form or newly introduced. By the early 1970s, drawing on this support, together with low-cost steel production and still relatively cheap labor, Japanese companies became the world's lowest-cost producers of ships, achieving some 50 percent of total world production. At that point the government's support measures were largely withdrawn.

Success was short-lived, however. The first oil shock hit in late 1973. The following year, the world tanker market collapsed. The global shipbuilding industry was suddenly faced with severe excess capacity and excess labor. This led shipbuilders in other advanced industrial countries, particularly in Europe, where shipping industries were in even worse shape than Japan's, to exert strong political pressure on the Japanese industry to cut back production. To compound the difficulties of the moment, which in one sense seemed largely cyclical, the collapse of the tanker market brought to light a structural problem in the form of competition from producers in the NICs. The drastic decline in orders for Japanese yards for ships over 2,500 gross tons gives some sense of the magnitude of the collapse—from 33.8 million gt in 1973 to 9.4 million gt in 1974, a drop of more than 70 percent. By 1978, orders had fallen to 3.22 million gt, only 10 percent of the 1973 peak.[15] Once again, Japanese government support measures were brought into play; steps were instituted with the close cooperation of both the shipbuilding companies and the major unions.

The Shipping and Shipbuilding Industries Rationalization Council, an MOT advisory group, issued a report in December 1974 recommending various measures to aid the industry. In June 1976, in an effort to avoid what was euphemistically referred to as "confusion" in the industry, the council outlined a proposal to reduce working hours for FY 1977 and FY 1978, based on a consensus ten-year forecast of demand and supply. This plan called for average working-hour reductions to 67 percent of capacity for FY 1977 and 63 percent for FY 1978 (from the peak operating hours registered for each firm from FY 1973 to FY 1975), balanced across the industry.[16] Market conditions continued to deteriorate, however, and the ministry had to force the industry to accept even more scaled down estimates of viable production levels. In 1978 the MOT made two additional recommendations: for the remainder of fiscal 1978, production should be cut from an earlier target of a 72 percent operation ratio to 67 percent of average; and subsequently in 1979 and 1980, to 39 percent.[17]

The MOT's requests that the industry cooperatively reduce operating ratios triggered the usual debate with the FTC over possible infringements of the antimonopoly law, particularly since the companies had previously organized an intraindustry committee to discuss the MOT's recommendations and, on acceptance of these as modified in the continuing discussions, to work toward achieving the targets. But

---

15. Japan Confederation of Shipbuilding and Engineering Workers Union, *Labour Union's Adaptation to the Structural Change in the Shipbuilding Industry* (Tokyo: Japan Confederation of Shipbuilding and Engineering Workers Union, August 1980), p. 24.

16. These figures are for large firms (over 1 million gt launching capacity); enterprises with less than 100,000 gt launching capacity were requested to cut working hours by less than those enterprises with either 100,000 to 1 million gt launching capacity or over 1 million gt. See ibid., pp. 31–32.

17. This production decline is an industry average distributed as follows: the 7 largest companies were to operate at 34 percent of capacity, the 17 middle-ranking companies at 45 percent, and the 16 smallest companies at 49 percent. Ibid., p. 32.

even the modified recommendations soon became moot, with the increasing recognition that the industry faced a structural, not a cyclical, decline, and for this reason needed a stabilization plan that would specifically exempt it from antimonopoly legislation. As eventually agreed upon in late 1978, a new plan recommended closure of some firms, capacity cutbacks in all others, scrapping of givernment ships ahead of schedule, export of excess ships to developing countries as a form of foreign aid, and, finally, a redesign of the industry itself to encourage companies to focus on new products such as floating factories, offshore oil drilling equipment, and liquefied natural gas (LNG) tankers. The planned cutbacks totaled at least 35 percent of existing shipbuilding capacity.

The MOT's recommendations for the plan were not advanced in isolation. They were the result of extensive discussion and negotiation with the parties most directly affected—namely, the companies and the unions; no single stabilization or restructuring plan was accepted as a matter of course. Moreover, the smaller firms in the industry, which tended to concentrate on shipbuilding alone, had much less scope for diversification than the large firms. Capacity reductions for them were all the more painful. Consequently, while there was general industry agreement on the need for capacity reductions, firms disagreed vehemently over which of them should bear the burden of these reductions. Some sought temporary financial assistance directly from the government, in the hope that excess capacity could be maintained until market conditions changed. In a famous case, political pressure was applied to rescue one particularly hard-hit company, Sasebo Heavy Industries. One account described the Sasebo case as follows:

> Sasebo Heavy Industries is the eighth largest shipbuilder in Japan. Its major stockholders are Nippon Steel and Nippon Kokan, Japan's two largest steel companies, and its major bank is Daiichi Kangyo. It is a major employer in the City of Sasebo, so its announcement in early 1978 of financial difficulty and its intention to seek voluntary early retirement by one thousand employees produced concern. Concern later became crisis when the major stockholders decided not to guarantee future loans, and the banks refused additional funds without guarantees. Confidence in the company's management was low and could not be restored. The major ministries involved—Finances and Transport—and the Bank of Japan chose not to arrange a rescue, and were prepared to see the company declare bankruptcy. The consensus of the regular policymaking ap-

paratus was that the company should be allowed to fail.

This became politically unacceptable, however, when the work force and the Sasebo community petitioned members of the Diet, including the Prime Minister, to intervene. The Prime Minister requested the two ministries to find a solution. It was not forthcoming. Then the Prime Minister *ordered* that a solution be found. Eventually the banks, major stockholders, and ministries put together a package which the banks grudgingly accepted. It included some government financial relief, a hastily arranged American ship repair business to bolster demand, a syndicated bank loan from eighteen different banks, and a modest new capital infusion from the major stockholders. All of this was premised on a carefully negotiated change of management.[18]

In 1978 the shipbuilding industry was designated as "structurally depressed," thereby becoming eligible for assistance under the Depressed Industries Law. One form of this assistance was access to funds under the Depressed Industries Credit Fund. Initial monies, totaling ¥2 billion (or $9.1 million at ¥220 = $1), were provided equally by the government and firms in the industry and handled by a special nonprofit corporation set up by the industry for this purpose. The special corporation was to use its paid-in capital to leverage loans for the acquisition of assets from those firms that were reducing capacity. Government guarantees could be granted on these loans up to a total of ¥96.5 billion (or $439 million at ¥220 = $1)—70 percent of this to be provided by the JDB, and the remaining 30 percent by commercial banks. To pay off the loans, the assets acquired by the corporation were to be sold off and converted to other uses. Interest payments were to be met by a levy on each shipbuilding firm's new orders (0.1 percent in 1979, 0.15 percent in 1980, and 0.2 percent in 1981). Adjustment was also facilitated by a series of measures taken to expand domestic demand for ships, including a ship-scrapping program, acceleration of a long-term

---

18. Ira Magaziner and Thomas Hout, *Japanese Industrial Policy*, Institute of International Studies Monograph (Berkeley: University of California Press, 1980), pp. 86–87. Emphasis is in the original. To bring the case up to date, after some assistance was provided, the new management was able to make numerous adjustments, including increased repair work for the U.S. Navy. Today, Sasebo Heavy Industries is operating profitably. For some details, see "Japan's Lazarus," *The Economist*, March 31, 1984, pp. 70–72.

plan to expand Japan's commercial fleet, acceleration of long-term purchase plans for the Maritime Self-Defense Force and the Maritime Safety Agency, and various measures to reduce the cost of financing the acquisition of new ships (perhaps most important, an interest rate subsidy of 2.5 to 3.5 percent).[19]

Although these government measures were important, it was the shipbuilding industry itself that vigorously sought and carried out the necessary adjustments. In fact, the industry's actions were so effective that by March 1980 its basic stabilization plan had been more than achieved, utilizing only ¥37 billion of the ¥96.5 billion funding available under the credit fund. Most of the money that was used went to smaller companies in the industry; the larger firms used internal funds. The seven largest companies provided the bulk of the funds to the non-profit corporation that bought up excess capacity; the seven also bore the brunt of the capacity reductions (40 percent of their own capacity, equivalent to some 70 percent of the total industry reduction). On the other hand, some 49 smaller shipbuilding companies went bankrupt. Since a 35 percent capacity reduction also meant close to a 35 percent reduction in employment and the unions effectively prevented firing, the companies were forced to use various other means to reduce the labor force. For the large companies, transfers to other lines of business was an important method of dealing with the problem. For both the larger and the smaller firms, "voluntary retirement" (that is, leaving the company, not early retirement) was also encouraged, in part through one-year salary premiums on top of the normal separation allowances. Firms also took various cost-cutting measures in addition to capacity reductions, including cutting wages, curtailing annual wage hikes, and cutting semiannual bonuses; they also restructured production toward plant exports and other new activities.[20]

In general, the Japanese shipbuilding industry provides an excellent example of how an industry has adjusted to new conditions, albeit painfully but largely through its own initiative, with government support facilitating but not actually directing the process. To be sure, the

---

19. Some of these measures to expand demand fell under the auspices of the Emergency Measures for Building Up Japan's Ocean-Going Shipping Fleet (FY 1977–81).

20. For example, in FY 1978/79, Nippon Kokkan "rid" itself of 1,100 workers; 100 were transferred from shipbuilding to steel, 600 were retired early, and the remainder were transferred to affiliated companies.

shipbuilding industry was able to take advantage of certain special conditions seldom present in other declining industries. First and foremost, Japanese shipbuilding was—and still is—generally the most efficient in the world. This meant that whatever happened the Japanese shipbuilding industry would have an easier time adjusting to new conditions than most other declining industries. Second, the immediate problem facing the industry in the mid-1970s was a collapse in demand, particularly for tankers; since Japanese producers had a large share of the world shipbuilding market (more than 50 percent), they also had the power to stabilize prices and market share. In the wake of various OECD-sponsored discussions, Japanese producers made a unilateral decision to take no more than roughly 50 percent of what was then becoming a much smaller world market. They could certainly have sought a larger market share; by limiting themselves in this way, Japanese producers indicated a willingness to stabilize the global market through an informal depression cartel, hoping thereby to minimize the economic and political frictions that would surely have arisen in the absence of some sort of coordinated countermeasures.[21] Within Japan, agreement on capacity reductions was reached—again albeit painfully—once it became obvious that the global industry was structurally, not cyclically, depressed.

The Japanese shipbuilding industry clearly hoped—and guessed—that it would emerge from this adjustment as still the most competitive in the world—as it has in most sectors of the industry. In hindsight, although this phase of the adjustment process in shipbuilding can easily be characterized as successful, it is also clear that Japanese producers underestimated the increasing competitiveness of the shipbuilding industries in South Korea, Taiwan, and other NICs. In other words, the process of adjustment is necessarily one that continues in some form indefinitely. This much is built into the logic of economic development. Even in a case like this where the domestic adjustment process is implemented exceptionally smoothly, no more than a temporary equilibrium point can be reached, and further adjustments will be needed as new factors change the comparative advantages of different industries in different countries.

---

21. As it was, Japanese producers subsequently felt cheated when, in their view, Western European producers seemed to be trying to take advantage of Japanese self-restraint.

Petroleum Refining and Petrochemicals

In contrast to the shipbuilding industry, the structural problems of
Japan's petroleum refining and petrochemical industries have proved
difficult to resolve even in the short term. Like shipbuilding, both industries were considered strategic in their early years and built up with
the help of government intervention. More recently, while the government has sought to protect petroleum refining and petrochemicals from
fundamental changes in the world economic environment, it has been
unable even to facilitate (let alone guide) these industries into positions
of predictable profitability. A specific example of the difficulties encountered in the government's policy program for the petroleum refining
and petrochemical industries is the conflict, discussed below, between
the refining industry's desire for higher prices for naphtha, which it
produces, and the petrochemical industry's desire for lower prices to
buy the naphtha that it uses for feedstock. This conflict—centered on
the petrochemical industry's desire to purchase cheaper naphtha from
abroad and thereby to reduce or cease compulsory purchases of more
expensive domestically produced naphtha—has arisen as a direct con-
sequence of changed market conditions. The resulting price differentials between imported and domestically produced naphtha have made
the previously stable relationship between the refining and petrochemical
industries uneconomic.[22]

Because in the early postwar years both petroleum refining and
petrochemical manufacturing were earmarked as strategic industries,
both benefited from direct government assistance. The petrochemical
industry got off the ground in the 1950s, when a number of chemical
companies sought and obtained MITI's permission to move into
petrochemicals. Government assistance came in the usual forms available at the time: favorable tax treatment for the licensing of foreign technology, foreign exchange allotments for the purchasing of equipment,
indirect subsidies through tariff schedules, and the provision of land at
nominal prices.[23] Partially because of such assistance, the industry

---

22. This discussion does not try to address in detail the world economic
conditions facing these industries. Nor does it address various additional legislative and other government measures aimed at derivative petrochemical industries, such as plastics and synthetic fibers.

23. For further detail, see Chalmers Johnson, *MITI and the Japanese Miracle* (Stanford, Calif.: Stanford University Press, 1983), p. 236.

quickly became too big. In the high-growth period of the 1960s and early 1970s, no individual firm wanted to miss what each perceived to be highly profitable business opportunities. In spite of recommendations from MITI and from an advisory council designed to function as a clearinghouse for new investment in the industry as a whole, each petrochemical firm prepared its own plans for capacity expansion, and—backed by its investment group— each expanded capacity rapidly. Ethylene production is perhaps the best indicator of this expansion: it nearly tripled between 1967 and 1972.[24]

The history of the refining industry, which has always been more heavily regulated, is more complex. In 1949, under direction from occupation authorities, the Japanese government began a program to promote the onshore refining of imported crude oil, in lieu of buying refined products from abroad. Four international oil firms—Mobil, Shell, Esso (now Exxon), and Getty—formed joint ventures to develop refinery capacity; no wholly Japanese-owned refineries were permitted. In 1952, with the end of the occuption and the Japanese government's resumption of control over industrial development policy, MITI launched a program to develop so-called independent, that is, fully Japanese-owned, oil refining and marketing companies. The idea was to lessen what business and government officials perceived as an undesirable dependence on foreign-based firms, although the crude oil going into the domestic-based refineries came almost entirely from foreign-owned sources. Gradually, three categories of oil companies emerged: (1) Japanese subsidiaries of Western-owned "majors" (these were mainly American-owned operations, and they undertook mainly, although not exclusively, marketing activities); (2) foreign-affiliated Japanese firms—that is, firms with part Japanese and part foreign ownership (these companies were involved in both refining and marketing, with the foreign firm generally supplying the latest refining technology in exchange for a share of the profits and, indirectly, the privilege of operating their own marketing channel, supplied of course by the joint venture refinery); and (3) wholly

---

24. The various petrochemical companies, known in Japanese as *kombinato*, typically built a string of plants grouped around an ethylene plant—in some cases with a nearby refinery, utility station, and port facility as well. These integrated complexes made economic sense at the time they were first constructed, but when market conditions changed, it became extremely difficult to reduce capacity in such large-scale facilities, even if all parts of them were no longer needed.

Japanese-owned firms (these companies also engaged in both refining and marketing; some later developed independent exploration activities, although only very slowly).

All firms in the industry were closely regulated, albeit in ways that proved acceptable to each type of firm. The Western-owned majors, although forced to give up some percentage of market share to partly or wholly Japanese-owned firms, obtained a captive market for the share of production or distribution they did have and thus a continuing foothold in one of the world's largest and fastest-growing markets. Moreover, they supplied crude oil to Japanese-owned or foreign-affiliated firms. They were also able to concentrate on higher margin product lines, for example, gasoline and distillates rather than fuel oil, which greatly improved their profitability.[25] Japanese interests also accepted this structure because, in the case of the affiliates, they had access to the best available technology; and in the case of both the affiliates and the independents, they (and thus the country as a whole) had access to as stable and cheap a supply of oil as any in the world. MITI was also satisfied; the structure entailed little risk, given the circumstances facing Japan at the time.

In 1962, MITI strengthened its direct control over the refining industry by introducing and obtaining approval of the Petroleum Industry Law (*Sekiyu gyōhō*), which remains in force today. It includes the following wide-ranging provisions, among others:

1. Direct MITI control over entry, capacity, and production. Any firm, foreign and domestic, has to get a MITI license to enter the refin-

---

25. In some ways, the compromise positions taken at the time by the Western-owned majors might be considered another example of the propensity of Western (especially American) firms to put a higher value on short-term profits than on long-term market position. Alternatively, the majors might have sought a larger share of either the Japanese market itself (since MITI has direct control over the number of sales outlets a company can set up) or their equity position in various joint ventures—and justified this "tougher" stand on grounds that the refining technology they were making available to their Japanese partners was worth much more than the compensation they were initially being offered. Yet any such second-guessing has to take account of the inability of even the most visionary executives to ignore short-term considerations. The point here is less to bemoan what the Western-owned majors failed to do in the past than to consider what alternative courses of action they might take in the future, based on a clearer understanding of the past.

ing business, and MITI must approve import levels of crude oil and any expansion of refining capacity.

2. Refineries are required to file annual production plans, and MITI is empowered to require changes in these plans.
3. MITI is empowered to set standard prices for oil and oil products.
4. MITI is required to prepare annual five-year rolling plans for oil imports, production levels, and refining capacity—these might be considered a consensus forecast, and they serve as a kind of indicative plan or guide, although changes are made frequently.

The law also has various corollary effects. For example, under the umbrella authority of this law, MITI uses administrative guidance to require domestic petrochemical firms to purchase domestically produced naphtha at a standard price determined in negotiations between MITI and the industries concerned.[26] This has been one of the most contentious issues in recent policy debates.

Like the petrochemical industry, petroleum refining became considerably fragmented during the high growth years of the 1960s. As one account of this period described the situation:

> As the oil glut continued into the second half of the 1960s, MITI's initial interest in keeping down the number of refineries in Japan disappeared. Crude oil was readily available and MITI increasingly succumbed to political pressures from petrochemical firms, trading companies, public utilities, and other business interests that wanted to enter the wholesale stages—the success of which required uncertain investments in the building of distribution networks and the creation of brand new images to withstand the fierce competition with the existing thirteen firms—new entrants swarmed to the refining operations, for which plants could be purchased on a turnkey basis. The manufacturing expertise and technologies of oil refining operations were readily procured from independent foreign engineering firms. Foreign major oil firms, seeking captive customers for their crude oil as well as supply sources for oil products for their sales subsidiaries in Japan, gladly extended technological aid to new oil refineries in Japan.[27]

Yet as late as 1973, MITI's goal of a strong market position for the wholly Japanese-owned companies was still a long way off; the latter

---

26. In recent years, this standard price has meant a tax on domestically produced naphtha of roughly ¥3,000 per kiloliter.

27. Yoshi Tsurumi, "Japan," *Daedalus* 104 (Fall 1975): 117.

remained almost entirely limited to refining and marketing (at the wholesale and retail level), and foreign-based majors still supplied more than 80 percent of the country's crude oil. Japan's continued dependence on foreign-owned sources of crude oil became readily apparent with the so-called *oiru shokku* ("oil shock"), the fourfold increase in the price of crude oil imposed by Organization of Petroleum Exporting Countires (OPEC) in 1973/74.[28] Price effects were keenly felt throughout the economy, and security of supply was thought—not necessarily correctly—to be seriously threatened. Concern over the latter led the Japanese government to announce a pro-Arab posture in the Arab-Israeli conflict in November 1973.[29]

From 1974 until 1979, the Japanese government paid considerable attention to the concept of a new, comprehensive energy policy but

---

28. Edith Penrose, Robert Stobaugh, and Zuhayr Mikdash argue that crude oil shortages were in fact recognizable by the late 1960s. MITI appeared not to respond to these changes in supply conditions because the majors had not passed these costs on to Japanese consumers. See "The Development of Crisis," "The Oil Companies in Crisis," and "The OPEC Process," in *Daedalus* 104 (Fall 1975). In 1970, after the Tehran Agreement, price rises became imminent, but MITI still did not respond with any particular policy change. However, the wholly Japanese-owned refining companies did respond, banding together between 1971 and 1973 to try to win authorized price increases, meanwhile fixing price increases among themselves higher than those established on crude, doubtless in expectation of retroactive authorization from MITI. Foreign-affiliated refining companies followed suit but did not participate in collusive price fixing. As noted in Chapter 3, the FTC in 1974 charged Japanese-owned refineries with price fixing and unauthorized production cartels; after six years of deliberations, a court judgment in 1980 ruled against the firms.

29. The aim of this foreign policy move was to induce Arab oil producers to authorize favorable export arrangements for Japan through so-called direct deals with Japanese-owned refineries—on the assumption that foreign-owned majors would be treated harshly and thereby become unreliable suppliers. Despite initial claims in the Japanese press that the majors were directing oil supplies to their home countries and concurrent fears expressed by the Petroleum Association of Japan that crude oil supplies would soon be some 70 percent below normal, specialists quickly realized that the majors were in fact allocating oil more or less in proportion to previous patterns—or in effect, fairly. Some reports claimed that the five American-owned majors actually supplied Japan more generously than either their home countries or Western Europe. See Stobaugh, "Oil Companies in Crisis," p. 193.

actually took measures in only a few areas—that is, legislation was passed to increase oil stocks, and MITI-sponsored research projects were launched in search of alternative energy sources.[30] The single most effective energy policy measure did not involve a special government program at all. Instead, market forces were harnessed in the simplest possible way: energy-consuming industries were encouraged to pass cost increases on to final consumers. In this way, Japanese energy prices rose with world prices, thereby automatically creating an incentive to conserve energy use and/or to switch to non–oil energy sources. In fact, once the initial shock of 1973/74 had been taken account of, world prices in real terms began a five-year slide; because exchange value of the yen was also greater then than it had been before 1973, domestic energy prices fell even further—some 50 percent from their peak in 1974. This decline in prices had the effect of easing pressure to conserve energy use or to diversify energy sources—at least in the calculations of major energy users at the time the slide was occurring.[31] Thus, not until the second oil shock of 1979/80, when the Iranian revolution and subsequent Iraq-Iran war led to roughly a doubling in prices from an already high base, did the actual practices of energy users result in demonstrable change, leading in turn to a significant movement toward the policy goals enunciated since the first shock.[32] As one account of the effects of the second oil shock described the situation:

---

30. These included the Sunshine and Moonlight projects referred to in Chapter 5.

31. Residential consumers, being less sophisticated about differences between nominal and real prices, typically did take conservation appeals to heart, but this represented no great change in traditional Japanese habits of frugality. In any case, industrial use of energy is greater in Japan, as a percentage of total energy consumption, than in any other OECD country, and it is much greater than residential use.

32. MITI bureaucrats continually produce supply and demand projections, which, coupled with MITI's vaunted reputation, sometimes created a misleading impression of government omniscience. In fact, these projections have rarely been more than ballpark estimates and, in any case, have usually been overtaken by events. For example, in 1970 the government set a production target for nuclear power of 60 million kilowatts in place by 1985. In 1976, that is, after the first oil shock and thus at a time when energy policy was nominally trying to promote diversification, this target was scaled down to 49 million kilowatts. It was scaled down again in 1977 to 30 million kilowatts and reduced further to 26 million kilowatts in 1980.

As majors were cut off from their traditional sources of crude oil by Iran and other OPEC countries, they had to curtail sales to third parties in order to supply their own affiliate refineries. Since Japan had discouraged large refining efforts by the majors, many of the third parties cut off were independent Japanese refineries. Whereas the majors provided 70 percent of Japan's supplies in 1978, they had fallen to 56 percent in September 1979 and 44 percent at the beginning of 1980. . . . The result was a sense of intense vulnerability and panic on the part of Japanese firms who were willing to pay extreme spot market prices and to submit to extraordinary contract terms. . . . The 1979 Iran crises produced a renewed commitment to reducing oil dependence and devising a strategy to cope with the unavoidable security problems.[33]

Once again, however, market forces confounded planners. The price increases of 1979/80 led to a considerable decline in demand for oil worldwide. In Japan, oil consumption fell from 233,171,791 kiloliters in 1979 to 194,799,491 kiloliters in 1981. As a source of total energy demand, oil dropped from 71.1 percent of primary energy use in 1978/79 to 65 percent in 1980/81, largely as a result of a major shift from oil-based processes to coal or LNG by several basic manufacturing industries, notably steel and cement. These shifts in energy use created extensive underutilization of refining capacity, which declined from 72.3 percent in 1979 to 59.5 percent in 1981. Far from being in a strong position in an energy-short world, Japanese refineries were faced with an environment of low demand, weakened domestic prices, overcapacity, and, at the same time, continued MITI resistance to the granting of relief through a system of industrywide floor prices such as imposed in 1975. This refusal to sanction floor prices implies that consumer pressures to keep prices low in such areas as gasoline, kerosene, and jet fuel have outweighed producer pressures for price increases.

MITI has, however, tried other ways to help the refining industry survive the adjustments forced upon it by changed market conditions. In 1981, MITI created an artifical tightening of the domestic mar-

33. Joseph S. Nye, "Energy and U.S.-Japan Relations," *Appendix to the Report of the Japan-United States Economic Relations Group* (Tokyo and Washington: Japan–United States Economic Relations Group, April 1981), p. 81.

ket through mandatory refinery production cuts.[34] Meanwhile, the Petroleum Subcommittee of the Industrial Structure Council argued in December 1981 for a major voluntary program aimed at further scrapping excess capacity.[35] The subcommittee stressed the need to consolidate the current fragmented system in which numerous small-scale companies compete intensively—and unprofitably. As in the auto industry case in the 1960s, MITI began to promote mergers into so-called leading companies, meaning in this case four primarily sales-oriented groupings centered around Idemitsu Kosan, Kyodo Oil, Maruzen/Daikyo, and Nippon Oil.[36]

More important, perhaps, changes in the composition of demand—away from heavy oil toward gasoline and other light oils—created a need for new refining facilities that could convert heavy oil to light oils. This need for an expansion of capacity in one area coincided with a need to cut capacity in another area and to cut total capacity to take account of the decline in overall energy demand. In terms of overall capacity reductions, MITI drew up a mandatory plan that called for an approximately 20 percent reduction in 1983/84, from 4.97 million barrels per day to 3.97 million, which was nearly fulfilled within 9 months of the 12-month period of the plan. To assist in the conversion and construction of new refining capacity for light oils, which MITI also authorized under the Petroleum Industry Law, the JDB drew up an expanded program of low-interest loans.[37] The MOF began consideration of special depreciation measures for these new facilities.

---

34. On the other hand, MITI has also induced some refineries to continue purchasing crude oil in excess of current demand in order to implement government stockpile targets. MITI's policies, when firmed up to the point of suggesting that companies take specific, concrete steps to fulfill policy objectives, often have unintended effects later on—and effects that leave the companies in the lurch. For example, when oil prices began to decline dramatically 1981, those refineries that had earlier been encouraged by MITI to enter into long-term direct deal supply contracts were especially hard-hit.

35. Earlier deliberations had indicated that cuts of 10 to 20 percent were required. By later 1981, 22 of Japan's 86 topping facilities had already been shut down, but excess capacity still remained.

36. For an excellent summary of trends in 1980/81, see Jeffrey Segal, "Losses Force Downstream Shape-up," *Petroleum Economist* 49 (February 1982): 45–48.

37. Previously, only members of the so-called Kyodo Group, a loose marketing/refining consortium formed at government behest in 1965, were eligible for loans for capital construction.

The refining industry's problems were eased somewhat by the decline in the world price for crude oil in 1983. Price differentials between domestically produced and imported petroleum products remained, however. The continuing debate on naphtha prices illustrates the kinds of difficulties that MITI encountered—and will increasingly encounter—in trying to maintain a system of administered prices in an environment in which the influence of world oil and other commodity prices cannot be controlled.

The specific reasons for the recent naphtha war are clearly related to world market conditions. Since mid-1976, the international price of naphtha has been lower, on average, than the domestic Japanese price.[38] Both the Petroleum Subcommittee of the Industrial Structure Council and the Petroleum Industry Association have gone on record as saying they expect such price discrepancies to remain for the foreseeable future, not only in naphtha but also in ethylene, a major chemical feedstock derived from naphtha. Naphtha imports, although supposedly strictly regulated, increased from roughly 30 percent of total consumption in fiscal 1979 to 45 percent in 1981. This was occasioned by the actions of a number of petrochemical companies, so-called chemical-line firms, that favored freer importation of foreign-source naphtha as a way of obtaining lower-priced feedstock. These firms formed a special company, the Petrochemical Feedstock Import Company (PFIC), in September 1978 to handle direct importing. The initial plan was to import relatively small amounts of naphtha and other petroleum products directly—approximately 250,000 kiloliters in the first year, as against the usual 10 million kiloliters imported through the refining companies—and gradually to increase the volume. MITI interpreted the move as an assault on its authority and on the whole framework of the Petroleum Industry Law, with the prospect of stimulating other consuming groups to seek direct imports.[39] After in-

---

38. For example, in 1977 the domestic naphtha price was ¥28,300 (per kiloliter); the import price ¥25,000. Comparable prices in 1981 were ¥57,630 and ¥53,660, respectively. See Hiroya Ueno, "Materials Industry in Recession," *Economic Eye*, Keizai Kōhō Sentā [Japan Institute for Social and Economic Affairs], March 1982, pp. 13–17; and *Nikkan Kagaku Keizai*, no. 5488, January 8, 1982. Although Japanese rarely complain about it, one reason for this gap is the continuation of regulated prices for U.S. natural gas.

39. The other sectors that might be particularly interested in direct imports include airline companies, which purchase jet fuel, fishing cooperatives, which purchase gasoline and diesel fuel, and consumer cooperatives, which purchase kerosene.

tense negotiations between MITI's Agency for Natural Resources and Energy (ANRE) and the PFIC in 1979, ANRE finally permitted the consortium to serve as an importing agent for member firms, while still requiring that the imports themselves be channeled through domestic refineries. Although MITI was forced to give some ground to the petrochemical companies, its basic policy framework, centering around the Petroleum Industry Law, remained intact.

This compromise proved short-lived, however. The petrochemical companies continued to argue that the high cost of domestically produced naphtha was the single most important factor undermining their competitiveness. Since 1980, the petrochemical companies have sought a variety of changes in existing procedures, including:

1. Removal of the petroleum tax on domestically produced naphtha;
2. Reductions in mandatory naphtha stockpiles;
3. Total liberalization of naphtha imports; and
4. Lowering of petroleum product prices.[40]

MITI's initial response to these initiatives was to set up various study groups and to appeal to the industry for patience. By late 1981, however, an intensification of the conflict could no longer be avoided. In January 1982, ANRE announced that the petrochemical companies' demands could not be met in full because free importation of naphtha would undermine the previously established—and in MITI's view, delicately balanced—system for importing oil and oil products and would probably lead to supply uncertainty.[41]

The petroleum refineries opposed the petrochemical industry's demands because any liberalization of naphtha imports would reduce the quantity of crude oil they would be called upon to process, thereby in-

---

40. *Nikkan Kogyo Shimbun*, January 29, 1982, p. 1; and ibid., February 4, 1982, p. 1.

41. Other considerations contributed to ANRE's reluctance to accede to the petrochemical companies' requests: Domestic naphtha taxes are an important revenue source for MITI's energy R & D programs, which are administered by ANRE. Moreover, consumer groups, which have traditionally borne a disproportionate burden of price increases in kerosene and home heating oil in order to limit previous increases in naphtha prices, would oppose any liberalization of naphtha imports that might force the refining companies to seek further price increases in other products. As indicated earlier, free importation of naphtha might also set a precedent leading to the dissolution of MITI's control over oil imports and energy policy generally.

tensifying their capacity utilization problems. In early April 1982, under further pressure from the petrochemical companies, ANRE came up with several proposals that again settled the dispute only temporarily. It continued to reject demands for free importation of naphtha, exemption from the petroleum tax for domestically produced naphtha for FY 1982, and removal of mandatory stockpile requirements for FY 1982. However, ANRE did concede that the scope of PFIC's activities could be expanded to include various additional petrochemical products, that direct imports of naphtha could increase, and that stockpile requirements and the petroleum tax would be reassessed in FY 1983. Most important, ANRE came up with a new method of determining prices that linked the price of domestically produced naphtha more directly to world prices; by effectively lowering the price of Japanese naphtha and thus reducing the earlier gap between international and domestic prices, this new formula represented a major departure from past MITI policy and a significant gain for the petrochemical industry.

Still, this move failed to resolve the problems of overcapacity facing the petrochemical industry. Only in the second half of 1983, after difficult negotiations among industry, labor, MITI, and the MOF, was consensus on future action agreed upon. The separate petrochemical companies were organized into four joint sales companies—led by Mitsubishi, Mitsui, Sumitomo, and Showa Denko. This reduced the cost of sales activities and strengthened incentives to avoid price wars. Second, production costs for petrochemical plants were to be lessened through capacity reductions in various products—that is, ethylene production was to be cut from 6.34 million tons to 4.05 million tons by 1985, a reduction of 36 percent; and low-density polyethylene was to be cut from 1.6 million tons to 978,949 tons, a reduction of 38 percent. MITI officials estimated that this degree of reduction would raise the capacity utilization ratios of remaining plants to about 80 percent. By the second quarter of 1984, with the recovery in the United States boosting petrochemical demand there and consequently reducing pressure for U.S. firms to export, a recovery in Japan was increasing demand at home. Because this upturn was occurring while capacity reductions were under way, capacity utilization did soon rise to nearly the 80 percent goal. Third, the price of domestically produced ethylene was initially set at the international market price plus 5 percent. This move was recognized as no more than a short-term measure since all parties concerned realized that if international prices increased or decreased significantly, the target price would have to be reset. MITI has also designated petrochemicals as a depressed industry under the revised Depressed Industries Law, thereby making the adjustment efforts outlined above supportable by various specific tax, loan, and other assistance measures.

Further compromises on naphtha policy leave MITI's influence over the petroleum refining or the petrochemical industries more or less intact but still constrained by world market conditions. As before, the refineries are still obligated under the Petroleum Industry Iaw to submit production plans for MITI's approval. Through administrative guidance, MITI continues to require petrochemical companies to purchase some naphtha from domestic refineries; import ceilings on naphtha remain, albeit at a higher level than before. MITI continues to coordinate Japan's overall energy policy. Finally, if these industries seek still greater government support under the revised Depressed Industries Law, they would then be obligated to negotiate nearly all aspects of their business operations with MITI.

Clearly, Japan's petroleum refining and petrochemical industries have both benefited from direct government assistance, particularly in the early postwar years of industrial expansion. However, both industries, and the economy as a whole, have also paid a price for this assistance and, subsequently, found themselves saddled with considerable overcapacity. Since government policy fostered both sectors as strategic industries, the government found itself unable either to curtail overinvestment as it was taking place or, worse yet, to introduce effective remedial measures once the excess capacity became obvious. Indeed, Japanese government decisions in the early 1950s to promote onshore refining and petrochemical capabilities can in large part be held responsible for encouraging what emerged as a highly fragmented and uncompetitive industry. Moreover, by favoring Japanese-owned refineries over foreign-owned firms, MITI prevented the latter from expanding capacity as much as they were requesting at the time. Ironically, these firms are now in a stronger position than the Japanese-owned refineries because they are less burdened with overcapacity.

The costs of the price control system authorized by the Petroleum Industry Law are more obvious now than in earlier stages of Japan's economic development. Artificially high prices for naphtha hurt the petrochemical industry, even as they helped support the refining industry. Now, with some partial deregulation of naphtha prices, the refining industry will be harder hit. But neither industry is in good shape; both are being forced to undertake significant capacity reductions, which still may not restore long-term profitability. The petrochemical companies, although they have succeeded in obtaining partial MITI acquiescence to lower naphtha prices through increased imports, may have opened the door to similar moves by other interest groups unwilling to assume the costs of artifically high prices for petrochemical products. The refining industry can still count on MITI's support to keep it from collapsing altogether (Japan's desire for some degree of "energy independence" will ensure this much), but the actual structure of the industry and the critical question of just how much government support would be forthcoming in exchange for what degree of acquiescence in MITI-designed plans remain in flux.[42] In the short term, MITI can be expected to continue to "plug holes in the dike," as it tries to mollify various competing interest groups. In the long term, if market conditions continue to generate sharp price discrepancies between domestically produced and foreign-produced petroleum products, still more imports can be expected to enter the Japanese market whether MITI or the affected industries like it or not.

Aluminum and Other Nonferrous Metals

Recent developments in the Japanese aluminum industry show that it has undergone a rapid and irrevocable decline. The industry's loss of competitiveness has occurred largely as a result of increased electricity costs, which become considerably higher than those in most other advanced industrial countries (see Table 6.1) after the oil price increases of the 1970s. For example, the average energy component of aluminum produced in Japan is roughly 45 percent greater than the average energy component of aluminum produced in the United States. Taking energy and other costs into account, the average price of Japanese-produced aluminum has been 17 to 18 percent higher in recent years that the average price of landed imports from the United States. Basically, the impact of higher energy costs in Japan has meant that only those few domestic aluminum refineries whose electricity is generated from coal or hydroelectric power remain competitive.

Basic demand and supply data from 1976 through 1983 show the degree of the aluminum industry's decline in the wake of worldwide

---

42. For recent discussions on a possible relaxation of direct government control over the refining industry, see *Nihon Keizai Shimbun*, June 5, 1984, p. 1; and ibid., June 6, 1984, p. 2.

Table 6.1

INTERNATIONAL COMPARISON OF AVERAGE
ELECTRICITY COSTS FOR ALUMINUM REFINING

	¥ per Kilowatt Hour
Japan	16.0–17.0
West Germany	7.0– 8.0
Canada	1.0– 1.5
Australia	3.5– 5.0
United States	4.0– 5.0

Source: Data as of September 1983 from conversations with Basic Industries Bureau, Ministry of International Trade and Industry, Tokyo, October 1983.

energy price increases (Table 6.2). Domestic production declined 72.2 percent (from 919,425 metric tons [mt] to 255,900 mt). Consumption increased only 12.4 percent (from 1,600,981 mt to 1,800,287 mt). Imports nearly quadrupled, increasing 276.7 percent (from 375,538 mt to 1,415,021 mt). Imports as a percentage of domestic production increased from 41 percent in 1976 to 553 percent in 1983. Exports have all but disappeared. The enormous increase in imports, to a level nearly six times that of domestic production, makes aluminum the first case in Japan's postwar history in which a basic manufacturing industry has been almost completely replaced by imports. The short time in which the surge in imports and corresponding fall in domestic production took place makes the decline of the Japanese aluminum industry one of the most dramatic examples of structural change on record anywhere.

Although the industry's problems of excess capacity, high production costs, and increased competition from imports are now perceived as structural and permanent, there is little evidence that either government or industry representatives anticipated how quickly this state of affairs would come about; the idea that increases in aggregate demand could revitalize the industry remained alive until the early 1980s.[43] In 1975 an Industrial Structure Council report on the aluminum indus-

---

43. Some MITI and industry officials may well have recognized privately that a drastic structural change was under way, but there is little evidence of efforts to make such thoughts known publicly or to initiate industry adjustment before the market literally necessitated it.

Table 6.2
DEMAND/SUPPLY CONDITIONS FOR ALUMINUM, 1976–83
(In Metric Tons)

	Production	Production Index	Imports	Import Index	Imports as a Percentage of Production	Exports	Export Index	Domestic Consumption	Domestic Consumption Index
1976	919,425	100.0	375,538	100.0	40.8	52,024	100.0	1,600,981	100.0
1977	1,188,197	129.2	466,696	124.6	39.3	86,924	167.1	1,417,625	88.5
1978	1,057,710	115.0	674,050	180.0	63.7	45,438	87.3	1,654,972	103.4
1979	1,101,409	119.9	601,797	160.7	54.6	1,764	3.4	1,802,024	112.6
1980	1,091,477	118.7	736,596	196.7	67.5	4,067	7.8	1,636,786	102.2
1981	770,602	83.8	924,712	246.2	120.0	8,319	16.0	1,568,000	97.9
1982	350,706	38.1	1,289,617	343.4	367.7	4,223	8.1	1,637,038	102.2
1983	255,900	27.8	1,415,021	376.7	552.9	1,679	3.2	1,800,287	112.4

Note: The index base is: 1976 = 100.

Sources: 1976–81: Ministry of International Trade and Industry; and Ministry of Finance. 1982 and 1983: U.S. Department of the Interior, Bureau of Mines.

try forecast that domestic production capacity in 1980 would equal 1,900,000 mt and imports 600,000 mt, or 32 percent of production. In 1978 the council, with MITI backing, revised this estimate to 1,141,000 mt of capacity for 1985 and 1,250,000 mt of imports, which again proved optimistic. In late 1981 the council came up with yet another stabilization plan based on expected domestic capacity of roughly 700,000 mt for 1985 and expected imports of 1,500,000 mt. By April 1982, this plan had also become moot, as by then MITI expected imports for fiscal 1982 (ending in March 1983) to surpass 1,000,000 mt and domestic capacity to be roughly 700,000 mt. Even this last projection proved overly optimistic, as imports increased to 1,415,021 mt in 1983, whereas domestic production fell to 255,900 mt. In its 1978 estimate, the council did recognize that the high energy price increases imposed on Japan signaled a need for major steps of some sort. But the council argued that aluminum refining could recover its competitiveness in five years if the industry were to undertake certain reforms, such as reducing electricity costs, improving labor productivity, and scrapping some excess capacity. To achieve this restructuring, the council recommended that the industry be designated as structurally depressed and be included under the Depressed Industries Law, which it was.

In hindsight, it is now clear that the industry never had the capability to reduce production costs to levels that would be competitive with those in other countries. Accordingly, the industry began taking equity positions in new aluminum refineries being built in Canada, the United States, Australia, New Zealand, Indonesia, Venezuela, and Brazil.[44] Industry executives quickly began adjusting to the idea of importing so-called *ekuitei metaru* ("equity metal"), meaning finished metal products manufactured abroad in facilities in which Japanese interests would hold equity positions. Such investments appeared to be motivated by national security considerations and a desire on the part of the existing firms to survive.[45]

As the precipitous decline in domestic production levels was taking place, the government, the producers, the unions, and the electric

---

44. The installation of some of this new capacity was subsequently delayed by the fall in aggregate demand occasioned by the 1980–82 global recession.

45. By exempting equity metal imports from duties, the government provides an incentive for firms to increase such imports rather than maintain domestic production.

power utilities were unable to agree on various relief measures proposed by one or another group, that is, electricity price changes, capacity reductions, or tolerable import rates. Some of the producers favored reversible, short-term measures, such as a production cartel (that is, a capacity freeze), rather than permanent capacity reductions. Others advocated various measures unacceptable to MITI, such as an electricity subsidy large enough to permit the continued supply of competitively priced aluminum to the domestic market. MITI rejected this on grounds that such blatant protectionism would be politically unacceptable, both inside and outside Japan, and would be unable in any case to solve the industry's basic problems. On the other hand, MITI advanced a number of proposals rejected by the producers, such as an idea offered in 1978 to combine the then-existing producers into two large groups, with the crucial decisions on capacity reductions to be made at the group level.

Another plan, agreed to by the producers and MITI in 1981 but opposed by other parts of the government (notably the MOF) and by the U.S. government, called for removal of a 9 percent tariff on aluminum imports entering the country under long-term contracts, while keeping the tariff on imports purchased in the spot market (where prices were below those on then-existing long-term contracts). Concurrently, Japanese producers were to contribute an amount equal to the tariff savings to an industry association, which would then plough this money back to the industry to finance rationalization efforts. The MOF balked at the plan because it would have resulted in revenue losses to the government. The U.S. government objected to the plan because it appeared to be a backdoor route to increased protectionism. For one thing, the price differential between long-term and spot prices was estimated to be more than the 9 percent tariff, which meant that the tariff cut could not be expected to increase significantly the demand for imports under long-term contracts. Meanwhile, the aluminum producers would be getting an indirect subsidy from their tariff-equivalent contributions to the industry association, a procedure that is probably prohibited under the GATT. Moreover, discriminatory purchases by the length of a contract would establish an entirely new form of protectionism. After much negotiation, a "temporary" tariff plan was approved in December 1981 by MITI and the MOF, allowing imports to be exempt from tariffs for a temporary period of three years starting in April 1982, regardless of the means of import (that is, whether through long-term contracts or through spot market purchases) but with an import ceiling of 400,000 mt per year eligible for full exemption.

By the end of 1982, when total imports had reached 344 percent of domestic production and one refining firm, Sumikei Aluminum, had gone bankrupt and four smelting plants in other companies had closed down, the situation had become so grave that the remaining refining companies requested additional MITI support. MITI agreed to guarantee interest payments on loans to the five companies from various commercial banks and to purchase and stockpile some 100,000 tons of domestically produced aluminum for no more than ¥45 billon (or $204 million at ¥220 = $1). Meanwhile, imports continued to increase, leading to further reductions in domestic production. Although domestic producers continue to hope that a world economic recovery would strengthen aluminum prices enough to stabilize the industry at a somewhat higher level than the roughly 250,000 mt produced in 1983, this has not happened as yet.

High Japanese energy costs have begun affecting the competitiveness of other metal production as well. These industries have yet to suffer as severely as aluminum, but some of them have also seen imports increase. Even though energy prices are unlikely to rise in the 1980s as much as in the 1970s (in real terms they may continue to fall), the absolute level of energy costs in Japan, relative to costs in other countries, is already high enough to militate against construction of new production capacity in most base metals. By implication, imports of these metals, on average, are also likely to increase.

To look by way of example at copper and nickel, as seen in Tables 6.3 and 6.4, production of copper metal from 1976 to 1983 increased 26.3 percent (from 864,351 mt to 1,091,929 mt), whereas consumption increased 30.3 percent (from 1,050,287 mt to 1,368,555 mt). Except for 1983, imports increased more or less proportionately.[46] No copper smelters or refineries have been built in Japan since 1974. In the aftermath of the 1973/74 increase in oil prices, capacity utilization fell precipitously (from 81.5 percent in 1974 to 66.9 percent in 1975) and

---

46. The falloff in metal imports in 1980 can be attributed to the unusually large increase in exports. To fill these orders, Japanese producers increased metal output, which had the corollary effect of dampening demand for imports. Similarly in 1983, there was a dramatic increase in copper exports, nearly 50 percent of which went to China. As before, Japanese producers sharply increased their output through inventory reductions and scrap utilization. In 1984, however, capacity utilization and production levels fell off significantly, from 88 to 77 percent, and exports were expected to decline to roughly their previous levels.

Table 6.3
DEMAND/SUPPLY CONDITIONS FOR COPPER METAL, 1976–83
(In Metric Tons)

	Production	Production Index	Imports	Import Index	Imports as a Percentage of Production	Exports	Export Index	Domestic Consumption	Domestic Consumption Index
1976	864,351	100.0	200,515	100.0	23	28,611	100.0	1,050,287	100.0
1977	933,703	108.0	205,174	102.3	22	43,487	152.0	1,182,631	112.6
1978	959,070	111.0	258,104	128.7	27	50,853	177.7	1,241,438	118.2
1979	983,700	113.8	305,408	152.3	31	46,934	164.0	1,330,136	126.6
1980	1,014,292	117.3	227,660	113.5	22	205,728	719.1	1,325,466	126.2
1981	1,050,120	121.5	241,146	120.3	23	38,301	133.9	1,353,966	128.9
1982	1,074,974	124.4	295,795	147.5	27	44,620	155.9	1,333,212	126.9
1983	1,091,929	126.3	109,385	54.5	10	177,509	620.4	1,368,555	130.3

Note: The index base is: 1976 = 100.

Sources: 1976–81: Ministry of International Trade and Industry; and Ministry of Finance. 1982 and 1983: U.S. Department of the Interior, Bureau of Mines.

Table 6.4

DEMAND/SUPPLY CONDITIONS FOR NICKEL METAL, 1976–83

(In Metric Tons)

	Production	Production Index	Imports	Import Index	Imports as a Percentage of Production	Exports	Export Index	Domestic Consumption	Domestic Consumption Index
1976	24,010	100.0	12,392	100.0	52	2,663	100.0	27,675	100.0
1977	24,140	100.5	11,982	96.7	50	4,176	156.8	26,723	96.6
1978	21,637	90.1	11,790	95.1	54	3,386	127.1	27,895	100.8
1979	25,030	104.2	20,775	167.6	83	2,077	78.0	31,960	115.5
1980	24,798	103.3	17,023	137.4	69	1,454	54.6	36,539	132.0
1981	23,790	99.1	19,188	154.8	81	1,325	49.8	34,114	123.3
1982	23,328	97.1	21,368	172.4	91	472	17.7	32,768	118.4
1983	23,812	99.1	30,184	243.5	126	563	21.1	39,601	143.0

Note: The index base is: 1976 = 100.

Sources: 1976–81: Ministry of International Trade and Industry; and Ministry of Finance. 1982 and 1983: U.S. Department of the Interior, Bureau of Mines.

only returned to around an 80 percent level in 1980. While Japanese metal producers typically expanded production in the pre-1973 period when capacity utilization exceeded 80 percent, they have since been unwilling to expand production facilities even after exceeding this level.

Higher energy costs have had a still stronger effect on nickel and ferronickel. Consumption of nickel from 1976 to 1983, as seen in Table 6.4, increased, whereas domestic production remained constant. Nickel imports rose sharply in 1979, and again in 1983. Consumption of ferronickel, as seen in Table 6.5, declined 32.1 percent (from 316,679 mt to 218,309 mt); production declined 26 percent (from 244,215 mt to 180,826 mt). However, imports more than doubled (from 14,307 mt to 36,750 mt), whereas exports were irregular.

As in aluminum, although to a lesser extent, recent years have brought increases in imports of copper (except in 1983), nickel, and ferronickel, with generally flat or declining domestic production. In time, a slow but steady decline in the competitiveness of Japanese base metal production will force these industries to shift toward more specialized segments of the market. Three factors are promoting this shift:

1. Energy costs are the most important single factor. Generally, the higher the energy input for the conversion of ore or concentrates to metal, the greater the likelihood that production of that metal in Japan will become uncompetitive, compared with production in a country with lower energy costs. Of the nonferrous metals, aluminum is the greatest energy user and has less profitable by-products, followed by ferronickel, nickel, and copper.

2. The financial condition of Japanese metal producers has been generally weak since the 1974/75 recession. Whereas most major producers had returned to a position of net profitability by 1980, their level of profits and capacity utilization was too low to warrant major new investments. Even when macroeconomic conditions improved in 1982 and might have appeared to justify new investment, Japanese base metal producers have been less willing (or able) to make such investments than they were in the pre-1973 years. Whatever investments are made have been, and are likely to continue to be, in facilities abroad, that is, where energy costs are lower and supply sources are closer by.

3. Although the efficiency of some Japanese base metal production processes is still relatively high, thanks to an infusion of investment just prior to 1973, this capital stock is maturing steadily. In time,

Table 6.5
DEMAND/SUPPLY CONDITIONS FOR FERRONICKEL, 1976–83
(In Metric Tons)

	Production	Production Index	Imports	Import Index	Imports as a Percentage of Production	Exports	Export Index	Domestic Consumption	Domestic Consumption Index
1976	244,215	100.0	14,307	100.0	5.9	13,262	100.0	316,679	100.0
1977	265,672	108.8	19,858	138.8	7.5	2,268	17.1	268,549	84.8
1978	235,863	96.6	20,485	143.2	8.7	21,773	164.2	273,014	86.2
1979	346,854	142.0	33,152	231.7	9.6	13,193	99.5	338,459	106.9
1980	324,109	132.7	31,119	217.5	9.6	17,125	129.1	316,065	99.8
1981	284,440	166.5	26,493	185.2	9.3	20,742	156.4	265,138	84.0
1982	214,523	87.8	29,758	207.9	13.8	21,405	169.6	257,711	81.3
1983	180,826	74.0	36,750	256.8	20.3	13,369	100.8	218,309	68.9

Note: The index base is: 1976 = 100.

Sources: 1976–81: U.S. Consultants, Inc., Tokyo, *1980 Nickel Statistics*; and Ministry of International Trade and Industry. 1982 and 1983: U.S. Department of the Interior, Bureau of Mines.

new investments made in other countries are likely to be more competitive than the then-older Japanese plants, in which most of the post-1973 investment has been for maintenance or rationalization designed to extend their useful lives.

IMPLICATIONS FOR THE FUTURE

Despite a widely held view that the Japanese market is "closed," the industries discussed above—shipbuilding, petrochemicals and petroleum refining, and aluminum and other nonferrous metals—show the Japanese companies, like those in other countries, are unable to sustain significant price/cost differentials vis-à-vis competition elsewhere. When this turning point is reached is naturally a matter that depends on the particular circumstances of time and place governing each industry. Much depends on macroeconomic conditions as well as factors affecting comparative advantage or the degree of government support. In shipbuilding, for example, the industry began to diversify when it perceived that its future prosperity would depend on capacity reductions that took account of the collapse in the world tanker market following the 1974/75 recession. Once the industry reached a consensus on this point, encompassing the views of management and labor, the actions it took were extremely decisive. In petrochemicals and petroleum refining, the petrochemical companies faced (and still face) an unalterable constraint: They cannot afford to limit their feedstock supplies to higher-priced, domestically produced naphtha. This salient fact of market conditions—not appeals for patience and further study—eventually led MITI to accept a partial deregulation of naphtha prices and a consequent loss to the refining industry of its previously captive share of this market. In aluminum the gap between higher-priced domestic aluminum and lower-priced imports led to dramatically increased imports, to an equally dramatic fall in domestic production, and to Japanese investments in offshore production facilities. In other nonferrous metals, imports are also likely to increase, although less dramatically than in aluminum.

These cases also show that Japanese business executives and government officials have been willing to change their approach to problems of structural adjustment. Despite strategic industry or national security arguments that are often used to try to justify subsidies to basic manufacturing industries, when price differentials become too great, imports increase anyway, and the degree of subsidies required to maintain a domestic industry becomes too great even for strategic industry advocates. As in other countries, cartellike behavior on the part of domestic producers and national security arguments will doubtless continue to be used to try to keep some manufacturing industries—or parts of some industries—alive indefinitely. In general, however, the greater the price differentials between domestic and imported products, the greater the pressure to import and, correspondingly, to contract the size of even so-called strategic industries. Moreover, as in other economies, the greater the importance of an uncompetitive good as an input to an otherwise competitive downstream industry, the greater the pressure to acquire that input from cheaper sources, including imports.[47]

In this regard the government's role in dealing with declining industries has generally been one that supported or facilitated structural adjustment, although this has sometimes involved efforts to hold back imports. Even when seeking to restrict imports, however, the government has rarely taken the initiative and has been prepared to modify its original trade-restricting proposals. The government's moves have been largely in response to moves being made by the affected industries themselves and in line with industry efforts to adapt to world market conditions. Government efforts have focused primarily on monitoring developments closely and then mediating among industries or firms when conflicts have arisen or when industry efforts at adjustment have faltered. Under the 1978 Depressed Industries Law and its 1983 successor, the government can offer concrete inducements to support capacity reductions, provide worker assistance programs in addition to those offered by management, and activate a special pool of funds for hard-hit sectors. These positive incentives to declining industries are

---

47. To date, the cases of declining industries in Japan have been mainly in producer goods—and in agriculture, which is protected in almost all countries, although more so in Japan than in most other advanced industrial countries. The differentials that exist between the domestic and overseas prices of many consumer goods suggest considerable room for imports of the latter as well. But the insularity of the Japanese market, as well as the attitudes of many potential exporters to the Japanese market, has left most Japanese consumer goods manufacturers with commanding market positions. When combined with various macroeconomic factors at work since 1973, these formidable market positions have deterred many U.S.-based consumer goods exporters from trying to compete in the Japanese market.

usually provided only in return for an explicit, enforceable plan agreed to by most members of the industry and requiring capacity reductions or other specific changes. In other words, government assistance has been clearly linked to mandatory industry adjustment. This link provides a positive incentive for the movement of capital and labor away from declining industries or product lines into growing industries or product lines, that is, by providing adjustment assistance only if and as industries (including labor) agree to use this assistance to facilitate their redeployment, rather than to cushion their remaining in place indefinitely.

The key reason for whatever success these programs have had is not their existence per se, or even the amount of money available in such programs, but the degree to which government leverage has reinforced market conditions. In shipbuilding, government assistance supplemented programs the industry itself had already initiated, based on its own analysis of world market conditions and its greater-than-50-percent share of the world market. At its new slimmed-down level, the Japanese shipbuilding industry remains extremely competitive in the product lines it is concentrating on, even as new industries in other countries make further inroads in the world market. In petrochemicals (especially ethylene production), petroleum refining, aluminum, and other nonferrous metals, Japanese industries remain at a competitive disadvantage vis-à-vis other producers. Since the main problem in these industries is the high energy content of their production costs, the problems they face cannot be solved by capacity reductions per se. The closure of relatively inefficient plants would improve the average cost position of the industry and help maintain the viability of the remaining capacity. But Japanese producers would still remain worse off, in absolute terms, than other producers with lower-priced and more abundant energy sources and raw materials. Thus, in these areas the government's primary efforts have been directed at trying to facilitate intraindustry agreements on which plants would close, in hopes thereby of minimizing the spillover costs to the rest of the economy—in the form of subsidies or higher prices—stemming from continued domestic production in a noncompetitive industry.

The examples discussed above suggest that even so influential a government body as MITI has been able to play its facilitating role only with great difficulty. As still more basic manufacturing industries become less competitive and the reasons for their decline become more structural than cyclical, the financial and import-restricting measures sometimes used to delay adjustment will become all the more costly, in addition to the political cost involved in worsened trade relations. As noted earlier, protectionism for declining industries in Japan was hardly an issue until after 1973, when, in the wake of oil price increases, it became evident that some of the basic manufacturing industries that Japan had been promoting since the end of World War II had to be phased out. Now, when a number of industries have already lost competitiveness, still others, including parts of the steel and auto industries, are likely to face much increased competition by the end of the decade. As a result, protectionism for these mature industries, as well as for other declining industries, will probably be sought. MITI's recent broadening of the scope and duration of the Depressed Industries Law is an indication that the government expects the problem of declining industries to worsen. The government is likely to offer additional carrots and sticks to firms and industries that are facing serious competitive pressures. Japan's problems with declining industries will thereby come to resemble U.S. and European patterns in which the intractable issues are those of facing up to permanent declines in competitiveness, of retraining older workers, and of reestablishing stable employment opportunities in hard-hit regions (for example, in areas where a manufacturing facility in a declining industry is the single major source of employment). For these reasons the whole process of structural adjustment in Japan is likely to become more difficult.

At the same time, U.S. resentment of past Japanese trade restrictions suggests that the introduction of new industry support measures that could in turn amount to increased trade barriers (or be seen as such) would almost certainly lead to increased U.S.-Japanese trade friction. Meanwhile, the U.S. government, while criticizing Japanese trade restrictions, has introduced many trade-restricting measures of its own, especially so-called voluntary export restraints in hard-hit manufacturing industries such as textiles, steel, and sutomobiles. Nonetheless, U.S. resentment of past Japanese trade restrictions exists and is a political reality that Japanese themselves recognize. Also, as the discussion in Chapter 2 suggests, the degree of adjustment that Japanese firms seek, as well as the degree of bilateral tension that arises as a result of disputes in specific sectors or firms, depends to a large extent on macro- as well as microeconomic conditions.

Chapter 7
THE CHANGING JAPANESE ECONOMY: POLICY AND BUSINESS IMPLICATIONS

The only thing permanent, as the fifth century Greek philosopher Heracleitus noted, is change. Preceding chapters have shown the Japanese economy has undergone dramatic change in the 40 years since the end of World War II. The physical scars of the immediate postwar years are gone. The scarcities and related frugality of still later years have been replaced by increasing affluence. The once significant exports of earlier years—toys, textiles, and other light manufactured goods—have given way to exports of automobiles and computers and to *imports* of toys, textiles, and other light manufactured goods, in addition to the raw materials that Japan has always lacked. As the first non-Western nation that consciously set out to catch up to the economic level of the predominantly Western countries, Japan has now achieved this goal in many areas. In terms of broad indices of economic performance, such as per capita income, living standards, technological capabilities, and industrial structure, Japan is now on par with most other advanced industrial countries.

Gaps remain, however. The overall convergence between Japan's economic achievements and the average of advanced industrial countries still leaves important differences in specific areas. Most Japanese seem to us to view these remaining gaps—for example, in housing, leisure time, wealth per capita, and the like—as a motivation to continue working harder, on average, than their counterparts in other advanced countries. At the same time, most Japanese also appear to be working less hard than they used to. This is part of the phenomenon of evolutionary change that is a central characteristic of contemporary Japan.

Interpretations of Japanese economic achievements depend to a considerable extent on one's attitude toward change in general. To those Americans (or Europeans or Canadians or Australians) who see lower-priced and higher-quality Japanese goods as primarily threatening their own livelihood or who perceive such Japanese successes as primarily resulting from seemingly unfair practices, Japanese achievements seem like a serious intrusion on a style of life they would otherwise prefer not to have "disrupted." To others in these advanced countries whose livelihoods have been improved by trade or investment with Japan or who attribute Japanese successes primarily to efforts made by Japanese themselves, Japanese accomplishments are much admired.

Indeed, such alternative interpretations can be drawn from the simplest comparisons of U.S. and Japanese economic performance. Figure 7.1 shows how Japanese productivity growth has raised Japanese productivity levels in the private sector generally and in manufacturing in particular to a point steadily closer to U.S. levels, while failing to show comparable gains in agriculture and services.[1] From a Japanese perspective, many gains have been made, but there is still plenty of room for improvement. From a U.S. perspective, the advantages of already being rich—of having achieved high productivity levels earlier than other countries—are readily apparent, and the implications of current trends are also obvious: If the United States continues to record lower rates of productivity growth than Japan, an increasing share of U.S. manufacturing would become less competitive than Japanese manufacturing. The well-known examples of Japanese steel and automobile manufacturing would be repeated in many other products.

FUTURE DIRECTIONS IN THE JAPANESE ECONOMY

Chapters 2 through 6 trace the evolution of the Japanese economy, and correspondingly the evolution of Japanese government policies, over the course of the postwar period. From the immediate postwar years to the

---

1. These data show productivity levels in services (classified here as nonfarm nonmanufacturing) to have declined in recent years in both the United States and Japan. This is primarily a result of the business cycle downturn in 1980/81. Although the point is a subject of considerable current discussion among economists, we suspect that productivity in services, if properly measured, would show greater increases over time in both the United States and Japan, but particularly in the United States. This much is implied, at least, by the recent development of a financial services industry in the United States based in part on new electronic technologies.

Figure 7.1.

LEVELS OF OUTPUT PER HOUR, 1970-81 (In Constant 1975 $ per Hour)

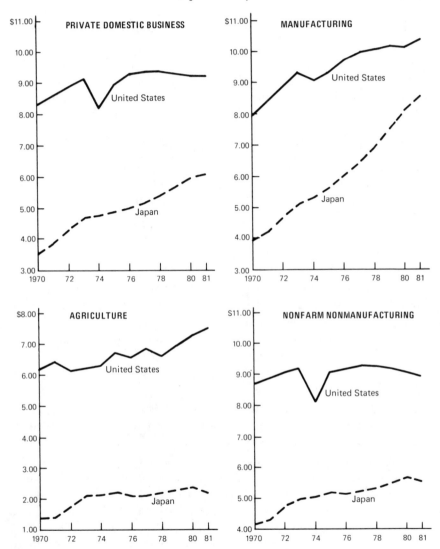

Sources: Elliot S. Grossman and George E. Sadler, *Comparative Productivity Dynamics: Japan and the United States* (Houston: American Productivity Center, November 1982), pp. 82–83; and Elliot S. Grossman, *Productivity and International Competition: United States and Japanese Industries*, HRS-298-P (Croton-on-Hudson, N.Y.: Hudson Strategy Group, June 1984).

mid-1960s, Japanese economic activities were focused almost exclusively on reconstructing the physical damage of the war and rebuilding the basic manufacturing capabilities of an industrial economy. The economy was essentially closed to imports other than foodstuffs, industrial raw materials, and technology and capital equipment. Consumer goods and other finished products, whether for the consuming or the producing sector, were either manufactured in Japan or simply done without. Besides providing for a protected home market, the Japanese government gave domestic industries other extensive support, directly or indirectly. One way or another, government policies had a hand in almost all areas of economic activity.

Over time, these patterns have changed considerably. Particularly since the early-1970s, market-based pressures at home and abroad have led to a slow but steady decline in government influence over the economy, including a slow but steady liberalization of trade restrictions and of international financial transactions. Japan's gradual but continuing shift from a "hothouse economy" toward a more open economy is well illustrated by the evolution of Japanese industrial policies (Chapter 3), by changes in the structure of the Japanese financial system (Chapter 4), by changes in the impact of government support to new industries (Chapter 5), and by the adjustments made by Japan's declining industries (Chapter 6). These changes are summarized below.

As shown in Chapter 3, the Japanese government's role in promoting industrial development through the specific application of narrowly targeted measures—so-called industrial policies—has clearly declined. Many of the broad instruments of government policy that gave officials considerable leverage over the private sector, such as MITI's authority to allocate foreign exchange, have either greatly diminished or been removed altogether. Moreover, the effectiveness of most of the specific instruments of industrial policy has also declined as the economy itself has matured. For example, since the early 1970s the benefits available to corporations from special tax measures have fallen off dramatically. This represents the loss of a key instrument of MITI influence. All along, the government's (notably MITI's) role has been especially significant in the early stages of an industry's development. This pattern continues today—albeit with less impact than in the past. Some high priority sectors, such as information processing, continue to be supported by vestiges of a once extensive system of industrial policies. Government assistance can also be important to declining industries, although here, too, market pressures are forcing industries to cut capacity and make other adjustments. Overall, despite these specific exceptions, a combination of market forces, budgetary constraints, and political pressures have made industrial policies less important than they used to be in influencing the evolution of the Japanese economy.

Given the important domestic as well as foreign pressures for change in key areas of economic policy, the Japanese government now faces continuing problems of trying to reconcile conflicts between groups pushing for change and those that benefit from the status quo. Recent disputes between petrochemical companies and petroleum refiners; between banks and securities companies; and among department stores, supermarkets, so-called superstores, and the traditional "mom and pop" stores are all vivid illustrations of the kinds of domestic policy disputes that arise as an economy has become more developed and thereby more complex. Special attention has been given in Chapter 4 to the prolonged discussions over further deregulation of the financial system that have taken place to date and in Chapter 5 to a similarly dogged battle over barriers to entry into information processing. In both of these areas, domestic conflicts were at the heart of the issue and the reason why foreign interests could not be satisfied easily or straightforwardly. Meanwhile, because industry and bureaucratic groups found themselves unable to resolve their differences, normally aloof politicians were called in to try to settle the disputes. This trend, too, is likely to continue, without supplanting the traditionally stronger voice of the bureaucracy in the Japanese policy-making process. While high economic growth and industrial development still remain important goals in Japan, they must now compete with goals broadly categorized by the term quality of life. In the face of more heterogeneous goals, the detailed industrial policies that the Japanese government followed in earlier postwar years are no longer as acceptable as they once were. New, typically more general policies have had to be implemented, with correspondingly less specific impact on industrial development.

As discussed in Chapter 4, a combination of domestic and international pressures has contributed to dramatic and continuing changes in the structure of the Japanese financial system. During the mid-1970s, the boundaries of the segmented and highly regulated financial system that had been in existence for most of the postwar period began to crumble. A major shakeout in the financial system is now under way, as public and private institutions and their corresponding regulatory agencies are in fierce debate over the latitude each is to be permitted. For example, a partial deregulation of administered interest rates has been forced into existence as a direct result of inefficiencies stemming from the earlier segmentation among different kinds of financial institutions. Further deregulation is only a matter of time. Similarly, banks have been given some latitude to participate in capital markets—formerly the domain of the securities firms—whereas the latter are seeking the right to issue commercial paper. New joint ventures and other cooperative arrangements are under way between Japan-based and foreign-based financial institutions. In short, the extensive changes occurring in the Japanese financial system since the mid-1970s have resulted in a change in kind rather than degree, which in time will lead to Tokyo's becoming a major world financial center comparable with New York and London.

As discussed at length in Chapter 5, the strength of the postwar system for the development of new industries in Japan stemmed from at least four interrelated factors. First, the government helped foster an environment favorable to investment generally, while also providing specific incentives for investment in certain priority areas—such as computers and electronics—through subsidies, preferential loans, cooperative R & D projects, tax breaks, and the like. Second, except in the crucial area of import protection, the government did not try to replace the market mechanism. Rather, it encouraged competition among Japan-based firms in an effort to bring these firms up to international standards.[2] Third, infant-industry restrictions sheltered domestic firms from foreign pressures. These began to be removed in a formal sense in the early 1970s, although a legacy of their impact remains even today in the commanding positions most Japan-based firms hold in the domestic market. Fourth, Japanese firms and the country as a whole benefited from a period of rapid economic growth worldwide and a related high degree of tolerance of Japan's discriminatory practices.

---

2. Admittedly, this competition was fostered primarily among large firms. If viewed as a group, which is how Japan-based firms look to foreign-based firms when the latter are excluded froom the market as a matter of policy, large-size Japan-based firms have held a certain degree of monopoly power. Until recently, such monopoly power was widely viewed in Japan as necessary to prevent "excess competition" from undermining the still nascent development of various industries. Now, however, this traditional attitude toward monopoly power is changing and leading to a greater acceptance of increased competition. See Masu Uekusa, *Sangyō no shoshikiron* [Essays on industrial organization] (Tokyo: Chikuma Shobo, 1983).

As Japan's level of technological sophistication has caught up to, and in some areas even surpassed, that of other advanced industrial countries, most of the factors mentioned above have experienced significant change. In the same way that Japan's industrial policies play a less important role in the economy than in the past, some specific instruments of industry support, such as the JECC, have become less important. Moreover, with official import restrictions reduced and foreign governments and foreign-based firms now watching developments in Japan much more closely than in the past, discriminatory practices—particularly via government policies—are that much more difficult to pursue. Most important, as Japanese economic performance has more or less caught up to that of other advanced industrial countries, Japan-based firms and the Japanese government have begun to experience serious limitations in the effectiveness of previous approaches to the development of new industries. In "frontier work," more funds have to be spent on basic research even as support for applied R & D continues. Technological change is inherently uncertain. No one, least of all government officials who are generalists in administrative procedures, can be sure of what direction to take. Thus greater decentralization than has been typical of Japanese research methods in the past is now being viewed as essential to continued progress. The privatization of NTT and the emergence of new and competing value-added communication networks—some of them involving foreign-based firms—are but two examples of how *deregulation* and *decentralization* have become watchwords of Japan's new industries.

In this environment, many foreign-based firms that are developing new technologies, especially in information processing, are now aggressively seeking a larger share of the Japanese market than they either sought or were granted in the past. Although the ground rules under which such participation will occur are still very much in flux, some Japan-based firms are clearly finding their own interests served by cooperative ventures with foreign-based firms—many of which have superior technology, marketing, or other experience to bring to bear. Such joint ventures or other cooperative arrangements in new industries are increasing because they serve the interests of both Japan-based and foreign-based firms. Similarly, cooperative R & D projects are no longer seen as offering a tremendous boon only to domestic firms. Foreign-based firms are finding less resistance than before to efforts to break through the implicit discrimination involved in the selection of firms eligible to participate in some of those projects. In some cases,

Japanese participants in a cooperative R & D project are seeking foreign participation in hopes of making the project more successful. This has been the record, for example, in the so-called Fifth Generation Computer Project, which is reportedly seeking new ideas to enable it to show more than mixed results.

As discussed in Chapter 6, after the various external shocks experienced in the 1970s the Japanese economy has found itself increasingly facing the same kind of strains that have troubled other advanced industrial countries. For the first time in Japan's modern history, a number of basic manufacturing industries began to experience serious declines in competitiveness, either because of pressures from firms in NICs or from firms in other advanced countries with lower energy costs. Japanese business, government, and political leaders have long supported the notion that a growing economy must phase out uncompetitive industries to make room for new industries. As a result, Japanese firms and the Japanese government both sought and, in the late 1970s established, a systematic process to facilitate the phasing out of old industries. Even with this system in place, the adjustment process has major political and economic costs. Indeed, the burdens likely to be placed on Japanese industries and on government policies in the future will almost certainly increase. The rest of the world now takes events within Japan more seriously than in the pre-1973 years; for this reason it is likely to react to declines in the competitiveness of Japanese industries more quickly.[3] Strongly protectionist adjustment policies will face serious political resistance from trade partners. In short, Japan will be forced, by domestic as well as by foreign pressures, to continue to scale down many of the basic manufacturing industries that once contributed so much to its economic development and to shift into still more knowledge-intensive industries and more modern service activities.

In fact, both the U.S. and Japanese economies are evolving in this direction. Both countries face increasingly similar economic challenges. As advanced industrial countries, both seek sustainable, noninflationary economic growth. Both face increased competition from developing countries and increased resistance to imports in previously dominant manufacturing industries, among other things. As each moves

---

3. For an illustration of increased American awareness of Japan as an export market, but also of various problems encountered in breaking into the Japanese market, see U.S.-Japan Trade Study Group, *Progress Report: 1984* (Tokyo: US-Japan Trade Study Group, September 1984). Chapter 7 of this report deals with Japan's declining industries.

toward more specialized manufacturing activities and more modern service activities, both also face increasingly similar opportunities, and each country will deal with the other in both a cooperative and a competitive manner.

COMMON PROBLEMS OF THE
U.S. AND JAPANESE ECONOMIES

For the U.S. economy to achieve sustainable, noninflationary growth, it must find ways to increase its continually low savings rate and to direct that savings into productive investments. Increased domestic savings are needed to fuel the increased rate of private investment that in turn is needed to raise productivity growth for an extended period of time. For the past three to four years, an unsustainable proportion of U.S. savings has come from foreign investors, including Japanese. In part these capital inflows have been attracted to dollar-denominated savings instruments with higher yields than alternatives available in their own or third countries, although the magnitude has exceeded what might have been expected on the basis of interest rate differentials alone. This is attributable in part to foreign (and American) perceptions of investment opportunities in the U.S., but also in part to different expectations of inflation. High U.S. interest rates are usually thought to reflect fears of renewed inflation on the part of Americans, but foreign, particularly European, investors appear to have judged that control of inflation was more likely in the United States than in Europe. Whatever the mix of motives behind the extensive capital inflow to the United States in recent years and the sharp drop in capital outflows since early 1983—and economists are disturbingly uncertain as to what this mixture might be—money supply growth in the United States did fall sharply after the Federal Reserve Board announced in late 1979 that it would no longer expand the money supply in an effort to control nominal interest rates. Interest rates then rose to unprecedented heights. A year later the economy went into the most severe recession of the postwar period. But inflation rates also began to fall—dramatically so, as indicated in Figure 2.4. Indeed, if the 1981/82 recession had a virtue, it was the signal contribution it made to downward pressure on wage and price growth.[4] For some 25 years, each recession had ended with a

---

4. This was President Reagan's "defense" of the recession during the 1984 election campaign, in answer to former Vice-President Walter Mondale's claim that the president's economic policies were harming the country.

higher rate of inflation than any preceding recession. The break in this ratcheting upward of inflation rates contributed significantly to the spread of positive expectations for the 1980s, relative to the 1970s, that began to show results in the United States and elsewhere in 1983.

Fears of renewed inflation remain strong, however. Such fears are reflected in the continuing concern that U.S. government budget deficits will be financed by an inflationary expansion of the money supply— lest they otherwise cause another major recession by crowding out investment. Thus, as long as the prospect of high government budget deficits hangs over the U.S. economy, U.S. saving and investment behavior is unlikely to produce the sustained increases in productivity growth needed to convert the 1982–84 cyclical recovery into a sustained *and* noninflationary expansion.

With appropriate policy changes—some recently implemented, such as deregulation of interest rates and expansion of tax-deferred individual retirement accounts (IRAs), and many others under discussion in the debate over tax reform—the U.S. savings rate is likely to rise. Even if this increase is so slight as to keep the savings rate within the range of historical levels, such policy changes would contribute to productivity growth by redirecting savings away from tax shelters and toward more productive investments. Meanwhile, the capital inflows that have been attracted by high U.S. interest rates and cushioned the United States against a credit crunch have also held the exchange value of the dollar high, relative to what would otherwise be implied by comparative inflation rates and increasing U.S. current account deficits. This, too, is worrisome because an apparently over valued dollar holds down U.S. exports and has been particularly damaging to the U.S. manufacturing sector.

On the other hand, if foreign investors became convinced that U.S. government deficits will continue indefinitely, they might suddenly transfer investment funds to their own or third countries, and the exchange value of the dollar could fall precipitously. In fact, as foreign portfolios become "saturated" with dollar-denominated assets, capital inflows to the United States are likely to slow down even without declines in interest rates; at that point the exchange value of the dollar would almost certainly fall. This, in turn, would cause U.S. inflation rates to rise as the prices of imports and import-competing goods rise. A decline in the value of the dollar would also decrease the value of dollar assets that foreign investors hold, putting further downward pressure on the dollar. At some point in this sequence of events, however, U.S. interest rates would stop falling; indeed, they might even rise again as fears of crowding out increase. Whether the countervailing forces of rising interest rates would then tend to stabilize the exchange value of the dollar depends largely on investor expectations of the overall health of the U.S. economy. In this regard, expectations about U.S. government budget deficits and how they might be reduced are critical. A belief that such deficits will decline, even if slowly, is more likely to result in a soft landing for the dollar and a sufficient supply of investment funds than a projection of increasing deficits.

The Japanese economy, for its part, must increasingly concern itself with the opposite side of the same problem: a need to strengthen domestic demand, particularly consumption demand, in the face of much higher savings rates than the United States and other advanced industrial countries. In effect, the Japanese economy saves too much and spends too little on itself, either in private consumption or in government investment in domestic infrastructure. Since Japanese government budgets have registered large deficits for almost a decade now—to the point where, as Figure 2.7 noted, accumulated debt as a percentage of GNP is greater than in the United States—the government's willingness to spend public funds is not the issue. Rather, from the viewpoint of other countries, Japanese government spending has been at least partially misdirected. Certainly Japanese government spending has been less productive than it could have been—for example, subsidizing uneconomic railway lines and high-cost rice and beef rather than developing much needed infrastructure that would in turn stimulate growth at home *and* abroad.

As noted in Chapter 2, a continued business-as-usual approach to government spending in Japan produces trade and current account surpluses that will eventually cause the exchange value of the yen to rise, thereby restraining exports and stimulating imports. But the point when this equilibration will occur is highly uncertain since it depends in part on the level of U.S. government budget deficits and the exchange value of the dollar. Nonetheless, the price paid for a continued delay in directing Japanese savings toward more productive uses is considerable: by Japanese who live less well than their per capita income might otherwise justify and by those in other countries whose own growth rates would be improved by a higher growth rate in Japan. Some means of stimulating domestic demand, without triggering inflation, is sorely needed if Japan is to avoid creating constant strains on the international trading system. Prime Minister Nakasone, more than most Japanese leaders, has the individual flair required to propose and lead a program that would utilize Japan's excess savings for domestic development. But even he has been unable to find ways to deal with the possible inflationary consequences of increased government spending, particularly in light of the projected increases in government bond issues scheduled for 1985. Thus a *de facto* form of macroeconomic "beggar-thy-neighbor" policies continues in Japan with no solution in sight.[5]

The problems of a high U.S. government budget deficit and Japan's high savings rate may or may not lead to the undoing of the global economic recovery that began with the U.S. cyclical upturn in late 1982. Much depends, as noted in Chapter 2, on more or less unquantifiable factors (political events, expectations, and the like), which are the Achilles heel of the "science" of economics. However current issues are tackled in the course of 1985, U.S., Japanese, and global eco-

---

5. Japanese sometimes argue that U.S. government budget deficits are also an example of macroeconomic beggar-thy-neighbor policies, roughly comparable with allegations that the United States was exporting inflation in the 1960s. The trouble with these counterarguments is that while in the narrow sense they may be right, they are essentially debaters' points that overlook comparably beggar-thy-neighbor policies or actions going on in Japan. Justifiably or not, most Japanese political and governmental leaders continue to argue that Japan is either too "small" or too psychologically unsure of itself to stimulate world growth by stimulating domestic demand; meanwhile, these same leaders consider criticism of the way U.S. policies in effect lead the world as fair game. Many, if not most, American political and governmental leaders are clearly less tolerant of such Japanese arguments than they were in the past.

For further discussion of the notion that Japan could do more than it has done to stimulate domestic demand, see Herman Kahn and Thomas Pepper, *The Japanese Challenge: The Success and Failure of Economic Success* (New York: Thomas Y. Crowell, 1979), especially chaps. 6 and 7; Morgan Guaranty Trust Company, *World Financial Markets*, "Japanese Trade Frictions and the Yen," January 1982, pp 6-12; idem, "The Undervalued Yen: Causes and Policy Options," *World Financial Markets*, December 1982, pp. 1-7; idem, "Japanese Financial Liberalization and Yen Internationalization," *World Financial Markets*, June 1984, pp. 1-11; Jai-Hoon Yang, "Yen/Dollar Accord: Implications on Yen and Bilateral Relations," Part 1, *Japan Economic Journal*, September 24, 1984, pp. 19, 24; idem, "Yen/Dollar Accord: Implications on Yen and Bilateral relations," Part 2, *Japan Economic Journal*, October 2, 1984, pp. 19, 24.

nomic prospects for the second half of the 1980s are still unlikely to be as problem-prone as the ten years of stagflation from 1973 to 1982. The oil price increases, loose monetary policies, and expansive social welfare expenditures (particularly in Western Europe) prevalent at that time contributed to an unprecedented combination of high inflation and high unemployment.[6] For the rest of the 1980s oil prices are unlikely to increase as sharply or to have as damaging effects on the world economy as they did a decade ago. A commitment on the part of all advanced industrial countries to keep their money supplies under greater control than in the 1970s remains strong (some would say too strong). Growth in social welfare expenditures has tapered off, even in Western Europe. These changes in economic conditions and in underlying attitudes can, and in our view will, make a difference.

Where the economic problems of the 1970s were exacerbated by widespread pessimism about the benefits of economic growth, today's economic problems are excessive optimism about the ability of the current recovery to solve major problems without requiring difficult policy choices. For example, some supply-side economists in the United States believe that budget deficits can both disappear with growth and not restrain growth. Correspondingly, some Japanese government economists believe that Japan's chronically high trade surpluses can be eased by measures taken primarily in other economies. We believe that high U.S. government budget deficits and high Japanese savings rates are real and serious problems, but we also believe that if progress can be made in dealing with these major macroeconomic issues, the underlying strengths of both economies would promote the sustained, noninflationary growth that Americans, Japanese, and the rest of the world are seeking.

---

6. For an excellent discussion of the events contributing to the global stagflation following the 1973 oil price increases, see Paul W. McCracken, Guido Carli, Herbert Giersch, Attila Karasomanoglui, Ryutaro Komiya, Assar Lindbeck, Robert Marjolin, and Robin Matthews, *Towards Full Employment and Price Stability* (Paris: Organisation for Economic Co-operation and Development, June 1977). Analyses of events since then, which track the key policies and variables identified in that report, can be found in the *OECD Economic Outlook*, issued twice annually. For an interpretation of lessons to be learned from the 1973–82 decade, especially regarding the limits of economic analysis, see Stephen Marris, "Managing the World Economy: Will We Ever Learn?" *Essays in International Finance*, no. 155, International Finance Section, Department of Economics, Princeton University, Princeton, N.J., October 1984.

POLICY AND BUSINESS IMPLICATIONS

As the above discussion implies, macroeconomic conditions in both the United States and Japan will continue to have decisive effects on the relative competitiveness of different industries. The current U.S. recovery has led and initially has been more vigorous than Japan's. One effect has been to expand U.S. imports from Japan while depressing Japanese imports from the United States. This trend will continue for at least another year, since exchange rate changes influence trade flows some 12 to 18 months after they occur, and will be exacerbated by the lagged effects of a strong dollar, which decrease the price of Japanese goods relative to those produced in the United States in all markets. Thus, even if the yen strengthened significantly and soon, the trade effects on the U.S.-Japan bilateral balance would take some time to work themselves out.[7] Meanwhile, if a significant enough package of U.S. government spending cuts and revenue increases is agreed upon in 1985, U.S. interest rates would be likely to decline, with a corresponding and gradual decline in the exchange value of the dollar. When combined with a slowdown in U.S. growth that will occur for cyclical reasons (while Japanese and European growth is picking up), this gradual decline in the value of the dollar would lead to increased U.S. exports and to reductions in the U.S. trade and current account deficits. Trade and current account deficits would also be reduced, perhaps dramatically, if the U.S. economy went into a serious recession. However, this alternative is hardly preferable to the continued, if somewhat slower, growth and the gradual decline in trade and current account deficits projected above.

Assuming that a lengthy U.S. recession is avoided and improvements in the economic performance of other countries continue, both cyclical and structural trends will be working to reduce the overall U.S. trade deficit. As the Japanese recovery becomes more vigorous—and, as a separate matter, the yen strengthens somewhat—the U.S. trade

---

7. Some evidence suggests that Japanese exporters are basing their dollar prices and marketing strategies on a long-term yen/dollar exchange rate of ¥ 200 = $1. If this practice applies to a large volume of Japanese exports, an increase in the exchange value of the yen would not greatly affect the average dollar price of Japanese goods in the short term. As a result, adjustments in the trade balance could be smaller than expected and take much longer than the 12-to-18-month average.

deficit with Japan will also narrow. However, because Japan's growth rate is likely to remain higher, on average, than those of most other advanced industrial countries for some years hence, the associated high productivity growth will enhance prospects for Japan's leading edge industries by holding costs down and expanding markets. Under these circumstances, many U.S. industries would see Japanese competition intensify. By implication, political pressures for protectionism in some sectors will continue despite a likely reduction in the U.S. trade and current account deficits with Japan.

In this environment, Japanese policymakers will remain under continuing pressure to accelerate the opening of the domestic market by stimulating domestic demand and accelerating the pace of trade and financial market liberalization. These are steps the Japanese economy needs to take in any case if it is to maintain its above-average growth rate while continuing to catch up to other advanced industrial countries in housing, leisure time, wealth per capita, and so on. For U.S. policymakers, some measures that facilitate increased savings, investment, and productivity growth will remain critical. Only by continued attention to these goals can U.S. policymakers hope to neutralize the lingering effects of a strong dollar.

However these macroeconomic issues are dealt with, the evolution of the Japanese economy described in earlier chapters will enable U.S.-based firms to find increasing opportunities to export to Japan and to invest with Japan-based firms in new projects in the United States, Japan, and third countries. For their part, Japan-based firms will find it increasingly attractive to encourage various forms of foreign participation in the Japanese domestic market and to join with U.S.-based firms in investment activities in the United States, Japan, and third countries.

In financial services, for example, both Japan-based and foreign-based banks are developing new products to facilitate investment both in Japan and abroad. The gradual deregulation of Japanese interest rates brought about by the maturing of the economy and its increasing integration with the world economy has stimulated Japan-based banks to offer new and more flexible instruments of savings—if only to compete with foreign-based banks whose less regulated domestic markets enabled them to develop these instuments earlier than Japan-based banks and thus to attract deposits from an enormous pool of previously untapped Japanese savings. Efforts to apply U.S.-based techniques for pension fund management have offered such clearly improved rates of return that Japanese pension fund managers have begun to seek a wholesale change in the structure of pension fund management in Japan. Where Japanese trust banks and life insurance companies had previously held essentially monopoly rights to manage these funds without fear of competition from other financial institutions, they have now been forced by events to adjust to competition from both domestic and foreign financial institutions. A similar process is beginning to occur in the area of venture capital financings. U.S.-based venture capital funds are seeking Japanese money to enlarge the size of their asset base within the U.S., and set up preliminary or nascent venture capital efforts in Japan. Meanwhile, Japan-based financial institutions are seeking to invest in U.S.-based venture capital projects where U.S. market conditions and expertise are clearly superior. In other words, Japan-based firms are now seeking cooperative relationships with foreign-based firms to take advantage of the expertise the latter can offer abroad or the specialized knowledge they might provide to Japan-based firms that previously lacked such experience.[8]

Similar processes are also at work in manufacturing sectors. As the process of deregulation continues in information processing, some foreign-based firms with superior technological or marketing capabilities—as well as the willingness and ability to sustain investment costs that may only bear fruit over a medium- or long-term period—are teaming up with new or existing Japan-based firms. A leading example to date, as discussed in Chapter 5, is in the provision of value-added networks for communications services. Others are springing up to service an increasingly sophisticated information processing industry.[9] Merck Sharp & Dohme's purchase of Banyu Corporation is an example of a similar trend in the pharmaceutical area. In the past, most U.S.-based pharmaceutical companies operated in Japan through licensing agreements. Merck's purchase of Banyu was designed to give it direct access to a distribution system in the Japanese domestic market while providing a much greater R & D capability than was otherwise likely to be developed in a highly fragmented domestic industry.

Even in declining industries, there are increased opportunities for

---

8. For example, in August 1984 an international venture fund involving Japanese, British, and American firms was established. The participants in this fund are: Orient Leasing Co., Ltd.; Daiwa Securities Co., Ltd; Sanwa Bank, Ltd.; Dai-Ichi Mutual Life Insurance Co., Ltd.; Baring Brothers & Co.; and Hambrecht & Quist.

trade between U.S.-based and Japan-based firms. Foreign-based producers that have a distinct advantage over Japan-based producers because of lower energy or raw material costs or greater economies of scale should in principle be able to increase exports to the Japanese market. Japan-based producers will naturally resist increased import penetration, perhaps by selling at or below cost in an effort to hold market share and avoid the costs of exiting from an industry. But as the experience with aluminum suggests, when Japanese firms find themselves saddled with problems of long-term structural decline, even they must cut capacity in uncompetitive business or product lines and develop new products or production methods. Since the Japanese economy has now entered a stage when a number of basic manufacturing industries will have to adjust to changing conditions, other lower-priced imports are likely to penetrate the Japanese market when prospective exporters are able to bring the necessary resources to bear to make this happen.

Indeed, the general direction in which the Japanese economy has been evolving has been clear for more than a decade. A major issue for potential exporters to the Japanese market as well as for foreign governments has been the pace at which this evolution has occured. Once the impact of Japanese export successes became so visible, competing producers in other countries saw much more clearly than before both the dangers facing their own businesses and the potential opportunities for sales to the Japanese market. After many years in which U.S.

---

9. For example, in December 1984, Westinghouse Electric Corporation and Toshiba Corporation, both large-sized diversified manufacturers with extensive operations in each other's home market, announced a joint venture to produce color cathode-ray tubes in the United States for use in computer terminals and professional graphics equipment. Douglas D. Danforth, Chairman and chief executive officer of Westinghouse, was quoted as saying that Toshiba ''has the best technology in the world and we have the markets and the manufacturing infrastructure.'' See Carol Hymowitz and Linda M. Watkins, ''Westinghouse Plans Venture with Toshiba,'' *Wall Street Journal*, December 12, 1984, p. 8. For a comprehensive survey of changing technological, financial, and political conditions affecting the semiconductor industry, see Daniel I. Okimoto, Takuo Sugano, and Franklin B. Weinstein, eds., *Competitive Edge: The Semiconductor Industry in the U.S. and Japan* (Stanford, Calif.: Stanford University Press, 1984).

producers either neglected potential sales to Japan or tolerated the Japanese government's application of infant-industry protection to nascent Japanese industries, many U.S. business and government leaders began to try to rectify the disadvantages under which they realized they had to operate. Often they have reacted to the advantages that Japanese firms enjoy by demanding an immediate "right" to export to Japan under the spirit of the postwar reciprocal trading system. In Japanese eyes, however, the reciprocal trading system has never been an issue since the direction of change has always been toward increased openness. Moreover, the market-based advantages that Japanese firms might now enjoy, after many years of building up their technological, financial, and marketing capabilities, are factors that U.S. business and government leaders will have to consider as simply another part of contemporary reality—a fact of life that the Japanese see no need to nullify to make things easier for U.S.-based competitors.

Whatever the legacies of the past, in particular the remaining explicit barriers to foreign participation in the Japanese market, the only effective means of gaining entry is first of all to have a product with a clear competitive edge. Without this, no amount of government pressure to open the market is likely to be effective. Even with a product that has a clear edge, the success of any given venture depends on a whole panoply of business-specific factors—for example, whether a new entrant is trying to build sales in a fast-growing or a mature market, to sell components or finished products, or to seek success in a sector with few or many competitors.

The various market-based opportunities discussed above would be facilitated by a trade policy environment that reinforced long-term market trends. Indeed, the challenge facing U.S. policymakers, in their attempts to improve access to the Japanese market, is to seek goals that are achievable as well as desirable and to do so in ways that do not prove counterproductive to long-term U.S. interests. Frequent comments by some U.S. leaders suggesting that the primary responsibility for reducing U.S. trade deficits with Japan lies with the Japanese government, rather than with either the U.S. government or the U.S. economy as a whole, are almost beside the point except for their political effects. Public statements can sometimes be a useful prod to Japanese negotiators who have traditionally "relied" on U.S. pressure to help them make decisions that would otherwise be politically difficult at home. Usually, however, such political responses to basically economic problems exacerbate bilateral political relations without helping to solve economic problems. The emphasis should be on attaining practical results, which means in turn to create incentives for Japanese negotiators to see improved market access as a net gain, both to the Japanese economy and to themselves as government officials. Obviously this is no easy task, but it appears to have been accomplished in recent U.S. government initiatives involving financial market liberalization and information processing.

In six months of negotiations culminating in May 1984, officials from the Treasury Department and the Ministry of Finance agreed on a timetable for further liberalization of Japanese domestic interest rates, an expansion of ground rules governing Euroyen financings, and increased scope for U.S.-based financial institutions operating in Japan, including the right to engage in pension and fund management. The important lesson from these talks was the way negotiators from both countries found it useful to emphasize the long-term gains of continued liberalization of the Japanese financial system, even at the risk of possibly increasing U.S.-Japanese trade and current account deficits in the short term. Instead of imposing capital controls in a possibly futile effort to strengthen the exchange value of the yen vis-à-vis the dollar—a step that would have constituted a complete reversal of U.S. and Japanese claims to be seeking a steady liberalization of international financial transactions—officials from both countries put their faith in the ability of trade and financial markets to equilibrate soon enough to fend off protectionist pressures from U.S. export-oriented industries hurt by a high exchange value for the dollar. Once they were willing to bear that burden themselves, U.S. officials had the edge in arguing to Japanese officials that a definite timetable for further interest rate liberalization and increased Euroyen transactions could no longer be put off. The argument that a more market-based interest rate structure and increased Euroyen transactions would in time increase total demand for the yen and the exchange value of the yen in international financial transactions was accepted by both sides. Thus, Japanese officials, once they could no longer avoid these steps through the "self-sacrifice" of reimposing capital controls and other trade-restrictive moves in response to U.S. political demands, found themselves trapped by their own logic that Japan was gradually opening up. These arguments spilled over into the question of access to the Japanese market for U.S.-based financial institutions since this, too, appeared to be an all-too-reasonable request in light of the gradual liberalization that all sides had been saying was under way.[10]

Similarly, in recent developments in information processing, sustained attention and consultations by U.S. government officials with U.S.-based industry representatives as well as Japanese government officals contributed to an easing of potentially contentious issues over the ground rules governing VANs, and property rights for software. U.S. officials contended, correctly in our view, that proposed Japanese legislation in these areas had considerable international implications and could not, as Japanese officials initially contended, be considered as a purely domestic matter. After heated negotiations, Japanese officials accepted the principle that U.S. officials were trying to advance, although much disagreement remains about the implementing language.

In domestic political terms, perhaps the most vexing problems in both countries concern declining industries. As Americans continue to face problems of declining competitiveness, the stated Japanese preference for shifting out of declining industries into new areas is well worth

---

10. The actual negotiations culminating in the May 1984 agreement were hardly as smooth as the above account might imply. Some evidence suggests that Donald T. Regan, the U.S. Secretary of the Treasury, personally intervened to withhold U.S. approval of an increased Japanese contribution to the International Development Association, the soft loan arm of the World Bank, and a correspondingly increased Japanese role in policy making at the World Bank, as leverage to pressure the Ministry of Finance to be more forthcoming in bilateral U.S.-Japan talks. Since the MOF found itself in the awkward position of having previously assured the Japanese Diet that an increased Japanese role in the World Bank was in the offing, it stood to lose considerable face, in domestic political terms, if the United States carried through with its threat. This bit of extra leverage doubtless helped the U.S. negotiating position but would not have mattered much if the underlying market-based logic behind that position had not also been as strong as it was. Similarly, in gaining access for U.S. banks to engage in pension fund management in Japan, Treasury negotiators were operating in an environment in which market-based pressures had already created incentives for the MOF to accept the proposal. Japanese pension fund managers and U.S.-based financial institutions were privately considering ways to apply U.S.-based pension fund management techniques to the Japanese market through offshore facilities. Attempts to delay full-scale approval for U.S.-based banks to engage in pension fund management in Japan itself would probably have not worked.

emphasizing. When financial support has been given to declining industries in Japan, it typically has been given with strings attached—namely, the beneficiaries must reduce capacity in unprofitable areas and, to the degree possible, move into new areas that will not require government assistance. This conditionality has been successfully employed in the major examples of adjustment that have occurred to date. However, conditionality worked best in shipbuilding, where Japanese producers represented about half of total world production and were among the most competitive. For this reason, when exogenous factors (that is, the collapse in the tanker market following the 1973/74 oil price increases) required the industry to cut capacity, it could do so, albeit painfully, while still remaining highly competitive in the share of the world market that it retained. Conditionality in the provision of adjustment assistance worked as well as it did because the industry was competitive enough to be able to use the aid in the process of diversification. Other industries in Japan that now face major adjustment burdens but that are much less competitive in the world market than was shipbuilding are likely to run into greater difficulties even when receiving government assistance. To provide for adjustment assistance in the United States, the 1974 Trade Act requires U.S.-based firms to prove that their competitive decline is significantly affected by imports. This provision of U.S. policy has, on balance, not helped to revitalize declining industries or even to facilitate industry adjustment. For this reason, policymakers are currently discussing changes in adjustment policies, especially how the concept of conditionality might be applied in the United States. As the Japanese experience has shown, conditionality can be used most effectively under market conditions that prevail only rarely. Nonetheless, more attention to ways that conditionality can facilitate adjustment as well as broadening the criteria by which firms or workers can qualify for assistance is needed to make any adjustment program more than a mere drain on the public treasury.

In recent years, many Americans have seen Japan's overall system of industrial development as a model to adopt in the process of trying to revitalize the U.S. economy. This ignores an important lesson from the Japanese experience: The Japanese government's ability to provide detailed direction for industrial development has declined significantly over time. Those who argue that the United States should adopt an explicit industrial policy model along Japanese lines should ask themselves whether the adoption of a Japanese model is likely to work in the United States, given that in Japan itself it no longer works as it once did. In contrast to Japan, where the relationship between business and government has been and remains generally cooperative, this relationship in the United States has generally been more adversarial. Even if business-government relations in the United States improve, the United States will remain a much more heterogeneous country than Japan, and Americans would doubtless resist the kind of cooperative relationship implied by a Japanese model. For one thing, MITI's ability to use administrative guidance is based on a much more flexible legislative mandate than is customary in the United States. Thus quite apart from current arguments about the desirability of smaller versus larger government, an agency or department with the discretionary authority enjoyed even by a much-weakened MITI goes against deeply rooted U.S. political traditions.

Some advocates of a Japanese-style approach for the United States argue that a new Cabinet department, perhaps called The Department of Trade and Industry (DITI), could coordinate U.S. economic policies and thereby strengthen U.S. competitiveness. Better policy coordination and more internal consistency are eminently desirable goals, but to suggest that one Cabinet department can coordinate the work of others, on behalf of the executive branch as a whole, is to go against the record of numerous previous attempts to give one department responsibility for matters normally within the purview of another.

Even the Office of the U.S. Trade Representative (USTR), which was created more than 20 years ago to perform a coordinating function with regard to trade policy, cannot, as it is currently structured, perform a broad-based coordinating role. The role of the USTR, by now firmly fixed in the minds of other executive branch agencies, is that of a negotiating body. We see no easy way to expand these responsibilities to enable the USTR to take on coordinating functions but also no persuasive reasons to incorporate USTR's negotiating role into another agency or department. On the other hand, a small organization within the White House that could assume a role in policy coordination without trying to plan what new industries are likely or desirable would probably improve U.S. policy-making. Thus we suggest the formation of an Economic Policy Council comparable to the National Security Council (NSC), and propose that it have only a small to medium-size staff to prevent its becoming a separate constituency in itself. There have been previous coordinating bodies within the White House, but none have had a lasting impact on U.S. policy-making, for example, the Council for International Economic Policy, which operated during the Nixon administration, or the Domestic Council, which, although designed as a counterpart to the NSC, never acquired the latter's sustained authority. Earlier and current ad hoc Cabinet-level councils have been too informal to operate as effectively as the NSC. An institutionalization of a policy-making process that incorporates both macro- and micro-factors, that integrates analyses of both domestic and international conditions, and that has sufficient authority to do the job is sorely needed.

Whatever procedural improvements are made, because of the overriding importance of macroeconomic factors, many bilateral economic problems will remain intractable in the short term. Although political conditions sometimes call for dramatic steps, to expect immediate improvements in trade patterns only produces disappointment. Thus trade officials in both the U.S. and Japan would do both countries a service if they focused even more attention on the major macroeconomic issues that underlie other economic and trade problems and minimized or avoided actions that are primarily a political response to adverse macroeconomic conditions.

THE FUTURE OF U.S.-JAPANESE RELATIONS

For all the talk of "crises" in U.S.-Japanese relations over the years, these have led to and will continue to lead to an increasing degree of interaction between the two societies on virtually every level. The relationship is both cooperative and competitive, with the benefits of cooperation clearly outweighing the costs. This has sometimes seemed hard to realize because many of the positive effects of increased economic interdependence—larger markets for both countries, cheaper sources of supply, higher growth rates, a stronger Western alliance, and an emerging concept of a Pacific Community—all bring long-term benefits that are usually less visible than short-term and seemingly negative costs. Moreover, political relations between countries are often subject to more volatility than the underlying economic or cultural relations. Sharp swings in mood, based on any number of variables (such as, personality clashes between political or governmental leaders, intragovernmental "turf battles," and political pressures that are resolved by treating foreign interests as scapegoats), all affect intergovernmental relations, but without arousing much interest elsewhere in the country.

As suggested in Chapter 1, the strains that have occurred in U.S.-

Japanese relations—and there have been many—stem fundamentally from the change in the relative positions of the U.S. and Japanese economies. Once the Japanese economy had more or less caught up to the level of the U.S. economy, while Japanese politicians seemed to Americans to delay the assumption of additional the defense or economic responsibilities in terms of what Americans perceived to be common interests, political friction with the United States was inevitable. Similar political friction has plagued U.S. relations with allies in the North Atlantic Treaty Organization. In fact, the United States and its allies are all trying to have it both ways: The United States would like its allies to bear a greater share of what it sees as common burdens while leaving itself free to make various decisions on behalf of these alliances almost unilaterally. Meanwhile, U.S. allies recognize all too well their dependence on the United States for their security vis-a-vis the Soviet Union, but they also believe that assuming a greater share of common burdens would not necessarily lead to a proportionate increase in benefits. In other words, the Soviet threat is significant and lasting enough to give the United States its own reasons for maintaining existing alliances without increased contributions from allies.[11]

Such political friction notwithstanding, we believe that a continuation of existing trends in U.S.-Japanese relations implies a future that will remain, on balance, cooperative. Those aspects of the relationship

---

11. In seminal writings on coalition behavior, Mancur Olson argues that a "free ride" is a characteristic behavior pattern in large-size groups, including countries. In Olson's view, most behavior is motivated by the prospect of specific gains. In large groups, Olson argues that any single individual is likely to receive the benefits of actions taken by others whether he or she contributes to producing those benefits or not. In other words, in large-size groups, it is easy to get a free ride, and the larger the size of the group, the easier it is to benefit from a free ride. Applying this distinction to relationships between countries, Olson argues that in the absence of moral constraints to share a burden or the sense of community that in his view exists only in small-size groups, a free ride is all too easy to accept. By implication, U.S.-Japanese relations will continue to be bedeviled by arguments over burden sharing under almost any circumstances, and the relationship will flourish to the degree that concrete benefits are gradually built up in spite of continuing political differences. See Mancur Olson, *The Logic of Collective Action* (Cambridge, Mass.: Harvard University Press, 1971); and idem, *The Rise and Decline of Nations* (New Haven, Conn.: Yale University Press, 1982).

that are indeed competitive—that is, economic competition between U.S.-based and Japan-based firms in their respective markets and in third-country markets and, more important perhaps, political disagreements between the two governments over the ground rules governing economic competition—are likely to be kept within certain limits by the array of cooperative economic and political interests that have also been built up in the postwar years. Thus, a basically cooperative pattern of relations is likely to be preserved more or less indefinitely by a self-correcting process. This need not necessarily restore the particular equilibrium point that previously prevailed, but simply take sufficient account of a too-sharp movement in a destabilizing direction to bring bilateral relations back toward their previous pattern. In this sense a projection of a basically cooperative pattern of U.S.-Japanese relations can encompass a wide range of cooperative and competitive (or even acrimonious) relationships.[12]

Under these circumstances, the phenomenon of evolutionary change in postwar Japan has profound implications for the rest of the world. Once Japan is seen by itself and others primarily in terms of its record of sustained economic development, rather than for its military and political record before and during World War II, Japan will then be seen—by Japanese as well as others—as a world leader. It will be the pioneering example that other nations will seek to follow in their own efforts to make the transition from historic poverty to contemporary affluence. Already, Japan's emphasis on economic development is being pursued (and improved upon) by South Korea, Taiwan, Hong Kong, and Singapore, sometimes called the "New Japans." South Korea, for example, achieved an average real growth of 8.1 percent a year from 1961 to 1982. As happened 10 to 20 years earlier in Japan, this high and sustained growth has wrought a "quiet revolution," not only in per capita income but also in social structure.[13] Similar changes, with differences in detail, are apparent in the other three high-growth

---

12. This argument is developed in greater detail in Thomas Pepper, Merit E. Janow, and Jimmy W. Wheeler, *Alternative Futures in U.S.-Japanese Relations*, (Washington, D.C., and Tokyo: United States-Japan Advisory Commission, September 1984).

13. The landed gentry and government officials that held privileged positions in Korean society for centuries are being replaced by a nouveau riche group of business executives.

countries of East and Southeast Asia. Indeed, the 20 to 25 years of sustained economic development in South Korea, Taiwan, Hong Kong, and Singapore—none of them well endowed with natural resources and all facing one or another kind of national security threat—have now become an example that the larger, resource-rich countries of East and Southeast Asia are also trying to follow. Even more important, in terms of the magnitude of potential impact on the rest of the world, is the recently enhanced commitment of Chinese leaders to make economic development through an increased reliance on market forces China's most important goal. If these efforts prove successful and politically sustainable, the entry of another quarter of the world's population into increased trading and investment relationships with other countries would stimulate growth throughout the global economy.

In a world environment in which the United States is economically dynamic and militarily strong enough to maintain the basic dimensions of postwar international relations, the kind of economic achievements that Japan has made for the past 40 years could be repeated by many other countries. As this process occurs, all the advanced industrial countries, including Japan, would then face the same choices that the predominantly Western advanced countries have had to face as a result of Japan's economic success: what goals to seek in light of the achievements of others; whether to try to be at least as economically dynamic as other countries to keep pace with changes taking place elsewhere in the world.

APPENDIX A

**Tax Schedules
and Government
Financial Assistance**

Table A.1

TAX REVENUE ESTIMATES BY ITEM, 1983

	National Taxes			Local Taxes	
Tax Item	Amount (¥ 100 million)	Percent	Tax Item	Amount (¥ 100 million)	Percent
General account			Ordinary taxes		
Direct taxes			Prefectural taxes		
Income tax	138,050	40.5	Prefectural inhabitants tax	24,227	12.5
Corporation tax	94,970	27.8	Enterprise tax	30,734	19.2
Inheritance tax and gift tax	7,930	2.3	Real property acquisition tax	3,617	1.7
			Prefectural tobacco consumption tax	2,836	1.5
Indirect taxes and the like			Local entertainment tax	999	0.5
Liquor tax	18,600	5.5	Tax on consumption at hotels and restaurants	4,618	2.4
Sugar excise tax	410	0.1	Automobile tax	8,635	4.5
Gasoline tax	16,530	4.8	Mine-lot tax	10	0.0
Liquified petroleum gas tax	150	0.0	Hunters license tax	32	0.0
Aviation fuel tax	520	0.2	Prefectural property tax	87	0.0
Petroleum tax	4,290	1.3			
Commodity tax	13,140	3.9	Municipal taxes		
Playing-cards tax	10	0.0	Municipal inhabitants tax	52,430	27.5
Bourse tax	150	0.0	Municipal property tax[a]	36,215	19.0
Securities transaction tax	2,570	0.8			
Travel tax	750	0.2			

Admission tax	80	0.0
Motor vehicle tonnage tax	4,690	1.4
Customs duty	7,200	2.1
Tonnage due	80	0.0
Stamp revenue	13,030	3.8
Monopoly profits	9,878	2.9
Light vehicle tax	499	0.3
Municipal tobacco consumption tax	4,983	2.6
Electricity and gas taxes	4,541	2.4
Mineral product tax	43	0.0
Timber delivery tax	25	0.0
Special landholding tax	546	0.3

Special Accounts

Local road tax[b]	2,973	0.9
Liquefied petroleum gas tax[b]	150	0.0
Aviation fuel tax[b]	95	0.0
Motor vehicle tonnage tax[b]	1,563	0.5
Special tonnage duty[b]	100	0.0
Customs duty on oil	1,360	0.4
Promotion of resources development tax	1,757	0.5

Earmarked taxes

Prefectures[c]	7,696	4.0
Cities, towns, and villages[d]	7,916	4.2

Total	341,026	100.0
Total	190,689	100.0

[a]Municipal property tax includes charges on national assets and public corporation's assets.
[b]Distributed to the local governments.
[c]Automobile acquisition tax, light-oil delivery tax, and so on, are included.
[d]Bathing tax, business office tax, city planning, and so on, are included.
Source: Ministry of Finance, *An Outline of Japanese Taxes, 1983* (Tokyo: MOF, 1983), pp. 15–16.

Table A.2

SHARES OF CORPORATION TAX AND INCOME TAX IN TOTAL NATIONAL TAX REVENUE, 1950–81

	Total National Tax Revenue (¥ 100 million)	Corporation Tax Amount (¥ 100 million)	Corporation Tax Percent	Income Tax Amount (¥ 100 million)	Income Tax Percent
1950	5,708	838	14.7	2,201	38.6
1955	9,369	1,921	20.5	2,787	29.7
1960	18,015	5,734	31.8	3,906	21.7
1965	32,797	9,271	28.3	9,704	29.6
1970	77,754	25,672	33.0	24,282	31.2
1975	145,068	41,279	28.5	54,823	37.8
1980	283,731	89,227	31.4	107,996	38.1
1981	304,622	88,225	29.0	119,804	39.3
Revised budget 1982	320,056	90,560	28.3	127,690	39.9
Budget 1983	341,026	94,970	27.8	138,050	40.5

Source: Ministry of Finance, *An Outline of Japanese Taxes, 1983* (Tokyo: MOF, 1983), p. 291.

Table A.3
RATES OF INDIVIDUAL INCOME TAX

Taxable Income (¥) (A)		Marginal Tax Rate (percent) (B)	Cumulative Tax for Each Bracket (¥) (C)	Average Tax Rate (at bracket maximum) (percent)
Over	But Not Over			
—	600,000	10	—	10.0
600,000	1,200,000	12	60,000	11.0
1,200,000	1,800,000	14	132,000	12.0
1,800,000	2,400,000	16	216,000	13.0
2,400,000	3,000,000	18	312,000	14.0
3,000,000	4,000,000	21	420,000	15.8
4,000,000	5,000,000	24	630,000	17.4
5,000,000	6,000,000	27	870,000	19.0
6,000,000	7,000,000	30	1,140,000	20.6
7,000,000	8,000,000	34	1,440,000	22.3
8,000,000	10,000,000	38	1,780,000	25.5

Table A.3 (Continued)

Taxable Income (¥) (A)		Marginal Tax Rate (percent) (B)	Cumulative Tax for Each Bracket (¥) (C)	Average Tax Rate (at bracket maximum) (percent)
Over	But Not Over			
10,000,000	12,000,000	42	2,540,000	28.2
12,000,000	15,000,000	46	3,380,000	31.7
15,000,000	20,000,000	50	4,760,000	36.3
20,000,000	30,000,000	55	7,260,000	42.5
30,000,000	40,000,000	60	12,760,000	46.9
40,000,000	60,000,000	65	18,760,000	52.9
60,000,000	80,000,000	70	31,760,000	57.2
80,000,000		75	45,760,000	—

Note: The tax liability is obtained by multiplying the taxable income in excess of the amount (A) by the rate (B) and adding the amount (C). For example, income tax due on taxable income of ¥ 25 million is: [¥ 25,000,000 − ¥ 20,000,000 (A)] × 0.55 (B) + ¥ 7,260,000 (C) = ¥ 10,010,000.

Source: Ministry of Finance, An Outline of Japanese Taxes, 1983 (Tokyo: MOF, 1983), p. 53.

Table A.4
LOCAL INCOME LEVIES

Prefectural Tax Rate		Municipal Tax Rate	
¥ (Thousands)	Percent	¥ (Thousands)	Percent
Not over		Not over	
300	2	300	2
500	2	450	3
800	2	700	4
1,100	2	1,000	5
1,500	2	1,300	6
2,500	4	2,300	7
4,000	4	3,700	8
6,000	4	5,700	9
10,000	4	9,500	10
20,000	4	19,000	11
30,000	4	29,000	12
50,000	4	49,000	13
Over		Over	
50,000	4	49,000	14

Source: Yuji Gomi, *Guide to Japanese Taxes, 1981–82* (Tokyo: Zaikei Shōhō Sha, 1981), p. 32.

Table A.5
TAX BURDEN ON CORPORATE INCOME
(Effective Tax Rate in Percent)

	Up to ¥ 3.5 Million	¥ 3.5 Million to ¥ 7 Million	¥ 7 Million to ¥ 8 Million	Over ¥ 8 Million
Corporate	26.60	25.88	25.18	34.82
Inhabitant taxes				
Prefectural	1.33	1.29	1.26	1.74
Municipal	3.27	3.18	3.10	4.28
Enterprise tax	5.66	8.26	10.71	10.71
Total	36.86	38.61	40.25	51.55

Note: The enterprise tax is deductible in computing the tax basis for the corporate tax and the enterprise tax itself. Indirectly it is also deductible in computing the inhabitant tax as well. It is assumed that 30 percent of corporate income before tax is distributed as dividends—to which a lower marginal tax rate is applied.

Source: Yuji Gomi, *Guide to Japanese Taxes, 1982–83* (Tokyo: Zaikei Shōhō Sha, 1982), p. 26.

Table A.6
USEFUL LIVES OF SELECTED FIXED ASSETS
(In Years)

Description of Assets	Useful Life
Tangible fixed assets other than machinery and equipment	
Reinforced concrete buildings (for office)	65
Wooden buildings (for office)	26
Steel vessels (2,000 tons or more)	15
Steel tankers (2,000 tons or more)	13
Steel fishing vessels (500 tons or more)	12
Elevators	17
Airplanes (for international service)	10
Electronic computers	6
Desks, chairs, or cabinets made of metal	15
Air conditioners or heaters	15
Typewriters	5
Trucks (for transport business)	4
Passenger automobiles (taxis)	4
Machinery and equipment	
Chemical condiment manufacturing plants	7
Sugar refinery plants	13
Beer brewery plants	14
Raw silk manufacturing plants	10
Worsted spinning plants	10
Pulp manufacturing plants	12
Chemical fertilizer manufacturing plants	10
Polyethylene manufacturing plants	8
Synthetic fiber manufacturing plants	7
Rayon yarn or rayon staple manufacturing plants	9
Plate or sheet glass manufacturing plants	14
Cement furnaces	13
Iron and steel manufacturing plants	14
Metallic machine tool manufacturing plants	10
Electrical machinery and appliances manufacturing plants	11
Automobile manufacturing plants	10
Lens or other optical instrument manufacturing plants	11
Radio or television broadcasting equipment	6
Hydraulic power generation plant for electric utilities	22
Intangible fixed assets	
Patent rights	8
Utility model rights	5

Source: Ministry of Finance, *An Outline of Japanese Taxes, 1983* (Tokyo: MOF, 1983), p. 84.

Table A.7
SPECIAL DEPRECIATION ALLOWANCES

	Allowance[a] (percent)
I. Increased initial depreciation	
A. Energy-saving equipment (April 1, 1981 to March 31, 1984)	30[b]
B. Designated plant and equipment	
1. Used for the prevention of environmental pollution	25
2. Designed not to cause environmental pollution	18
3. For industrial water supply, constructed in lieu of a well in designated areas	18
4. For recycling that may contribute to the promotion of efficient use of resources	18
5. And other depreciable assets that are newly developed to use the energy resources effectively	18
6. Composing an integrated system, such as combination of electronic equipment for data analysis and industrial machinery	10[b]
7. Certain assets used for the structural adjustment of the specific basic material industries	18[b] (8 other than machinery)
8. Steel vessels used by ocean transportation enterprises	15
9. Aircraft used by air transportation enterprises	11
10. Buildings for stores and shops jointly operated by retailers	8
C. Designated plant and equipment in developing areas whose prices are more than ¥ 15 million	
1. Underdeveloped areas, coal mining regions, agricultural areas, depopulated	

Table A.7 (*Continued*)

	Allowance[a] (percent)
areas, severely depressed local industrial areas, and industrial development areas	18 (equipment) 8 (plant)
2. Okinawa Industrial Development Region[b]	34 (equipment) 20 (plant)
3. Okinawa Free Trade Zone[b]	50 (equipment) 25 (plant)
D. Assets used for earthquake disaster prevention	18
E. Machinery and equipment	
1. Acquired by small- or medium-sized enterprises or agricultural cooperative associations, and the like, and whose prices are more than ¥ 1.4 million	14
2. For medical use acquired by medical corporations and whose prices are more than ¥ 1.4 million	18
F. Specific shafts and lifts for mining use	100
G. Forestation	
1. Special initial amortization on forestation expenses in the year in which the expenses are incurred	27
2. Special initial depreciation of the acquisition cost of the specific constructions for forestation	20
H. Special initial depreciation of the acquisition cost of facilities for members' mutual benefits (for buildings, the allowance is 16 percent, or 8 percent of the acquisition cost) acquired by a designated association that accumulates (a)	

Table A.7 (*Continued*)

	Allowance[a] (percent)
reserves for structural improvement projects of small- and medium-sized enterprises, (b) reserves for promotion of small- and medium-sized enterprises as subcontractors, or (c) reserves for promotion of traditional craft industries	25
I. Special amortization of expenditures for R & D purposes paid to specified associations mainly engaged in a research work	100
J. Special initial depreciation on assets acquired by small- and medium-sized enterprises according to the rationalization program under the Law on Extraordinary Measures for small and medium enterprises located together in specific areas	18 (equipment) 8 (plant)
II. Accelerated depreciation	
A. Houses newly built for rent	
1. Useful life under 45 years	47/5[c]
2. Useful life 45 years or over	70/5
B. Construction eligible for requirements of law concerning redevelopment of metropolitan area	14/5
C. Newly constructed storage for crude liquefied petroleum gas	34/5
D. Specified fireproof warehouses used for trade purposes and silos for grains	30/5
E. Machinery used by members of the commercial and industrial cooperatives, textile industry, and so on, which execute the plan for promotion of rationalization of small- and	

Table A.7 (*Continued*)

	Allowance[a] (percent)
medium-sized enterprises or the structural improvement project of textile industry	30/5
F. A corporation where not less than 25 percent of the employees at the end of accounting period are handicapped persons	18/life 25/life (factory buildings)
G. Miscellaneous other accelerated depreciation benefits are given, including designated equipment for small- and medium-sized enterprises changing their business in order to cope with the grant of a preferential tariff, the facilities for a qualified international tourist hotel, and for various mining and forestry industries	

[a]These allowances are in addition to the regular depreciation schedule.
[b]This item was reported on in one of the two sources used.
[c]This designation is defined to mean that the firm is permitted to add 50 percent to ordinary depreciation for the first five years. Subsequent use is interpreted analogously.

Sources: Ministry of Finance, *An Outline of Japanese Taxes, 1983* (Tokyo: MOF, 1983), pp. 85–88; and Yuji Gomi, *Guide to Japanese Taxes, 1982–83* (Tokyo: Zaikei Shōhō Sha, 1982), pp. 316-22.

Table A.8
REVENUE LOSSES ATTRIBUTABLE TO SPECIAL TAXATION MEASURES

	1972	1973	1974	1975	1976	1977	1978	1979	1980	1981
I. Promotion of savings, and the like										
1. Exemption for interest on small (minor) deposits	69	71	87	97	109	131	147	159	206	263
2. Separate taxation on interest income	28	27	22	11	12	7	8	7	9	13
3. Separate taxation on dividend income	41	53	49	50	34	30	35	42	51	58
4. Life insurance premiums deduction	76	88	89	106	111	147	152	156	163	191
5. Other	5	7	6	7	8	9	10	11	11	12
II. Environmental development, regional development, and the like										
6. Reduced taxation for obtaining houses	40	74	106	84	83	81	97	102	110	106
7. Reduced taxation for overpopulated city relief measures	3	4	3	0	2	1	0	3	1	3
8. Reduced taxation for regional development	3	5	8	12	12	14	12	13	8	11
9. Reduced taxation for pollution control	34	38	49	61	37	24	29	37	28	33

III. Resource development, and the like									
10. Overseas investment loss reserve	14	15	19	26	20	12	7	0	0	0
11. Atomic power plant construction reserve	5	10	1	1	0	15	8	18	19	21
12. Expenditure in prospecting for mineral deposits	1	2	4	2	2	3	0	0	0	0
IV. Promotion of technology, modernization of equipment									
13. Experimental and research expenses tax credit	9	20	21	21	14	17	15	21	24	27
14. Overseas technical service transactions	4	5	10	12	8	12	10	13	14	15
15. Electronic computer repurchase loss reserve	10	6	3	5	5	3	0	3	2	2
16. Special depreciation for specified plant and equipment	31	13	17	12	11	9	15	14	16	16
17. Special depreciation of machineries for small enterprises	47	52	54	60	54	50	45	62	53	57
18. Other	1	2	1	1	4	6	9	8	4	5
V. Fulfilling internal reserves and strengthening corporate profile									

Table A. 8 (*Continued*)

	1972	1973	1974	1975	1976	1977	1978	1979	1980	1981
19. Price fluctuation reserve	15	2	12	19	2	3	0	0	0	0
20. Unusual casualty reserve	13	20	17	18	13	18	1	3	3	5
21. Security transaction responsibility reserve	0.2	0.2	0	0	0	0	0	3.0	1.0	0
22. Reserve for overseas market development by small enterprises	8.0	3.1	7.0	12.0	12.0	8.0	9.0	7.0	5.0	4.0
23. Allowance for blue return	20.6	28.4	20.0	28.0	27.0	25.0	28.0	32.0	38.0	42.0
24. Bad debt reserves by small enterprises	1.6	4.4	5.0	7.0	7.0	7.0	6.0	5.0	0	0
25. Other	5.2	5.2	5.0	5.0	6.0	6.0	6.0	8.0	6.0	7.0
VI. Other										
26. Special computation of medical income based on social insurance	80.0	88.0	105.0	132.0	158.0	189.0	226.0	157.0	168.0	141.0
27. Special allowance for old and dependent	—	—	—	—	—	—	—	14.0	15.0	17.0
28. Other	13.8	3.5	7.0	7.0	8.0	13.0	20.0	23.0	26.0	27.0
29. Additional taxation on entertainment expenses	129.7	180.5	207.0	235.0	267.0	396.0	416.0	512.0	543.0	638.0
Total	450.7	464.5	520.0	561.0	492.0	444.0	479.0	409.0	438.0	438.0

Source: Material from an interview with the Tax Bureau, Ministry of Finance, Tokyo.

Table A.9

SOURCE AND USE OF FUNDS OF THE FISCAL INVESTMENT AND LOAN PROGRAM

(In ¥ Billion)

	FY 1979	FY 1980	FY 1981	FY 1982	FY 1983	FY 1983 (U.S.$ million)
Source of funds						
Total	16,832.7	18,179.9	19,489.7	20,288.8	20,702.9	85,851
Trust Fund Bureau Fund	13,666.7	14,889.4	15,980.2	16,068.9	15,435.3	64,007
Other	3,166.0	3,390.5	3,509.4	4,219.9	5,267.6	21,844
Use of funds						
Total	16,832.7	18,179.9	19,489.7	20,288.8	20,702.9	85,851
Public investment, and the like	4,842.4	4,975.6	5,545.1	5,796.4	5,866.6	24,328
Policy implementation financing	8,229.5	9,193.6	9,793.9	10,111.7	10,515.6	43,606
Local governments	3,760.8	4,010.7	4,150.7	4,380.7	4,320.7	17,917
As a percentage of total						
Public investment, and the like	28.8	27.4	28.5	28.6	28.3	
Policy implementation financing	48.9	50.5	50.3	49.8	50.8	
Local governments	22.3	22.1	21.2	21.6	20.9	
Total	100.0	100.0	100.0	100.0	100.0	
Government bonds subscribed for by Trust Fund Bureau Fund (initial program)	1,500.0	2,500.0	3,500.0	3,500.0	3,700.0	15,343

Source: Japan Development Bank, *JDB Fact Book 1983* (Tokyo: JDB, 1983), p. 29.

Table A.10
JAPAN DEVELOPMENT BANK:
NEW LOANS BY INDUSTRY
(In ¥ Billion)

		Cumulative	
	FY 1980	FY 1976–80	Distribution (percent)
Nonmanufacturing			
Agriculture and fisheries	4.0	19.3	0.44
Mining	9.8	31.6	0.73
Construction	2.6	20.7	0.48
Wholesale and retail trade	9.9	84.6	1.95
Real estate	30.7	287.5	6.62
Transport and communi- cation	216.8	803.3	18.51
Electricity, gas, thermal sup- plies, and water supplies	419.7	1,511.9	34.83
Services and other non- manufacturing	72.9	364.0	8.39
Subtotal	766.4	3,122.9	71.95
Manufacturing			
Foodstuffs and beverages	6.9	58.0	1.34
Textile products	7.8	39.3	0.91
Pulp, paper, and related products	7.5	47.7	1.10
Chemical products	29.0	217.1	5.00
Petroleum refining	47.0	220.6	5.08
Ceramic, stone, clay, glass, and related products	29.8	87.3	2.01
Iron and steel	33.7	258.0	5.94
Nonferrous metals	10.4	61.0	1.40
Fabricated metal products	6.7	26.3	0.61
General machinery and apparatus	3.8	15.8	0.36
Electrical machinery and apparatus	14.7	42.6	0.98
Transportation machinery and equipment	4.2	68.7	1.58
Other manufacturing	5.5	75.4	1.74
Subtotal	207.0	1,217.8	28.05
Total	973.4	4,340.7	100.00

Source: Japan Development Bank, *Facts and Figures about the Japan Development Bank* (Tokyo: JDB, 1981), p. 18.

Table A.11

JAPAN DEVELOPMENT BANK LOANS FOR DEVELOPMENT OF TECHNOLOGY

(In ¥ Billion)

	FY 1977	FY 1978	FY 1979	FY 1980	FY 1981	FY 1982	FY 1982 (U.S.$ million)
New loans	71.2	129.0	108.5	96.4	96.1	110.4	458
Development of electronic computers	38.2	55.3	47.1	55.4	45.1	50.9	211
Domestically manufactured computers	35.5	53.5	45.0	54.0	44.0	49.5	205
Computer manufacturing plants	0.4	0.2	0.4	0.6	0.5	0.9	4
Data processing systems	2.3	1.6	1.7	0.8	0.6	0.5	2

Table A.11 (Continued)

	FY 1977	FY 1978	FY 1979	FY 1980	FY 1981	FY 1982	FY 1982 (U.S.$ million)
Use of high technology in certain electronic and machinery industries	8.3	7.8	10.2	14.5	12.0	13.4	56
Electronic industry	3.8	2.1	7.0	12.0	9.8	11.3	47
Machinery industry	4.5	5.7	3.2	2.5	2.2	2.1	9
Development of domestic technology	24.7	65.9	51.2	26.5	39.0	46.1	191
Development of new technology	20.4	57.4	40.9	22.6	35.5	38.0	158
Trial manufacture for commercial use	0.9	4.0	1.2	0.3		0.1	0
Development of heavy machinery	3.4	4.5	9.1	3.6	3.5	8.0	3

Source: Japan Development Bank, Facts and Figures about the Japan Development Bank, Tokyo, JDB, 1981, p. 26; and Japan Development Bank, JDB Fact Book 1983 (Tokyo, JDB, 1983), p. 17.

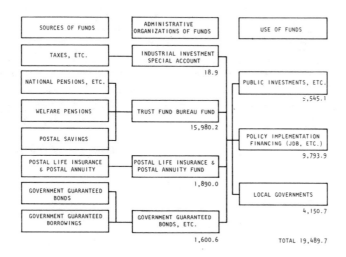

Figure A.1
STRUCTURE OF FISCAL INVESTMENT AND LOAN
PROGRAM: INITIAL FY 1981 PROGRAM (IN ¥ BILLION)

Source: Japan Development Bank, *Facts and Figures about the Japan Development Bank* (Tokyo: JDB, 1981), p. 40.

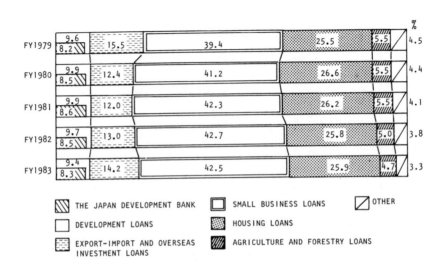

Figure A.2

COMPOSITION OF FUND DISBURSEMENT PROGRAMS
OF POLICY IMPLEMENTATION
FINANCING INSTITUTIONS

Source: Japan Development Bank, *JDB Fact Book 1983* (Tokyo: JDB, 1983), p. 35.

APPENDIX B

Research and
Development Projects
for New Industries

OUTLINE OF THE RESEARCH AND DEVELOPMENT PROJECT ON BASIC TECHNOLOGIES FOR NEW INDUSTRIES

FY 81 budget was allocated to three subjects:

1. New materials (six themes):   ¥ 1,356 million
2. Biotechnology (three themes):   ¥ 675 million
3. New function elements (three themes):   ¥ 673 million

(The total budget including clerical expense was ¥ 2,714 million.)

List of Companies That Have Applied, By Area

Fine ceramics (15 R & D–associated member companies):
      Toshiba Corporation (chair company)
      Showa Denko, K.K.
      Asahi Glass Co., Ltd.
      Kobe Steel, Ltd.
      Kyoto Ceramic Co.
      Toyota Motor
      Ishikawajima-Harima Heavy Industries Co., Ltd.
      Shinagawa Refractories
      Inoue Japax
      N G K Spark Plug Co., Ltd.
      N G K Insulators, Ltd.
      Toyoda Machine Works, Ltd.
      Denki Kagaku Kogyo K.K.
      Kurosaki Refractories Co.
      Sumitomo Electric Industries, Ltd.

Macromolecule materials (11 R & D–associated member companies):
      High-efficiency separation membrane material
      Conductive macromolecule material
      Crystallinity macromolecule material

      Toray Industries, Inc. (chair company)
      Teijin, Ltd.
      Asahi Glass Co., Ltd.
      Mitsubishi Chemical Industries, Ltd.
      Sumitomo Electric Industries, Ltd.
      Toyobo Co., Ltd.
      Daicel Chemical Industries, Ltd.

Kuraray Co., Ltd.
Mitsubishi Petrochemical Co., Ltd.
Asahi Chemical Industry Co., Ltd.
Sumitomo Chemical Co., Ltd.

New materials (17 R & D-associated member companies including):
High-efficiency crystal control alloy
Composite material

(The starting fund was ¥ 50 million; the FY 1981 subsidy, ¥ 370 million).

Fuji Heavy Industries Ltd. (chair company)
Kobe Steel, Ltd. (subleader)
Toray Industries, Inc. (subleader)
Ishikawajima-Harima Heavy Industries Co., Ltd.
Hitachi Metal, Ltd.
Hitachi, Ltd.
Mitsubishi Metal Corp.
Daido Steel Co.
Sumitomo Electric Industries, Ltd.
Teijin, Ltd.
Mitsubishi Chemical Industries, Ltd.
Kawasaki Heavy Industries, Ltd.
Toshiba Machine Co., Ltd.
Toyota Motor Co., Ltd.
Mitsubishi Electric Corporation

Biotechnology (14 R & D-associated member companies including):
Bioreactor for industrial use
Technology for mass cultivation of cells
Gene-splicing technology

(The FY 1981 subsidy was about ¥ 670 million.)

Mitsubishi Chemical Industries, Ltd. (chair company)
Daicel Chemical Industries, Ltd. (reactor)
Kao Soap Co., Ltd. (reactor)
Mitsubishi Gas Chemical Co., Ltd. (reactor)
Mitsui Petrochemical Industry, Ltd. (reactor)
Takeda Chemical Industry Ltd. (biomass)
Ajinomoto Co., Inc. (biomass)
Kyowa Hakko Kogyo Co., Ltd. (biomass)
Asahi Chemical Industry Co., Ltd. (biomass)
Toyo Jozo Co., Ltd. (biomass)

Table B.1

SUNSHINE PROJECT ACTIVITIES PLANNED
FOR FISCAL 1981

(In ¥ Million)

Project Name	Budget for FY 1980	Budget for FY 1981	Points in 1981 Plan
Solar energy	9,544	7,961	Operational testing of solar thermal power generation plant (Two 1,000 kw systems)
			Construction of facilities to utilize photovoltaic power generation technologies
			Expansion of R & D on new type solar cells and low-cost solar panel production process
			Development of solar systems for industrial process heat, etcetera (including solar systems for industrial process heat)
Geothermal energy	8,006	9,223	Technology for exploration and extraction of geothermal energy
			Technology for 10,000 kw class binary cycle geothermal power generation test plant and total flow pilot test plant utilizing hot water
			Technology for deep geothermal water supply systems
			Technology for multipurpose utilization of geothermal energy and environmental preservation
			Demonstration environmental protection program for development of large-scale power plant using deep geothermal reservoirs
Coal conversion	8,553	13,514	Operation of 40 t/D low-calorific gasification plant

			Construction of high-calorific gasification plant with a capacity of 7,000 m/D
			Operation of 1 t/D solvolysis liquefaction plant and design of 40 t/D plant
			Operation of 1 t/D solvent extractive liquefaction plant
			Operation of 2.4 t/D direct liquefaction plant
Hydrogen energy	951	948	Construction of high-temperature high-pressure water electrolysis pilot plant (20 Nm²/hour)
			Expansion of research on hydrogen utilization technology
Supporting research	551	1,233	Expansion of research on ocean thermal energy conversion technology
			Development of wind energy conversion system (100 kw)
Other	364	112	Implementation of research facilities
			Office expenses, etcetera.
International cooperation	679	668	U.S.-Japan joint research on geothermal energy utilization technologies
			U.S.-Japan joint research on coal liquefaction technologies
			IEA countries—Japan multilateral cooperation
Total budget	28,648	33,659	

IEA = International Energy Agency

Source: Ministry of International Trade and Industry, Tokyo.

Table B.2

R & D ON LARGE-SCALE CONSERVATION TECHNOLOGY—MOONLIGHT PROJECT

(In ¥ Million)

Project Name	R & D Period (FY)	Total R & D Expenditure	Budget for FY 1981	Outline of Project	Main R & D Activities in FY 1981
Advanced gas turbine	1978–84	About 21,000	5,920	Development of a gas turbine that will raise heat efficiency to a remarkable 55 percent-plus in a combined generating cycle with a steam turbine. R & D on ultra-high-temperature-resistant materials and elementary technology will enable the temperature at the turbine inlet to be raised to 1,500°C, and so on.	A pilot plant (generation efficiency 50 percent) of the 100,000 kw class will be designed and manufactured.
Waste heat utilization technology systems	1976–81	About 4,000	887	R & D on elementary technologies and total systems for the	Pilot plants and equipment are being manufactured

Magneto-hydrodynamic power generation	1976–82 (second phase) 1966–75 (first phase)	About 12,000 First phase: about 6,400	624	Under this system, high-temperature combustion gas is transformed directly into electrical energy, by being passed between powerful magnets at high speed. R & D is being conducted on MHD electric power generation	utilization of waste heat, including heat recovery, heat exchange, heat transmission, heat storage, etcetera, with a view to conserving resources and energy in industry and promoting the effective utilization of waste heat by the community.	Construction of the Mark VII test facility (using ordinary magnets) has been completed, and experimental runs of 200 hours at 100 kw are underway.

and practical experiments will be performed.

Table B.2 (*Continued*)

Project Name	R & D Period (FY)	Total R & D Expenditure	Budget for FY 1981	Outline of Project	Main R & D Activities in FY 1981
				technology, which can be combined with thermal power generation in order to vastly increase thermal efficiency.	
Advanced battery energy storage system	1980–90	About 17,000	646	The development of highly efficient batteries to store electrochemically surplus power at off-peak periods and release it at peak periods.	Studies will be conducted into basic technology for a new-type 1 kw class batteries (Na/S, Zn/Cl_2, Zn/Br_2, redox flow), systems analysis of electrical networks using simulation mechanisms, and total systems for battery storage of energy.

| Fuel cell genera-tion technology | 1981–86 | About 11,000 | 239 | Fuel cell generation is ideal in that power stations employing it can be located in urban areas, and it is expected to make a major contribu-tion to generational efficiency. R & D into fuel cell sys-tems and feasibility studies on practical applications, relia-bility, and economy are now underway. | Commenced in 1981 as a new project. |

Zn/Br_2 = zinc/bromide

Source: Minister of International Trade and Industry, Tokyo

Table B.3
NATIONAL RESEARCH AND DEVELOPMENT PROGRAM—LARGE-SCALE PROJECT
(In ¥ Million)

Project Name	Period (FY)	Total Expenditure	Outline of Project
Super-high-performance electronic computer	1966–71	10,124	Large-scale computer system with super-high performance.
Desulfurization process	1966–71	2,675	(1) The efficient removal of the SO_2 contained in the gases exhausted from power plants or other industries that consume a great deal of heavy oil. (2) The direct removal of sulfur from heavy oil.
Seawater desalination and by-product recovery	1969–77	9,966	Economical large-scale production of fresh water and economical by-product recovery technology.
Electric car	1971–77	5,692	Various types of electric cars to replace ordinary vehicles in urban areas.
Comprehensive automobile control technology	1973–79	7,406	Integrated control technology with a view to relieving traffic congestion, reducing automobile pollution and traffic accidents, etcetera.
Pattern information processing system	1971–80	22,073	Computer technology for the recognition and processing of pattern information such as characters, pictures, objects, and speech.

| Direct steelmaking process using high-temperature reducing gas | 1973–80 | 13,998 | | Direct steelmaking technology with a view to solving the pollution problems that accompany present-day methods and reducing the dependence on coal as a raw material. The new technology aims at a closed system that uses the heat energy from a multipurpose high-temperature gas-cooled reactor in the steelmaking process; this new reactor is scheduled for development in the near future. | |
| Remotely controlled undersea oil drilling rig | 1970–75 | 4,507 | | The development of remote-control oil drilling rigs for undersea use. | |

Ongoing National Research and Development Projects

Project Name	R & D Period (FY)	Total R & D Expenditure	Budget for FY 1981	Outline of Project	Main R & D Activities in FY 1981
Olefin production from heavy oil as raw material	1975–81	About 13,800	3,156	R & D on the technology for manufacturing high-value-added olefin (commonly known as ethylene, propylene, etcetera, and used as a raw material for syn-	Operation of the large-scale pilot plant.

Table B.3 (*Continued*)

Project Name	R & D Period (FY)	Total R & D Expenditure	Budget for FY 1981	Outline of Project	Main R & D Activities in FY 1981
				thetic resin, synthetic rubber, synthetic fibers, etcetera) using a high sulfur-content heavy oil fraction (so-called asphalt), which is difficult to desulfurize, as the raw material.	
Jet engines for aircraft	1976–81 (second phase)	About 13,000	1,901	R & D on a high-performance civil aircraft fan-jet engine that causes less environmental damage—that is, less noise and less atmospheric pollution—and features high overall efficiency, high	Engine tests and simulated high-altitude anticing tests.
	1971–75 (first phase)	First phase: about 6,900			

durability against
frequent takeoffs
and landings and
easy maintenance.

High-speed computer system for scientific and technological uses	—	—	30	R & D on high-speed computer system for processing and computation of scientific and technological information (processing of image information from satellites, simulation of nuclear fusion, etcetera), which present computers cannot handle in realistic time.	Planning of the R & D program for the entire project. Inauguration of R & D on high-speed logic and memory devices such as Josephson and GaAs FET devices and conceptual design work on high-speed parallel processing systems.
Subsea oil production system	1978–84	About 15,000	3,515	R & D on subsea oil production system (in which production from small-scale oil fields is	Test manufacture of some of the equipment for comprehensive marine experiments; final

Table B.3 (*Continued*)

Project Name	R & D Period (FY)	Total R & D Expenditure	Budget for FY 1981	Outline of Project	Main R & D Activities in FY 1981
				possible without any adverse effects on the fishing industry, which is effective for subsea oil production in deep waters (over 300 meters deep) and suitable for use in the sea areas surrounding Japan.	design and production work on other experimental equipment. Detailed planning for experiments.
Optical measurement and control system	1979–87	About 18,000	2,419	R & D on measurement control system that uses optics and makes possible the systematic measurement, integrated observation, and control of mass information, including visual informa-	Detailed design of functional subsystems for various functions; research on essential technology.

				Description	Goal
				tion arising in specific areas, such as industrial parks, large-scale plants, etcetera, even under adverse conditions such as those where electromagnetic induction, etcetera, prevail.	The inauguration of R & D on projects aimed at promoting a switch on chemical technology to basic materials other than oil resources.
C_1 (monocarbon) chemical technology	1980–87	About 15,000	902	R & D on technology for the stable and economic production of such basic chemical products as ethylene glycol, acetic acid, and ethanol, with C_1 compounds such as carbon monoxide obtained from alternative carbon sources such as natural gas coal, and tarsand as their basic raw materials.	

Table B.3 (*Continued*)

Project Name	R & D Period (FY)	Total R & D Expenditure	Budget for FY 1981	Outline of Project	Main R & D Activities in FY 1981
Manganese nodule exploitation system	—	—	50	R & D on efficient and reliable methods for exploiting, by means of hydraulic mining systems, deep-sea deposits of manganese nodules containing economically important metals (Ni, Cu, Co, Mn, and so on).	Conceptual design of the entire system and subsystems such as collectors, lifting pumps, pipe strings, handling apparatus, and instrumentation; basic experiments on vertical slurry transportation and the geotechnology of deep-sea sediments.
Resource recovery technology	1976–82 (second phase) 1973–75 (first phase)	About 11,000 First phase: about 1,300	1,501	R & D on technical systems for the disposal of solid urban waste, centered on resource recycling with a view to promoting the effi-	Comprehensive research on the operation of materials-recycling-type facilities and energy-recycling-type facilities.

			...cient utilization of resources and facilitating the smooth application of solid urban waste treatment.	
Flexible manufacturing system complex provided with laser	1977–83	About 13,000	R & D on complex production system in which mechanical components for small-batch production of diversified products can be flexibly and rapidly produced from metallic materials in an integrated system.	Detailed design of manufacturing system complex test plant.
		2,745		

Source: Ministry of International Trade and Industry, Tokyo.

APPENDIX C

**Laws on
Government Assistance
Regarding
Declining Industries**

Figure C.1

OUTLINE OF THE LAW ON TEMPORARY MEASURES
FOR SPECIFIC DEPRESSED INDUSTRIES

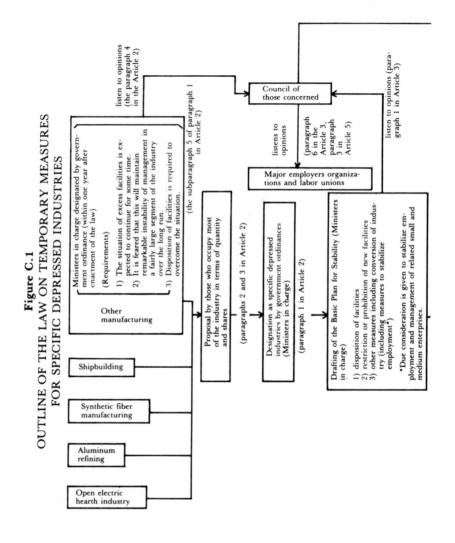

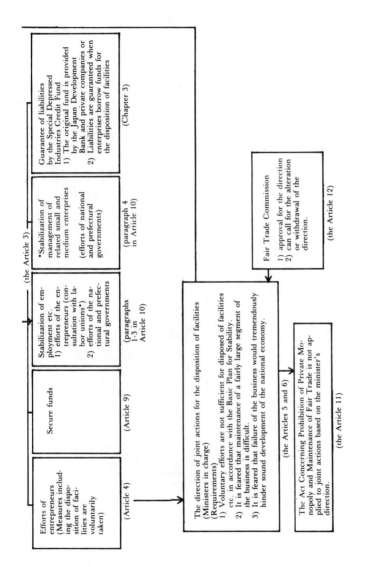

* Prefectural governors can submit their opinions to the ministers in charge where they recognize that disposition of facilities, etc., will have a profound affect on the local economy.
* The ministers in charge and Labor Minister must communicate and cooperate closely on matters related to employment.
* This law shall be abolished by June 30, 1983.

Source: Ministry of International Trade and Industry, Business Behaviour Division.

Figure C.2

OUTLINE OF MAJOR UNEMPLOYMENT MEASURES

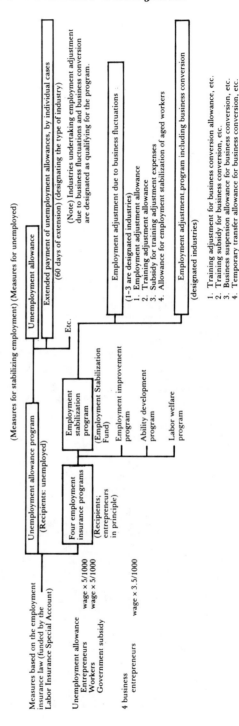

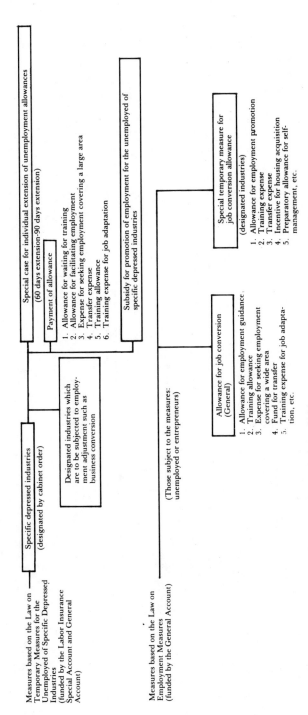

Source: Ministry of International Trade and Industry, Business Behaviour Division.

Figure C.3

LAW ON TEMPORARY MEASURES FOR UNEMPLOYED OF SPECIFIC DEPRESSED INDUSTRIES

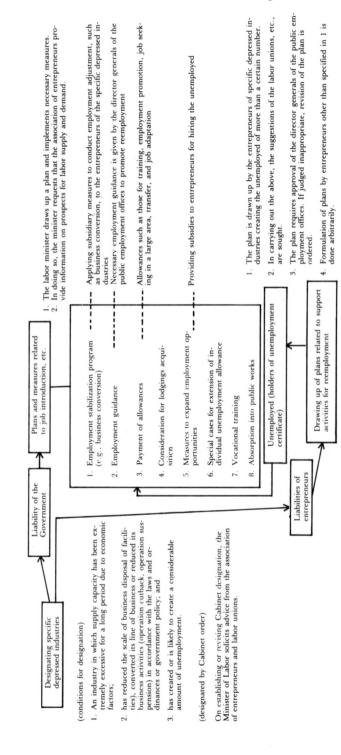

Source: Ministry of International Trade and Industry, Business Behaviour Division.

GLOSSARY OF JAPANESE TERMS

amakudari. Literally, "descent from heaven." A custom whereby government officials retire at around age 55 and often enter senior management positions in business.

chihō ginkō. "local banks." These have the same range of activities as city banks, but their business is usually concentrated in one prefecture.

chukoku. A money market fund based on a medium-term government bond.

Daini Dendensha. Literally, "second telephone/telegraph company." A group led by Kyocera that has proposed to create a company competing with NTT in the VAN market.

Denshinhō. Law on Extraordinary Measures for the Promotion of Electronic Industries.

doru shokku. "Dollar shock." In August 1971 President Nixon announced that the United States would no longer exchange dollars for gold at a fixed price of $35 per ounce, demanding in effect a realignment of major currencies against the dollar.

ekuitei metaru. Literally, "equity metal". Finished metal products manufactured abroad in facilities in which Japanese interests hold equity positions.

Fukkō Kinyū Kinkō. Reconstruction Finance Corporation.

fukyō sangyō. "Depressed industry."

gensaki. A repurchase contract that serves as a lending or borrowing instrument.

geta. Japanese-style wooden clogs.

hikiatekin. Tax-free reserves justified by general accounting principles—for example, the bad debt reserve.

hojōkin. "Conditional loans" provided by the Japanese government. Payback tends to be conditional upon success of the project.

itakuhi. "Consignment payments" for government contracted work in R & D projects usually.

junbikin. Tax-free reserves introduced to achieve certain economic policy goals.

Keidanren. Federation of Economic Organizations.

keiretsu. A pattern of industrial organization that has descended from the prewar *zaibatsu* system.

kenkyū kumiai. Literally, "research association." This is a legally constituted nonprofit entity.

kenkyukai. Literally, "study groups." Informal or formal groups that meet regularly to discuss new developments in their area of research.

Kidenhō. Law on Extraordinary Measures for the Promotion of Electronics and Machinery Industry.

Kijōhō. Law on Extraordinary Measures for the Promotion of Specific Machinery and Information Industry.

Kōkōgyō gijutsu kumiai hō. Industrial Technology Association Law.

kokuryoku. "National strength."

Kokusai Denshin Denwa. Japan's international telecommunications monopoly.

kombinato. Refers to petrochemical production complexes.

kondankai. Literally, "roundtable."

kutabare GNP. "Down with GNP."

madoguchi shidō. "Window guidance." Refers to the BOJ's own version of administrative guidance.

oiru shokku. "Oil shock." The fourfold increase in the price of crude oil imposed by OPEC in 1973/74, which greatly affected the Japanese economy.

Sekiyu gyōhō. Petroleum Industry Law.

shingikai. "Advisory councils" that sometimes resemble kenkyū kumiai in the sense that both may be formed under the auspices of the government, and both tend to meet regularly to keep abreast of new developments in their areas of research.

sōgō anzen hoshō. Literally, "comprehensive security."

sōgō shōsha. General trading companies such as Mitsui & Company.

terakoya. "Temple schools."

Tokutei fukyō sangyō antei rinji sochihō. Law on Temporary Measures for the Stabilization of Specified Depressed Industries (1978). Also known as the Depressed Industries Law. In 1983 the law was extended and the name was changed to the Law on Temporary Measures for the Structural Improvement of Specific Industries.

toshi ginkō. "City banks." These handle the bulk of the country's short-term and trade financing.

zaibatsu. "Financial groups." In effect, holding companies that included a commercial bank.

zaidan hōjin. Generally defined as a nonprofit organization.

INDEX

ABOUT THE AUTHORS

THOMAS PEPPER, MERIT E. JANOW, and JIMMY W. WHEELER are members of the senior research staff of Hudson Institute, a public policy research organization with headquarters in Indianapolis, Indiana. The three authors have worked together on studies of economic issues in the Asia-Pacific region for more than four years, including a major study of Japanese industrial policies for the U.S. government.

Pepper was director of Hudson's Asia-Pacific Office in Tokyo from 1977 to 1981; prior to that he was a correspondent for the *Baltimore Sun* and the *Economist*. He is coauthor, with the late Herman Kahn, of *The Japanese Challenge: The Success and Failure of Economic Success* (1979) and *Will She Be Right? The Future of Australia* (1980), and a consultant on business development in the Asia-Pacific region.

Janow worked in Hudson's Asia-Pacific Office from 1980 to 1981. She has coauthored two Hudson reports on economic and political conditions on the Korean Peninsula and a number of Asian strategic planning studies.

Wheeler has directed Hudson studies on international economic issues since 1977. He is coeditor, with Irving Leveson, of *Western Economies in Transition: Structural Change and Adjustment Policies in Industrial Countries* (1980).